Philosophy as World Literature

Literatures as World Literature

Can the literature of a specific country, author, or genre be used to approach the elusive concept of "world literature"? **Literatures as World Literature** takes a novel approach to world literature by analyzing specific constellations—according to language, nation, form, or theme—of literary texts and authors in their own world-literary dimensions. World literature is obviously so vast that any view of it cannot help but be partial; the question then becomes how to reduce the complex task of understanding and describing world literature. Most treatments of world literature so far either have been theoretical and thus abstract or else have made broad use of exemplary texts from a variety of languages and epochs. The majority of critical work, the filling in of what has been traced, lies ahead of us. **Literatures as World Literature** fills in the devilish details by allowing scholars to move outward from their own areas of specialization, fostering scholarly writing that approaches more closely the polyphonic, multiperspectival nature of world literature.

Series Editor
Thomas O. Beebee

Editorial Board
Eduardo Coutinho, Federal University of Rio de Janeiro, Brazil
Hsinya Huang, National Sun-yat Sen University, Taiwan
Meg Samuelson, University of Cape Town, South Africa
Ken Seigneurie, Simon Fraser University, Canada
Mads Rosendahl Thomsen, Aarhus University, Denmark

Volumes in the Series
German Literature as World Literature, edited by Thomas O. Beebee
Roberto Bolaño as World Literature, edited by Nicholas Birns and Juan E. De Castro
Crime Fiction as World Literature, edited by David Damrosch, Theo D'haen, and Louise Nilsson
Danish Literature as World Literature, edited by Dan Ringgaard and Mads Rosendahl Thomsen
From Paris to Tlön: Surrealism as World Literature, by Delia Ungureanu
American Literature as World Literature, edited by Jeffrey R. Di Leo
Romanian Literature as World Literature, edited by Mircea Martin, Christian Moraru, and Andrei Terian
Brazilian Literature as World Literature, edited by Eduardo F. Coutinho
Dutch and Flemish Literature as World Literature, edited by Theo D'haen
Afropolitan Literature as World Literature, edited by James Hodapp
Francophone Literature as World Literature, edited by Christian Moraru, Nicole Simek, and Bertrand Westphal
Bulgarian Literature as World Literature, edited by Mihaela P. Harper and Dimitar Kambourov
Philosophy as World Literature, edited by Jeffrey R. Di Leo

Philosophy as World Literature

Edited by
Jeffrey R. Di Leo

BLOOMSBURY ACADEMIC
NEW YORK • LONDON • OXFORD • NEW DELHI • SYDNEY

BLOOMSBURY ACADEMIC
Bloomsbury Publishing Inc
1385 Broadway, New York, NY 10018, USA
50 Bedford Square, London, WC1B 3DP, UK

BLOOMSBURY, BLOOMSBURY ACADEMIC and the Diana logo are trademarks of
Bloomsbury Publishing Plc

First published in the United States of America 2020

This paperback edition published 2022

Volume Editor's Part of the Work © Jeffrey R. Di Leo, 2020
Each chapter © Contributors, 2020

For legal purposes the Acknowledgments on p. ix constitute an extension
of this copyright page.

Cover design by Simon Levy / Levy Associates

All rights reserved. No part of this publication may be reproduced or
transmitted in any form or by any means, electronic or mechanical,
including photocopying, recording, or any information storage or retrieval
system, without prior permission in writing from the publishers.

Bloomsbury Publishing Inc does not have any control over, or responsibility for, any
third-party websites referred to or in this book. All internet addresses given in this
book were correct at the time of going to press. The author and publisher regret any
inconvenience caused if addresses have changed or sites have ceased to exist, but can
accept no responsibility for any such changes.

Library of Congress Cataloging-in-Publication Data
Names: Di Leo, Jeffrey R., editor.
Title: Philosophy as world literature / edited by Jeffrey R. Di Leo.
Description: New York : Bloomsbury Academic, 2020. | Series: Literatures as world
literature | Includes bibliographical references and index. |
Summary: "Explores the intersections between philosophy and literature through a
transnational, comparative lens"– Provided by publisher.
Identifiers: LCCN 2020019017 | ISBN 9781501351877 (hardback) |
ISBN 9781501370717 (paperback) | ISBN 9781501351884 (epub) |
ISBN 9781501351891 (pdf)
Subjects: LCSH: Literature–Philosophy. | Literature and philosophy.
Classification: LCC PN49 .P465 2020 | DDC 100–dc23
LC record available at https://lccn.loc.gov/2020019017

ISBN: HB: 978-1-5013-5187-7
PB: 978-1-5013-7071-7
ePDF: 978-1-5013-5189-1
eBook: 978-1-5013-5188-4

Series: Literatures as World Literature

Typeset by Newgen KnowledgeWorks Pvt. Ltd., Chennai, India

To find out more about our authors and books visit www.bloomsbury.com
and sign up for our newsletters.

The separation of philosophy from literary study has not worked to the benefit of either.
　　　　　　　　　—Geoffrey Hartman, *De-construction and Criticism* (ix)

Contents

Acknowledgments — ix

Philosophy as World Literature: An Introduction — 1
Jeffrey R. Di Leo

Part I World, Worlding, Worldliness

1 The World, the Text, and Philosophy: Reflections on Translation
   Brian O'Keeffe — 23

2 Plato as World Literature   *Paul Allen Miller* — 47

3 Worlding Interpretation, or Fanon and the Poetics of Disalienation   *Nicole Simek* — 59

4 Alluvia: The Palimpsest of African Memory   *Michael Stern* — 71

Part II Migration and Difference

5 Feminism as World Literature   *Robin Truth Goodman* — 91

6 Astonishing Worlding: Montaigne and the New World   *Zahi Zalloua* — 105

7 Literature of the World, Unite!   *Peter Hitchcock* — 115

8 Transatlantic Thoreau: Henry S. Salt, Gandhi, and British Humanitarian Socialism   *David M. Robinson* — 129

Part III Philosophy, Religion, and the East

9 Nietzsche and World Iterature: The Eternal Recurrence of Dualism in *Thus Spake Zarathustra*   *Jeffrey S. Librett* — 145

10 Asian Philosophy, National Literatures, and World Literature Anthologies   *Junjie Luo* — 173

11 The Dharma of World Literature   *Ranjan Ghosh* — 185

12 Olive-Red in Orhan Pamuk and Anton Shammas: Deconstruction's Eastward Dissemination *Henry Sussman* 197

Part IV Philosophy versus World Literature

13 Existentialism as World Literature: De Beauvoir, Heidegger, and Tolstoy *Robert Doran* 233

14 Jorge Luis Borges and Philosophy *Efraín Kristal* 247

15 Philosophy for the Masses: Haldeman-Julius, Durant, and *The Story of Philosophy* *Jeffrey R. Di Leo* 261

List of Contributors 279
Index 281

Acknowledgments

My primary debt of gratitude goes to the contributors to this volume for sharing their thoughts on philosophy as world literature. I have benefitted greatly from my conversations with them about this topic and others, and appreciate their willingness to engage this topic from a number of different theoretical perspectives and disciplinary positions.

I am also grateful to Vikki Fitzpatrick for her administrative assistance and to Keri Ruiz for the help she has given me in preparing this manuscript for publication. At Bloomsbury, I would like to thank Katherine De Chant, Amy Martin, and Harris Naqvi for his help steering this manuscript through the peer review and publication process; and series editor, Thomas O. Beebee, for his helpful suggestions and steadfast encouragement.

Finally, I would like to thank my wife Nina, for her unfailing encouragement, support, and patience.

Philosophy as World Literature: An Introduction

Jeffrey R. Di Leo

The relationship between philosophy and literature has been a traditional topic of debate. On one side of the debate are those who push for a strict separation between philosophy and literature; on the other are those who blur the lines between them. These lines are often demarcated by differing sets of oppositions: if philosophy is concerned with universality, then literature is concerned with particularity; if philosophy deals with reason, then literature deals with imagination; if philosophy is about detachment, then literature is about engagement; if philosophy favors insight, then literature favors emotion; and so on.[1] The question pursued in this collection though is a twist on this traditional topic of debate: namely, how does a consideration of "*world* literature" (rather than just "literature") alter its relationship with philosophy?[2] Furthermore, does this consideration push us also toward the conclusion that all philosophy is or should be considered "world" philosophy?

Philosophy considered as just "literature" often reduced the terms of the debate to ones of mere philosophical style. That is, the difference between philosophy and literature amounted to a difference in the style of their respective writing—or, if you will, the relationship between its form and its content. Anglo-American analytic philosophy hijacked philosophical style for most of the twentieth century by emphasizing a style of writing that reduced philosophical investigation to arid argument—and excluding as philosophy writing where "arguments" could not be readily discerned.[3] In the United States, this led to the widespread exclusion of "literature" from the philosophy classroom except in advanced undergraduate courses such as "Philosophy of Literature."[4]

What was forgotten or ignored during this period by the Anglo-American tradition was that historically speaking, much of the most influential philosophy in the world *was* a form of literature: from Plato's dialogues and Augustine's confessions to Nietzsche's aphorisms and Sartre's plays, philosophy has always had a close relationship with literature—and, arguably, by extension—"world" literature. At the same time, however, continental traditions in philosophy ranging from existentialism through post-structuralism largely ignored or rejected the Anglo-American approach to philosophical style and provided a much more complicated portrait of the relationship between philosophical and literary writing, namely, one that established fluid lines between "philosophy" and "literature."

However, today we live in an age of "worlded" literature. Not the world literature of nations and nationalities considered from most powerful and wealthy to the least. And not the world literature found with a map. Rather, the worlded literature of individuals crossing borders, mixing stories, and speaking in dialect. Where translation struggles to be effective and background is itself another story. The "worlded" literature of the multinational corporate publishing industry where success in the global market is the primary determinate of aesthetic and literary value.[5]

Consequently, the essays in this collection ask what it means for philosophy to be considered as a species of not just "literature" but "world" literature—and vice versa. They offer a complex and authoritative account of what it means to consider philosophy as world literature by exploring philosophy through the lens of the "worlding" of literature, that is, the ways in which we might regard philosophy as connected and reconnected through global literary networks of increasing complexity and precarity. In the process, "philosophy" itself becomes much more "worldly" and projects such as an "Anglo-American" or "Continental" approach to it less capable of meeting the demands of both "world literature" *and* "world philosophy." The question too of whether "philosophy as world literature" is also "post-literature" and "post-philosophical" comes to the fore.

Nevertheless, what is not up for debate in this volume is that philosophy today is more *worldly* now than ever. The issue of whether philosophy produced in various nations around the world is now more than ever preoccupied with worldly issues, be they global, international, cosmopolitan, or geopolitical, is important to this consideration but not essential. The story of philosophy back to its beginnings has always involved transnational considerations even if the Anglo-American analytic movement in philosophy appeared to push it in the opposite direction. Current concern with the "worlding" of philosophy is less about its tendency to bring the world overtly to bear in its subject matter than the ways in which philosophy has become indistinguishable from world literature when regarded from a more cosmopolitan, transnational perspective.

Under such conditions, what it means to be an African, American, or Asian "philosopher"—let alone a French, German, or Spanish one—in the new millennium is as complicated (or simple) as what means to be "African," "American," or "Asian." Our charge now as "world philosophers" is less to be "authorities" on national philosophies and to differentiate philosophy from literature than to explore the many "worlds" each open up for readers and in readings. As such, those who consider themselves philosophers have a huge task ahead of them, namely, what it means when not just literature needs an account relative to philosophy, but when the world comes between both literature *and* philosophy. The essays in this volume offer a variety of accounts of the ways in which the worlding of literature problematizes both the national categorizing of philosophy (e.g., American philosophy, German philosophy, etc.) as well as brings new meanings and challenges to the traditional topic of the coming together of philosophy *and* literature.

Philosophy against Literary Theory

During the late 1970s and the mid-1980s, the works of Jacques Derrida,[6] Paul de Man,[7] and Geoffrey H. Hartman[8] prompted thinkers to reconsider the relationship between philosophy and literature as well as the relationship of style, writing, and rhetoric to philosophy.[9] The main points of contention were the following:

1) *All Texts Are Equal*: Literary theorists claimed that philosophical texts should be considered as equal to all other texts and forms of textuality, whereas philosophers rejected this proposal and argued for differentiation between philosophical and literary texts.
2) *All Texts Can Be Read Equally*: Literary theorists claimed that philosophical texts should be read no differently than other texts, whereas philosophers rejected this proposal.
3) *The Textuality of Philosophy*: Literary theorists claimed that considerations of writing, style, and rhetoric have a direct bearing on what philosophy is, whereas philosophers rejected issues concerning the textuality of philosophy as philosophically insignificant.
4) *Reconsideration of the Philosophical Canon*: Literary theorists suggested that there were a body of philosophical texts in support of their views concerning the textuality of philosophy and that this tradition should be considered in addition to the dominant analytic philosophical tradition, whereas philosophers were hesitant to acknowledge the contemporary significance of this alternative philosophical tradition. And
5) *The End of Philosophy*: Philosophers inferred from the aforementioned points that the end of philosophy was at hand, whereas literary theorists regarded this transition as a problem to be handled by philosophers and philosophy.

The promise of a fuller collaboration between philosophers and literary theorists on these matters seemed particularly probable during this period in the 1970s and 1980s. The work of Derrida and others suggested that a closer collaboration between literary studies and philosophy was imminent, and that we should look back to previous collaborations between philosophy and literature for insight and instruction.[10]

In 1979, Hartman noted the excitement and anticipation of the time in his brief "Preface" to a collection of articles by the "hermeneutical Mafia":

> Since the era of the German Romantics, however, and of Coleridge—who was deeply influenced by the philosophical criticism coming from Germany around 1800—we have not seen a really fruitful interaction of these "sister arts." Yet the recent revival of philosophical criticism associated with such names as [Georg] Lukács, [Martin] Heidegger, [Jean-Paul] Sartre, [Walter] Benjamin, [Maurice] Blanchot, and even [I. A.] Richards, [Kenneth] Burke and [William] Empson, is like a new dawn that should not fade into the light of common day.[11]

Furthermore, as the quote from Hartman used as the epigraph to this volume indicates,[12] the hope was that this newly found (or rediscovered) integration between philosophy and literature would affect *both* disciplines. While such a collaboration ran the risk of confusing the domains of philosophy and literature, Hartman and others were claiming that confusing the realms of philosophy and literature was a danger worth experiencing.

Yet, what Hartman and other literary theorists at the time failed to recognize was that what *they* projected from *within* literary studies as a potentially positive situation resulting from the integration of literary studies and philosophy would be viewed from the *outside*, particularly by philosophers, as a potentially negative situation for philosophy. Some philosophers at the time were discussing philosophy as an institution in crisis, while other were even opening up the possibility of the "end" of philosophy.[13] Richard Rorty, commenting on this very passage, writes that Hartman is "simply being courteous to a defeated foe"[14] but really does not believe that philosophy and literary theory will ever fruitfully interact. The future collaboration between philosophy and literature suggested by literary theorists is perceived as a threat to philosophy. Given the continual denial of the significance of textuality to philosophical practice and the strong codification of this belief through the prevailing analytic traditions of the late 1970s and early 1980s, it is not surprising that the work of Derrida, de Man, Hartman, and others had only a minor impact on the *dominant* philosophical communities in the United States and Britain.[15]

The work of Derrida, de Man, Hartman, and others did, however, compel a reconsideration of the philosophical canon and the grounds for division in American philosophy departments. The European philosophical tradition was searched and subdivided in the United States into at least two distinct parts: the "continental tradition" and the other traditions derived from European philosophy like Empiricism and Rationalism. This "continental tradition" in the United States came to be the "other" tradition—a tradition that was seldom viewed as crossing paths with the sources of the dominant analytic traditions of the time. Moreover, in cases where analytic philosophers found themselves claiming that their work was also grounded in "continental philosophy," a further division between *their* continental tradition and the *other* continental tradition was made: given their formative role in the development of Anglo-American analytic philosophy, sources like Bernard Bolzano's *Scientific Doctrine* (1837), Gottlob Frege's *Begriffschrift* (1879), Franz Brentano's *On the Origin of Moral Knowledge* (1889), Edmund Husserl *Logical Investigations* (1900), Alexius Meinong's *On Object Theory* (1904), and Rudolf Carnap's *The Logical Construction of the World* (1928) came to be the "real" continental philosophy, whereas sources like Immanuel Kant's *Critique of Judgment* (1790), Georg Wilhelm Friedrich Hegel's *Phenomenology of Spirit* (1807), Søren Kierkegaard's *Concluding Unscientific Postscript* (1846), Friedrich Nietzsche's "On Truth and Lying in an Extra-Moral Sense" (1873), Edmund Husserl's *Phenomenology of Internal Time-Consciousness* (1928), Heidegger's *Being and Time* (1927), Jean-Paul Sartre's *Being and Nothingness* (1943), Maurice Merleau-Ponty's *Phenomenology of Perception* (1945), Georges Bataille's *On Nietzsche* (1945), Alexandre Kojève's

Introduction to the Reading of Hegel (1947), Emmanuel Levinas's *Time and the Other* (1948), and Maurice Blanchot's *The Space of Literature* (1955) came to be the "other" continental philosophy. The "other" continental philosophy was deemed as such in part because of its *indirect* influence on the dominant analytic traditions in the United States and Britain, and in part because of its "negative" association with the development of deconstruction and other types of mid- to late-twentieth-century literary theory.

Furthermore, departments in the United States were sometimes literally divided between the "analytic" and the "continental" philosophers. While the "continental/analytic" divide in philosophy departments predates "deconstruction,"[16] the arrival of deconstruction in America only intensified the divide. Some programs specialized in only one side; others contained "divided" faculties; some departments even fractured into different tracks. The result of all this division was that the "premier" departments in the United States were primarily "analytic" and discouraged students from studying the "other" philosophy. French departments and comparative literature programs quickly became the locus for the orphaned "literary theory."

In this climate, professional philosophy in the United States was effectively able to contain and control indirectly the possibility of the collaboration of philosophy and literature as well as to ensure that it did not become part of the dominant tradition in American philosophy departments. The works of Derrida and others were marginalized into a philosophical tradition that was for the most part alien to or disregarded by the dominant traditions of the time. Moreover, many philosophers still did not acknowledge Derrida's work as "philosophically" grounded.[17]

Richard Rorty, however, presented his own work as a serious effort to bridge continental theory and analytic philosophy. Even though Rorty was one of the few major contemporary American philosophers at the time to acknowledge a possible relationship between philosophy and literature, like most contemporary philosophers he remained unconvinced of the benefits of collaboration between literary and philosophy scholarship, and seemed keen on maintaining a division between them. Rorty's argument against the integration of philosophy and literature was based on the claim that the "vocabularies" of literature and philosophy are radically different, leaving them little in common. Whereas philosophy, like science, is "the sort of activity in which ... one can agree on some general principles which govern discourse in an area, and then aim at consensus by tracing inferential chains between these principles and more particular and more interesting proposition,"[18] literature, on the other hand, does not lend itself readily to argumentation. "Literature," for Rorty, concerns the "areas of culture which, quite self-consciously, forego agreement on an encompassing critical vocabulary, and thus forego argumentation."[19] As such, philosophers and literary theorists may share ideas with each other, but they will remain unable to argue with each other. For Rorty, on the basis of their relative "natures," there is little hope for their ever joining to share a discipline.

Rorty's more contentious claim is that despite their pretext of collaboration, literary theorists are actually asserting their superiority to philosophers. To exacerbate matters further, they are doing it on *philosophical* grounds. In addressing a conference at Johns

Hopkins in 1980[20]—just a year after Hartman's optimistic assessment of a future of collaboration between philosophy and literature—Rorty says that

> the *weakest* way to defend the plausible claim that literature has now displaced religion, science, and philosophy as the presiding discipline of our culture is by looking for a philosophical foundation for the practices of contemporary criticism. That would be like defending Galilean science by claiming that it can be found in the Scriptures. ... Science did not *demonstrate* that religion was false, nor philosophy that science was merely phenomenal, nor can modernist literature or textualist criticism *demonstrate* that the "metaphysics of presence" is an outdated genre.[21]

In Rorty's mind, literary theory cannot be granted a philosophical foundation—or, at best, a feeble one. Not only are literary theory and philosophy strictly distinct from one another in a way that would forever preclude the rapprochement between them suggested by Hartman, but, furthermore, literary theory can never become philosophy or philosophical. The two disciplines are strictly distinct, and any claim to the contrary by literary theorists should be viewed as an attempt to seize the role of presiding discipline of our culture.

For Rorty, anyone who defends the position that philosophy is a "text" is a proponent of the view that there are "nothing but texts."[22] Rorty calls such a person a "textualist," and in his mind they are all alike: "the so-called 'Yale school' of literary criticism centering around Harold Bloom, Geoffrey Hartman, J. Hillis Miller, and Paul de Man, 'post-structuralist' French thinkers like Jacques Derrida and Michel Foucault, historians like Hayden White, and social scientists like Rabinow" in Rorty's mind all hold exactly the same, singular view of text. Rorty's grouping is a clear distortion. While these thinkers share an affinity for a contemporary sense of text, they are by no means all proponents of Derrida's version, nor is their collective notion of textuality the only one.[23]

While it is uncertain why Rorty assembled these thinkers together, either out of ignorance or intentionally, the effect of this conflation was undeniable: it allowed him to dismiss both literary theory and textuality in a single assertion. Rorty's stance was not uncommon among the foes of literary theory and textuality at the time. Literary theory was presented in direct opposition to philosophy: literary theory meant "no argumentation" and "no philosophical foundation," and textuality meant a position much like Berkeley's idealism "where nothing exists but ideas."[24]

Portrayed as such, "textualism" in Rorty's opinion is merely an exaggerated romantic and pragmatic approach to textuality. A Derridean approach to textuality adds nothing to

> romanticism and pragmatism save instances of what can be achieved once one stops being bothered by realistic questions such as "Is that what the text really *says*?" or "How could one *argue* that that is what the poem is really *about*?" or

"How are we to distinguish between what is in the text from what the critic is imposing upon it?"[25]

For Rorty,

> the *only* force of saying that texts do not refer to nontexts is just the old pragmatist chestnut that any specification of a referent is going to be in some vocabulary. … the practices of the textualists have nothing to add save some splendid examples of the fact that the author of a text did not know a vocabulary in which his text can usefully be described.[26]

While Rorty is to be admired for attempting to situate and understand the work of the Yale school and post-structuralist thinkers, his efforts are nothing less than a vulgar distortion of their respective views. Like Gerald Graff and other critics of "textualism" of this period (1976–83),[27] Rorty thinks that not only do the proponents of textualism not argue for their positions, but that they also are really just paraphrasing old ideas: for Rorty, "textualism adds nothing save an extra metaphor to the romanticism of Hegel and the pragmatism of [William] James and Nietzsche,"[28] and for Graff, deconstruction is just the current refashioning of New Criticism.[29]

From Texting to Worlding

The late 1970s and the mid-1980s were the theoretical heyday of discussions of the relationship between philosophy and literature. And, as we have seen, it was a conversation largely conducted through the concept of *textuality* and whether or not philosophy and literary theory could join forces to explore the multifarious ways in which textuality impacts philosophical practices. Moreover, as far as one can determine such intangible things as disciplinary configurations, philosophy departments have by and large been able to avoid the influences of literary theory and, from their perspective, its major antagonists, deconstruction and poststructuralism. This compels students interested in studying the relationship between philosophy and literature[30] to turn away from them and toward history, politics, comparative literature, rhetoric and communications, and English and language departments.[31]

Rorty saw this clearly in 1981, at the height of the textualism in philosophy controversy. "One will not be encouraged," says Rorty,

> to go to a prestigious American graduate philosophy department if one does not have this particular intellectual virtue. Even if one loves to study Plato, Augustine, Spinoza, Kant, Hegel, etc., but lacks this skill at argumentation, one will not be encouraged to pursue a career in philosophy. One will wind up studying, instead, in a comparative literature department, or a politics department, or a history department. The result is gradually to strengthen the analytic philosophers' image

of themselves as, not specialists in a certain area of scientific inquiry, but rather a *corps d'élite* united by talent rather than a list of shared problems and prior results.[32]

Again, Rorty holds up argumentation as the distinguishing characteristic of philosophy in contrast to other disciplines. From within the philosophical community, the distinction is made between those who can argue (philosophers) and those who cannot (casual readers of Plato); from outside the philosophical community, the distinction is between those who view philosophy as text (historians, cultural theorists, rhetoricians, and comparatists) and those who do not (philosophers and scientists).

Rorty rightly adds that this environment in philosophy makes it "less and less important for analytic philosophy to have a coherent metaphilosophical account of itself"[33]—in other words, for philosophers to ask the kind of questions that literary theorists have asked about philosophical textuality. In fact, many philosophers regard projects that explore the textuality of philosophy as *merely* exercises in metaphilosophy. As one exposes issues relating to the textuality of philosophy—issues concerning writing, style, rhetoric, history, and culture—it becomes difficult to maintain a coherent metaphilosophy for analytic philosophy (or even professional philosophy in general) that excludes textuality as an important philosophical issue.

Now, two decades into the new millennium, there are still no major shifts in the philosophy curriculum nor are there any research trends that would indicate that literary theory changed the analytical emphasis of philosophy departments. While philosophy departments are a little less ahistorical today than they were in 1975, they still show very little interest in the relations between philosophy and literature. There is not much research today at the crossroads of philosophy and literary theory, philosophy and rhetoric, and philosophy and style by professional philosophers. Of the latter, Charles Altieri puts this absence into perspective commenting, "I do not think anyone in the heyday of modernism could have imagined how little style matters now as a topic of academic discourse in the arts and philosophy."[34] Moreover, textuality continues not to be a major preoccupation of philosophers or philosophy departments and still evokes the same dismissive response it received some forty years ago.

But philosophy departments are not alone today in their lack of interest in the relations between philosophy and literature. By the turn of the twentieth century, English and comparative literature departments seemed to also have had their fill of this debate and have looked toward "studies" (cultural and otherwise) as the way of the future. In more general terms, literary theory (as an area of inquiry concerned with the relations between philosophy and literature) became their recent past, and *studies* (as an area of inquiry concerned with everything *other than* the relations between philosophy and literature) their near future. Evidence: the booklists of major publishers reveal that decreasing numbers of literary theory books are being published today, while increasing numbers of studies books—cultural and otherwise—are being published by the selfsame publishers. The rise in the number of studies manuscripts published is inversely proportional to the decrease in the number of literary theory manuscripts published today. While quantity of manuscripts is not a good indicator of intellectual merit, it is a good indicator of scholarly and professional interest.[35]

What this indicates is the passing of a prominent "place" for the study of the relationship between philosophy and literature. If philosophy departments do not have an interest in it, and English and comparative literature programs are not interested in these "old" literary theory discussions from the 1970s and 1980s anymore, then where will discussion of the relations between philosophy and literature come from today? The answer is perhaps found in the essays in this volume, that is, in the shift from an emphasis on text and textuality to one on world and worlding.

As I have argued before, a strong case may be made that post-structuralist responses to social and political events, such as Jean Baudrillard's to the Gulf War in *La Guerre du Golfe n'a pas en lieu* (1991) and then again to the events of September 11, 2001, in "L'esprit du terrorisme" (2002) and "Requiem pour les Twin Towers" (2002), were some of the straws that broke the camel's back of "literary-philosophico" agenda of late-twentieth-century theory—and presaged the major changes in the temper of theory to come, which is to say, decidedly turned the academic momentum from theory to studies, or, alternately, from critique to criticism.[36] Vincent Leitch notes that the opposition to high theory of the type exhibited in the work of Derrida and others came "from not only conservative scholars, but also a broad array of contending liberal and left theorists, indicting it (particularly post-structuralism) for philosophical idealism, nominalism, obscurantism, and quietism, charges early made famous by certain Marxists, feminists, critical race theorists, and cultural studies scholars."[37] Work like Baudrillard's in the wake of the events of September 11, 2001, only added fuel to the fire.

But all of the blame for the changes in the temper of theory in the twenty-first century need not only be attributed only to opposition to high theory. Growing concern with and recognition of the ideology of neoliberalism that champions consumerism, global trading, and international free markets all aimed at producing a "better" world was gradually attracting more theoretical and philosophical attention. Though neoliberalism as an economic and political project that rose to prominence in the 1980s during its "first wave" in the United States with President Ronald Reagan (1981–8) and in the United Kingdom with British prime minister Margaret Thatcher (1979–90), both of whom shared the neoliberal belief that government is inefficient and strove to end the Keynesian era of "big government," and continued in its "second wave" in the 1990s with the market globalism of US president William "Bill" Clinton (1993–2001) and the Third Way of British prime minister Tony Blair (1997–2007), both of whom continued the neoconservative agenda of hyper-patriotism, militarism, neglect of the environment, and rejection of multiculturalism of first-wave neoliberalism, the critique of neoliberalism gained a lot of steam after the events of September 11, 2001.[38] Now globalization and neoliberalism brought the world and worlding to bear on all areas of academic inquiry including philosophy and literary studies. In short, in an era marked by global neoliberalism and terrorism, the textuality and literariness of philosophy took a backseat to seemingly more urgent and pressing "worldly" concerns.

Philosophy, Literature, and the World

Hindsight, though, is a funny thing. When we look back at the relations between philosophy and literature as discussed in the 1970s and 1980s, we might see that concerns with the "world" and "worlding" were more present in conversations that were dominated by discussions of texts and textuality than perhaps previously acknowledged. For example, Derrida (along with Juri Lotman) viewed the world as text[39]—a position that has entirely different connotations when emphasis is placed on the former term rather than the latter. We also may see the degree to which these high theorists (e.g., Derrida) and "their" continental philosophical tradition (e.g., Nietzsche, Heidegger, and Sartre) play a key role in many of the contributions to this volume. A good example is an interview Derrida gave in April 1989.

Published as "'This Strange Institution Called Literature': An Interview with Jacques Derrida," it is peppered with discussions of "texts"—literary and otherwise. However, when asked whether "a text is 'literary' or 'poetic' when it resists a transcendental reading," Derrida responds,

> Literature perhaps stands on the edge of everything, almost beyond everything, including itself. It's the most interesting thing in the world, maybe more interesting than the world, and this is why, if it has no definition, what is heralded and refused under the name of literature cannot be identified with any other discourse. It will never be scientific, philosophical, conversational.[40]

While the traditional debate between philosophy and literature still takes center stage, and he goes on to say if literature "did not open onto all of these discourses, if it did not open onto any of those discourses, it would not be literature either,"[41] the relationship between literature and *the world* is called upon to aid him in his response.

It in this same spirit of recalling "the world" in considerations of the relationship between philosophy and literature that the essays in Part I, entitled "World, Worlding, Worldliness," take their cue. The first, "The World, the Text, and Philosophy: Reflections on Translation" by Brian O'Keeffe, argues that philosophy cannot associate itself to the "world" without passing by a reflection on translation. The choice, as O'Keeffe sees it, is this: either philosophy quarantines itself behind a privileged idiom, or it exposes itself to multiple languages, such an exposure being, for him, the condition of possibility of philosophy—its texts, at least—encountering the "world," in all its variegated plurality, at all. Yet philosophy, argues O'Keeffe, has often been strategically hesitant to foreground the topic of translation, perhaps because aware of the risk that something—something vital to truth, to the universality of the concept—will be lost in translation. By pursuing that topic, with and against philosophy (with and against its putative other, namely literature, moreover), he aims to interrogate the complicated relation philosophy has to its own idiom, to language in the singular, and to languages in the plural.

The principal thinker at issue in his essay is Heidegger, he for whom the idioms of philosophy are rather sacrosanct but for whom literature has a privileged place. But, as

O'Keeffe shows, it is a privilege that depends on a discreet but consequential reflection on translation. His essay concludes with an invitation to philosophy that it enhance its scope by acknowledging its necessary debt to translation and thereby its debt to readers who are capable of the bilingual task of reading both in the original and in their own languages. Capable, that is, of transplanting that original into other languages, into other discourses and genres, including that of literature, that transplantation being, he argues, the only way philosophy can find its way to the "world." To be sure, O'Keeffe's essay serves as an important bridge between the "textuality" arguments of the 1970s and 1980s, and the emerging "worlding" ones of the new millennium.

The next essay, "Plato as World Literature," by classicist Paul Allen Miller acknowledges that while there are many senses in which Plato is world literature, he wants to argue for a specific and unique one. For Miller, Plato is world literature because the world as we know it, as we experience it, is constructed from a certain reading of Plato. This is true in terms of our continuing conviction that justice is something that transcends immediate utility, that beauty is more than sensuous gratification, and that truth is not purely contingent, that it perdures beyond the moment. Perhaps more fundamentally, argues Miller (following Heidegger like O'Keeffe), our very concept of being, the way in which we experience the world qua world is Platonic. For Miller, this is as true in New York as it is in Paris or Tehran or Beijing.

In "Worlding Interpretation, or Fanon and the Poetics of Disalienation," postcolonial theorist, Nicole Simek discusses worlding in some of the writings of French West Indian psychiatrist, revolutionary, and political philosopher Frantz Fanon. Drawing on Fanon's *Black Skin, White Masks* and the recently published collection *Alienation and Freedom* (which includes two previously unpublished plays by Fanon), this essay examines Fanon's poetico-philosophical forms of argument, and in particular his investment in interpretive forms that serve the project of disalienation by engaging both material and psychic conditions, cognitive and affective concerns. Simek argues that for Fanon to world interpretation is to take up the challenge of making sense of postcolonial life with an eye for the global processes with which it enters into relation. Worlding interpretation yields a knowledge that is both relational and skeptical. Foregrounding "the quite simple attempt to touch the other, to feel the other, to explain the other to myself," Simek sees the project of disalienation as an intersubjective and perpetual activity, poetically captured in Fanon's last line from *Black Skin, White Masks*, "O my body, make of me always a man who questions!"

The final essay in Part I, "Alluvia: The Palimpsest of African Memory" by Michael Stern, continues the discussion of colonial worlding. In the spring of 1885, proximate to the conclusion of the *Berlin Conference*, which divided the African continent into European colonies, Friedrich Nietzsche wrote two notebook entries describing how the "human being," a creature driven to make shapes and rhythms, creates worlds through the exercise of power. In the years that followed, European forms were imported to Africa and imposed on local populations in the name of "civilization." Stern's essay creates a dialog between Nietzschean notions of *worlding* and the Kenyan writer Ngugi Wa Thiong'o's critique of colonial education. For if Nietzsche would later argue that naming marks the possessions of sovereign individuals, then Ngugi, for Stern, provides us with a salient riposte, describing how the colonial practice of renaming imposes alien memory as an erasure of indigenous culture.

The essays in Part II, "Migration and Difference," opens with an essay by Robin Truth Goodman entitled "Feminism as World Literature." Feminist theory, argues Goodman, has traditionally positioned femininity in its relation to "home." Simone de Beauvoir, for example, wrote of women's gender role as "imminent," meaning that she was grounded in the physicality of her own body, especially in her reproductive, care, and familial capacities. Partha Chatterjee has analyzed women's position in colonialized societies as preserving indigenous national culture against foreign impositions and bureaucracies. Recently, however, trends in feminist theory have pivoted against these suppositions and increasingly begun to consider women's place as what Gayatri Spivak has called "worlding." Judith Butler, for example, has considered how gender and sexuality are being constructed to justify torture in global war. Areas of investigation that have also taken this turn include migration, translation, new technology, and social reproduction. In this chapter, Goodman discusses the various ways that feminist theory and femininity itself are becoming part of the worldly imagination and its literature.

In "Astonishing Worlding: Montaigne and the New World," Zahi Zalloua moves the discussion back to the origins of modern philosophy. In *The Passions of the Soul*, René Descartes blames philosophy's failure to attain a "better state" on an unhealthy excess of wonder: "Astonishment is an excess of wonder which can never be anything but bad." Philosophy, for Descartes, ought to be about successful translation: the translation of the new into a mastered and well-digested familiar. Michel de Montaigne for his part is skeptical of any return on philosophy's cognitive investment. Rather, Montaigne, in his *Essays*, argues Zalloua, yearns for and thrives on astonishment, the endless, multiple, and joyful pursuit of his subject matter (including his self and others).

Zalloua's essay turns to Montaigne's writing on the New World, exploring the essayist's ambivalent figuration of the Cannibal of the New World. Though the designation of "Cannibal" became coterminous with the enslavement of the indigenous population of the New World, Montaigne arguably co-opts the term for its astonishing value—the Cannibal is, after all, the image of the radical other *par excellence*. At the same time, Montaigne is all too aware that the radical alterity of the Cannibal has been synonymous with the latter's assumed lack of humanity. For Zalloua, Montaigne's *essaying* of the Cannibal constitutes an act of worlding—an act that gestures toward an alternative reception and configuration of the radical other, toward a heterology that stresses cultural otherness without simultaneously evacuating the other's claims to universality.

The next essay in this section is "Literature of the World, Unite!" by Peter Hitchcock. This essay explores the critical tension between a political philosophy primed to encourage global transformation and the effulgence of a literary system that is often read to be the effect of that project's sublation. The ambivalent worldliness of Marxism is not just a measure of its constitutive limits of politics in given historical crises but also a condition of its status as philosophy, as worlding. This contribution attempts to show how a materialist critique of world betrays the "unity" it is intended to proffer. Clearly, this has implications for the "world" in "world literature" and beyond. It also has, as Hitchcock shows following O'Keeffe, implications for translation and translatability in the production of a "world" literature.

The final essay in Part II is "Transatlantic Thoreau: Henry S. Salt, Gandhi, and British Humanitarian Socialism" by David M. Robinson. In his contribution, Robinson shows how the transatlantic migration of Thoreau's political philosophy through his first British biographer contributed to political activism in both Britain and India. In 1890, Henry S. Salt published the first British biography of Henry David Thoreau, adding an influential voice to the radical circles associated with Salt's Humanitarian League. Best known for his advocacy of animal rights and vegetarianism, Salt sought to make the Humanitarian League a means of linking pacifist, socialist, anti-imperialist, and similar causes in a shared mission. Salt's biography, still highly respected in Thoreau studies, attempted to provide a contemporary example of an engaged and principled, yet simple, life. Of particular importance to Salt and his associates was Thoreau's incisive exposition of the philosophical grounding of ethical resistance to unjust governmental actions in "Civil Disobedience." Thoreau's argument appealed to both the peaceable and resistant aspects of Salt's thinking. These same principles appealed to Gandhi, who corresponded with Salt, read Salt's Thoreau biography early in his political development, and consistently cited Thoreau as one of his key influences.

The essays in Part III, entitled "Philosophy, Religion, and the East," continue to push our discussion of philosophy as world literature eastward. In "Nietzsche and World Iterature: The Eternal Recurrence of Dualism in *Thus Spake Zarathustra*" by Jeffrey S. Librett, we again return the philosophy of Nietzsche. In his essay, Librett provides a reading of Nietzsche's *Thus Spake Zarathustra*—a text that takes the manifest form of an extended impersonation of the ancient Persian prophet Zoroaster—in order to lay bare the main contours of Nietzsche's response to the orientalist tradition in German philosophy and literature, especially in Johann Wolfgang Goethe and Arthur Schopenhauer. Librett places particular emphasis on the way in which Nietzsche displaces Schopenhauer's concept of "world" by taking up Goethe's suggestion to pursue a "world-literature" perspective. Whereas Schopenhauer's ethics of the negation of the world (seen as a will-to-live) privileged Hindu culture as a model to be both imitated and realized in the West, Nietzsche's paradoxically nihilistic and optimistic later poetic thinking privileges Persian culture as a model to be both imitated and actively forgotten by the creatively independent individual. The essay concludes with the implications of Nietzsche's text (including its complex reception history) for "world-literature" in the age of cultural globalization.

The next essay, "Asian Philosophy, National Literatures, and World Literature Anthologies" by Junjie Luo, moves our discussion of philosophy as world literature even further eastward in its discussion of Asian philosophy. According to Luo, some early world literature anthologies include Asian philosophical texts such as the *Bhagavad Gita* and Confucius's *Analects* instead of examples of other Asian literature genres. These Asian philosophical writings were used to represent their national literatures and civilizations. Contemporary world literature anthologies, however, include a more diverse body of Asian texts. The Asian philosophical traditions are often treated as the foundation and beginning of their respective national literatures. These contemporary anthologies seek to construct dialogues between Asian philosophical texts and the other types of texts and to explore the dynamic interactions between philosophy and literature. Luo concludes that Asian philosophy plays a pivotal role in connecting Asian literatures to world literature. During this process, these philosophical texts have also become part of world literature.

Ranjan Ghosh's "The Dharma of World Literature" focuses on Rabindranath Tagore's essay "Visva Sahitya" (world literature) where he works out a philosophical-critical understanding of sahitya's comradeship and the problematic notion of "totality." Ghosh reinterrogates the notion of sahitya with its Sanskritic origin and epistemological identity, and extends its meaning outside its own culture and tradition of thinking. Ghosh's fresh reading of this major essay then situates Tagore's idea of "visva" around the concept of sahitya. Even though Tagore's visva sahitya owes much to a philosophical tradition and a culture of thinking, it cannot help evoking correspondences with traditions outside it too. Ghosh's discussion of "worlding" concludes on the potency and poesis of Tagore's transcultural understanding with resonances derived from across cultures both within the Indian subcontinent and outside it. Visva sahitya cannot restrict itself to its Indic understanding only, argues Ghosh. Sahitya is too encompassive and immanental to allow such restrictive, walled-in, experience of reading literature.

In the final essay in this section is nothing less than a tapestry of philosophy, religion, and literature magisterially woven by Henry Sussman through his examination of deconstruction's eastward dissemination in the work of two novelists. "Olive-Red in Orhan Pamuk and Anton Shammas: Deconstruction's Eastward Dissemination" discusses in sequence novels by Orhan Pamuk, the Nobel Prize-winning Turkish novelist, essayist, and curator; and by Anton Shammas, the Israeli-Arab-Christian poet, novelist, and scholar. Sussman describes deconstruction's eastward dissemination into the Muslim framework of Turkey via Pamuk's *My Name is Red* and into the complexities of Middle Eastern politics via Shammas's Hebrew-language novel *Arabesques: A Novel* as "an oozing, not an earthquake but a mudslide, a slow sink." Furthermore, Sussman warns that such "an eastward diffusion or extension of a specialist's set of readerly and philosophical bearings incubated on Montparnasse is just as much an act of return as it is colonization, an incursion into new territory." Derrida's comments about "his Algerian beginnings, about the impact of growing up in Arab society, irrespective of his familial Jewish ethnicity" serve as the context for "deconstruction's tending, its *Neigung*, toward the Muslim, the Arab, the Algerian, the Persian—deconstruction's always already pitching a tent in the Middle East and utterly thriving among the self-negating and self-effacing codes of hospitality and honor—is also its turning homeward back toward its base position of full-throttle critical engagement." Sussman's readings of works that establish philosophy (in this case, Derrida's) as world literature (in this case, works by Shammas and Pamuk) add layers of meaning and complexity as well as complement and expand our understanding of philosophy as world literature.

The final section of this collection is devoted to the tensions and dialectics that come to the fore when world literature is regarded as philosophy and when works of world literature are treated as philosophical. Part IV, entitled "Philosophy versus World Literature," begins with a look at existential writing, which is perhaps the most commonly recognized form of philosophy as world literature. In "Existentialism as World Literature: De Beauvoir, Heidegger, and Tolstoy," Robert Doran reminds us that existentialism has always been an intellectual movement that transcended national boundaries. Its main philosophical progenitors—Søren Kierkegaard, Nietzsche, Karl Jaspers, Heidegger, Sartre, Simone de Beauvoir, José Ortega y Gasset, and Fanon—cover a wide range of styles, languages, and cultural contexts over a roughly one-hundred-year period. This is no less true of the literary engagements with existentialism, from Fyodor Dostoevsky in Russia and Franz Kafka in Germany, in the nineteenth century, to Sartre and Albert Camus in France and Ralph Ellison in the United States, in the twentieth. That these literary engagements reverberated globally is signaled by the Nobel Prize in Literature awarded to Sartre (1964, refused) and Camus (1957, accepted).

Doran's essay approaches this vast expanse of work by focusing his discussion on the problem of the philosophy-literature relation as explored by the French novelist and philosopher de Beauvoir, and following it with a "case study" on how a Russian fiction writer (Leo Tolstoy) and a German philosopher (Heidegger) treat the subject of death in an existentialist manner. Doran concludes that existentialist philosophy and fiction have had an enormous impact on world literature and even on the concept of world literature itself—if one privileges a thought-based rather than a generic approach to the subject.

The next essay looks at the problem of the philosophy-literature relation through the work of one of the most respected writers in the world, the Argentinian short-story writer, essayist, poet, and translator, Jorge Luis Borges. In "Jorge Luis Borges and Philosophy," Efraín Kristal claims that Borges was not and did not consider himself to be a philosopher, and that it would be misleading to draw on his short stories as a coherent philosophical system. And yet, philosophical ideas and observations abound in his short stories, essays, and poems; he was interested in the lives and circumstances of a select number of philosophers; and his works have inspired commentary and meditation by major philosophers in the continental *and* analytic traditions. In this chapter, Kristal focus attention on Fritz Mauthner and Macedonio Férnandez, who were decisive in Borges's approach to philosophy, and discusses some of Borges's philosophical commentaries. For Kristal, Borges conducts his thought experiments through a range of mutually exclusive philosophical ideas, which are all part and parcel of his literary world.

The final chapter, "Philosophy for the Masses: Haldeman-Julius, Durant, and *The Story of Philosophy*" by Jeffrey R. Di Leo examines the philosophy-literature relationship through an examination of one of the most "popular" philosophy books in the world. After the First World War, there was a fear that if the masses were not more educated in history, philosophy, literature, and other critical areas of knowledge, the world was doomed for catastrophe. This resulted in a publication boom of books for the general reader with titles that began with "The Outline of" and "The Story of." The first was H. G. Wells *The Outline of History* (1919–20), which was explicitly written to educate the masses about history in order to avoid "catastrophe"—or more simply put, to save the world. In a similar vein, Will Durant started publishing pamphlets on the history of philosophy in 1923, which were compiled into *The Story of Philosophy* in 1926, a best-selling book that by 1953 already had been translated into German, French, Swedish, Danish, Jugo-Slavian, Chinese, Japanese, and Hungarian, and was read worldwide. Though it helped to popularize philosophy worldwide, it was an assault on analytic and professional philosophy, and was and still is widely dismissed by professional philosophers. Part of the reason for its dismissal was Durant's efforts to make his story read more like a "romance" or "literature" than an analytic treatment of the arguments of the philosophers. This essay examines *The Story of Philosophy* as a work of "world literature" rather than "philosophy" and speculates on its role as both an agent against the rise of authoritarianism worldwide and the analytic movement in twentieth-century philosophy.

Conclusion

Philosophy as world literature offers the opportunity for a new rapprochement between philosophy and literature. However, while many of the key arguments regarding the relations between philosophy and literature that dominated the academy in the 1970s and 1980s may be behind us, many of the key thinkers are not. A reconsideration of the relation between philosophy and literature from the position of the world and the worlding of literature invites us to broaden both the concepts of literature *and* philosophy. It also shifts considerations of philosophy and literature from topics such as universality versus particularity, reason versus imagination, detachment versus engagement, and insight versus emotion to ones of colonization, translation, migration, transnationalism, disalienation, and resistance.

In sum, the essays in this collection reveal philosophy as world literature to involve global networks of increasing complexity and precarity. They also show how the establishment of this new rapprochement between philosophy and literature has the potential to again open up pathways between the study of philosophy and the study of literature albeit under the guise of world theory—a theory that invites speculation that crosses borders, mixes stories, and speaks in dialect. Where translation is a key part of the story and migration is always already in play. Since the era of deconstruction, we have not seen another really fruitful interaction of the "sister arts" of philosophy and literature. But philosophy as world literature has this potential as it requires *cooperative* disciplinary relations rather than competitive ones. It is a nod to a future where the disciplines of philosophy and literary studies work toward understanding and resolving the issues facing the world—*our* world—rather than hiding from them in their disciplinary outposts.

Notes

1 See Richard Eldridge, "Introduction—Philosophy and Literature as Forms of Attention," in *The Oxford Handbook of Philosophy and Literature*, ed. Richard Eldridge (New York: Oxford UP, 2009), 3–18.

2   There has been an active debate of late both for and against "world literature." See, e.g., David Damrosch, *What Is World Literature?* (Princeton: Princeton UP, 2003); Pascale Casanova, *The World Republic of Letters*, trans. M. B. Debevoise (Cambridge: Harvard UP, 2007); Emily Apter, *Against World Literature: On the Politics of Untranslatability* (New York: Verson, 2013); Pheng Cheah, *What Is a World? On Postcolonial Literature as World Literature* (Durham: Duke UP, 2016); and Aamir Mufti, *Forget English! Orientalisms and World Literatures* (Cambridge: Harvard UP, 2016).

3   The question of style in philosophy is an interesting one. It is both everywhere and nowhere in the history of philosophy. Berel Lang, ed., *Philosophical Style: An Anthology about the Reading and Writing of Philosophy* (Chicago: Nelson-Hall, 1980), for example, collects selections from Plato, Aristotle, Augustine, Hume, Kant, Kierkegaard, Peirce, Collingwood, and Merleau-Ponty on philosophical style. However, while these selections show that many of the classic philosophers grappled with issues of style, none of them attempt to define style or to pursue its domain and range in philosophy. One good source for this topic is Caroline van Eck, James McAllister and Renée an de Vall, eds., *The Question of Style in Philosophy and the Arts* (Cambridge: Cambridge UP, 1995), which challenges us to look to studies of style in the arts for a conception of style for philosophy given that art theorists and historians have been grappling with these issues for over two hundred years, and philosophers have only been marginally interested in the prospect of style in philosophy.

4   Some current examples of undergraduate courses that combine philosophy and literature from philosophy departments in the United States include: Philosophy 2024—Philosophy in Literature (Louisiana State University), Philosophy 252—Philosophy and Literature (George Mason University, which offered eight sections of this course in Fall 2018), Philosophy 320—Philosophy and Literature (Princeton University), Philosophy 306—Philosophy and Literature (John Carroll University), Philosophy 204—Philosophical Fiction (Virginia Wesleyan University), Philosophy 215—Philosophy of Literature (University of Southern Maine), Philosophy 217—Philosophy and Literature (Trinity College, San Antonio, Texas), Philosophy 226—Philosophy and Literature (SUNY, Geneseo), Philosophy 226—Philosophy of Literature (Lafayette College), Philosophy 3161—Philosophy and Literature (George Washington University), Philosophy 360—Philosophy and Literature (Marymount University), and Philosophy 81—Philosophy and Literature (Stanford University).

5   See Jeffrey R. Di Leo, ed., *American Literature as World Literature* (London: Bloomsbury, 2018), for a survey of some of the different ways of "worlding" American literature.

6   Particularly, *Of Grammatology* [1967], trans. Gayatri Spivak (Baltimore: Johns Hopkins UP, 1976), *Writing and Difference* [1967], trans. Alan Bass (Chicago: University of Chicago Press, 1978), *Dissemination* [1972], trans. Barbara Johnson (Chicago: University of Chicago Press, 1981), *Margins of Philosophy* [1972], trans. Alan Bass (Chicago: University of Chicago Press, 1982), *Positions* [1972], trans. Alan Bass (Chicago: University of Chicago Press, 1981), and *Glas* [1974], trans John P. Leavey and Richard Rand (Lincoln: University of Nebraska Press, 1986).

7   Particularly, *Allegories of Reading: Figural Language in Rousseau, Nietzsche, Rilke and Proust* (New Haven: Yale UP, 1979) and *Blindness and Insight: Essays in the Rhetoric of Contemporary Criticism* (Minneapolis: University of Minnesota Press, 1971; 2nd ed. 1983).

8 Particularly, *Criticism in the Wilderness: The Study of Literature Today* (New Haven: Yale UP, 1980) and *Saving the Text: Literature/ Derrida/Philosophy* (Baltimore: Johns Hopkins UP, 1981). By 1979, Harold Bloom, Paul de Man, Jacques Derrida, J. Hillis Miller, and Hartman had come to be referred to as the "hermeneutical Mafia," with Bloom and Hartman referred to as the most "moderate" of the deconstructors and de Man, Derrida, and Miller as the "boa-deconstructors."

9 Between 1976 and 1983, there were an extraordinary number of studies on the possible interrelations between philosophy and style, rhetoric, and writing. Even the philosophy journal *The Monist* got into the act by publishing a special issue on "Philosophy as Style and Literature as Philosophy" in October 1980 (vol. 63, no. 4). Nevertheless, while just a speculation, it seems as though "deconstruction in America" caused an extraordinarily high amount of interest in the "borders" of philosophical practice both in and out of the philosophical profession.

10 At the time, particularly after the 1977 exchange between J. L. Austin and Derrida over the work of J. L. Austin, there were a number of well-intended collections of essays published concerning the tensions and commonalties between analytic philosophy, deconstruction, and literary theory. See, especially, Reed Way Dasenbrock, ed., *Redrawing the Lines* (Minneapolis: University of Minnesota Press, 1989), as well as Donald Marshall, ed., *Literature as Philosophy / Philosophy as Literature* (Iowa City: University of Iowa Press, 1987). These collections capture well the spirit and issues of the times regarding the relationship between philosophy and literature.

11 Harold Bloom, Paul de Man, Jacques Derrida, Geoffrey Hartman, and J. Hillis Miller, *De-construction and Criticism* (New York: Continuum, 1979), ix.

12 "The separation of philosophy from literary study has not worked to the benefit of either. Without the pressure of philosophy on literary texts, or the reciprocal pressure of literary analysis on philosophical writing, each discipline becomes impoverished. If there is the danger of a confusion of realms, it is a danger worth experiencing" (Hartman, "Preface," in *De-construction and Criticism*, ix).

13 See John Rajchman and Cornel West, eds., *Post-Analytic Philosophy* (New York: Columbia UP, 1985); Kenneth Baynes, James Bohman, and Thomas McCarthy, eds., *After Philosophy: End or Transformation?* (Cambridge: MIT Press, 1987); and Avner Cohen and Marcelo Dascal, eds., *The Institution of Philosophy: A Discipline in Crisis?* (La Salle: Open Court, 1989). If Blaise Pascal is right that "not to care for philosophy is to be a true philosopher," then the late 1980s (1985–9) saw an exponential growth in philosophers: voices from many different quarters were telling us that we should not care about philosophy and that it had ended.

14 Richard Rorty, "Nineteenth Century Idealism and Twentieth-Century Textualism (1980)," in *Consequences of Pragmatism* (Minneapolis: University of Minnesota Press, 1982), 159n7.

15 Nevertheless, around this time, a rebellion was staged against the dominance of the analytic tradition in the American Philosophical Association (APA). Led by Bruce W. Wilshire, a group of metaphysicians, continental, and pragmatic philosophers in the early 1970s demanded that the APA not treat their work as second-rate to the dominant analytic philosophy and include more of it in their conference programs. The work of this "pluralist movement" eventually changed the APA to be more inclusive of "non-analytic philosophy" in the conference program and laid the course for the inclusion as well of the work of women and racial and ethnic minorities in

APA conference programming. See Bruce W. Wilshire, "The Pluralist Rebellion in the American Philosophical Association," in *Fashionable Nihilism: A Critique of Analytic Philosophy* (Albany: State University of New York Press, 2002), 51–64.

16 One must remember that for some, Hans Reichenbach's publication of *The Rise of Scientific Philosophy* (Berkeley: University of California Press, 1951) was a benchmark in the history of the rise of analytic philosophy in the United States. From that time on, analytic philosophy clashed with differing forms of "continental" philosophy including but not limited to the existentialist and phenomenological movements of the late 1950s through the early 1970s.

17 Nevertheless, a very good introduction to some of the philosophical background of Derrida's literary theory is Mark C. Taylor's *Deconstruction in Context: Literature and Philosophy* (Chicago: University of Chicago Press, 1986).

18 Rorty, "Nineteenth Century," 141.

19 Ibid., 142.

20 The presentation was later published as "Nineteenth Century Idealism and Twentieth-Century Textualism" and was reprinted in Rorty, *Consequences of Pragmatism*.

21 Rorty, "Nineteenth Century," 155.

22 Ibid., 139. It should be noted here that Rorty is referring to Derrida's vision of the world as text wherein he argues that there is nothing outside of the text (*il n'y a pas de hors-texte*). See Jacques Derrida, *Dissemination*, 328.

23 Depictions of "text" can be generally divided into two distinct groups: the classical and the contemporary depictions. Broadly speaking, there are four main characteristics of the classical depiction of text: (1) Autonomy—text is isolated from the whole of signification; (2) Stability—text has a perfectly stable and unchanging aspect; (3) Coherence—text is totally coherent and definable; and (4) Identity—text has an entirely determinate identity. Contemporary depictions of text tend to define themselves in direct opposition to classical depictions of text. Thus, again broadly speaking, the contemporary depiction of text also has four main characteristics: (1) Non-Autonomy—text is regarded as coextensive or integrated with the whole of signification; (2) Non-Stability—text is *unstable* and *changing*; (3) Non-Coherence—text exemplifies a total lack of coherence and definability; and (4) Non-Identity—text has an indeterminate identity. See Jeffrey R. Di Leo, "Text," in *The Oxford Encyclopedia of Aesthetics*, 6 vols., ed. Michael Kelly, 2nd ed. (New York: Oxford UP, 2014), 6: 129–34, for an account of where the work of particular thinkers fall relative to this distinction.

24 See Rorty, "Nineteenth Century," 139ff. For some, the rejection of theory does not entail the adoption of another version of it. Rather, it is the simple and categorical rejection of theory—*all* theory, no exceptions. Vincent Leitch has said that this group of antitheorists includes "traditional literary critics; aesthetes; critical formalists; political conservatives; ethnic separatists; some literary stylisticians, philologists, and hermeneuticists; certain neopragmatists; champions of low and middlebrow literature; creative writers; defenders of common sense and plain style; plus some committed leftists" (Vincent Leitch, "Antitheory," in *Bloomsbury Handbook of Literary and Cultural Theory*, ed. Jeffrey R. Di Leo [London: Bloomsbury, 2019], 373). For a general introduction to the varieties and conditions of antitheory, see Jeffrey R. Di Leo, ed., *What's Wrong with Antitheory?* (London: Bloomsbury, 2020).

25 Rorty, "Nineteenth Century," 154.

26 Ibid.

27 A good primer of attacks on deconstruction from this time period is John M. Ellis, *Against Deconstruction* (Princeton: Princeton UP, 1989).
28 Rorty, "Nineteenth Century," 155.
29 Gerald Graff, "What Was the New Criticism?," *Literature against Itself* (Chicago: University of Chicago Press, 1979), 145.
30 I have discussed this in "On Being and Becoming Affiliated," in *Affiliations: Identity in Academic Culture*, ed. Jeffrey R. Di Leo (Lincoln: University of Nebraska Press, 2003), 101–14.
31 The major exception to this was the American philosopher Stanley Cavell, who was a distinguished and long-standing member of the Harvard University philosophy faculty. Cavell's work, though, went in a completely different and unique direction from the post-structuralists regarding the interrelations of philosophy and literature as it was influenced by the writings of Emerson, Thoreau, Kierkegaard, Nietzsche, Wittgenstein, Heidegger, and J. L. Austin. See, e.g., *Must We Mean What We Say?* (Cambridge: Cambridge UP, 1969; 2nd ed., 2002), and *The Claim of Reason: Wittgenstein, Skepticism, Morality, and Tragedy* (New York: Oxford UP, 1979).
32 Richard Rorty, "Philosophy in America Today," in *Consequences of Pragmatism*, 219–20.
33 Ibid., 220.
34 Charles Altieri, "Style," in *The Oxford Handbook of Philosophy and Literature*, 420.
35 A recent edited collection suggests that we might look to areas such as metamodernism, posthumanism, object-oriented ontology, new materialisms, ordinary language criticism, embodiment, and biopolitics for "new" directions in philosophy and literature. See David Rudrum, Ridvan Askin, and Frida Beckman, eds., *New Directions in Philosophy and Literature* (Edinburgh: Edinburgh UP, 2019). The jury though is still out as to whether these "new" directions achieve the level of interest in the relationship between philosophy and literature that was attained in the late twentieth century. Moreover, at least one of these areas, ordinary language criticism, is not all that recent. Stanley Cavell, as noted above, was working in this area for most of the latter half of the twentieth century.
36 See Jeffrey R. Di Leo, "The Ruins of Critique," in *Criticism After Critique: Aesthetics, Literature, and the Political*, ed. Jeffrey R. Di Leo (New York: Palgrave, 2014), 1–4.
37 Vincent Leitch, *Living with Theory* (Malden: Blackwell, 2008), 10.
38 See Jeffrey R. Di Leo, "Neoliberalism," in *Bloomsbury Handbook of Literary and Cultural Theory*, 587–9.
39 I make this argument in my article "Text" in *The Oxford Encyclopedia of Aesthetics* (2014). For Juri Lotman, see *The Structure of the Artistic Text* (1970), trans. Ronald Vroon and Gail Vroon (Ann Arbor: University of Michigan Press, 1977); for Derrida, see especially *Dissemination* (1972).
40 Jacques Derrida, "'This Strange Institution Called Literature': An Interview with Jacques Derrida," in *Acts of Literature*, ed. Derek Attridge (London: Routledge, 1992), 47.
41 Ibid., 48.

Part I

World, Worlding, Worldliness

1

The World, the Text, and Philosophy: Reflections on Translation

Brian O'Keeffe

My topic is philosophy's "world"—the concept philosophy makes of it and how philosophy encounters it in a real sense. But the world is a big place, so I begin on a smaller scale, with two small islands. Consider, first, Thomas More's *Utopia*: insularity protects utopia's borders from less-than-ideal encroachments—this society flourishes in secure isolation. Utopian language flourishes here too, and we may read a little example (in English translation): "The commander Utopus made me into an island out of a non-island / I alone of all nations, without philosophy / have portrayed for mortals the philosophical city."[1] How to make an island out of a non-island? Imagine digging a deep ditch, contoured to the island's profile, or making a moat out of the sea itself. Perhaps the easier way to insularize an island, however, is to erect a linguistic border: surely the hardest border is constituted by an *invented* language. Yet inasmuch as we have a translation, hasn't the deconstruction of this border already begun? As a thought experiment in imagining the ideal nation, in any case, it may well require an island to serve as the space wherein such experiments can occur: the ideal nation as an island where geographical, national, and linguistic borders map onto each other, presuppose each other. Plato take heed: "I alone … have portrayed for mortals the philosophical city." If so, experiments in construing the philosophical Republic require what Marc Shell calls an "islandology": the best way to idealize a nation, or a republic, is to maroon philosophical and political thought on an island of the mind—a circumscribed, *eutopian* place, immune from encroachment, bridgeless and without pier or jetty, alone and isolate.

My second island is Robinson Crusoe's. Robinson doesn't invent a new language, of course—the lingo of his scepter'd isle is English. But it took a Frenchman's flair to insert this English literary text into a sustained discussion of philosophical sovereignty. I refer, of course, to Jacques Derrida's *The Beast and the Sovereign*. Insularity is requisite to the discussion because Daniel Defoe's text, among other things, is an attempt to proffer a truly national literary work—no wonder an island serves this agenda, since its borders are geographically distinct, as distinct as one might hope a national literary work might be as well. Derrida cites James Joyce: "[Defoe was] the first English author to write without imitating or adapting foreign works."[2]

Islandology describes spaces immune from foreignness that serve the heuristic need for a tabula rasa where, in literature and in philosophy, ideal nationalisms, absolute sovereignties, and utopian communities can be imagined. We are far from the "world," therefore, or from the "non-island": connected landmasses or adjoined continents linked by internal borders (hard or soft) or by bridges and tunnels. So be it, if we wish to imagine the aboriginal, the indigenous, and a political philosophy of splendid isolation. Alas, moreover, "island" describes our own isolation as well—aren't we all Crusoes, marooned on separate islands because we are all different from one another? My world is not your world, my being in time and space is not your being in time and space:

> Between my world and any other world there is first the space and the time of an infinite difference, an interruption that is incommensurable with all attempts to make a passage, a bridge, an isthmus, all attempts at communication, translation, trope, and transfer that the desire for a world … will try to pose, impose, propose, stabilize.[3]

Every man is an island, then, islanded by a singularity that forbids transference, transposition, or *translation*, since no man can turn or trope himself into someone else. The isolate, desolate conclusion, *pace* John Donne's "no man is an island," is that "there is no world, there are only islands."[4]

Not that the word "island" is immune from translation. When Derrida asks "qu'est-ce qu'une île?" (what is an island?), and "qu'est une 'île'?" (what is an island?), he lets French speakers hear a different question, namely, "qu'est-ce qu'une 'il'?" (what is a he?), where the feminine article "une" introduces the masculine "il." None of this is really translatable into English, but Anglophone readers of Derrida ought not to miss the point. Every man is an island; no man is an island. Perhaps we ought to question the philosophical and literary sovereignty awarded to the masculine.

These two instances of islandology (three, if you add Joyce—a specialist of Irelandology, I think) give us a sense of the figurative and conceptual geographies to consider when philosophy's relation to the world is at issue. Perhaps philosophy would prefer to circumscribe its intellectual dominion thanks to an island, rather than emplace itself in the world. For on an island, philosophy's *logos* spreads unimpeded, transparently intelligible to all. Philosophical utopia wards off barbarians, translators, and inopportune writers, like Homer, writing in that foreign genre called "literature" (foreign to philosophy at any rate), knocking at the gates, seeking admission to philosophy's safe space.

World Philosophy

If philosophy is to leave its islands and encounter the world, we must imagine a voyage or at least consider the modes of circulation whereby philosophy travels worldwide. If "translation" describes one such mode, we might accordingly activate the maritime metaphor resident in *translatio* and contemplate journeying from a home shore to a foreign shore—envisage embarkation, the crossing, and disembarkation at that farther shore. But philosophy will eventually ask us to relinquish metaphors, cease referring to literary texts, and abandon these whimsical itineraries of translation in order to get serious: the philosophical treatment of the world, and indeed the "world analytic" philosophy offers, requires rigorous engagement with the *concept* of world. At issue, moreover, is the purchase philosophy gains on what it means to inhabit the world, to make or form "world," and besides, to survey the world from the position of philosophical universality. Then there's the matter of what philosophy conveys to the world: concepts, principles, hypotheses and theses, and, above all, Truths. If a truth is subject to the vicissitudes of a worldwide journey, it presumably wishes to arrive intact as the same truth it was when it departed. If translation is one of the journeys to be envisaged, nothing of a truth *as such* should be lost in translation. Thus, philosophy must idealize a model of perfect translation: as Derrida puts it in *The Ear of the Other*, "the origin of philosophy is translation or the thesis of translatability."[5]

I'll have more to say later concerning this provocative determination of philosophy's origin and its related thesis of translatability. I allude to it here in order to make the point that, if philosophy relies on a certain model of translation, it does so the better to secure for philosophy a distinction it doesn't apparently share with anything else, namely, the prerogative to establish, verify, and circulate truths. I insist on this. For it clarifies what philosophy's attitude might be to the proposal that philosophy be regarded as world literature. That is: if philosophy is to encounter a wider world, it might have to convey itself to that world *as literature*. If, on the contrary, philosophy has its own modes of circulation—one of which is afforded by a translation model that broadcasts philosophical truths without loss—then philosophy has no need of other conveyances and would therefore decline the invitation to transpose (or translate) itself into literature.

Nonetheless, in order to examine how the notion of "world literature" can serve as a touchstone for construing a corresponding (or opposing) notion of "world philosophy," it may be instructive to briefly describe how scholarship has treated the question of literature's worldliness, the dynamics of its "worlding," and its modes of worldwide circulation. For Edward Said, writing in *The World, the Text, and the Critic*, texts have a circumstantial reality, a "worldliness."[6] Once the horizons of such worldliness are discerned by the critic, texts become mobile—the world isn't static, so texts cannot be static either. In "Traveling Theory," moreover, Said calls for a study of the circulation not just of texts, but also of ideas, and indeed literary or philosophical theories. The starting point is an acknowledgement that "like people and schools of criticism, ideas and theories travel—from person to person, from situation to situation, from one period to another."[7] Said describes the four stages of the journey: there's a point of origin, this being a matter of the initial circumstances enabling an idea's birth. Then there's a "distance traversed, a passage through the pressure of various contexts as the idea moves from an earlier point to another time and place."[8] Then, at the other time and place, there's acceptance and resistance to that transplanted idea. Finally, once the accommodations have been made, the idea is transformed by the new uses being made of it.

David Damrosch shares Said's emphasis on a text's worldliness, and the motif of travel is also active in his *What Is World Literature?* But the specific context for Damrosch's account is Goethe's call for the advent of the age of world literature. If one wished to hasten world literature's advent, wouldn't that mean reading all literature and mastering all the languages of literature? For Damrosch, however, "world literature is not an infinite, ungraspable canon of works but rather a mode of circulation and of reading."[9] Moreover, "I take world literature to encompass all literary works that circulate beyond their culture of origin, either in translation or in their original language."[10] Let's translate already: world philosophy is a mode of circulation and of reading. World philosophy encompasses all philosophical works that circulate beyond their culture of origin, either in translation or in their original language.

But one question is how philosophy might react to the following: "In its most expansive sense, world literature could include any work that has ever reached beyond its home base."[11] *Any* work: presumably, therefore, any philosophical work as well. Philosophy, I imagine, would object to this "most expansive sense" and sharply ask by what right literary studies claims the world in the name of *literature*, and what expansive sense literary studies ascribes to the idea of "literature" in any case. Philosophy would be well within its rights to ask, "What is literature?" The response, I take it, would be that "world literature" isn't a *theory* of literature, that "world literature" is only to be understood as a mode of circulation. For philosophy, however, that's putting the cart before the horse, and so it will resist any idea that "world literature could include any work that has ever reached beyond its home base," not in order to resist the "worlding" of philosophical texts (all writers, philosophers included, wish for a wider audience) but in order to resist philosophy's subsumption under the general rubric of "world literature." But we can still envisage a variety of relations between philosophy and (world) literature. Let's borrow the title of Arthur Danto's essay "Philosophy as/and/of Literature" and re-title it "World Philosophy and/as/or World Literature." World philosophy *and* world literature is unproblematic enough—philosophy can assuredly *learn* from the world literature debate. But world philosophy *as* world literature is more problematic, since the difference between philosophy and literature risks collapse. In terms of the philosophical bid to ensure such differences are maintained, I offer world philosophy *or* world literature.

I therefore modify Danto's third option. Of course, there's a philosophy *of* literature, but Danto doesn't countenance a literature *of* philosophy, or rather a *literary theory of philosophy*, of the sort provided by Friedrich Schlegel or Paul de Man. Nor does he interrogate the move his title makes in advance of his own essay: those slashes already divide philosophy from literature. The title already presumes a stable difference between philosophy and literature. I prefer world philosophy *or* world literature not because I presume that same stability but because I want to register the tension and controversy as regards the difference between them—the quarrel is ancient indeed, and this invites caution when what is at stake—to invoke the title of the volume in which my essay is published—is the possibility of "Philosophy as World Literature."

Philosophy's Purview: The World

Any bid to describe the circumstances of "world philosophy" is defeated by the scope of the undertaking: too much to read, too many languages to master. One can seek assistance elsewhere, however, and view matters in terms of complex systems: within the ultimate complex system Niklas Luhmann calls "world society," philosophy carves out a distinctive space, and inasmuch as philosophy does circulate, and has identifiable *modes* of circulation, then it should be possible to describe how philosophy's system differentiates itself, to some extent at least, from other systems—the economic, scientific, or media systems, for instance. Another approach would be more sociological in orientation: we could be inspired by Bourdieu's account of the "literary field" and describe the world "philosophical field"—a jostle of ideas in competition, rivalrous philosophers, the formation of dominant schools of thought, cliques, and acolytes.

Pascale Casanova's *The World Republic of Letters* might provide a serviceable model here. Let's imagine a volume entitled *The World Republic of Philosophy* (or perhaps *The World Sovereignty of Philosophy*). Restricting matters to recent philosophical history, one would begin by studying philosophical influence—nodal points of preeminence centered in certain cities, and in certain universities, and then the spread of both philosophical ideas and philosophical renown across the globe. An interesting chapter might address Martin Heidegger's reception in Japan, for instance. Another chapter would examine the Anglo-American orientation in philosophy and its divorce from "Continental" philosophy. Then there's the question of "Paris" in the 1960s and how, when certain philosophical works produced there traveled worldwide, they were "translated" (in the United States especially) into works of "French theory." Much of this, however, has been well studied, and, at all events, the challenge—if the worldwide spread of philosophical ideas is under consideration—is whether we are prepared to claim that one philosophy "travels" more widely than another because it has better ideas to offer. Compared to Karl Jaspers, Heidegger is just in a different league.

But that coarse assessment still requires justification by way of philosophical argument. And it's disagreeable to view philosophy in terms of "leagues" as we do for sports like soccer—some philosophers play in the Premier League, some risk relegation (after the publication of the *Black Notebooks*, Heidegger risked permanent relegation), some from the lower leagues might get promoted, but many remain minor league material. Let's not enter into Monty Python territory (I allude to their sketch where the philosophical World Cup Final pits the Greeks against the Germans), but one can agree that some philosophical ranking is necessary nonetheless, otherwise the exercise risks becoming an expression of bland pluralism, where all philosophies have equal distinction. Casanova, in this regard, is more concerned to describe (like Bourdieu in some respects) unequal distributions of "capital," and accordingly, if one ventured a similar exercise for philosophy, there will have to be an acknowledgment of the unequal weight awarded to European philosophy, and also the weight given to only certain European languages—Greek, Latin, English, French, and German being the privileged *linguae francae* here. Thus, her own chapter on Emil Cioran shows how Cioran's French publications are better known than the works he wrote in Romanian.

One thinks also of the Czech philosopher Jan Patočka, now much better known because his work has been translated into English (but only recently), and although it would be provocative to say he traveled more widely by clinging to Derrida's coattails, I confess I first encountered Patočka when I read Derrida's *The Gift of Death*.

Other considerations concern how philosophy's "worlding" is enabled by a country's support for philosophy—institutional and publishing support, funding for translations, and so on. At issue, moreover, is the social regard enjoyed by philosophy in a given country. What counts is whether philosophy is held in high regard (as in France) or disregarded (by countries that distrust "intellectuals"). Then there's the question of how the worldwide perception of a nation is informed by the image the world has of that nation's philosophers. France: the country of Jean-Paul Sartre, Albert Camus, and Simone de Beauvoir. The *Rive Gauche* and the Café de Flore: the sites from which existentialism embarked on a worldwide journey enabled, to a significant degree, by the circulation of its literary works—examples of "Philosophy as World Literature" would surely be *Nausea* and *The Stranger*. In short, one can depict the philosophical world in terms of the image we have of philosophers themselves (Sartre's chic tweediness, Camus's debonair handsomeness, de Beauvoir's stern sensuality), and in terms of the idealized esteem that, to borrow a term from Frances Ferguson, "operationalizes"[12] philosophical texts and their authors.

But what hampers philosophy's "worlding" is surely philosophy's sheer difficulty. Whence the importance of undertakings that popularize philosophy: publications promising Plato or Immanuel Kant "in a nutshell" (or for "idiots"). Denis Diderot said, "Let us hasten to make philosophy popular," but there remains much work to do in that regard. The matter might involve "deconstructing" the borders between philosophy as produced and professed within a University and philosophy as practiced outside the University. Thus, we ought to read Derrida's *Who's Afraid of Philosophy?* and agree with him that it's not simply a matter of institutions, or "institutionality," but also of widening "right to philosophy" (and also, I think, of attending to the putative opposition between the philosopher and the nonphilosopher). Nonetheless, philosophy is *hard*: Ludwig Wittgenstein's terse profundities are mind-bending; Derrida's crafted undecidabilities and aporias are bewildering; Alain Badiou's recourse to mathematics is challenging. On the other hand, if one takes Derrida, for instance, he arguably "worlded" himself with more success than others because deconstruction seemed simple—take a binary and dispute the hierarchized terms of the opposition. One way philosophies "world" themselves is by offering vulgate versions of themselves—digestible formulas, handy methods, easily affixed labels (e.g., "deconstruction"). If there is a philosophical *bourse*, as Casanova says there is for literary values, a marketplace where a philosopher's stock goes up and down, then perhaps the philosopher who won the world jackpot was René Descartes because "I think therefore I am" seems unarguably true and packages philosophy so neatly that the *cogito* almost functions as a slogan. If "world philosophy" is a mode of circulation, the best mode is perhaps the slogan, the truth offered as a truism, retailed by philosophy to the world with almost aphoristic concision.

But if one were to describe the "World Philosophical Space" (to modify a section heading of Casanova's), we would surely wish to address how philosophy engages with the geographical features of the world. We might therefore return to the philosophical islands that obtrude into the vaster world-scape—besides More's, and Derrida's account of Crusoe's island, one could pay a visit to Heidegger's Aegean islands. "Zu den Inseln der Ägäis" is a philosophical travelogue that meditates on "das Erzmeer, das Meer der Meere,"[13] the archipelagic sea, the sea of seas, the chief sea. Heidegger describes his travels around the Greek islands, commenting all the while on Hölderlin's poem "The Archipelago." A further matter would concern the basic poles of home and abroad: Kant, notoriously, never left home.[14] Derrida, less *casanier* in his attitudes, published more than one book generated out of an exchange of postcards from his foreign travels—*Counterpath*, coauthored with Catherine Malabou, is one example. When presenting a lecture, moreover, Derrida almost always began with remarks acknowledging the place he's in—Strasbourg, New York, Oxford. Many of his books are self-consciously located in the margins, situated offshore, looking for the other heading, or, as in *Faith and Knowledge*, confined to yet another island (Capri). Such registrations of place and displacement, however, should not be taken as signs of oikophobia, as Roger Scruton does. Mark Dooley characterizes Scruton's position as follows: "Derrida is a classic *oikophobe* insofar as he repudiates the longing for home that the Western theological, legal and literary traditions satisfy. ... Derrida's deconstruction seeks to block the path to this 'core experience' of membership, preferring instead a rootless existence founded 'upon nothing.'"[15] What would be the philosophical gesture of such "repudiation"? Given Derrida's intricate entanglements in the vast configurations of Western philosophy, I don't see Derrida simply *leaving*, packing his bags and embracing a footloose philosophical nomadism. And, if one wishes to apprehend Derrida's relation to "home," to France, and to his native language, at the least it requires a patient reading of *Monolingualism of the Other*.

As for the world itself, there are many philosophical accounts to consider. For Derrida, one world that matters is Heidegger's: in *The Fundamental Concepts of Metaphysics*, Heidegger describes the world as a domain available to active engagement, especially insofar as other beings can be interacted with *as* beings. Humans have the greatest capacity for such interactions—we are "world-forming." A stone is "without world" because its engagement is null. As for an animal, like a bee, it engages with the little precinct of the world allotted to it, buzzing from flower to flower, flying to and from the hive. But the bee's busy interactions prevent it from gaining any greater access to the world: the animal is "poor-in-world."

Strange that one of the fundamental gestures of metaphysics involves allocating "world" to man, the animal, and a stone. But inasmuch as philosophers will presumably not want to duck the fundamentals of metaphysics, then a reckoning with Heidegger's *Welt* (and what he means by "die Welt weltet" (the world worlds)) is unavoidable. It is for Derrida, at least, which is why he is alert to the difficulty of translating *Welt* into *monde*, particularly when the discussion shifts to the processes and dynamics of globalization, internationalization, or *mondialisation*. "Worlding," for a Heideggerian, means something very specific, and Derrida, in turn, is keen to retain the reference to Heidegger—whence another question of translation. To respect Derrida's preference, a preference he is barely able to assert in French, his English translators offer "worldwide-ization."

Arguably, the only *Welt* that matches Heidegger's for scale and philosophical elaboration is Georg Wilhelm Friedrich Hegel's. If one envisaged a chapter entitled "The Hegel Paradigm," the preliminary observation to be made is this: what enables Hegel to incorporate all extant world knowledge is the power of dialectics. That power is wielded especially potently in the *Phenomenology of Spirit*, and it's no exaggeration to say that the world was "worlded" by that very text—the supreme text, surely, of "world philosophy." In the context of Hegel's survey of history, universal history is the aim. But there's no universal history without particulars to be incorporated into this universal history. Whence Hegel's attention to particular societies, cultures, and nations, or rather Hegel's dialectical particularization of such things. For instance, the "nation" becomes salient as a means of offering a specificity for universal history to contemplate. Furthermore, to each nation is ascribed a "spirit," which is then contemplated by the "world spirit." At issue is accordingly the dialectical relation between national spirits and the world spirit. But the question then becomes how each nation partakes of world spirit—whether "sublation" preserves national spirits in their difference, or whether they are subsumed, absorbed, or transcended by world spirit. And, finally, what to do with the fact that, after dialectics has discerned, and *named* something called "world spirit," Hegel grants it the prerogative to judge the waxing-and-waning spirits that diversely animate world history? For the world spirit, Hegel claims, constitutes the world's court of judgment (its *Weltgericht*).

Attitudes to Hegel's account vary. For some, the problem is that while a given nation offers an "objectification" of a national spirit, Hegel also equates a nation with a political state and indeed offers further elaborations that end up with the deeply questionable characterization of various "races." For others, it is a matter of the sheer ambition of Hegel's project. What is it about philosophy that it presumes to *think* world history, no less? What is it about philosophy that it presumes to override history, sociology, anthropology—every discipline, in fact—as if to clasp knowledge of the world's past, present, and future to philosophy's bosom and subject it thereby to "dialectic"? "World philosophy," in that sense, designates an *ambition*, an aim that is intelligible as a matter of "worlding" only if one is prepared to state what philosophy's ultimate objective actually is. Is it the Hegelian project to achieve absolute knowledge? Does any other manifestation of thinking, any other intellectual discipline, have such an ambition? Possibly not, and if so, then "worlding" becomes a matter of the ambition (or pretention) distinguishing philosophy from all else. For Derrida, it's a matter of "philosophical discourse, the mastery of every other possible discourse," and "even if this takes this express form only in Hegel, absolute knowledge is indeed the truth of the philosophical project."[16] "World philosophy" is profiled against the project to produce absolute knowledge, and hence the only modes of circulation philosophy of this sort knows is either the circulation of world spirit or else the dialectical movements of an undertaking that doesn't orbit the world so much as suborn it to the conceptual requirements of philosophy itself: Sameness and Difference, Universal and Particular, Thesis, Antithesis, Synthesis.

Philosophy's Purview: The Universe

But philosophy doesn't just speak of the world or purport to master it thanks to dialectics. Philosophy also speaks for, or at least holds in its conceptual purview, the "universe." For philosophy deems itself capable of establishing and describing *universal truths*. "Universe" is philosophy's other realm—the "world" designates the place where universal truths are acknowledged as such. But what is a truth? For Badiou, there are four domains wherein a truth can occur: art, politics, science, love. The event of falling in love, or the revolutionary event, utterly changes things, and that utterness has, Badiou claims, the nature and impact of truth. These domains lie outside philosophy, however—philosophy isn't the fifth domain. But philosophy describes the nature of such truths insofar as what gives rise to them are *events*. Philosophy's task is to operate a relay between truths and philosophy's own principal categories—Being, Subject, Event. A truth obtains in a particular situation, or indeed a certain "world," but a truth isn't reducible to the particular circumstances that give rise to it: "although it is situated in a world, a truth does not retain anything expressible from that situation."[17] Badiou thus rejects the skeptical attitude that, for its part, declares there can be no interpretive settlement on the ultimate nature of a putative "truth." Hermeneutic skepticism accordingly casts a truth back into the context whence it came. These contexts can be cultural, religious, or historical, and thus the menace to philosophy and its command of truth appears—relativism, hermeneutics, and worse, the prospect that philosophy bends the knee to sociology, anthropology, cultural studies, and so on. Badiou resists the "thoroughgoing skepticism which reduced the effects of truth to particular anthropological operations,"[18] since this devolves to a "linguistic sophistry legitimating the right to cultural difference against any universalist pretension on the part of truths."[19] For Badiou, "if truths exist, they are certainly indifferent to differences."[20] Truths cannot be relativized away, vaporized by an endless respect for difference. For Badiou, "the universality of a truth is that which constitutes an exception to the anthropological hold of a particularity or to the hold of a historical and cultural world, to the hold of the context in which it is constructed."[21]

We see why Badiou, in defense of universal truths, wishes to prize the grip of particularity. But one also detects philosophy's desire to *not be* anthropology, sociology, historical studies, and so on. If this is what menaces philosophy's specificity from without, menacing philosophy from within is "linguistic sophistry" and hermeneutical skepticism, since this compromises philosophy's capacity to articulate a truth and hampers philosophy's ability to immunize the singular event from repetition, reproduction, or iteration. At stake, then, is philosophy's identity, and that returns us to *philosophia*—to Parmenides' association between thinking, being, and nonbeing. So is the "worlding" of philosophy an exercise in furthering the spread of *philosophia*? Is "world philosophy" a matter of ensuring these Greek determinations are retained, wherever one is in the world, doing philosophy?

For Badiou, "there is well and truly a Greek historicity to the birth of philosophy, and, without doubt, that historicity can be assigned to the question of being."[22] Thus, Badiou awards Heidegger special privilege, insofar as he forthrightly reopens the great ontological dossier: "Heidegger is the last universally recognizable philosopher."[23] But Badiou tracks away from Heidegger because his "poetic ontology" is overly reliant on poets like Hölderlin and Trakl to describe a world haunted by the dissipation of Presence and the loss of origin. Moreover, as Badiou sees it, for all that Hölderlin and Trakl are European poets, the problem is that we find expressions of our ontological predicament in poetic traditions throughout the world. The following remark is extremely revealing: "Similar sentences pronounced on being and non-being within the tension of the poem can be identified just as easily in India, Persia or China."[24] So there's no scope for "Philosophy as World Literature," if that means philosophy borrowing poetry to express matters of being and nonbeing. We might read a poem from China, and appreciate its lyrical expression of the metaphysical fundamentals, but we have strayed too far from philosophy—which is, Badiou asserts, well and truly rooted in Greece.

In Greece, we find a philosophical language that isn't translatable into poetic "sentences," be they rendered in German, Bengali, Farsi, or Mandarin. We find the language of mathematics and recover a conjunction between philosophy and mathematics that *Greek* philosophy first established:

> If philosophy—which is the disposition for designating exactly where the joint questions of being and of what-happens are at stake—was born in Greece, it is because it is there that ontology established, with the first *deductive* mathematics, the necessary form of its discourse. It is the philosophico-mathematical nexus—legible even in Parmenides' poem in its usage of apagogic reasoning—which makes Greece the original site of philosophy.[25]

Thanks to this philosophico-mathematical nexus, philosophy resists any transposition that would "world" it beyond the Greek determinations Badiou wishes to preserve as a corollary of his own elaboration of a "mathematical ontology" in opposition to Heidegger's "poetic ontology." But any retrieval of Greek philosophy eventually has to reckon with the great quarrel mentioned by Plato's *Republic*: can philosophy, even in its mathematical guises, ward off literature? Consider: "Let us do battle for the conflicted respite, we philosophers, forever torn between the norm of literal transparency of mathematics and the norm of singularity and presence of the poem."[26] Alas that philosophers should be so "torn" between the literal transparency of mathematics and a poem that *will not* let itself be translated into a piece of algebra. Badiou continues, "Apagogic reasoning ... supports itself with nothing but the imperative of consistency, and turns out to be incompatible with any legitimation by way of storytelling."[27] Philosophy needs no Story to tell its tale of truth. Its apagogic reasoning is not comparable to the episodic coherence of a well-formed Plot—it cleaves instead to the sequences of logical and mathematical deduction. Moreover, while mathematics writes itself out on a page, it does so without that writing ever being ascribed to an authorial presence, or voice: "The matheme ... is that which, making the speaker disappear, emptying its place of any and all mysterious validation."[28] Impersonality is the authentic guise of philosophical writing, the absence of speakers its ideal, the relinquishing of Story its prerequisite. All this implies the primacy of philosophy's Greek determination: "Philosophy began in Greece because there alone the matheme enabled the interruption of the sacral exercise of validation by way of the story (by the mytheme, Philippe Lacoue-Labarthe would say)."[29]

I retain from Badiou the following: first, the specificity of philosophical discourse is secured if it rejects Story—any conveyance that risks the transposition of philosophy into literature (or fabulation in general). Second, to muster such resistance, Badiou adverts to Greek philosophy the better to deploy mathematics as a bulwark against literary contamination (and it is supposed that the mathematical *item*—the matheme—cannot be transposed or translated into a mytheme). Third, while the philosophico-mathematical nexus seemingly gives us a "writing" that cannot be treated by Aristotle's *Poetics*, it can resonate with Plato's *Republic*, insofar as Plato's preference is also for an unmuddled narrative voice. What clearer voice can one imagine than the depersonalized, neutral articulation of mathematics, and what clearer format for writing can one imagine than the dianoetic modalities of mathematical or logical thinking? Badiou: "What Plato says above all is that the poem ruins discursivity. In Greek: *dianoia*. What is opposed philosophically to the poem [is] *dianoia*—discursive thought that proceeds by putting arguments in a chain, the paradigm for which is mathematics."[30]

I don't have the philosophical competence to determine whether philosophy can, thanks to mathematics, immunize itself from its others (literature, fabulation, mimesis) or whether philosophy can resist availing itself of Story, Plot, and the mytheme. I note only Badiou's wish that it be so. Thus, we can return to the question of "world philosophy" and suggest that philosophy's "worlding" would ideally be achieved by the universal translatability, which is to say the *literal transparency* of mathematics. If the matter additionally concerns the "worlding" of truths, the scenario here would be akin to mathematical work carried out on a given "set"—set theory tells us that the ultimate closure of a given set is impossible, and so, likewise, "truths travel through time and space—not just because their universality is recognized, but because they are pursued and further developed."[31] Truths travel through time and space recognized *as* truths, as universal truths moreover. While philosophy, partnered to mathematics, still has journeys to envisage and its own work to do as regards universal truths, the circumstance and endeavor of such work is best described by how set theory engages with infinite incompleteness. Philosophy's world is thereby calibrated to the mathematical environment of Number and the infinite. With the exception, perhaps, of Stéphane Mallarmé, this isn't literature's domain, nor is it the world of "world literature."

Philosophy's World Language

Any attempt to establish a philosophical discourse of literal transparency is stopped in its tracks by an elementary problem: philosophy (unlike mathematics) is written in natural languages. Philosophy cannot deny this, whatever be its desire for absolutely formalizable languages. We might therefore heed Ordinary Language Philosophy (OLP) and, like it, attend to the ordinary uses we make of language ("ordinary language is all right," Wittgenstein reassures philosophers[32]). Beyond OLP, however (and the question of whether its version of ordinary language is particularly "ordinary"), the difficulties multiply. Depending on one's point of view, the increased attention to language turns philosophy back into the teeth of the "linguistic turn," and, for Badiou, into "linguistic sophistry," or it deprives philosophy of a special idiom, a non-ordinary language it can claim for itself.

Consider, as an aspect of philosophy's "worlding," therefore, its fantasies of a universal philosophical language: if the context is that of the expression of mathematical, scientific, and metaphysical concepts, we will be revisiting Gottfried Wilhelm Leibniz's proposals for a universal symbolic language. If the matter concerns speculations on the origins of language, we will be examining the various attempts to revert to a pre-Babelic, "Adamic" vision of language and naming, and reading Walter Benjamin—he who also announces the prospect of *reine Sprache* (pure speech) in "The Task of the Translator." In his notes on the "Theses on the Philosophy of History," moreover, Benjamin's "messianism" informs his view of a universal history twinned with a universal language: "The messianic world is a world of total and integral actuality. In it alone is there universal history. What goes by the name of universal history today can only be a kind of Esperanto." As Giorgio Agamben remarks, "universal history presupposes or, rather, *is* the universal language that puts an end to the Babelic confusion of tongues."[33] Where the context is philosophy's desire for a *logos* resembling God's Word, we will be engaging with Jacques Rancière's argument, in *The Flesh of Words*, that philosophy shares the same dream as literature—the dream of a Word that can make flesh: "Philosophy, which wants to separate its language from all the glamour of mimesis and its effect from all 'literary' vacuity, does so only at the price of uniting with the most radical forms by which literature mimics the incarnation of the word."[34] While philosophy desires a language distinct from the mimetic "language" (or medium) of literature, resists the empty glamour of literature's vivid reproductions of worldly reality, when philosophy rejects literature's empty word and envisages a putatively full word, it edges close to a sort of Cratylism spliced with theology. But literature, particularly nineteenth-century French literature from Honoré de Balzac to Mallarmé, also edged into this terrain. So, even as philosophy rejects literary mimesis, philosophy enters into a mimetic logic whereby philosophy finds a model for its own desires in literature. Philosophy and literature both risk René Girard's scenario of mimetic desire, whereby they both triangulate, or indeed "cathect," on theology.

Or, quite simply, we will be returning to Plato's *Phaedrus* and considering how philosophy faces down the threat of writing itself. The passage is famous: "Once a thing is put into writing, the composition … drifts all over the place, getting into the hands not only of those who understand it, but equally of those who have no business with it; it doesn't know how to address the right people, and not address the wrong."[35] True, philosophy gets out and about thanks partly to "writing," but, as Badiou insists, such writing, when construed as mathematical writing, would neither be self-reflexive about its status *as* writing nor engaged in any specular relation (for instance, or above all) with literary writing. Writing of this sort need not contemplate Plato's errant scenarios therefore, because it cannot in any case: it hasn't the capacity for self-contemplation at all, and this, in fact, is its privilege. *Pace* Plato, in any case, Rancière regards errancy as a good thing: when readers who aren't supposed to be reading whatever drifts into their hands do read that material, they do something discreetly but potently political. Politics happens when people refuse to be told their own business, by Plato or anyone else. Whence *The Flesh of Words* and its account of "excursions of the word,"[36] where the emphasis bears upon the political consequences of writing's capacity to address itself to anybody. Writing enjoys such excursions because it cannot be tracked back to the oral utterances of incarnate human beings. Writing's disincarnate status is such that Rancière can speak of "the adventure of writing alone, of the body-less letter, addressed to someone who doesn't know that she—or he—is the addressee."[37]

Rancière thus invites us to revisit Plato and moreover juxtapose the bodyless letter and an incarnate (appreciably Catholic) Word. He also invites us to regard the novel as the literary genre that travels the best, since "[Le roman] est le genre qui s'adresse à n'importe-qui" (the novel is the genre that addresses itself to anyone).[38] One imagines philosophy being less keen on such excursions, however, and disinclined to borrow (or become) the novel in order to circulate more widely. But Rancière raises the important questions: What is philosophy's attitude to writing and reading? Does philosophy want to be read by *n'importe-qui*, or does it prefer to be read only by those whose business it is to read philosophy? When a philosophical text is sent into the world, starts to travel, if not to drift, can it ensure that it will still be read *as* philosophy, once it completes its journey toward the reader?

In a pragmatic sense, it surely can: in the introductory moments of a given philosophical text, certain rhetorical protocols are put in place so as to specify, and indeed anticipate, the audience for whom it is written. Yet, to adduce two examples at this point, there remain significant doubts. Danto ends his essay by criticizing philosophers for forgetting that their texts are meant to be *read*: "We pay a price for forgetting this in the current style of writing, since it enables us to depict worlds in which readers cannot fit. Contemporary philosophies ... may be striking examples of an oversight which is encouraged by a view of philosophical reading which makes the reader ontologically weightless."[39] But that oversight might be strategic, even if it makes philosophy's worlds ill-fitting for human beings, since it nullifies the problem of unintended readers. Curiously, in wanting to retrieve the reader, Danto then says "so philosophy is literature in that among its truth-conditions are those connected with being read."[40] When philosophy is read, it apparently becomes tantamount to literature, as if "literature" is the paradigm for readability itself. It might have been better to say: "philosophy is *writing*, in that among its truth-conditions are those connected with being read." But, Rancière (or Plato) might observe, that doesn't solve the issue: once philosophy becomes writing, it *will* start to drift and might therefore end up read by anybody.

My second example is more philosophically radical, and doubtless Danto would be alarmed by the juxtaposition, but Jean-François Lyotard's *The Differend* also attempts to box philosophy into a specific genre, allocate it a distinctive style, mode, or format, and envisage a scenario where one can determine the readers of a given philosophical text (if that's how it "identifies"). Lyotard envisions discourses separated into genres, or better, a cluster of "phrases" obeying a set of rules, those rules constituting its "regimen": "Phrases from heterogeneous regimens cannot be translated from one into another."[41] His discussion of phrases and regimens dovetails with the attempt, in the prefatorial "reading dossier," to establish his own book as philosophical book: its "mode" is "philosophic."[42] The reader is designated as a *philosophical* reader. Yet he also says "philosophers have never had instituted addressees,"[43] which reintroduces the problem we saw in connection with Danto. In fact, Lyotard's book is more uncertainly pitched even than that, because his own "phrases," he admits, cannot ascertain where they will end up, or if they end up anywhere at all: it's not just that "he will never know whether or not the phrases happen to arrive at their destination,"[44] it's that an author perforce addresses himself, and his text, to happenstance itself: What's happening over there? Does my book, do my phrases make anything happen at all? "In writing this book, the A. [author] had the feeling that his sole addressee was the *Is it happening?*"[45] One cannot foresee all eventualities as and when phrases travel towards their "destination" because destination is an "arrival" that takes place as an *event*—and no true event can occur when its eventualities and outcomes are predictable.

Traveling Philosophy

If we are to speak of "traveling philosophy" (to invoke Said), we must admit that the journeys can be unpredictable, the destination uncertain. Can philosophy travel as itself, in a distinctively philosophical mode? Can it fend off translation by declaring itself governed by a "regimen," heterogeneous and therefore untranslatable into any other phrase regimen? Perhaps the issue is that philosophy differentiates itself less because it has a stable mode, genre, idiom, or regimen, but because *what* philosophy conveys *as* philosophy can be distinguished, namely, its truths. Instead of asserting a thesis of untranslatability, therefore, philosophy might wish to assert, on behalf of its truths, a thesis of translatability, and indeed regard philosophy's very origin in terms of that thesis. Back to Derrida:

> What matters is truth or meaning, and since meaning is before or beyond language, it follows that it is translatable. Meaning has the commanding role, and consequently one must be able to fix its univocality or, in any case, to master its plurivocality. If this plurivocality can be mastered, then translation, understood as the transport of a semantic content into another signifying form, is possible. There is no philosophy unless translation in this latter sense is possible. Therefore, the thesis of philosophy is translatability in this common sense.[46]

Philosophy desires translation in the "common sense"—translation bidden to respect original meaning, forbidden to creative reworkings. Truths must withstand adjustment or modification: a truth is a truth is a truth—verity brooks no loss in translation, resists recontextualizations that might relativize a truth into something less than *the* truth. Philosophy thus desires ideal translatability so that a truth travels intact—comes out the other side as true as it had been when it departed from "home."

For a truth is univocal, or it is not. The *meaning* of a truth mustn't be dispersed to the linguistic four winds. The translator must be faithful to such meaning, to meaning that has the "commanding role," being "before or behind" the language expressing that meaning. Translation must render what is meant in one language to what is still meant, and not meant otherwise, in another language. If philosophy's task is to communicate truths to whoever in the world is disposed to acknowledge them, it must credit translation as a vehicle that can preserve the integrity of truths *as such*. If "the origin of philosophy is translation or the thesis of translatability," it is so because the universal validity philosophy claims for a given truth can only be confirmed *as* universal if it passes the test of translatability. If philosophy's thesis is that such and such is a truth, then the proving of that thesis is assigned to translation, since translation traverses languages and tests thereby the presumptive univocality of a truth against the menace of plurivocality. World, or universal translatability, would accordingly be the condition of possibility of truth itself.

Derrida's remarks put into relief one of Damrosch's propositions concerning world literature: "World literature is writing that gains in translation."[47] Damrosch then distinguishes between literary language and nonliterary language, the latter being, he argues, less vulnerable to the translatory economy of loss and gain:

> Literary language is thus language that either gains *or* loses in translation, in contrast to nonliterary language, which typically does neither. The balance of credit and loss remains a distinguishing mark of national versus world literature: literature stays within its national or regional tradition when it usually loses in translation, whereas works become world literature when they gain on balance in translation, stylistic losses offset by an expansion in depth as they increase their range.[48]

Translating a literary text is challenging, and it's often said there will be an inevitable loss in translation. But that challenge frequently spurs creative re-renderings that offer the prospect of a gain in translation as well. A washing-machine manual doesn't present the same challenges, nor therefore does it spur the same creativity either. But where, in terms of the opposition between literary and nonliterary language, might we position philosophy's language? Might philosophy want to avoid a translatory economy that wagers a gain in translation against the risk of loss? Philosophy wishes to convey its truths intact, without loss—and without gain either, or at least it might hesitate to offer its truths to translation without further clarification of what a gain, and indeed a gain in *depth*, actually means. It cannot be a matter of offsetting "stylistic losses." The loss philosophy fears is a loss of meaning, the compromising of a truth. Thus, philosophy might prefer to be placed on the side of nonliterary language, and express itself in unstylish language, like Badiou's mathematical writing, so that no translator is prompted to impertinent acts of creative rewriting. If philosophy wishes to increase its range and avoid being restricted to a national or regional tradition, it needs a translation model that conveys philosophical truths to the world without any "economic" fluctuations of loss and gain.

That model, I suggest, is described by Derrida. In any case, one proposition philosophy would approve of, I think, is Damrosch's claim that "a work enters into world literature by a double process: first, by being read *as* literature; second, by circulating out into a broader world beyond its linguistic and cultural point of origin."[49] Doubtless, philosophy also wishes to depart from its point of origin, circulate out into a broader world, and emerge, wherever in the world it does emerge, intact and recognizable *as* philosophy. Yet the question remains whether literature and philosophy can defend their specificities *as* literature, *as* philosophy against the vicissitudes of worldwide travel—from translations, transpositions, or transferences that, accidentally or by design, don't respect the right of literature or philosophy to remain, from journey's beginning to journey's end, identifiable as "philosophy" or "literature."

Whatever a text (a literary text in Damrosch's case) gains in translation, "on balance," as he puts it, when it expands its depth and increases its range, there is no sense in which that gain might be afforded by the conversion of literature into something else entirely. Or to put it the other way, the loss in translation never becomes a loss of literature's own identity. Philosophy would presumably like to see similar scenarios obtain when it too is subject to "worlding" and to translation. Yet, while Damrosch insists on literature's retaining its identity *as* literature, it's not clear whether his characterization of "world literature" can secure, for example, philosophy's identity *as* philosophy. For Damrosch, we recall, says that "in its most expansive sense, world literature could include any work that has ever reached beyond its home base." Perhaps a certain transposition has already occurred, insofar as "world literature" designates something applicable to "any work," including, presumably, a philosophical work. Will philosophy agree to barter away the specificity of philosophy for the price of the world (and at the uncosted price of a putative "gain" in both depth and reach afforded by translation)? Literature might be comfortable with such vague economies, but would philosophy?

Philosophy and/as/or Translation

For philosophy, translation is a risky business. Whence its interest in deeming its concepts untranslatable—the best defense against translation is the categorical assertion that some things cannot be translated. I refer, of course, to Barbara Cassin's *Dictionary of Untranslatables*. A different approach, however, asks why translation doesn't find a place in the conceptual armory of a given philosophy. Take Hegel's *Phenomenology*: when he inspects excerpts from the *Iliad* and the *Odyssey*, he translates. But translation is not operative in the Hegelian dialectic, perhaps because the "lateral" logic of translation is incompatible with the upward movement of sublation. Yet can we not pose the same questions to dialectics as we do to translation? The question for translation is whether it erases the original, or preserves something of the original, particularly when the translation is forced to "foreignize" itself. Does dialectics likewise preserve elements of the foreign at the elevated level of the synthetic moment, or erase that foreignness? Does Hegel preserve the foreignness of art and religion, allow art to remain *as* art, religion to persist *as* religion, even as both are taken up into philosophical discourse? Is there any sense in which philosophical discourse foreignizes itself because its task is to *sublate*, but not to *subsume* the artworks and religious texts of which it speaks?

These are some questions one might put to Hegel. Consider, moreover, the letter he drafted in 1805 to the translator Johann Heinrich Voss. In "Yes-Yet-Hegel's Oracle," Kristina Mendicino quotes it as follows:

> Luther made the Bible talk in German; you, Homer,—the greatest gift that can be made to a people; for a people is barbaric and does not see the preeminence that it knows as its true property, so long as it has not learned it in its own language;—if you will forget these two examples, so I will say of my striving that I will try to teach Philosophy to speak German.[50]

Translation teaches people the true significance of a property—their own language—that was theirs to own all along. Hegel will teach philosophy to learn the true language of philosophy (German) in order that philosophy appropriate its own true property. This wouldn't be translation as a *conversion* of one philosophical language into a foreign philosophical language, but translation as a *reversion* to what was always proper to philosophy in the first place, even if it didn't know it—the proper "possession" of philosophy by German. Yet if there is learning to be done, the question is whether philosophy has to speak not only German but also a German that isn't yet spoken. Thus, Mendicino reads the *Phenomenology* "not only as a translation project, but also as a prophecy of a (German) language to come, which would also be the language of Philosophy herself."[51] Philosophy would *come into its own* if and when German—Hegel's German, a German not yet spoken even by Germans—becomes Philosophy's universal language. Translation: less a way of dealing with the Babelic plurality of philosophical languages, more an adherence to the ambitions of the tower builders—removing the necessity for translation by achieving a "universal or polyvocal German, a philo-logical masterpiece or a philosophical labor of the most complex kind, the language of God or of Babel."[52]

If the *Phenomenology* can be regarded as a translation project, rather than a dialectical undertaking, or if both projects are in tension with each other, or if the logic of translation undergirds the dialectical undertaking, as if translation is an operation upon which dialectics relies, what would be the starting point for that operation? If *Übersetzen* implies a "crossing-over," then what is philosophy taking up and taking over, appropriating and redeploying *as* philosophy? God's language, perhaps, or as Mendicino suggests, oracular language: both teach philosophy what a universal, prophetic, and always-already self-fulfilling language looks like. But inasmuch as dialectics appropriates what is different to philosophy the better to establish what is proper to philosophy alone, dialectics will hardly accept to be ex-appropriated (to borrow a term from Derrida) by the precedence it would presumably have to ascribe to God's Word or to oracular speech. It cannot be that their status as potential starting points is too strongly noted; it cannot be that they represent the home shore from which the *Phenomenology*, if read as a translation project, will have departed, the shore from which it journeys to philosophy proper. Philosophy must not have been "started" by anything other than itself, unless it be that what "begins" the dialectic is what it both acknowledges and elides, as if it is triggered by the inspiration it finds in the spirit that speaks in the Bible and in the example of oracular language, but is unwilling, for all that, to admit that it, and therefore philosophy proper, will have been a "translation" of improper models that preceded philosophy itself.

If it's difficult for Hegel to make a place for translation, one philosophical approach that willingly embraces translation is hermeneutics. The basic scenario, in Gadamerian hermeneutics, concerns the interpretive dialogue occurring between two interlocutors, where hermeneutic success involves finding common ground. Overcoming the difficulty that obtains where the participants are speaking foreign languages would accordingly be an exemplification of hermeneutic achievement: the overcoming, or conquest of alienness itself. "The fact that a foreign language is being translated," Hans-Georg Gadamer writes in *Truth and Method*, "means that this is simply an extreme case of hermeneutical difficulty—i.e. of alienness and its conquest."[53] But how "extreme" might that case be before translation cannot serve as a paradigm or epitome of hermeneutic achievement *tout court*? For if translation is shadowed by the dilemma of untranslatability, translation might discover interpretation's *limits*, locate those places where common ground cannot be found, where the conquest of alienness is impossible. This caveat duly entered, the hermeneutic investment in translation remains significant. For hermeneutics, describing interpretive interactions (translation is one such) is the first and indeed last philosophical order of business: only the solipsist refuses to engage with the world, and so hermeneutics regards itself as a universal practice—interpretation, dialogue, and translation are activities we all perform, of necessity, inasmuch as the world gives itself to be interacted with, other people likewise, other cultures, languages, historical, literary, and philosophical traditions as well. Whence Jean Grondin's claim for the "universality of hermeneutics": all philosophy is hermeneutical. Hermeneutics-as-philosophy worlds the world, therefore, insofar as to be active in the world is to be practicing the various interpretative interactions hermeneutics describes.

Consider, finally, the Rilke poem that provides the epigraph to *Truth and Method*: "Catch only what you've thrown yourself, all is / mere skill and little gain; / but when you're suddenly the catcher of a ball / thrown by an eternal partner / with accurate and measured swing / towards you, to your center, in an arch / from the great bridgebuilding of God: / why catching then becomes a power—/ not yours, a world's."[54] Hermeneutics sees itself as the catcher of God's curveball. Once it's caught, another span is thrown across the great gulf separating God's farther shore and ours. Thus do we participate in the world-making and bridgebuilding of God—the riverbanks get a little closer, the *translatio* between God and Man becomes more possible. Hermeneutics envisages crossing-points, rather than an untranslatable abyss. This is bridgebuilding, or translation, as I prefer to put it, that builds nothing less than the world: spanning divides and overcoming differences are the very acts of worlding.

Philosophy's World to Come

But whose world (besides God's)? Heidegger's or Hegel's, or indeed the worlds of Badiou's *Logics of Worlds*? Which concept? What truth? For Badiou, whatever truth emerges from the four domains, and whenever it then travels in time and space, there is still an ongoing process—a proving process—buttressing that truth's validity. For Derrida, the proving processes are different, but one process he deploys is precisely translation. Yet what concept to select as a candidate for translation unto the world? What idea does philosophy want to subject to the test of recontextualization, grafting, or transplantation? A test which, if passed, would enable that concept, idea, or ideal to claim legitimate purchase world-wide—the legitimacy of something universal and univeralizable, something proved against relativism. Somewhat self-consciously, I want to select that "something" from Greek philosophy in order to address the question of philosophical Eurocentrism, and address, by the same token, the "worlding" of European philosophy in particular. What does European philosophy hope to convey to the world? Would it be the idea of democracy, born in Greece, given philosophical profile in that same place, and then broadcast to the world as the one political framework worthy of the world (since it unconditionally guarantees the freedom everyone in the world ought to enjoy)?

Or would it be reason itself—the ultimate "product" of philosophical thought as such? If we imagine reason undertaking a world-wide journey and doing so in order to prove its rationality against whatever recontextualization occurs as and when other cultures—philosophical or otherwise—encounter it, then we need to ask where reason starts from. Here is Derrida:

> The great question of reason would already begin to unfurl its sails for a geopolitical voyage across Europe and its languages, across Europe and the rest of the world. Is reason (*logos* or *ratio*) first of all a Mediterranean thing? Would it have made it safely to port, with Athens or Rome in view, so as to remain until the end of time tied to its shores? Would it have never really lifted anchor or been set adrift? Would it have ever broken away, in a decisive or critical fashion, from its birthplaces, its geography, and its genealogy?[55]

Reason's geopolitical voyage first traverses Europe and its *languages*—already reason is traveling in translation. But will reason sail toward destinations beyond Europe and the Mediterranean? Will reason subject itself to a critique that implies breaking with the securities of reason's putatively European genealogy? Can reason really embrace translation if it never leaves the home shores or always tarries in the offshores and *parages* of philosophical Europe? These are the world-philosophical questions to be answered. This is the journey European philosophy must make, if it is to "world" itself to the world and still retain reason as both the medium and the message it conveys to the elsewhere-world of "non-Europe." Derrida then speaks of "an experience of translation that ... takes upon itself the entire destiny of reason, that is, of the world universality to come."[56] On the one hand, translation holds the key to reason's legitimate universalization, but that legitimacy seems predicated on translation's overcoming of its own Babelic difficulties and achieving for reason such transparency that the world acknowledges reason's universality, its sovereignty, its righteous dominion as the one idiom to reign over us all. On the other hand, translation does the opposite: it gives other, non-European languages the chance to have their say on what is to be retained of that European genealogy and what is not. Perhaps reason will *gain* in translation once other philosophical cultures work on it. Perhaps reason will thereby find new vistas for its own rationality, or reasonableness, as it journeys to unforecastable shores.

The hope would be, at all events, that once the translation test is passed, it is then possible to promote a version of reason that *deserves* universalization, warrants *mondialisation*, or worldwide-ization. So when Derrida invokes a translation that "takes upon itself the entire destiny of reason, that is, of the world universality to come," and then gestures "towards a hypothetical and problematic universal translatability that is one of the fundamental stakes of reason, of what we have called, and will still call tomorrow, reason, and reason in the world,"[57] the stakes couldn't be higher. "Problematic" is an understatement, given the imperative to preserve reason's name (at least for "tomorrow") and the ambition of a "world universality" reason regards as its "entire destiny."

But that's precisely what translation has always been asked to preserve—it's philosophy's "thesis" of translatability, as we have seen. Here it would be a matter of (European) reason becoming translatable throughout the world, but never lost in translation, always meaningful as the intact dignity of philosophical thought as such. One can perhaps assert the same "thesis" for *demokratia*—require that its original Greek meaning not be lost even as it is translated into different political frameworks worldwide. In the meantime, since tomorrow is another day, reason and *demokratia* remain "to come." Thus, world philosophy, assuming it wishes to travel in the name of *demokratia*, or in the name and mode of reason, also remains "to come." It accordingly shares that temporal horizon with "world literature": commenting on Goethe's call to hasten the advent of world literature in "The Stakes of a World Literature," Gayatri Spivak rightly says that "the category of 'world literature' is in the mode of 'to come.' "[58] As for philosophy, we might recall that it hasn't yet learned to speak Hegel's German, so there's another "not yet" to contend with. As for the task of further refining the philosophical vision of "Europe," Rodolphe Gasché views the undertaking as necessarily "infinite." "To come" doesn't mean permanently postponed, however: it means that while we abide with the *prospect* of world literature, or world philosophy, the "gap" between the present and the future—the future Derrida calls *the* "to-come"—creates a time lag during which critique (and I would like to add "translation") has sufficient time to ensure that philosophy and literature's world ambitions don't curdle into a new imperialism, colonialism, or a renewed Eurocentrism.

So it's not a matter of putting off until tomorrow what can be accomplished today. Still, reason, for its part, presumably hopes that the tomorrows of philosophical reason will resemble reason's todays. But it will only find out if it undertakes the maritime journey Derrida envisions as a journey of translation. On the way, we might linger on Crusoe's island and undertake thought experiments in philosophical sovereignty. We will also let a critical islandology address the temptations of nationalism, chauvinism, and the matter of borders: hard borders and border walls erected to keep out the foreigner. As the ship sails by, we might see archipelagos come into view—island chains that connect and that thus represent *relation*, not separation—this point is beautifully made by Édouard Glissant in *Poetics of Relation*. We might, inspired by Glissant, then ask philosophy (and Heidegger, still circuiting with Hölderlin around the Aegean archipelago) to "creolize" itself—to diversify its languages, mix things up a little more, rather than persist in welding philosophical thought ever tighter to the ideal language of logocentrism. (Spivak, in "World Systems and the Creole," endorses Glissant, calling for a "creolization of the world's past,"[59] an endeavor philosophy might wish to participate in.) But these desiderata clash with philosophy's desire to establish reason's sovereignty and enhance the prospects of universal transparency—the unimpeded transmission of philosophy's truths. Universality would still measure the extent of world philosophy's ambitions, and the horizons of such universality might well be political in the last instance. But if the true temporal dimension of world philosophy, *and* reason, *and* democracy is the "to-come," then we do not know whether such "worlding" can be accomplished by a definitive universalization or an ultimate politics. Time will tell, and translation, I think, will tell as well.

Notes

1 *Utopia* was originally written in Latin of course. As for the Utopian language, the examples we have of it are sometimes claimed to be the work of More's friend Peter Giles. The line that interests me, "The commander Utopus made me into an island out of a non-island," is also rendered into Latin as "Utopus me dux ex non insula fecit insulam." See Thomas More, *Utopia* (Cambridge: Cambridge UP, 2002), 119.
2 Jacques Derrida, *The Beast and the Sovereign II*, trans. Geoffrey Bennington (Chicago: University of Chicago Press, 2009), 15.
3 Ibid., 9.
4 Ibid.
5 Jacques Derrida, *The Ear of the Other*, trans. Peggy Kamuf (Lincoln: University of Nebraska Press/Bison Books, 1988), 120.
6 Edward Said, *The World, the Text, and the Critic* (London: Vintage Press, 1991), 34.
7 Ibid., 226.
8 Ibid., 227.
9 David Damrosch, *What Is World Literature?* (Princeton: Princeton UP, 2003), 5.
10 Ibid., 4.
11 Ibid.
12 Frances Ferguson, "Planetary Literary History: The Place of the Text," *New Literary History* 39.3 (Summer 2008): 666.
13 Martin Heidegger, "Zu den Inseln der Ägäis," in *Gesamtausgabe, Band 75* (Frankfurt am Main: Vittorio Klostermann, 2000), 249.
14 Kant may not have traveled much, but there are interesting moments in his work where colonialism emerges—problematically to be sure—as a touchstone for thinking about the acquisition of knowledge itself. See Willi Goetschel's essay "Epilogue: 'Land

of Truth—Enchanting Name!' Kant's Journey at Home," in *The Imperialist Imagination: German Colonialism and its Legacy*, ed. Sara Friedrichsmeyer and Sara Lennox (Ann Arbor: University of Michigan Press, 1998), 321–36.
15 Mark Dooley, *Roger Scruton: The Philosopher on Dover Beach* (New York: Continuum, 2009), 83.
16 Jacques Derrida, "Dialanguages," in *Points…Interviews, 1974–1994*, ed. Elisabeth Weber, trans. Peggy Kamuf, Verena Andermatt Conley, Peter Connor, Marian Hobson, Michael Israel, Christopher Johnson, John P. Leavey Jr., Christie V. McDonald, and Avital Ronell (Stanford: Stanford UP, 1994), 140.
17 Alain Badiou, *Being and Event*, trans. Oliver Feltham (London: Bloomsbury, 2015), xvi.
18 Ibid., xv.
19 Ibid.
20 Ibid.
21 Alain Badiou and Jean-Claude Milner, *Controversies*, trans. Susan Spitzer (Cambridge: Polity Press, 2014), 80.
22 Badiou, *Being and Event*, 10.
23 Ibid., 1.
24 Ibid., 11.
25 Ibid.
26 Alain Badiou, *The Age of the Poets*, trans. Bruno Bosteels (London: Verso, 2014), 35.
27 Ibid., 37.
28 Ibid.
29 Ibid.
30 Ibid., 33.
31 Badiou and Milner, *Controversies*, 73.
32 Ludwig Wittgenstein, *Major Works* (New York: Harper Perennial, 2009), 119.
33 Agamben quotes these lines from Benjamin. See Giorgio Agamben, *Potentialities*, trans. Daniel Heller-Roazen (Stanford: Stanford UP, 1999), 48.
34 Jacques Rancière, *The Flesh of Words*, trans. Charlotte Mandell (Stanford: Stanford UP, 2004), 5.
35 Plato, *The Collected Dialogues* (Princeton: Princeton UP, 2005), 521.
36 Rancière's book opens with a section entitled "The Excursions of the Word."
37 Ibid., 137.
38 Jacques Rancière, *Et Tant Pis Pour Les Gens Fatigués* (Paris: Éditions Amsterdam, 2009), 562.
39 Arthur Danto, *The Philosophical Disenfranchisement of Art* (New York: Columbia UP, 2005), 161.
40 Ibid., 161.
41 Jean-François Lyotard, *The Differend*, trans. Georges Van Den Abbeele (Minneapolis: University of Minnesota Press, 2002), xii.
42 Ibid., xiv.
43 Ibid., xv.
44 Ibid., xvi.
45 Ibid.
46 Derrida, *The Ear of the Other*, 120.
47 Damrosch, *What Is World Literature?*, 288.
48 Ibid., 289.

49 Ibid., 6.
50 Kristina Mendicino, "Yes-Yet-Hegel's Oracle," *Differences* 25.5 (2015): 14.
51 Ibid., 18.
52 Ibid., 19.
53 Hans-Georg Gadamer, *Truth and Method*, trans. Joel Weinsheimer and Donald G. Marshall (New York: Continuum, 1996), 387.
54 Ibid., v.
55 Jacques Derrida, *Rogues*, trans. Pascale-Anne Brault (Stanford: Stanford UP, 2005), 119.
56 Ibid.
57 Ibid., 122.
58 Gayatri Chakravorty Spivak, *An Aesthetic Education in the Era of Globalization* (Cambridge: Harvard UP, 2012), 461.
59 Ibid., 454.

2

Plato as World Literature

Paul Allen Miller

When I gaze upon the world, I assume an attitude toward it. I direct my attention to it in a certain definite fashion that in many ways determines how that world appears to me. Yet that attitude itself does not normally appear as such. I do not experience my attitude toward the world as a stance, a position, or a thesis. The unspoken assumptions that structure my perception of the world must remain just that if I'm not to be estranged from what seems be the natural attitude toward the world, if I am not to fall into an infinite regress in which I come to question the ground of my assumptions, by making certain assumptions about my ability to perceive their ground.

The natural attitude goes something like this.[1] I look at objects. Those objects have names, and those names refer to the ideal instantiations of those objects. I identify the objects in the world by referring my perceptions to those objects' ideal instantiations. This is a dog, this is a tree, this is a cat. As Ferdinand de Saussure taught us, the signifier "tree" does not refer to the tree I stand before but to an idea of a tree that should be equally applicable to all the objects I denominate "tree."[2] There is thus a not insignificant sense in which the idea of the tree must preexist my perception of it.

Still, I do not simply name objects or perceive objects in terms of the categories their names denote; I also advance propositions concerning those objects, that is, "The cat is on the mat," creating and deploying syntactical relations that imply an organized system and logic of being. All men are mortal. Socrates is a man. Therefore, Socrates is mortal. I may even create fictions about those objects and the worlds they inhabit, which while not real remain intelligible precisely because they refer to ideal rather than real objects: "The cat of Socrates is flying on a mat."

Nothing could seem more natural than to be a perceiving subject within this world. The activity of recognizing objects and referring to the ideal models that make them intelligible is not something we choose to do. We do not simply wake up one day and say, "We are going to understand and experience being (and beings) in this way." That world is something that surrounds us. It is something that structures us. It is something into which we are thrown. It is the basis of our "ideology." And what could be more natural? How could it be otherwise? How could we think differently?

Nonetheless, what I want to argue is that this is in fact a very Platonic world, that is, the world as it is pictured by Platonism. And while in other places I would want to argue that the Platonic texts in fact problematize this world picture even as in a certain measure they create it,[3] there can be little doubt that the attitude that I described above is not only that of Platonism—the conventional philosophy abstracted from the texts of Plato (*inter alia*)[4]—but it is also the world that generally undergirds our assumptions about what it means to do science, what it means to have an evidence-based attitude toward the world, and what we understand to constitute the truth: a correspondence between my perception of objects in the world and the categories we use to define them. I will pursue this argument in two parts. First, we will turn to Martin Heidegger's argument that we currently live under the Platonic "world picture," and that this governs the way we do science, the way we define truth, and our interactions with the object world. Second, I will expand this argument beyond the object world of traditional science to the more abstract world of social justice. I will contend that there remains an implicit Platonist ontology that governs many of our most basic political and social interactions. Note that I am not contending that the texts of Plato directly underwrite modern political philosophy. Rather, what I am contending is that in our everyday social interactions with the world, we operate as if a Platonist ontology governs (or should govern) those interactions.

I

One of Heidegger's most important contributions—in what was undoubtedly both an important and deeply problematic legacy—was the way in which he made us aware of how many ancient Greek concepts are still active within what he termed Western "metaphysics" and, consequently, within the entire scientific and technical worldview that has come to dominate the global system.[5] We can see the presence of this heritage on a number of levels—whether in democracy, equality before the law, or freedom of speech, all of which receive their first articulations in Greek—even if the precise meaning and value of those terms continue to be debated. One of the most important and enduring of these legacies is the opposition between subjects and objects, which founds the modern epistemic universe. Notions like scientific objectivity and the difference between subjective experience and objective truth are predicated on the separability of the object of perception from the perceiving subject. It is through this foundational opposition, Heidegger contends, that the world of "beings" is initially constituted, as a set of objects and their corresponding categories. One of Heidegger's fundamental points is that, while the constitution of our world in this way allows for us to manipulate our environment in particularly powerful ways through technology, it does not allow the larger unity out of which those beings arise, as well as the subject who perceives them, to be thought. Rather, the world of beings that emerges in opposition to the subject causes us to forget the question of Being, to forget the problem of the undifferentiated one out of which the phenomenal many arise, a one whose presence is still felt in the thought of the pre-Socratics, as well as in Confucian, Buddhist, and Taoist forms of thought.[6] The subject of Western philosophy, Heidegger argues, has little to do with the concrete experience of any particular "I" but instead names a function within the larger metaphysical game of truth that characterizes our world.

The subject names "that-which-lies-before, which, as ground, gathers everything into itself" so that the world, as "world," becomes the reflection of that subject and of the categories of its thought.[7]

For Heidegger, the story of Western philosophy as metaphysics begins with Plato, and by "metaphysics" he means representational thinking, as described at the beginning of this essay, in which truth is defined as the adequacy of the representation possessed by the subject in relation to the object.[8] One consequence of Heidegger making Plato, or at least Platonism,[9] the beginning of the thought-world he labels metaphysics is that this understanding of philosophy, this understanding of truth, and consequently of what we labeled the "natural attitude," is in fact anything but natural.[10] It is particular mode of being a subject, limited in time and space. In Foucauldian terms, we might characterize it as the *épistémé* of a given age,[11] whose genealogy we are asked to trace:

> In metaphysics reflection is accomplished concerning the essence of what is and a decision takes place regarding the essence of truth. Metaphysics ground an age, in that through a specific interpretation of what is and through a specific comprehension of truth it gives to that age the basis upon which it is essentially formed. This basis holds complete dominion over all phenomena that distinguish the age.[12]

The origin of metaphysics in Plato, as Heidegger describes it, is less a philosophical event than the event that makes philosophy as we understand it possible. Indeed, it is less something Plato or Socrates argues for than something Platonic philosophy imagines. In one of the great ironies, the invention of metaphysics is essentially a poetic act, an act of creation that make other forms of discourse and reasoning possible.[13]

What we see in Plato, Heidegger argues, is fundamentally a new concept of truth, in which the world is grasped as a "picture." What is only *is* to the extent it enters representation, and that representation can be more or less correct.[14] As we shall see, this new vision of truth as "vision" is for Plato not the exclusive way in which truth is constituted either for him or for the Greeks, who at the time the *Republic* is being written still possess an earlier notion of truth as what Heidegger translates "unhiddenness," but which might be more accurately termed "that which escapes oblivion" or *alētheia*.[15] The truth of the *Iliad* is not fundamentally that Plato imagines in the Myth of the Cave, nor is it the truth of Confucius or Shakyamuni. The "evidence-based" world of modern science and of technological domination, and indeed I would argue the secret ontology of capitalist commodity production itself, presumes a certain attitude of the subject toward the object world. This is an attitude that we first see codified in the Myth of the Cave and most fully realized in the dream of a world whose objects can be fully expressed digitally or in terms of what Karl Marx terms the "universal equivalent" or "exchange value," a form hollowed out of all irreducibly individual or unrepeatable experiences, in which the sensuous and the concrete have been fully sublimated into the abstract and universal.[16]

In the Myth of the Cave, we have two environments. The first is the world of our everyday experience. In that world, subjects look at objects as projections on a screen, objects whose essences remain hidden.[17] Still, those subjects are either more or less correct in their recognition of the identity of those objects, and they are able to label them either appropriately or not in accordance with whether they can recognize the realities to which those representations correspond. Their experience is what is referred to above as "the natural attitude." Now, the subjects in this particular telling are limited in some very specific ways through their being bound in place within the cave, and the nature of those limitations and how they can be overcome is what receives much of the emphasis in the story. Nonetheless, the basic model of truth as the adequacy of the act of knowing both to the represented object and to a reality beyond that specific representation remains fundamental to the concept of truth first fully imagined here.[18] Thus, Heidegger writes,

> Taking the essence of truth as the correctness of the representation, one thinks of all beings according to "ideas" and evaluates all reality according to "values." That which alone and first of all is decisive is not which ideas and which values are posited, but rather the fact that the real is interpreted according to "ideas" at all, that the "world" is weighed according to "values" at all.[19]

And while such an attitude may appear in the movement of our experience to be natural, it is in fact a decision, even if not a personal one. What remains unsaid in the Myth of the Cave and throughout Plato's thought is that this way of "thinking is a change in what determines the essence of truth."[20]

In Greek culture prior to this moment, truth was that which "escaped oblivion," that which persisted in its "unhiddenness," or *alētheia*, based on the alpha privative plus *lēthē* as in the River Lethe, the river of oblivion in the underworld.[21] It was not a correspondence between the thought or perceptions of an autonomous subject, the object of that subject's thought or perception, and the underlying nature of that object as a being, but a powerful and tangible story, a narrative capable of infinite repetition.[22] Achilles is not dishonored (*atimos*) in the *Iliad* because there is an agreed-upon abstract concept of honor to which his and the other Greek leaders' behavior is supposed to correspond and he has failed to be treated accordingly. He is dishonored because his portion (*timē*) of the loot captured in warfare, in the person of Briseis, has been taken from him.[23] He has been deprived of the portion he should have received in accord with his status (*a-timos*). There is no possibility in the *Iliad* of dissociating the concept, and hence the judging subject, from the concrete acts and situations in which they occur. As Charles Stocking has recently shown, the funeral games for Patroklos in Book 23 of the *Iliad* enact a powerful calculus of both who is the most skilled in the various feats performed and of where those actors stand in relations to the social hierarchy.[24] There is no abstract concept of honor that would allow the judging subject to consider honor/reward apart from the object of perception, and therefore there is no possibility to reconstruct from these scenes our "natural" triangular relation of truth. Instead, there are a series of individuals performing actions in deeply socially embedded relations that produce meanings that are both recognized by others and unable to be separated from the actors and their contexts. If in the "natural attitude" the subject's relation to the object is always mediated by the concept, which exists on a plane above the act of perception, in the Homeric world there are only actions in the world, produced by multiple overlapping actors, who vary in status, whose meaning and hence reality is produced by their continuing recognition by others.

With the Myth of the Cave and the analogy of the good to the sun in Book Six of the *Republic*, however, what becomes dominant in place of truth as that which is not forgotten, *alētheia*, as the powerful story capable of infinite repetition, is precisely, Heidegger argues, the *idea*. This is true in two senses: for the word *idea* in Greek in the first instance means simply that which has been seen, and in the second refers to the mental image of past things seen or perceived, that is to say, the concept or the idea. The word *idea* in Greek is in fact cognate with both the Latin word *video* and such English words as *wit* and *wisdom*. The image of the projection of shadows on the wall, and the subsequent exit from the cave and eventual recognition of objects illuminated by the sun, captures both sides of this ambiguous poetic image, grasping both the fact of our perception and the identification of that perception with a preexisting conceptual category: the whole of which is illuminated by the *idea agathou* or "the idea of the good." Thus, Heidegger observes,

> This "allegory" contains Plato's "doctrine" of truth, for the "allegory" is grounded in the unspoken event whereby *idea* gains dominance over *alētheia*. The "allegory" puts into images what Plato says about *idea tou agathou*, namely that *autē kuria alētheian kai noun paraskhomenē* (517 c4), "she herself is mistress in that she bestows unhiddenness (on what shows itself) and at the same time imparts apprehension (of what is unhidden)." *Alētheia* comes under the yoke of the *idea*.[25]

In this way, truth comes to be defined by our perceptions of objects in the world, of a set of beings, and not by the ground against which those objects are defined and projected, a ground that defines the subject every bit as much as the object and yet which remains invisible to all those who remain within the cave. This ground is what Heidegger terms "Being."[26] The world, which the sun illumines outside the cave, is not only the world of objects but also the world of light, the world of the sun not presented against a single uniform background as in the wall of the cave, against which the projections of objects are made visible, even as the wall itself, the screen remains invisible. It is this enveloping light of the sun that constitutes the second environment introduced by the Myth of the Cave: the possibility of escaping the enclosure that frames our perceptions, our current vision.

And here there is a turn in the story whose importance cannot be overemphasized: for, while Plato's text introduces this new concept of truth as idea, a concept that comes increasingly to dominate and even create our world through an extraordinary act of poetic invention, an act of imagination that becomes "world" "literature" in an almost unparalleled sense, the image of the idea of the good as the sun is also squarely cognate with the idea of truth as the "unhidden," of truth as not only the objects of our perception and their presumed correspondences to their conceptual essences but also as the larger field from which those objects emerge, that is to say, as not only "beings" but also "Being." In the turning of the subject, the literal conversion of the prisoner from gazing upon the enclosed space of the cave wall, and in his or her emergence into the light of a world that is initially blinding, is found also the recognition that the set of objects to which our perception corresponds, even if adequately identified, is always but *a* set of objects whose very visibility obscures the field of possibilities from which they emerge, whose very visibility constitutes a decision as to how the objects of the world are apportioned in the field of our vision.[27] There is a preexisting source of illumination that makes their envisioning possible. It is when that decision is forgotten that the world comes to exist as a set of objects that are subjected to man (and the gendering is both accidental and telling), as a set of technological problems for the subject to solve, and the object world becomes the correlate of the "natural attitude."[28]

II

The Platonic texts and the profound act of imagination those texts represent are complex and multifaceted phenomena. The very ontological assumptions, which Heidegger and others would argue have led to the creation of our epistemic universe of technological subjection and commodification, I would contend, can also serve as some of the primary tools our modern world offers for resistance to a kind of unthinking domination of scientific and technical reason. There is, in fact, an ironic reversal of the first order in this recognition. When we normally think of Plato and Platonism, we do not in fact think of the object world. Shortly after the Myth of the Cave in Book 7 of the *Republic*, Plato tells us that astronomy is not the study of individual stars, that geometry does not measure the triangle drawn in the sand, and that harmonics is not the adjustment of the pegs on a lyre to produce consonance (522b–531c). The word Platonic does not automatically evoke our evidence-based universe in which data ("the things given") are sorted, organized, and brought into correspondence with categories of analysis so that truths are produced, realities stabilized, and objects able to be manipulated in predictable fashions, but it should. Astronomy is no more the study of individual stars than zoology is of the mouse beneath my window. This is what Louis Althusser means when he argues that empiricism is an idealism and why that statement, like Heidegger's initial observation, seems so counterintuitive. The object world is not a set of things or perceptions but the recognition by a subject of those things in relation to a logically elaborated set of categories.

Instead, the idea of Platonism in common usage leads us to think of the world of transcendental ideals: most prominently the good, but also the just, and the beautiful. We recall the *Symposium*'s "Ladder of Love," Socrates' great speech in the *Phaedrus*, or the Demiurge hard at work in the *Timaeus*. But there is a profound sense in which Platonism underwrites the most salient concepts of our social and political world every bit as much as Heidegger argues its Metaphysics structures our epistemic universe. We both want and need our moral and political universe to be structured around transcendental norms. Human rights, whether as articulated in *Les droits de l'homme* or the United Nations Universal Declaration of Human Rights, only exist qua rights if they are said to be equally applicable in all places and times. They must transcend every concrete instantiation in order to function as a critical tool available in all contexts, which means to say their activation must have much the same structure as the epistemic realities we examined in section one. That is to say, there must be a judging and perceiving subject, an object (in this case often an act rather than a thing), and a transcendental set of norms that allows the subject to categorize and judge a given act as just or unjust, fair or unfair, respecting or disrespecting of recognized rights. But where in the first instance, as Heidegger notes, the Metaphysical universe imagined by Platonism works to install a kind of scientific and technical domination of the object world, the second offers a form of leverage to resist it.[29] We call out the manifest injustice, the lack of veracity, the sheer ugliness or disharmony of the world as we live it, and we seek to change it accordingly. Like Socrates before his judges in Athens or Plato before Dionysius in Syracuse, we speak truth to power (*parrhesia*).[30] We do so not in the name of our passing whim but always in the name of an *idea* that transcends our experience of the immediate.

Now, I am well aware of the dangers of simply accepting the traditional reading of the forms, and I have written extensively about the way such a reading does not do justice to the Platonic texts, which problematize any simple notion of a two worlds theory in which the world of our experience is definitively and ontologically separated from the world of the intelligible. Nonetheless, the traditional reading remains true in important and significant ways. The notion of *ideai* as moments that unify the sensible manifold into a series of intelligible wholes is absolutely necessary not only to any philosophy bearing the label Platonic but also to any modern understanding of intellectual experience as more than a cascade of disjoined sensory impressions.[31] If we truly believe there is no such thing as justice, however we may define it, lying behind just acts, beauty behind beautiful deeds, or goodness behind good deeds, then we are saying that the world and our experience of it is, on a fundamental level, unfounded and arbitrary. That of course may well be true![32] But if so, then the projects of philosophy, politics, and culture as more than assertions of power and preference are nullified from the start, and no one save the sociopath truly acts and, therefore, on the most existential level, truly believes, that that is the case.[33] Thus, whenever we complain about a lack of fairness, whenever we complain about injustice, whenever we aspire to a standard of beauty or truth, we live very much in a world imagined by Platonism, which is to say we live in the modern world. To behave otherwise is to live in the manner of the tyrant described at the beginning of Book 9: a person who, in his or her assertion of absolute power, becomes a slave to even the most momentary desires and, therefore, fears as well.[34] The tyrant is also accordingly in thrall to the world of immediate appearance, to the way things seem at the moment. We can all think of leaders who fall into this category. There is, then, at least according to Plato, but also according to virtually the entire history of Western philosophy, a necessary yet also very practical moment of transcendence in which thought and experience must go beyond the immediate, if rationality and criticism are to have any purchase.

Moreover, these *ideai* must, as Plato recognized, exist outside of space and time, at least as conventionally conceived. Justice cannot be "just" only on Tuesday or only in

Cleveland, none of which means that a given just act might not in a different context be unjust or even shameful. And this is why a person who insistently confuses the individual action bearing a predicate with the predicate itself is, Plato says, like someone having a dream or a hallucination.[35] The difference between appearance and reality has completely collapsed. For such a person, all is visible and the visible is all.

This strong reading of the theory of forms represented in the myth of the cave is, as even Derrida contends, the necessary positive moment of abstraction on which the Platonic and philosophic edifice depends.[36] But, it is only one moment in the Platonic text.[37] It does not authorize us, according to Plato, to posit a positive ontology for the forms, let alone another world in which they exist,[38] nor even less can we say that any one person has access to them, let alone possesses them with sufficient knowledge so as to be able to demand or force others to adhere to their vision. Instead, we are always dealing with semblances, always dealing with likenesses.[39] Indeed, it is only the knowledge that the object of perception and the category under which we judge it are not the same and therefore that we must posit a moment of difference, which separates the lover of wisdom not only from the object of perception but also from the dreamer and ultimately the madman and tyrant.[40] It is the preservation of this moment of difference in the assertion of identity that underwrites the structure of both our epistemic and ethical universe. It is predicated on the separation of subjects from objects and is as a consequence a product of representational thinking.

III

Thus, within the Platonic world picture there are set up two contrary movements. On the one hand, we see the abstraction of the object world from the subject and, as a consequence, that world being reduced to a collection of things. This abstraction has certain undeniable benefits and is at the base of what we sometimes term the scientific method. Who would want to return to a world without antibiotics? Who among us seriously believes that the presence of phlogiston in objects is a better explanation of their flammability than that of oxygen in the atmosphere? Yet we pay a certain price when our separation from the object world is taken to its logical (and often commercial) extreme. Food is no longer a recognition of our deep implication within the material world, a moment affirming both our social ties and our elemental relation with soil, rain, pastoral life, as well as material traditions stretching back millennia, but it becomes a collection of nutrients, or a disaggregated set of qualities—crunchiness, chewiness, flavor profiles—to be reengineered and mass-produced. Education is no longer the cultivation of personality, of empathy, and of a deeper awareness of one's place in the cultural, historical, and material world, but a set of quantifiable skills, learning outcomes, and outputs. The world is no longer where we live but a set of objects subjected to our use, a collection of technical problems to be solved, a field of potential commodities.

On the other hand, this same moment of abstraction produces a notion of beauty that extends beyond any one beautiful person or thing, that asks us at least to contemplate the possibility of something being beautiful not because of its specific utility[41]—a screwdriver that turns screws, an algorithm that identifies potential consumers—but because it is beautiful beyond any one context of consumption or use:[42] a Ming vase, the Goldberg Variations, a fragment of Sappho. It asks us at least to contemplate a notion of justice that is not simply about the efficiency and consistency of judicial procedure or a personal desire for retribution but is about substantial justice, about a recognition of what is just that transcends any one person's individual and unrepeatable circumstances. In each case, these notions, these *ideai*, go beyond the identification of isolated individual instances, which can never in themselves be critical, which can never signify beyond themselves, to offer the leverage that permits us to ask why things cannot be better, more just, more beautiful, and more true.

What is crucial to recognize is that these two contrary movements are on a certain level one and the same. The moment of abstraction that separates out the object from the subject to create the world of representation, the closure of our Metaphysics, is also the world that posits its own beyond. There is nothing necessary about this world. People can and have lived in other worlds. But those worlds are structured in different manners. In the world of the *Iliad*, gods and men intermingle but there is no transcendental realm. The gods are not ontologically different from humans.

Plato, then, is world literature not simply because he is read all over the world. There are extremely important translation and commentary projects in China. Plato remains a significant source of inspiration for the Iranian revolution,[43] and his works are read in every major university throughout the Western world. But Plato is world literature because, as Heidegger recognized, our world is in significant ways Plato's and that world was not simply deduced. It was not the product of a syllogism. It was imagined. It was created through an almost inconceivable poetic act that gave birth to the parameters and assumptions that make our syllogisms possible on which we bestow Plato's name.

Notes

1   The term originates from Edmund Husserl, *Ideas for a Pure Phenomenology and Phenomenological Philosophy: First Book General Introduction to Pure Phenomenology*, trans. Daniel O. Dalhstrom (Indianapolis, IN: Hackett, 2014).
2   Ferdinand de Saussure, *Course in General Linguistics*, trans. Wade Baskin (New York: Philosophical Library, 1959), 65.
3   Paul Allen Miller, "Queering Plato: Foucault on Philosophy as Self-Fashioning and Resistance in Plato's 7th Letter," *Trans: Revue de Littérature Générale et Comparée* 23 (2018); Paul Allen Miller, "Dreams and Other Fictions: The Representation of Representation in Republic 5 and 6," *American Journal of Philology* 136.1 (2015): 37–62; Paul Allen Miller, "The Platonic Remainder: *Khora* and the *Corpus Platonicum*," in *Plato and Derrida*, ed. Miriam Leonard (Oxford: Oxford UP, 2010), 321–41.
4   Jacques Derrida, *Khôra* (Paris: Galilée, 1993).
5   Catherine H. Zuckert, *Postmodern Platos: Nietzsche, Heidegger, Gadamer, Strauss, Derrida* (Chicago: University of Chicago Press, 1996), 37.

6 Th. C. W. Oudemans and A. P. M. H. Lardinois, *Tragic Ambiguity: Anthropology, Philosophy, and Sophocles' Antigone* (Leiden: Brill, 1987), 229; Rachel Jones, *Irigaray: Towards a Sexuate Philosophy* (Cambridge: Polity Press, 2011), 189. For notable attempts to think beyond the classic subject/object dichotomy in contemporary science, see Christopher Whitmore, "Symmetrical Archaeology," *Encyclopedia of Global Archaeology*, ed. Claire Smith (New York: Springer, 2014); and Bruno Latour, "Circulating Reference: Sampling the Soil in the Amazon Rainforest," *Pandora's Hope: Essays on the Reality of Science Studies* (Cambridge: Harvard University Press, 1999), 24–79.
7 Martin Heidegger, "The Age of the World Picture," in *The Question Concerning Technology and Other Essays*, trans. William Lovitt (New York: Harper Torchbooks, 1982), 128; cf. Alain Renaut, *Sartre: Le dernier philosophe* (Paris: Grasset, 1993), 137; Luce Irigaray, *Speculum, De l'autre femme* (Paris: Minuit, 1974), 383, 412–16.
8 Martin Heidegger, "Plato's Doctrine of Truth," trans. Thomas Sheehan, in *Pathmarks*, ed. William McNeill (Cambridge: Cambridge UP, 1998), 181; Ellen Mortensen, *The Feminine and Nihilism: Luce Irigaray with Nietzsche and Heidegger* (Oslo: Scandinavian UP, 1994), 80–2; Jones, *Irigaray*, 43.
9 As I have argued elsewhere, Plato's text presents a much more complex and ambivalent picture that can be profitably compared to Confucianism. Paul Allen Miller, "Wisdom as Knowledge and Wisdom as Action: Plato, Heidegger, Cicero, and Confucius," in *Wisdom and Philosophy: Contemporary and Comparative Approaches*, ed. Hans Georg Mueller and Andrew K. Whitehead (London: Bloomsbury, 2016), 75–92.
10 Heidegger, "The Age of the World Picture," 145.
11 Michel Foucault, *Les mots et les choses* (Paris: Gallimard, 1966), 171–9.
12 Heidegger, "The Age of the World Picture," 115.
13 Max Statkiewicz, *Rhapsody of Philosophy: Dialogues with Plato in Contemporary Thought* (University Park: Penn State UP, 2009), 57.
14 Heidegger, "Plato's Doctrine of Truth," 129–31.
15 Ibid.
16 Irigaray, *Speculum*, 301, 306–7.
17 Jones, *Irigaray*, 40.
18 Heidegger, "Plato's Doctrine of Truth," 177–8.
19 Ibid., 182.
20 Ibid., 55.
21 Ibid., 172, 182.
22 The bibliography here is immense and more often concerned with concepts of writing and speech than what we see in Heidegger's direct concern with metaphysics. But clearly these bodies of thought are more complementary than they are exclusive, and Plato is as much concerned with the nature and impact of "writing" as he is with philosophy's birth from a new concept of truth. See e.g. Bruno Snell, *The Discovery of the Mind in Greek Philosophy and Literature*, trans. Thomas G, Rosenmeyer (New York: Dover, 1953), 20; Eric A. Havelock, *Preface to Plato* (Cambridge: Harvard UP, 1963); Jack Goody and Ian Watt, "The Consequences of Literacy," in *Literacy in Traditional Societies*, ed. Jack Goody (Cambridge: Cambridge UP, 1968), 53; Jacques Derrida, *Of Grammatology*, trans. Gayatri Spivak (Baltimore: Johns Hopkins UP, 1976), 27; Walter J. Ong, *Orality and Literacy: The Technologizing of the Word* (London: Methuen, 1982), 172–3; Paul Allen Miller, *Lyric Texts and Lyric Consciousness* (London: Routledge, 1994), 1–36; and Arnold Davidson, "Ethics as

Ascetics: Foucault, the History of Ethics, and Ancient Thought," in *The Cambridge Companion to Foucault*, ed. Gary Gutting (Cambridge: Cambridge UP, 1994), 126-7.
23 Gregory Nagy, *Best of the Achaeans: Concepts of the Hero in Archaic Greek Poetry* (Baltimore: Johns Hopkins UP, 1979).
24 Charles Stocking, *Homer's Iliad and the Failure of Force* (Forthcoming).
25 Heidegger, "Plato's Doctrine of Truth," 176.
26 Zuckert, *Postmodern Platos*, 56.
27 Heidegger, "Plato's Doctrine of Truth," 167-8, 180, 182; Zuckert, *Postmodern Platos*, 49-50.
28 Heidegger, "The Age of the World Picture," 133; Alisson Stone, *Luce Irigaray and the Philosophy of Sexual Difference* (Cambridge: Cambridge UP, 2006), 96-7.
29 Foucault on tactical polyvalence. See Michel Foucault, *La volonté de savoir: Histoire de la sexualité*, vol. 1 (Paris: Gallimard, 1976), 132-3.
30 Cf. Michel Foucault, *Le Gouvernement de soi et des autres: Cours au Collège de France 1982-83* (Paris: Haute Études, Gallimard, Seuil, 2008), 42-65, 98-9, 318-26; John Rajchman, *Truth and Eros: Foucault, Lacan, and the Question of Ethics* (London: Routledge, 1991), 119-21, 128-9.
31 *Parmenides* 132b-d. Cf. Auguste Diès, "Notice," in *Platon, Oeuvres completes*, Tome 9.2, *Philèbe* (Paris: Société d'Edition Les Belles Lettres, 1966), xx; A. J. Festugière, *Contemplation et vie contemplative selon Platon*, 2nd ed. (Paris: Vrin, 1950), 230; Nicolas-Isidore Boussoulas, *L'être et la composition des mixtes dans le Phlèbe* (Paris: Presses Universitaires de France, 1952), 143-4; and Jean-François Pradeau, *Platon, l'imitation de la philosophie* (Paris: Aubier, 2009), 105-10.
32 This is the fundamental insight of the existential philosophy of the absurd found in Albert Camus's *Mythe de Sisyphe* (1965) and Jean-Paul Sartre's *Nausée* (1981).
33 This is also Socrates' wager in his battle with Callicles in the *Gorgias* and Thrasymachus in the *Republic*.
34 *Rep.* 9.571-79.
35 *Republic* 5.476c1-5.
36 Cf. Eric Alliez, "Ontologie et logographie: La pharmacie, Platon et le simulacre," in *Nos Grecs et leurs modernes: Les Stratégies contemporaines d'appropriation de l'antiquité*, ed. Barbara Cassin (Paris: Seuil, 1992), 221; Derrida, *Khôra*, 83; Zuckert, *Postmodern Platos*, 235; Luc Brisson et Jean-François Pradeau, ed., *Dictionnaire Platon* (Paris: Ellipses, 2007), 64-8; and Jones, *Irigaray*, 43.
37 Francis Wolff, "Trios: Deleuze, Derrida, Foucault, historiens du platonisme," in *Nos Grecs et leurs modernes: Les Stratégies contemporaines d'appropriation de l'antiquité*, ed. Barbara Cassin (Paris: Seuil, 1992), 241-2; Derrida, *Khôra*, 81-2; Jones, *Irigaray*, 43.
38 Cf. Hans-Georg Gadamer, "Reply to Nicholas P. White," trans. Roger C. Norton and Dennis J. Schmidt, in *Platonic Writings, Platonic Readings*, ed. Charles L. Griswold Jr. (New York: Routledge, 1988), 260; Zuckert, *Postmodern Platos*, 73; John Sallis, *Chorology: On Beginning in Plato's Timaeus* (Bloomington: Indiana UP, 1999), 48-9.
39 Even a relatively traditional reader of Plato like Goldschmidt contends that while the sensibles reflect the intelligibles as imperfect copies of ideal types, those same sensibles provide the paradigms for understanding the intelligibles (Victor Goldschmidt, *Le paradigme dans la dialectique platonicienne* [1947] [Paris: Vrin, 1985;

2nd ed. 2003], 87). Compare Cynthia Hampton, *Pleasure, Knowledge, and Being: An Analysis of Plato's Philebus* (Albany: SUNY Press, 1990), 92.
40 Pradeau, *Platon*, 163. Thus, in the *Sophist*, Being is not absolute unchanging self-identity but that which is beyond change and rest (249c–250c).
41 What Kant termed *pulchritudo adhaerens* (*Critique of Judgement* §16). See Paul Allen Miller, "Kant, Lentricchia, and Aesthetic Education," *Kant Studien* 83 (1992): 454–66.
42 What Kant termed *pulchritudo vaga*, and Plato gestures toward with the idea of the beautiful in itself (*Critique of Judgement* §16).
43 Sadakat Kadri, *Heaven on Earth: A Journey through Shari'a Law from the Deserts of Ancient Arabia to the Streets of the Modern Muslim World* (New York: Macmillan, 2012), 95.

3

Worlding Interpretation, or Fanon and the Poetics of Disalienation

Nicole Simek

In his 1951 medical dissertation investigating the interrelationship between neurological and psychological elements of mental illness, Frantz Fanon (1925–1961) gives a succinct and telling characterization of madness: "*Ultimately, the mad person is someone who can no longer find his place among people.*"[1] This relational understanding of health reflects Fanon's epistemological "caution," as Jean Khalfa puts it, his wariness of reification and insistence that "we should always be ready to think in terms of processes rather than entities."[2] The insight that individual patients cannot be treated in isolation from their social and cultural environments drove both the reforms he instituted in his psychiatric practice at the Blida-Joinville Hospital in Algeria, and, later, in Tunis, but also his philosophical and political work, which focused on treating a diseased social world: the "morbid universe" of colonialism, which requires "a complete lysis," as he put it in *Peau noire, masques blancs* (*Black Skin, White Masks*).[3] This work of lysis, of ending disease, must be complete in the strong sense: not only must the disease be thoroughly eradicated, but the process of healing must take place in all of reality's dimensions: the psychic, the socioeconomic, the political, and also the linguistic. "Reality requires total comprehension," Fanon stresses, arguing that while the subjective and objective, or psychic and social, levels of neurosis in a racist world are "mutually dependent, any unilateral liberation is flawed, and the worst mistake would be to believe their mutual dependence automatic."[4] The struggle against alienation, in other words, must be *worlded*. It must take account of the totality of the "massive psycho-existential complex" created by colonization,[5] and it must also open onto new worldings, new world-making processes and temporalities.

This essay focuses on Fanon's interest in poetic-philosophical form and the role he gives to poetics as a worlding mode of interpretation and address within this project of disalienation. If colonial powers narrate the colonized in such a way as to efface their histories and deny them the capacity to make meaningful worlds—thus committing what Pheng Cheah describes as "cultural genocide," or world-killing[6]—Fanon insists on the colonized's "right to narrate," to borrow an insight from Edward Said.[7] Intrinsic to the process of revolutionary decolonization is the act of reworlding, the act of setting time in motion again. It requires a new approach to past, present, and future.

"Disalienation," Fanon famously declared, "will be for those Whites and Blacks who have refused to let themselves be locked in the substantialized 'tower of the past,'" and for those who suffer in the present, "for many other black men," it "will come from refusing to consider their reality as definitive."[8] This work of poiesis, of creative invention, happens in dialectical relation to our social and material conditions. Poiesis is founded in human existential freedom, a freedom that, as beings-for-others, we can only realize in relation, in language. To speak of a poetics of disalienation is thus to draw attention to both to the creative dimension of worlding and the specific ways in which linguistic and aesthetic form matters to its achievement.[9]

I will begin here by reviewing Fanon's understanding of alienation and the role of language in psychosocial life, before turning to literature as a particular mode of analyzing and remaking the world. This poetic project takes form as an effort "to touch the other, feel the other, discover each other," an effort to develop knowledge that remains open to relation, as voiced in the final prayer closing *Black Skin, White Masks*: "O my body, always make me a man who questions!"[10]

The Place of Madness

In describing mental illness as a relational state in which one is out of place, deprived of social bonds, Fanon brings to the forefront the need to prioritize reintegration into community as a goal of treatment.[11] This treatment cannot proceed on an individual level alone, however, if the social world, the place of social relation, is itself diseased. Under colonialism, the place allocated to the colonized is a "zone of nonbeing," a zone of psychological and economic inferiority, and to remain in one's place, to obey the social injunction, "You, stay where you are," is to accept the status of inferior object, to deny one's subjectivity and freedom.[12] As he puts it more bluntly in *The Wretched of the Earth* (*Les Damnés de la terre*, published in 1961 during the Algerian War), colonization itself, even in what passes for peacetime, is "a great purveyor of psychiatric hospitals":

> Since 1954 we have drawn the attention of French and international psychiatrists in scientific works to the difficulty of "curing" a colonized subject correctly, in other words making him thoroughly fit into a social environment of the colonial type. Because it is a systematized negation of the other, a frenzied determination to deny the other any attribute of humanity, colonialism forces the colonized to constantly ask the question: "Who am I in reality?" ... When colonization remains unchallenged by armed resistance, when the sum of harmful stimulants exceeds a certain threshold, the colonized's defenses collapse, and many of them end up in psychiatric institutions. In the calm of this period of triumphant colonization, a constant and considerable stream of mental symptoms are direct sequels of this oppression.[13]

A colonized world has no meaningful place for the colonized as a fully human subject. It offers only disintegration, nonbeing. "Genuine disalienation," Fanon thus argues, "will have been achieved only when things, in the most materialist sense, have resumed their rightful place."[14]

Psychoanalysis, Fanon affirmed, would play a key role in analyzing this morbid social world and identifying the structural causes for its illness. "Only a psychoanalytical interpretation of the black problem," he went so far as to say in *Black Skin, White Masks*, "can reveal the affective disorders responsible for this network of [psycho-existential] complexes" plaguing the colonized subject.[15] The usefulness of psychoanalysis stems from two factors. First, in terming the effects of colonialism "affective disorders," Fanon was not simply drawing from psychoanalytic language for illustrative metaphors; in speaking of a diseased social world and the pathologies that result from it, Fanon was referring to actual symptoms observable in individual members of society, encountered in his own psychiatric practice, and reported by the other psychiatrists whose work he engaged in his writing. Second, psychoanalysis provided an interpretive model for investigating the complex, unknown, masked causes at the root of observable symptoms, symptoms that themselves were not readily apparent or even identifiable as indicators of disease in the racist colonial regime under which Fanon was born and was working. Psychoanalysis's ability to denaturalize or demystify that which is taken for granted (to question accepted social norms and prohibitions) and, conversely, to naturalize (to make sense out of) the seemingly abnormal or unacceptable, would prove extremely useful to bringing to light and thematizing the generalized malaise, the sentiments of inferiority, the discomfort with or shame of one's own body, the "epidermalization" of identity through race, as Fanon put it, in short, the desire, the striving to be white, to be other (the state which characterized the alienated colonized subject).[16]

These "diseased" thoughts are made to appear normal and logical in a culture where blackness and the negative traits associated with it were taken as fact, and where material conditions reinforced and helped perpetuate the belief in the aesthetic and intellectual superiority of whiteness. Psychoanalysis must also operate, then, as socioanalysis, as a means for locating and interpreting the material conditions that underpin alienation. "In some circumstances, we must recall, the *socius* is more important than the individual," Fanon points out in his discussion of the interpretation of dreams, maintaining as well that "the true disalienation of the black man implies a brutal awareness of the social and economic realities."[17] An understanding of a subject's psychic history will remain incomplete and ineffective as long as political, historical, and economic factors fail to be adequately incorporated in the analysis—as long, that is, as it fails to engage the place of madness as a world.

Importantly, such an engagement, one that is worlded and world-making, requires not simply a change of scale (from the individual to the society) but rather a rigorous, dialectical approach to local particularities, to individual organic bodies and psyches situated in precise and dynamic familial, cultural, regional, and global economic and political relationships all at once. This is a lesson Fanon learned well in the psychiatric context, as he and his colleagues discovered through trial and error the contours of their own Eurocentrism and worked to overcome it in developing specific sociotherapeutic methods appropriate for Blida's ethnically, linguistically, and religiously diverse population of patients.[18] Though colonization's global reach impacted colonized populations in similar ways, disalienation, as Fanon stresses, will unfold differently in different contexts. For the alienated bourgeois intellectual, the study of history and the rediscovery of a rich, effaced African culture may be an effective first step in disalienation, because anyone who "takes a stand against this living death" that is bourgeois society, "any society that becomes ossified in a predetermined mold, stifling any development, progress, or discovery," is, Fanon argues, "in a way a revolutionary."[19] Yet such a move does not have the same impact always and everywhere:

> It is obvious—and I can't say this enough—that the motivations for disalienating a physician from Guadeloupe are essentially different from those for the African construction worker in the port at Abidjan. For the former, alienation is almost intellectual in nature. It develops because he takes European culture as a means of detaching himself from his own race. For the latter, it develops because he is victim to a system based on the exploitation of one race by another and the contempt for one branch of humanity by a civilization that considers itself superior.
>
> We would not be so naive as to believe that the appeals for reason or respect for human dignity can change reality. For the Antillean working in the sugarcane plantations in Le Robert, to fight is the only solution. And he will undertake and carry out this struggle not as the result of a Marxist or idealist analysis but because quite simply he cannot conceive his life otherwise than as a kind of combat against exploitation, poverty, and hunger.[20]

If disalienation is to succeed, it must proceed through varied modes in order to address diseased relationality in its specificity wherever it obtains. Only such an attentive worlding can bring into being a place in which humans can become themselves, as subjects in creative relation to one another.

Poetics as Address

As an overwhelmingly important medium of relationality in human life, language represents a major concern for Fanon throughout his work, from its mediating role in the doctor-patient relationship to its alienating function under colonialism to its capacity to spark decolonial imagination and rally collectivities in the form of combat literature. *Black Skin, White Masks* opens with a wrenching study of language, a "phenomenon" Fanon describes as being of "fundamental importance," for it is through language that worlds are opened or foreclosed, that the status of human being in the eyes of others (and in one's own eyes) is achieved or denied; "to speak," Fanon asserts, "is to exist absolutely for the other. ... A man who possesses a language possesses as an indirect consequence the world expressed and implied by this language."[21]

Language serves as a lifeline to others, a means for constructing and maintaining a self. Dispossessing someone of language—be it in the institutional structure of the 1950s psychiatric hospital, frequently located outside city centers, isolating patients from society, or in the colonial context of Fanon's native Martinique, where "human" status is tied to speaking French and abandoning Creole—thus has catastrophic consequences. Reconstructing the self in language becomes, then, a key priority for Fanon, in therapy and in activism. "The discovery of writing," states Fanon in the inaugural issue of *Notre Journal (Our Journal)*, the weekly publication he established for the Blida-Joinville Hospital in the service of this reconstruction, "is certainly the most beautiful one, since it allows you to recall yourself, to present things that have happened in order and above all to communicate with others, even when they are absent."[22] The reflexive character of writing allows one to sort through memory and construct a self through narration, but most importantly ("above all") it is an act of connection, of hearing and being heard by the other. Fanon reiterated the importance of this act in a number of his editorials, advising, for example, that "the patient's place in society, in his or her family, must be maintained. This is why the patient has to have a social attitude: writing, receiving news and narrating are some of the most important social activities. ... If possible, each patient needs to write at least once a week."[23] Writing is not a mere pastime but an essential means of communication. "The boarders who write in the journal," Fanon stresses, "do not do it for the sake of doing something. They each express something that prevails for them. The act of writing is already a higher act. The act of reading as well."[24] These acts are "higher" because they allow one to form and reshape thought. Reading and writing are acts of analysis, creation, sharing, and revision—in short, acts of relational poiesis.

This conception of reading and writing as intimately connected to one another and to the formation of selves in social relation helps shed light on Fanon's extensive use of literary examples in his work. Motivated by the precise aim "to think and construct freedom as disalienation within a necessarily historical and political process," Khalfa and Young observe, Fanon sought out all possible sources of insight and "devoured in equal measure literature, philosophy, psychiatry, history, politics, sociology and ethnology." Yet, as they note, "everything in this thinker's work has its intelligibility."[25] Fanon's use of these resources was far from indiscriminate; he remained highly attuned to the specific historical, conceptual, and epistemological contours and contributions of the readings nourishing his thought, as well as to the effects created by the interplay or juxtaposition of various genres in his own writing, which can itself be described as poetic in its intense attention to language and aesthetic form.

Poetic discourse serves Fanon's project of disalienation in at least three interconnected ways. It provides a means for taking account of realities that have gone unseen from other vantage points, for better addressing those who would turn away from such realities and for articulating the precise relationships between the particular and the universal, a task necessary to political change. In his preface to the first edition of *Peau noire, masques blancs*, Francis Jeanson captures some of this force that the literary takes on in Fanon's writing when he describes Fanon's demands in the book as "unfitting, improper, ill-adapted, almost unspeakable, *unobjectifiable*."[26] Writing from a colonized position—that place of madness—creates a double bind: how to communicate something of this out-of-jointness which is antithetical to the very narrative and epistemological norms governing intelligibility?

Fanon's earliest surviving texts—two 1949 play manuscripts, *L'Œil se noie* (*The Drowning Eye*) and *Les Mains parallèles* (*Parallel Hands*)—explore this problem through theatrical forms that combine classical and contemporary genres, poetry and prose, conceptual abstraction and embodied affect.[27] As Robert J. C. Young explains in his close study of these works, Fanon's plays

> could be best described as philosophical dramatizations: they are primarily plays of ideas and expression not of character. However, as the emphasis on the body in the titles of both plays already suggests, they are not merely cerebral: as a result of the distinctive poetic-surrealist idiom of Fanon's language, they come across as "*lived* things," intensely physical, visceral, full of affect, with the sensations of the trembling dispersed body emphasized as much as that of the psyche and indeed often indistinguishable from it.[28]

Surrealism for Fanon, as for Aimé Césaire before him, whose work heavily influenced Fanon's thinking, "was exactly right for the irrational disjunctive world of coloniality," Young continues.[29] Unsettling and estranging, surrealism foregrounds incongruities, allows tensions and gaps to hang unresolved, defamiliarizes the world, and disrupts the unthinking use of language by shifting the ways it signifies, rendering it opaque or newly and differently significant. That it does so not merely by describing disjuncture but by enacting it is of great importance, for it allows Fanon first to test language and its relationship to reality,[30] but also to address the reader on an affective level, to reconstruct the diseased social relations of a morbid colonial universe, and elicit a response from those who are otherwise disinclined to listen.

The problem of readership—of reaching the other—is an epistemological and affective one that Fanon raises at the outset of *Black Skin, White Masks*, which begins with a lyric string of declarations bearing on the situation of address:

> Don't expect to see any explosion today. It's too early ... or too late.
> I'm not the bearer of absolute truths.
> No fundamental inspiration has flashed across my mind.
> I honestly think, however, it's time some things were said.
> Things I'm going to say, not shout. I've long given up shouting.
> A long time ago ...
> Why am I writing this book? Nobody asked me to.
> Especially not those for whom it is intended.[31]

As Robert Bernasconi points out, the identity of the intended audience remains ambiguous in the opening pages, but it is given more specificity when the speaker asserts, "My true wish is to get my brother, black or white, to shake off the dust from that lamentable livery built up over centuries of incomprehension."[32] "Black or white" signals the inclusion of differently situated readers while also pointing to that very difference, and throughout the volume, Fanon maintains a mode of dual address, demonstrating a concern for the ways in which the work of shaking off the "lamentable livery" of racialized subjectivities will need to proceed somewhat differently for blacks and whites.[33] Yet the analysis must address both at once, for they are locked in a "vicious cycle" of "dual narcissism": "Fact: some Whites consider themselves superior to Blacks. Another fact: some Blacks want to prove at all costs to the Whites the wealth of the black man's intellect and equal intelligence. How can we break the cycle?"[34]

One reason this cycle is so difficult to break is that it feeds on a gap between cognitive abstractions and lived experience, a gap disavowed by white consciousness in particular. Jeanson points to this in his preface when he imaginatively anticipates white readers' reactions to Fanon's aim to study black experience:

> Right-minded people take a dim view of these types of concrete description, which delve into the very flesh of consciousness and compromise the sangfroid of ideas by bringing in the murky confusion of *lived experience* [*le vécu*]. We can imagine some of their objections: "What does it matter if the author is black or white? Anyone can ask these questions henceforth. Besides, the black problem is a white problem, and its solution is also white. Undoubtedly, Blacks' complaints are quite moving, but they can no longer teach us anything. ... And after all, it's Western science we have to thank for objectively dismantling the myth of racism!"[35]

The Western reader schooled in the values of an abstract universalism finds in such an approach to truth a convenient excuse to turn away from particulars, to ignore any claim that human experience might be differentiated, while nevertheless implicitly upholding distinctions between "us" and "them," between Western science that teaches and emotional testimony which brings no new knowledge.

Such an orientation finds its roots in the historical structures that shape experience, for even well-intentioned white readers can mistake partial perspective for exhaustive knowledge, as Fanon makes clear in his critique of Jean-Paul Sartre's analysis of the Negritude movement as a stage to be subsumed in the dialectic. When Sartre "located Negritude in a dialectical history that has white racism for its first term," Bernasconi explains, his mistake in Fanon's eyes was not that he was wrong to grasp Negritude as a movement that shores up an essentialist conception of identity (a critique Fanon shared) but rather that his statement, written from the position of a white subject, "keep[s] intact the structure that serves to produce the problem," the structure within which "he, a white man, asks Blacks unilaterally to renounce the pride of their colour."[36] In pronouncing this, Fanon argues, Sartre "forgets" the specificity of black experience, the fact that "the black man suffers in his body quite differently from the white man," and that his needs—his need to "get lost in the night of the absolute," to draw from the wellspring of Negritude in order to become self-conscious—are different from those of whites.[37] In using the verb "forget," Bernasconi points out, Fanon suggests that Sartre "knows but does not know," a formulation he uses elsewhere in the book, that his knowledge of racism is limited by his *standpoint*, which allows him to forget an experience of suffering that can only and always be painfully present to blacks, who move through the world in bodies constantly subject to scrutiny and denigration.[38]

A crucial problem then, for Fanon, is to develop a mode of expression that, as Bernasconi puts it, "obliges white readers, like [himself], to consider what we prefer to ignore and what we too easily dismiss as beyond our understanding."[39] The challenge, then, lies not just in bringing to light the contours and limits of situated knowledge[40] but also in pushing readers to engage in the construction of new worlds from the place where they find themselves. While the sheer intensity (to use Bernasconi's description) and visceral quality (to use Young's) of Fanon's depiction of personal experience overcome to some extent the reader's defense mechanisms, Fanon remains all too aware that cries of pain do not necessarily lead to revolution.[41] To shift readers, the language of analysis must similarly refuse to remain in its place. The result, perhaps in *Black Skin, White Masks* most prominently, is a language that Jeanson characterizes as "quasi poetic."[42] Hovering between poetry and essay, autobiography, sociology, and psychoanalysis, Fanon's style pushes against accepted categories and terms of debate, bringing affect into realms where it is excluded, while insisting on the value of clinical study and argument.[43] If Jeanson's phrase points to the unsettling effects of this juxtaposition, it also reminds us that "poetic" is, in Fanon's work, a relational term, not one that can be defined once and for all through clearly identified formal characteristics. What matters is that expression breaks through inertia, that it finds a way to sustain unsettlement—epistemological and affective—and that it gives support to an inventive reworlding.

The fullest expression of this reworlding in the literary realm is what in *The Wretched of the Earth* Fanon calls "combat literature." If combat literature has evolved historically to take on particular forms—moving from the assimilation of Western styles to a poetry of revolt addressed to the colonizer to prose forms with an emphasis on clarity—this is precisely as a result of the particularities of a historical movement and not the expression of a transcendent and necessary progression. Ultimately, combat literature becomes combat literature—literature that "informs the national consciousness, gives it shape and contours, and opens up new, unlimited horizons," literature that "takes charge, because it is resolve situated in historical time"[44]—not when it takes shape in a particular generic telos but rather when it freely adapts and innovates form. Older forms, "congealed, petrified forms," are taken up again, but made anew: "oral literature, tales, epics, and popular songs, previously classified and frozen in time, begin to change."[45] Poiesis begins when expression comes alive, moving in a dynamic relation of address and exchange.

"By Way of Conclusion"

Fanon ends *Black Skin, White Masks* by marking, through the final chapter's title, the illusory character of any "conclusion." His last word wears the "guise" of an ending,[46] for writing, like the life of the author, is temporally bound, yet so long as life obtains, disalienation, or the exercise of freedom, can never be achieved once and for all. "Fanonian freedom," Jean Khalfa asserts, "presupposes the structural incarnation of all thought, and its essentially open temporality, in the endless construction of a world."[47]

The project of disalienation emerges in Fanon's work as poetic in the strong sense. Freedom and poiesis depend on one another and must be continually reinvented in the project of worlding. Expressive form is intimately tied to thought, feeling, and embodied particularity. In dialectical relation these can certainly regress into unfreedom or congeal through inertia into stasis—they come with no guarantee—yet it is this very open-endedness and unpredictability that provides the conditions for new imaginings to arise, for a poetics of freedom to remain at once necessary and viable.

Notes

1. Frantz Fanon, *Alienation and Freedom*, ed. Jean Khalfa and Robert J. C. Young, trans. Steven Corcoran (London: Bloomsbury, 2018), 224. Italics in the original. Fanon's dissertation was titled "Mental Alterations, Character Modifications, Psychic Disorders and Intellectual Deficit in Spinocerebellar Heredodegeneration: A Case of Friedreich's Ataxia with Delusions of Possession."
2. Jean Khalfa, *Poetics of the Antilles: Poetry, History, and Philosophy in the Writings of Perse, Césaire, Fanon and Glissant* (Oxford: Peter Lang, 2017), 221. Khalfa also makes this point in Fanon, *Alienation and Freedom*, 177.
3. Frantz Fanon, *Black Skin, White Masks*, trans. Richard Philcox (New York: Grove Press, 2008), xiv.
4. Ibid., xv.
5. Ibid., xvi.
6. Pheng Cheah, *What Is a World? On Postcolonial Literature as World Literature* (Durham: Duke UP, 2016), 195.
7. Edward Said uses the term "permission to narrate" in his discussion of Palestinian rights. "Permission to Narrate," in *The Edward Said Reader*, ed. Moustafa Bayoumi and Andrew Rubin (New York: Vintage, 2000), 243–66. See also Homi K. Bhabha, "On Writing Rights," in *Globalizing Rights: The Oxford Amnesty Lectures 1999*, ed. Matthew J. Gibney (Oxford: Oxford UP, 2003), 162–83.
8. Fanon, *Black Skin*, 201.
9. Though it will not be the focus of this essay, it is important to recall here that Fanon's work also belongs to world literature in the sense that it has circulated widely around the world and has been translated from the French into over twenty other languages, including Arabic, Japanese, Persian, Russian, Sindhi, Spanish, Swahili, and Tamil. For an insightful study of Fanon's global reception, in particular that of *Les Damnés de la terre*, see Kathryn Batchelor and Sue-Ann Harding, eds., *Translating Frantz Fanon Across Continents and Languages* (New York: Routledge, 2017).
10. Fanon, *Black Skin*, 206.
11. See Jean Khalfa, "Fanon, Revolutionary Psychiatrist," in Fanon, *Alienation and Freedom*, for an insightful discussion of Fanon's adoption of social therapies in his practice as well as the institutional reforms he carried out, including, in Blida, "the opening of a Moorish café, the celebration of traditional festivals, regular evenings with storytellers and local music groups" (191), as well as his critique of institutional confinement in itself and his creation of a psychiatric day center in Tunis as an alternative structure allowing patients to remain connected to their families and social environment.

12 Fanon, *Black Skin*, xii, 17. It is first through language that the corruption of social relations takes place. "You, stay where you are," Fanon observes, is the implicit message communicated to blacks when whites in France speak to them in pidgin French ("petit nègre"), for it conveys both an assumption that the person addressed is cognitively inferior and incapable of understanding the language, and also that this is his proper place and role in the status quo: the place of the grinning, fawning primitive grateful to have been given the gift of civilization—an assumption whose full violence is brought out when the addressee pushes back against it:

> You're sitting in a café in Rouen or Strasbourg and you have the misfortune to be spotted by an old drunk. He makes a beeline for your table: "You African? Dakar, Rufisque, whorehouse, women, coffee, mangoes, bananas …" You get up and leave; you are greeted with a hail of insults: "You didn't play big shot like that in your jungle, filthy nigger!" (*Black Skin*, 16)

13 Frantz Fanon, *The Wretched of the Earth*, trans. Richard Philcox (New York: Grove Press, 2004), 181–2.
14 Fanon, *Black Skin*, xv.
15 Ibid., xiv.
16 Ibid., xv.
17 Ibid., 85, xiv.
18 The Blida-Joinville hospital, as Jean Khalfa notes, was divided into two wards, one of European women and another of Algerian (Arab and Kabyle) men. This provided Fanon with a particularly instructive set of experimental conditions within which to continue testing the thesis developed during his doctoral studies, namely, as Khalfa summarizes it well, that "even when a mental illness has clearly its origin in neurological disorders, it generally develops in a socially determined relational space which in turn explains the form it takes" (Fanon, *Alienation and Freedom*, 173). In their article "Social Therapy in a Ward of Muslim Men: Methodological Difficulties," Fanon and his intern, Jacques Azoulay, analyze the reasons why the initial social therapies they instituted (European-style festivities, films, songs, and games) worked effectively for the European women but failed for the Muslim men. They conclude that through lack of objectivity, they had failed to take account of "the geographical, historical, cultural and social frames" of the indigenous society (Fanon, *Alienation and Freedom*, 362). Consequently, they reconfigured their approach to incorporate forms of sociability (Muslim religious observances, performances by indigenous musicians and storytellers, participation in café life) familiar to and valued by the Algerian patients.
19 Fanon, *Black Skin*, 199.
20 Ibid., 198–9.
21 Ibid., 1–2.
22 Fanon, *Alienation and Freedom*, 315 (*Our Journal*, December 24, 1953, no. 1, "Memory and Journal"). Fanon explains the mission of the journal (which was addressed to both patients and staff, and to which patients also contributed pieces) through the example of a ship:

> On a ship, it is commonplace to say that one is between sky and water; that one is cut off from the world; that one is alone. This journal, precisely, is to fight against the possibility of letting oneself go, against that solitude. Every day a

news-sheet comes out, often poorly printed, without photos and bland. But every day, that news-sheet works to liven up the boat. In it, you are informed about the "on-board" news: recreation, cinema, concerts, the next ports of call. You also learn, of course, about the news on land. The boat, though isolated, keeps contact with the outside, that is to say, with the world. Why? Because in two or three days, the passengers will meet up again with their parents and friends, and return to their homes. (315)

23 Fanon, *Alienation and Freedom*, 320–1 (*Our Journal* 23, May 27, 1954, "Patients' Relations with the Outside World").
24 Fanon, *Alienation and Freedom*, 330 (*Our Journal* 2, December 30, 1954, second year).
25 Jean Khalfa and Robert J. C. Young, "General Introduction," in Fanon, *Alienation and Freedom*, 5, 6.
26 Francis Jeanson, "Préface à *Peau noire, masques blancs*," in Frantz Fanon, *Peau noire, masques blancs* (Paris: Seuil, 1952), reprint, *Sud/Nord* 14 (2001): 179. https://www.cairn.info/revue-sud-nord-2001-1-page-175.htm. Translations from this piece are my own.
27 Robert J. C. Young, "Fanon, Revolutionary Playwright," in Fanon, *Alienation and Freedom*, 12–15.
28 Ibid.," 13–14. Italics in the original.
29 Ibid., 15.
30 Young situates Fanon and Césaire's concern for language, its role in ideology, and its capacity to produce material effects in a post–Second World War context:

> The direct experience of language's deceptions, the ways in which it can produce meaning that is at odds with reality and truth, detaching signifier from signified, meant that many writers after the war (among them Edouard Glissant, Yves Bonnefoy, Roger Giroux, Sartre) shared a sense of the emptiness (*vacuité*) of language and became preoccupied with re-attaching it to the material world and reworking its power in more forceful ways.

What the play manuscripts show us is the extent to which this work served as "an apprenticeship in writing that enabled Fanon to develop his own distinctive, visceral linguistic style closely related to his belief in the necessity of political action in his later work" ("Fanon, Revolutionary Playwright," 22).
31 Fanon, *Black Skin*, xi. Philcox's translation of the first line, "L'explosion n'aura pas lieu aujourd'hui" (which, more literally, reads "The explosion will not take place today") effectively brings out, through the imperative, the power dynamic and tension between readers' expectations and the speaker's concern to shake these preconceptions off that marks the whole passage.
32 Robert Bernasconi, "The European Knows and Does Not Know: Fanon's Response to Sartre," in *Frantz Fanon's Black Skin, White Masks: New Interdisciplinary Essays*, ed. Max Silverman (Manchester: Manchester UP, 2005), 101. I quote the passage Bernasconi cites from Philcox's later translation.
33 Ibid.," 101–2. "Throughout the book," Bernasconi observes,

> Fanon addresses Blacks and Whites very differently. He writes: "J'ai constamment essayé de révéler au Noir, qu'en un sens il s'abnormalise; au Blanc, qu'il est à la fois mystificateur et mystifié" ("I have constantly tried to show the

> Black that he is in a sense abnormalized; I have tried to show the White that he is at the same time a mystificator and mystified"). (101)

34 Fanon, *Black Skin*, xiv.
35 Jeanson, "Préface," 176. Italics in the original.
36 Bernasconi, "The European Knows," 108.
37 Fanon, *Black Skin*, 117, 112.
38 Bernasconi, "The European Knows," 107.
39 Ibid., 100.
40 Bernasconi argues cogently that Fanon's approach to knowledge is one that "today might be understood as a version of standpoint theory or the epistemology of provenance, but which was in its own time developed by him in terms of existential phenomenology" ("The European Knows," 101).
41 As he comments in *The Wretched of the Earth*, "a memorable example" of colonialist resistance to disalienation

> was the reaction of white jazz fans when after the Second World War new styles such as bebop established themselves. For them jazz could only be the broken, desperate yearning of an old "Negro," five whiskeys under his belt, bemoaning his own misfortune and the racism of whites. As soon as he understands himself and apprehends the world differently, as soon as he elicits a glimmer of hope and forces the racist world to retreat, it is obvious he will blow his horn to his heart's content and his husky voice will ring out loud and clear. (175–6)

42 Jeanson, "Préface," 179.
43 "This book is a clinical study," Fanon asserts in the introduction to *Black Skin, White Masks*. "The attitudes I propose describing are true. I have found them any number of times" (xvi).
44 Fanon, *The Wretched of the Earth*, 173–4.
45 Ibid., 174.
46 The original French reads "En guise de conclusion."
47 Khalfa, *Poetics of the Antilles*, 207.

4

Alluvia: The Palimpsest of African Memory

Michael Stern

Berlin, Germany, November 1884–February 1885

Berlin of 1884 was effected through the sword and the bullet. But the night of the sword and the bullet was followed by the morning of the chalk and the chalkboard.[1]

The delegates at the Conference of Berlin met with the intention of extending their world; they were blind to the world they unworlded. Most had never been to the continent whose raw materials they sought to extract, and what they knew mainly consisted of fictions describing it and its inhabitants as mere adjuncts to a destiny that had arrived in modern Europe first, and which from their perspective had yet to begin in Africa, that is, if they believed that the continent had any history at all.[2] Perhaps like Jean-Baptiste Labat, each of them they felt that "I have seen Africa but I have never set foot there."[3] This species of blind certainty carried over to the proceedings of the conference. As Adam Hochschild relates, "in snowy Berlin, almost none of the conference participants had seen more of Africa than the drawings of scenery on the menus for Bismarck's banquets."[4] Early in the proceedings, Henry Morton Stanley showed them a map depicting the Congo basin,[5] which I imagine must have looked like that cartographical temptress that first fascinated Joseph Conrad's Marlow as a young boy, serving as a serpentine snapshot of his ambitions, planting in his mind the intellectual blueprint that Africa was about him and (his place in) his own civilization. The delegates met for almost a third of the earth's journey around the sun, and in that time, they carved up that map and with it, the people who resided in the lands redescribed by its lines and its limits. The delegates knew that the agreements they would reach would launch the expeditions that would fill in the "many blank spaces on the earth"[6] not with what Jonathan Swift had earlier described as the "savage pictures" to "fill the Gaps"[7] but with the various colors that represented their claims to the land and its resources, and as a result the animals and monsters that were placed in the interior of earlier maps were erased, now filled in "with rivers and lakes and names."[8] However, there was another type of monstrosity that replaced the beasts; as the land was colonized and one form of life replaced another, the map of Africa would be traced in European vernaculars, her boundaries would be redrawn, and the places would be christened with new names, filling in the empty spaces where the monsters had been.⁹

The delegates drew the map guided by a Calabanic sense for cartography; it was as if a collection of Prosperos had renamed the features of Sycorax's island and imposed a language on her sons and daughters.¹⁰ In other words, for most of the conferees, Africa was a text cartographically displayed in the archive of an already existing cultural imaginary, an image of a continent that was theirs to define, theirs to extract from. Some of the European names for African places already reflected that: Ivory Coast, Gold Coast, and the Slave Coast, for example. And in a seeming contradiction that is really no contradiction at all, the cultural imaginary in which the delegates resided carried forward a notion of a *civilizing mission* in concert with their plunder, an enterprise that would create the notions of the Anglophone, the Francophone, and Lusophone in Africa, recreating Caliban's education, giving the gift of a language and the consequence of a debt of vocabulary.¹¹ This mission was described by *Article VI* of the final agreement, giving colonial paternal fantasies life by charging the nations attending the conference with the "care for the improvement of the conditions of … moral and material well-being" of Africans.¹² Imagine the degree of illusion necessary for the conferees to marry planning for the exploitation of a continent and her people with feeling qualified to care for their moral instruction. The delegates must have imagined themselves to be a collection of Crusoes naming their Fridays, enlisting those they considered to be unnamed into the rationality of a particular calendar and a particular clock.¹³ For that is what is often at stake in the colonial project: the articulation of space and time as form and rhythm, as a means to replicate conditions for the benefit of maximum extraction. This process begins with a renaming of that space.

Considering this, it is no small wonder that Frantz Fanon born in Martinique, who after having lived and having been educated in a world that saw no contradiction in these tethered drives to exploit and to civilize (the conjoined twins of the colonial project), declared that the colonizer performs the "fabrication" of the "colonized subject."¹⁴ For the filling of an empty map with European colors and names was happening at a moment when the historian A. Adu Boahen paints a very different picture of what of the continent, telling us that much of Africa was thriving, experiencing its own rather fruitful version of modernity.¹⁵ The Cameroonian philosopher Achille Mbembe reminds us of something that may well explain this willful ignorance of the forms of life lived by others, the result of a blindness to a blindness:

> The other foundation of the consciousness of empire has always been the tremendous will to ignorance that in every case seeks to pass itself off as knowledge.¹⁶

Perhaps the persistence of this willful ignorance in a culture that claims a scientific orientation can be explained by the way the knowledge was formed and re-formed during the period of the scramble for Africa. Mbembe writes,

To have power is therefore to know how to give and receive forms. But it is also to know how to escape existing forms, how to change everything while remaining the same, to marry new forms of life into new relations of destruction, loss, and death.[17]

The power to create forms is also a power to escape them, Mbembe's *dangerous perhaps*. I will return to this, but suffice to say here that the translation of a populated landmass into an empty map ready to be named was the prelude to a process where the African continent was reshaped by European military power, and retains its form to this day, continually shaped by foreign economic imperatives and known through a cartography shaped by the traces of economic imperatives. As Ngugi Wa Thiong'o reminds us in our epigraph, space on the African continent would be renamed, re-spoken, and knowledge of its spaces now marked by the doubleness signified by their new names would be taught in the full light of that duplicity in classrooms all over the continent to generations prompted to think through European forms, in the languages of the colonial powers. Ngugi writes elsewhere,

It is in the naming of the landscape that we can so clearly see the layering of one memory over another, a previous native memory buried under another, a foreign alluvium becoming the new visible identity of a place.[18]

The question remains: How is this alluvium embedded?

Sils Maria, Switzerland 1885: Consider the Midge

In the early days of the summer of 1885, sometime in June or July, four to five months after the delegates divided up Africa in Berlin, perhaps the most literary of German philosophers described how *worlds* are conceived in two remarkable notebook entries. What is remarkable about these notes emerges when we think of them as an internal challenge to the ideological principles, the fictions that allowed the attendees of the conference to divide up a continent in the absence of its inhabitants: namely, that the flow of time is unidirectional in a progressive sense; that within this temporal stream different geographical areas live at different stages of development; that the apogee of human progression is located in modern Christian Europe and therefore its people have the right to see themselves and their cultures as the template for historical development; and that despite these temporal historical disparities between peoples and cultures, there is *one world* regulated by a set of universal principles; and these principles, derived from nature, reason, history, or biology are embodied by enlightened Europeans.[19]

Our philosopher, Friedrich Nietzsche, had no patience for his culture's pieties. His critique of modernity excavates the roots of the philosophical, scientific, and ideological prejudices of its European form, exposing them as illusory. Nietzsche's peculiar understanding of Western modernity as a form of nihilism moved him to describe the relationship of power to knowledge and to consider how the creation of spaces and temporal compartments influence human understanding. In addition, Nietzsche's assertion that philosophy itself is a type of unconscious memoir in the form of a misunderstanding of the body[20] allows him access to a series of interrogations of seemingly abstract principles while bringing them back to relations between bodies as they move through space and time. His descriptions of social interactions cast them out from the coming paradise of the teleological, eudaemonic historical sense that guided the "civilizing mission" of Article VI in the conference protocols, exposing it to the light of a world where social forms are shaped through the exercise of power. Nietzsche illustrates how worlds are formed in excess of our experiences and how we are seduced into identifying with the very illusions that regulate our habituation, creating social facts out of fiction.

Preliminaries aside, entry number 10 in notebook 38 opens as follows: "Man is a creature that makes shapes and rhythms; he is practiced at nothing better and it seems he takes pleasure in nothing *more* than in *inventing* figures."[21] The original German reads, "*Der Mensch is ein Formen-und-Rhythmen-bildendes Geschöpf.*"[22] The symmetry of the German sentence describes the first principle for an aesthetics that trespasses upon epistemic ground with this simple equation: "The Human is a creature" (*Der Mensch ist ein Geschöpf*). Why would this be significant? Both *Geschöpf* and creature have similar etymologies. *Geschöpf* is a derivative of *Schöpfung* as "creature" derives from the Latin *creatura*. *Die Schöpfung* refers to the creation in the sense of a God creating the world or the human imagination creating works, adjectives like *Schöpferisch* describe a person or an act as being creative. The Latin *creatura* denotes a being created and of course the English adjective "creative" refers to acts of the imagination as well. So what kind of created creature is *Der Mensch?*: *ein Formen-und-Rhythmen bildendes Geschöpf: a creature who makes shapes and rhythms*, a being who through an integrated process connecting time and space creates shapes and reshapes, interpreting a world. For Nietzsche, it is not time that collapses into space as is often stated; it is more that compounded by the particularity of human sensations and activities, created space divides time into rhythm, while rhythm sets the pace for movements through space. This is not a matter of conflation but of relation.

In addition, form derives from the Latin *forma*, which carries many connotations that all relate to a gathering that gives shape, creating models and patterns out of or in existing space. Rhythm's etymology can be traced from the Latin *rhythmus*, a name describing movement in time, which in turn derives from the Greek *rhythmos*, whose primary meaning conveys a measured flow or movement with secondary meanings pertaining to proportion, symmetry, arrangement, form, manner, and disposition. Forms and shapes are not space categorically; they articulate space. Rhythms are not time categorically but time mediated by a body, an affect that divides, turning time's flow into the discernable shape of a tempo. This is not Immanuel Kant's conception of the human being intuiting categories as the conditions of possibility for apperception or G. W. F. Hegel's modern subject self-consciously and rationally understanding the movement of spirit through time as it manifests in the creation of forms, this is the human mediated by the experience of an aesthetic process that is intrinsic to her desires and energies (*Lust*), a human being creating the conditions of possibility as an activity rather than a receptivity. In other words, *der Mensch* who desires nothing more than the gathering that creates models, shapes, and patterns as an articulation of space also creates movements in a measured flow, forming a shape for time. While this seems quite promising, like most Nietzschean formulations there is a *dangerous perhaps*.

Thirteen years before penning this note, Nietzsche, then a young professor of classical philology in Basel, had written a sketch that remained unpublished during his lifetime. *On Truth and Lies in a Non-Moral Sense* begins: "In some remote corner of the universe, flickering in the light of the countless solar systems into which it had been poured, there was once a planet on which clever animals invented cognition (*erkennen*)."[23] This clever animal, the very same creature creating forms and rhythms, drunk on the dregs of her invention, carries the same delusion as a tiny midge traveling through the air thinking itself the "flying center of this world."[24] On one level, this statement speaks to a delusional self-centeredness, misrecognizing perspective for objectivity and consciousness for reality (the error of the delegates in Berlin, a sin they apparently share with the midge); but the *dangerous perhaps* remains in all its equivocal force as Nietzsche also seems to be inviting us to consider the midge as an opening, as a possibility for understanding that other beings are centered in the very same illusion that centers us, for the limits of our cognition do not constitute the extent of possible worlds; rather, they indicate the way we translate earth into a conception that exceeds our experience, calling it the world. In other words, Nietzsche's speculation about the parallel between the self-centered midge and the human intoxicated by the creation of cognition asks us to consider the possibility of multiple conceptions of the world, of multiple worlds. For even as Nietzsche wrestles with the implications of viewing knowledge as a creative act, he concedes that the particularity of human knowledge does not exhaust the possibilities of worlding despite a tendency to believe in the world as a singular, discernable, and absolute totality. In 1887, he would write,

> There is only perspectival seeing, *only* perspectival "knowing," the *more* affects we are able to put into words about a thing, the *more* eyes, various eyes we are able to use for the same thing, the more complete will be our 'concept' of the thing, our "objectivity."[25]

So, if we consider Nietzsche's *midge* metaphorically, as a substitution for others engaged in creating worlds through interpretative cognition, we world in a world where others are also worlding. Language carries a seductive trace of that multiplicity.

This raises another question: Midge metaphors aside, how does language multiply our eyes and ears? How do we account for different perspectives despite our tendency to regard ourselves as the *flying center of the world*? How do we get past our own limited vision and understand how others create worlds as well? Why doesn't cognition lead to the type of knowledge promised by idealism, that our picture of the world will progress through time to be a picture of the earth, of one true world? To answer this question, let us explore the rest of the notebook entry only to return to the syllogism, *Der Mensch ist ein Geschöpf*, for it is important to remember that if the earth has been and continues to have the possibility of being shaped into multiple worlds, each of these worlds leaves forms, traces, memorials, and indications of its movements through time. We respond to those shapes, those rhythms, which act as mediation for our own creative acts. We world in a world already worlded.

My reading of this hinges on an understanding that Nietzsche is not positing a metaphysical creator for our creature, *Der Mensch*. Worlding is not simply a matter of interpreting a clarified actuality through the recollection of an absolute foundation. It is also not a simple matter of stimuli and a creative response. The symmetry of the description of the human being in notebook entry 38 (10) allows us greater clarity when we consider that while anti-theistic thinking and creativity occupy central positions in Nietzsche's thought, he is also a thinker who understands the force and durability of established forms. The human who creates the articulation of space and time on the earth is herself also created,[26] historically and not divinely, and her appearance by extension occurs in a time and space always already articulated by others. Because of this, we never think alone, even if we may think particularly. Nietzsche explains this particularity in note 38 (10):

> There is something active about this process, in this, our way of "imposing shapes upon things," and we experience this shaping as "force, ... as a resisting and determining force—rejecting, selecting, shaping to fit, slotting into ... schemata.[27]

One could imagine that this creative being unfolding in a world already created experiences a tension as her propensity to shape provides only a partial picture of all the forms that guide her movement in space impacting her very sense of motion, cadence, and rhythm. These forms already created inculcate a sense of discipline in our bodies, and even if we are shaped through this, we experience life as a particular body that is also always already shaping. We both act and are acted upon, always shaping within a time and a space already shaped, and through education and experience these shapes and the narratives that accompany them become part of our inner life. As Nietzsche reminds us in Aphorism 19 in *Beyond Good and Evil*, "our body is afterall, only a society constructed of many souls—*L'effect c'est moi*"[28] ("unser Lieb ist ja nun rein Gesellschaftsbau vieler Seelen").[29] Whether it presents itself to our consciousness or not, we are, like Nietzsche in the sense of our situation, a result of all the names in history. We enter the world as a result of their living, experiencing conditions of possibility in their wake, and we learn about the world from their traces.

The human being articulates space and time by extending that which is already articulated by others and negotiating these shapes internally. We are enfolded by a world and then we unfold within it. Living in a world of names, one names after already being named by others who name after having been named by others themselves. We build worlds on top of other worlds and often mistakenly sanctify our world as the only one, as a shrine to our knowing. As Nietzsche reminds us, this is not an act of innocence: "If a shrine is to be set up, *a shrine has to be destroyed*."[30] For Nietzsche, forming shapes, like the act of sculpting, destroys in order to create. This description is related to colonial expansion. Our sense of the world is palimpsestic, and never completely innocent, perhaps even mediated by what Mbembe describes as the imperial will to ignorance, which is dressed in the garments of knowledge.[31] Understanding the role of illusion and exclusion becomes crucial to understanding what a conception of the world means to a creative, destructive, and forgetful creature like *der Mensch*; it reveals the relationship between the Conference in Berlin and a late-nineteenth-century European sense of *World Creation*. The Congolese philosopher V. Y. Mudimbe writes,

> Although generalizations are of course dangerous, *colonialism* and *colonization* basically mean organization, arrangement. The two words derive from the Latin word *colĕre*, meaning to cultivate or to design. Indeed, the historical colonial experience does not and cannot reflect the peaceful connotations of these words. But it can be admitted that the colonists (those settling a region), as well as the colonialists (those exploiting a territory by dominating a local majority) have all tended to organize and transform non-European areas into fundamentally European constructs.[32]

This is the crux of the danger of Nietzsche's conception of the process forming shapes and rhythms; it suggests a human propensity to create, to form sensual or aesthetic experience into worlds in excess of the experience of brute physicality, performing a shaping poetics concerned with tempo, augmenting the experience of time and space. The danger arrives when any individual or group of people regard their world as the only one, for worlds are always already in excess of the earth we share. This is the movement of the concept of the globe as it effaces the multiplicity of worlds.[33]

The second sentence of notebook entry 38 (10) extends this thought further into an explanation of how illusion could guide the conception of knowledge in an imperial sense by stating that in the absence of actual stimuli, our eyes and our ears continue to "create ... something (*schafft sich etwas*)" as if to "practice (*übt*)" this "transformation of the world."[34] In other words, even if we lack something external to mold, we create shapes and rhythms as possibilities by seeing what does not appear and hearing that which does not make a sound. The possibility of fiction in all its mediated particularity is always present even in the absence of actual phenomena. We carry these possibilities within us, which is one reason why Nietzsche utilizes metaphors of nourishment and digestion when discussing knowledge, which he sees as a process. In addition, the relationship of this thought to the arts emerges in even clearer relief when we remember that Nietzsche both claims that this shaping activity is not limited to interaction with actuality and that creating in a world that created you as well involves mediation, translation, or, if you prefer, interpretation. It is important to remember that for Nietzsche, these processes may involve appropriation.[35]

In other words, there is a double movement here: on the one hand, our experience of actuality is guided by a series of preexistent forms that rhythmically inflect and guide our experience of movement and temporality, and on the other, our imagination—that shaping in the absence of something to shape—creates forms that extend beyond any practical exigency into the realm of representing something adjacent to our experience of the external world. Nietzsche suggests that our ceaseless interpretative activity creates images in excess of raw experience, and that makes philosophy, art, and literature possible and necessary at the same time. Through an act of extension—a poiesis, a making one gives to the world—and an act of internalization—praxis, where we recreate and retain the image as a shape to guide our consciousness—our interpreting senses supplement both the physical earth and the history of the human presence upon it, allowing us to create and imagine other possibilities. It follows that both the rhythmic shaping of physical space and the way we practice this process in the absence of real interaction with the stuff of experience are part and parcel of how we create our perspectives. We are as much dependent on those sounds and sights we do not actually see in our conception of a world as on actual experience, when we consider the tradition of texts, archives, and citations from which we construe our sense for knowledge, perhaps even more so.[36] For this was a tradition that Nietzsche felt had run its course chiefly because the forms it had created no longer *nourished* the population due to its calcification of cruelty into the form of spirituality. Nietzsche explains how even this type of antiquated value system could endure in his further extension of note 38 (10): "Without the transformation of the world into figures and rhythms there would be nothing 'the same' for us, thus nothing recurrent, and thus no possibility of experiencing and appropriating, *of feeding*."[37] In other words, if language multiplies *our eyes* with *various eyes*, we also reduce our possibilities for the sake an impulse towards repetition.

That said, how do the related sensations of sameness and recurrence allow us to experience and appropriate, to feed? The simple answer is that according to Nietzsche, humans seek to delimit possibilities and create predictability. In Aphorism 230 from *Beyond Good and Evil*, he writes that the tendency "classify new things into old classes" for the sake "of the feeling of growth, the feeling of increasing strength" is a result of what he calls the spiritualization of knowledge. The *spirit*, Nietzsche claims, "resembles a stomach more than anything"[38] in that it can digest experience or experience dyspepsia. In the second essay of *On the Genealogy of Morals*, this gastro-metaphor extends to a discussion of what Nietzsche calls *nature's paradoxical task*, the *breeding* of an animal that can make and keep promises. On the surface, one could reasonably expect that the sense for creating shapes and rhythms, reworlding a world for the sake of calculability and recurrence would create a temporal comportment where anticipation of repetition would prevail, that our memories would need to be calibrated to "recollect forward," as Kierkegaard puts it in his own psychological experiment with repetition. However, it is important to remember that Kierkegaard points out a paradox as repetition seems to be dependent on a temporal comportment that anticipates something by someone who has forgotten that it recurs. His pseudonym Constantine Constantius denies repetition even as he repeats, cites, paces back and forth, and returns.[39] Nietzsche embraces this cloud, this paradox of a repetition in the form of a denial of repetition, in a specific way. He posits that this predictability based on a fidelity to memory is dependent on an active forgetting (*a willful ignorance*), an oblivion that allows digestion of experience, that enables assimilation and vitality. For Nietzsche, this active forgetting occurs when we "shut the doors and windows of consciousness for a while" to "make room for something new" for "ruling predicting, predetermining."[40] Nietzsche sees the ability to forget as part and parcel of assimilating and appropriating the shapes and rhythms created by others as possibilities essential to our sovereignty. The other possibility, the dyspeptic possibility, is *ressentiment*: where experience does not get digested and becomes "unforgettable"[41] and revenge is "sanctified ... with the term justice."[42] It is important to note that Nietzsche considers *ressentiment*, this inability to assimilate and incorporate as the process that created his contemporaries' sense of morality. As stated in Aphorism 229 in *Beyond Good and Evil*, "almost everything we call "higher culture" is based on spiritualization and deepening of cruelty."[43] These formulations from 1886 and 1887 were anticipated by the last line of the notebook entry which reads,

> But we are beings who are difficult to feed and have everywhere enemies, and as it were indigestibles—that is what has made human knowledge *refined*, and ultimately so proud of its refinement that it doesn't want to hear that it is not a goal but a means, or even a tool of the stomach—if not itself a type of stomach.[44]

I would argue that this points to two regimes of time for Nietzsche, a time structured through the creative activities that convey a somewhat obscured sense for recurrence, and the cultural enforcement of a regime of memory that posits progression as a type of spiritualized violence, as *ressentiment*, defined here simply as the internalization of a violence wearing the mask of a value. Perhaps this explains how the delegates of the conference could ever think they could legitimately educate the people they were exploiting in matters of "morality." However, there is more to this process than the blindness of the delegates.

The second remarkable notebook entry, number 38 (12) explains a thorny problem raised by our discussion. For if each particular human being has a propensity to form shapes and rhythms from stimuli both real and imagined, how does this spread from person to person and from culture to culture? How do some interpretations or translations become dominant? Why do we not live in a world determined by the creativity of those who are in our proximity? Why isn't all knowledge local or if not local, shared consensually? Why would we bother to posit universals at all? Is it a simply a matter of history, or is there something intrinsic to Nietzsche's experience of late-nineteenth-century European culture that better informs us? Is the *ego cogito* that Descartes described really the *ego conquiro* posited by the Argentinian philosopher Enrique Dussel or, even more radically, the library burning, language eradicating, god killing, epistecidal, *ego extermino* described by Puerto Rican sociologist Ramon Grosfoguel?[45] Suffice it to say that Nietzsche enfolded by and unfolding his imagination inside the existing cultures of late-nineteenth-century Europe provides his own answer, one that finds its contours, its horizon governed by the expanding world he inhabited. He ends this second notebook entry exclaiming, "*This world is will to power—and nothing besides!* And you yourselves are this will to power—and nothing besides."[46]

What is the will to power? On the one hand, Nietzsche, influenced by the second law of thermodynamics, posits its existence in a closed system "a determinate force set in a determinate space, and not into space that is anywhere empty," a force "which grows neither larger nor smaller, which doesn't exhaust but only transforms itself," eternally returning, "self-creating" and "self-destroying," "traveling in the form of a circle," "a solution for all riddles."[47] The connection between the will to power and the shape-and-rhythm-making creature of note 38 (10) becomes apparent here, the will to power operates in space that has already been articulated, not in empty space. It is the drive that divides and organizes that which is already differentiated; its raw material is the already shaped. It is the colonial impulse described by V. Y. Mudimbe expressed as a force that reconfigures someone else's land into the repeatable, the familiar, the calculable, that which is arranged to be suitable for appropriation.[48]

The key to understanding this appears in another less poetic and more straightforward entry from sometime between the spring of 1885 and the autumn of the following year: "The will to power *interprets:* … sets limits, determines degrees and differences of power … In truth, *interpretation is itself a means of becoming master of something.*"[49] This notion of mastery through interpretation and naming runs parallel to Nietzsche's understanding of translation as an adjunct of "an age's historical sense," as a process of creating hierarchies, as a function of the "best conscience of the *imperium Romanum*," and is congruent to the creation of a population of Calibans translated into the language and rationality of the metropole.[50] In other words, the *will to power* creates horizons as it expands, creating forms and rhythms that are the interpretations derived from a process of cognition establishing the epistemic limits of a horizon aesthetically, as a practice of the senses.[51] In its colonial expression, the *will to power* expands a regime of knowing in a way that displaces local knowledge, local forms of life.

This raises a question: If the *will to power* operates in already articulated space, delimiting in order to interpret, yet acting as an opening for the process of shaping forms and rhythms (possibilities for movement and tempo in the articulation of space), how do these forms spread? Why do these shapes and rhythms travel, how do they become dislocated? What is it that keeps us from creating new forms abandoning the shape of the old, interpreting our lives as individuals, oblivious to that which preceded us, oblivious to culture and history? How does a sense for calculation and repetition blind us to the midge providing scant insight to the midge's sense for shaping the world? For if the relationship between forms and rhythms creates a sense of relationship between space and time that is world creating, then the ability of rhythm to compel one's movements and thoughts becomes an issue. In other words, it is not only a matter of listening to the music but also a matter of who pays the piper and who writes the song. In 1881, Nietzsche pondered a partial response to these types of questions when he considered the affective power of rhythm in music and in verse. Aphorism 84 in *The Gay Science* entitled "The Origin of Poetry" describes how the poetic use of rhythm "gives thoughts a new color and makes them darker, stranger, more distant." In addition, rhythm helps us remember speech and Nietzsche claims that the ancient Greeks believed that tempo could be used to attract the attention of the gods:

> Above all, one wanted to take advantage of that elemental overpowering force that humans experience in themselves when listening to music: rhythm is a

compulsion; it engenders an unconquerable desire to yield, to join in; not only the stride of the feet but the soul itself gives in to the beat.⁵²

So, if rhythm compels our thoughts, it also has relation to space in that the establishment of forms divides it in a manner influencing and inflecting bodily movement. In addition, rhythm resides in our bodies, yet according to Nietzsche's description of how it was used to propitiate favor with the Gods, it calls the distant into proximity through an embodiment of an external temporal register. In other words, rhythm relates to the way we think about our existence and our relationship to that which resides beyond our sense of space, beyond our horizons through an internalization of an external tempo. Rhythm is infectious, it can make the time of the other seem like one's own comportment. Rhythm can make language seem like it addresses something supersensible, a principle beyond our experience. Nietzsche drives this point home when he reminds us that "hexameter was invented at Delphi–rhythm was supposed to exercise a compulsion." And it is for the sake of compulsion that the prophesies of the oracle were pronounced with "a rhythmic precision," to the advantage of "Apollo, who as god of rhythm can also bind the goddess of fate."⁵³ Rhythm not only settles in our bodies in the moment, compelling us to move to a certain cadence, but also ties us to a sense of anticipation, foreclosing infinite possibility, positing a future guaranteed by the deity reigning at Delphi, the God of poetry, dreams, individuation, representations, and for Nietzsche the God of appearance, of *schein*. Appearance, it seems, is not limited to bodies in space unfolding in time; it is not only the articulation of space that helps divide time in rhythm; the articulation of speech participates in the process as well. Rhythm not only moves our bodies but is also an element of mediation and of discourse and as such is tied to our voicing and the subsequent binding of the god to our destinies. And in speaking our destinies, poetry as the verbal articulation of rhythmic possibilities was seen by "the Pythagoreans as a philosophical doctrine and as an educational contrivance."⁵⁴ It seems that Nietzsche understood rhythm as a physical manifestation of the will to power that educates us about our fatality, to our relationship to the unfolding of time, pleasing both the sense of anticipation and predictability, the hallmarks of the individual in nineteenth-century Western culture; predictability for the Bourgeoisie was an indication of character in the sense that someone can be relied on or counted on to do something, and cultural mediations trace the parameters of what is expected.

Conclusion: Poetry and the *Dangerous Perhaps*

Nietzsche describes the origin of poetry as the gleaming razor's edge of a *dangerous perhaps*: as formal gathering, a rhythmic movement, a song, a petition to the gods, a pronouncement delivered, a comportment toward a shared destiny, and an expression of the will to power operating in already articulated space as a second type of world-making, a making attuned to that enfolding palimpsestic world it unfolds in.⁵⁵ Rhythm relates to the articulation of a space; it can compel one's movements or open one up to one's co-destining with another world. For if we regard poetry as the creation of a world within a world, a trace of the multiplicity embodied by that particular creature, *Der Mensch* within a world expanding and universalizing its claims, we can understand poetry as the moment when the world opens up to the possibility of a co-destination, a location where we can remember the midge, the other creating a world in which he too is its "flying center." Furthermore, if you recall Mbembe's formation, that power "gives" and "receives" existing forms, and knows how to escape them, it becomes apparent that poetic language alerts us to the possibility of that *Saturnalia* that "jumbles up metaphors and shifts the boundary stones of abstraction,"[56] mobilizing new metaphors and conceptions of the human being. Perhaps escaping these forms allows us to understand how our horizons have been shifted by the European colonial project, which began the process that replaced the multiplicity of worlds with the conception of a globe.

That said, allow me to close by offering another perspective. Perhaps Mbembe's version of the *dangerous perhaps* is born of a realization that can be put in conversation with Nietzsche's understanding of his expanding world, the world of European modernity. His insight that one can be formed and still create forms, that one unfolds in a world while he is being enfolded within a world speaking itself is a ray of hope born from an acquired doubleness, a duplicity that runs parallel to the "creolization of the west" described by the Martiniquan poet and philosopher Edouard Glissant in his description of the *Open Boat*, the location where the abyssal knowledge of poetic relations was born.[57] Glissant, Mbembe, Fanon, Ngugi, and others remind us that the articulation of space and the imposition of rhythms has a distinct relationship to power, to the stories that power endorses, and the stories that endorse power as they play upon the bodies that power inscribes itself upon. Power bends knowledge through time, and history has often been received as a hierarchy of lineages. But we can resist by unfolding new forms, in the guise of new relationships to that which enfolds us and that which destroys us. The Conference of Berlin gave Africa a new map with new names; it also created a Calabanic cartography where power gave the gift of language at the cost of a debt of vocabulary.[58] It also created a literary history where the literature of the metropole was always already seen as a precursor to the literary production of newly independent states. With that in mind, we should remember that this is an incomplete history, reconstructed from a perspective that is blind to the possibility of a precolonial lineage. This history serves as a metropolitan mirror that obscures rather than reveals, as it erases by virtue of its own construction, serving as extension of the epistemological prejudices of the metropole. Perhaps we should regard traditional notions about world literature as informed through that prism, as refracted by two terms that are as inextricably linked as Prospero and Caliban are to each other, modernity and colonialism.[59] Perhaps we would benefit to realize that the world-making that Nietzsche describes also unworlds, but that unworlding is always already incomplete. There are mnemotopic traces.

> The sprawling hills and fields of coffee and wheat the railway line generated spoke of white presence, but they also spoke eloquently of African loss. I was benefitting from a history that had come to negate my history.[60]

Ngugi wrote these words while reflecting on a pivotal moment in his own intellectual journey where he would begin to *decolonize his mind*. He was riding on a train from his home in Kenya to Makerere University located in what is now Kampala, Uganda. It was there that he would *become* a writer. His first novel, *Weep Not Child*, was published in English in 1964 and was written while he was still in college in Uganda. There he studied English literature and participated in productions of Shakespearean drama. Later, Ngugi would earn a master's degree at Leeds University, writing a thesis on Caribbean literature, and it was through this study that he found interlocution with the work of George Lamming, the writer who understood his own relationship to English and the possibilities of his writing as tethered to Caliban. Lamming expressed his own situation by exploring the relationship between *the gift of language* and the subsequent *debt of vocabulary*, that seeming inextricable bond that reveals a yawning abyss between Caliban and Prospero. Only Caliban can see this; Prospero is blinded by the difference he created. He thinks Caliban is his own creation. Yet Lamming understood that despite this, Prospero's language could not truly translate him, for Prospero's own inclinations were the source of his cruelty and blindness. Lamming writes that for Prospero,

> Caliban is man and other than man. Caliban is his convert, excluded by language. It is precisely this gift of language, this attempt at transformation that has brought about the pleasure and paradox of Caliban's exile. Exiled from his Gods, exiled from his nature, exiled by his own name. He is afraid because he knows his encounter with Caliban, is largely his encounter with himself.[61]

After Ngugi returned from his linguistic exile and returned to Kenya, he would later reject the English language as his preferred vehicle for composition and write in his first language, Kikuyu. It was as if he had realized that colonization and an education in the rationality of European modernity had tried but failed to translate his world completely despite the "best conscience of the *imperium Romanum*," as Nietzsche would phrase it. He saw underneath the velum to the palimpsest. He realized with Glissant that "imperialism (the thought as well as the reality of empire) does not conceive of anything universal but in every instance is a substitute for it."[62]

Ngugi even without the reference understood that when Nietzsche claimed that the world is "will to *power* and nothing besides!"[63] he was merely showing us "his own mirror,"[64] a glass held up to his European readers in the moment of the Conference of Berlin. Ngugi realized something that Glissant would later describe in these terms: "Transparency no longer seems like the bottom of a mirror in which Western humanity reflected the world in its own image."[65] According to thinkers like Ngugi and Glissant, the clarity with which Nietzsche saw the pulsating energy, the unrelenting interpretative and appropriating force of the will to power in his own reflection, has been gradually replaced by "a whole alluvium deposited by populations, silt that is fertile but, in actual fact, indistinct and unexplored even today, denied or insulted more often than not, and with an insistent presence that we are incapable of not experiencing."[66] Perhaps one day Prospero will learn the language of Caliban and learn the names of the things on his island from someone who has tilled that soil.

Notes

1. Ngugi Wa Thiong'o, *Decolonizing the Mind: The Politics of Language in African Literature* (Portsmouth, NH: Heinemann, 2005), 9.
2. See the geographical discussion in the introduction to G. W. F. Hegel's *Philosophy of History* (Mineola: Dover, 2004). After a rather ignorant and unflattering description of the continent and its inhabitants, Hegel writes, "At this point we leave Africa not to mention it again. For it is no historical part of the world" (99).
3. Achille Mbembe cites Labat in *Critique of Black Reason*, trans. Laurant Dubois (Durham: Duke UP, 2017), 70. Jean-Baptiste Labat, among other things, served as the colonial governor of Guadeloupe at the tail end of the seventeenth century. The quotation comes from the 1728, *Nouvelle relation d'Afrique occidentale, vol. 1* (Paris: G. Cavalier, 1728).
4. Adam Hochschild, *King Leopold's Ghost* (Boston: Mariner Books 1999), 85.
5. Ibid., 84–5. "Early on, reported one diplomat, Stanley went to a big map of Africa and immediately engrossed the interest of every delegate by a vivid description of the features of the Congo basin; and finally of the [adjacent] country."
6. Joseph Conrad, *Heart of Darkness* (London: Penguin Classics, 2007), 9.
7. Jonathan Swift, *Poems*, ed. Harold Herbert Williams (Oxford: Oxford UP, 1958) 2: 645–6, "On Poetry" (1733).
8. Conrad, *Heart of Darkness*, 9.
9. A. Adu Boahen writes,

    By as late as 1880, Africans were enjoying their sovereignty and were very much in control of their own affairs and destinies. However, within the incredibly short period between 1880 and 1900, all of Africa except Liberia and Ethiopia were seized and occupied by the European imperial powers of Britain, France, Germany, Belgium, Portugal, Spain, and Italy; and Africans were converted from sovereign and royal citizens of their own continent into colonial and dependent subjects. By the 1900s, in place of numerous African independent states and polities, a completely new and numerically smaller set of some forty artificially created colonies had emerged. (*African Perspectives on Colonialism* [Baltimore: Johns Hopkins UP, 1987], 27)

10. See William Shakespeare, *The Tempest* (New York: Penguin 1999), 19.
11. These are terms used by George Lamming in *The Pleasure of Exile* (Ann Arbor: University of Michigan Press, 1992), a book of essays organized around a confrontation with what Lamming understood as the legacy of Caliban visited upon the West Indies. He uses the phrases the "gift of language" and the "debt of vocabulary" to express the double edge of being educated in and speaking a colonial language.
12. Article VI reads, "All the powers exercising the rights of influence in the aforesaid territories bind themselves to watch over the preservation of native tribes, and to care for the improvement of the conditions of their moral and material well-being, and

to help in suppressing slavery, and especially the slave trade." The text can be found in William H. Worger, Nancy L. Clark, and Edward A. Alpers, eds., *Africa and the West: A Documentary History*, Vol. 1 (Oxford: Oxford UP, 2010), 238.

13 One could imagine Friedrich Nietzsche's famous parenthetical statement from *On the Genealogy of Morals* resounding in the hallways of the conference. It reads, "(The seigneurial privilege of giving names even allows us to conceive of the origin of language itself as a manifestation of the power of the rulers: they say 'this is so and so,' they set their seal on everything and every occurrence with a sound and thereby take possession of it, as it were)." This citation is found in section 2 of the first essay of *On the Genealogy of Morals*, ed. Ansell-Pearson, trans. Carol Diethe (Cambridge: Cambridge UP, 2007), 12.

14 Frantz Fanon, *The Wretched of the Earth*, trans. Richard Philcox (New York: Grove Press, 2004). The citation comes from the opening essay, "On Violence," 2.

15 Boahen, *African Perspectives on Colonialism*: see note 9 above.

16 Mbembe, *Critique of Black Reason*, 70.

17 Ibid., 132.

18 Ngugi Wa Thiongo, "Europhone or African Memory," in *African Intellectuals*, ed. Thandika Mkandawire (Dakar: Coderisa, 2005). The citation can be found on 157 of the same text.

19 Dipesh Chakrabarty sums up the historical dimension of the metaphysics of European modernity nicely: "Historicism—and even the modern, European idea of history—one might say, came to non-European people in the nineteenth century as somebody's way of saying "not yet" to someone else." See *Provincializing Europe* (Princeton: Princeton UP, 2000), 8.

20 See Friedrich Nietzsche, *The Gay Science*, ed. Bernard Williams, trans. Josefine Nauckhoff (Cambridge: Cambridge UP, 2001), 5.

21 Friedrich Nietzsche, *Writings from the Late Notebooks*, ed. Rudiger Bittner, trans. Kate Sturge (Cambridge: Cambridge UP, 2003), 37.

22 Friedrich Nietzsche, *Nachlaß 1884–1885*, *Kritische Studienausgabe*, vol. 11, ed. Giorgio Colli and Mazzino Montinari (Berlin: de Gruyter, 1988), 608.

23 Friedrich Nietzsche, "On Truth and Lies in a Non-Moral Sense," in *The Birth of Tragedy and Other Writings*, ed. Raymond Guess and Ronald Speirs, trans. Ronald Speirs (Cambridge: Cambridge UP, 1999), 141.

24 Ibid.

25 Nietzsche, *Genealogy*, 87.

26 Nietzsche is quite explicit about how the human being is both created and creative. See, e.g., Friedrich Nietzsche, *Beyond Good and Evil*, ed. Rol-Peter Horstmann and Judith Norman, trans. Judith Norman (Cambridge: Cambridge UP, 2002). In Aphorism 225, he writes, "In human beings *creature* and *creator* are combined" (Nietzsche, *Beyond Good and Evil*, 117). The German text can be found in Friedrich Nietzsche, *Jenseits von Gut und Böse, Zur Genealogie der Moral* (Kritische Studienausgabe, vol. 5, ed. Giorgio Colli and Mazzino Montinari [Berlin: de Gruyter, 1999], 161).

27 Nietzsche, *Late Notebooks*, 37.

28 Nietzsche, *Beyond Good and Evil*, 19.

29 Nietzsche, *Jenseits von Gut und Böse*, 33.

30 Nietzsche, *Genealogy*, 65–6.

31 Mbembe, *Critique of Black Reason*, 11.

32 V. Y. Mudimbe, *The Invention of Africa: Gnosis, Philosophy, and the Order of Knowledge* (Bloomington: Indiana UP, 1988), 1.
33 It is interesting to observe how, despite the expansion of the notion of the globe and the one-world theory that accompanies it, multiplicity is in a sense preserved online through a series of new communities dislocated in time and space but beholden to a sense for identities as mutual exclusivities. In this way, the web mimes a form of diaspora. As this is neither the subject of this essay or my expertise, I will leave it at that, as a suggestion about how "grand narratives" still persist.
34 Nietzsche, *Late Notebooks*, 37, and *Nachlaß 1884–1885, Kritische Studienausgabe*, vol. 11, 608.
35 Nietzsche, *The Gay Science*, Aphorism 83, "On Translation," 82–3.
36 See Jorge Luis Borges, *Ficciones*, ed. and trans. Andrew Kerrigan (New York: Grove Press, 1962). The following citation comes from "The Library of Babel" and can be found on page 79: "In the entrance way hangs a mirror, which faithfully duplicates appearances. People are in the habit of inferring from this mirror that the library is not infinite (if it really were, why this illusory duplication?); I prefer to dream that the polished surfaces feign and promise infinity." I understand Borges's story as an allegory about how textual knowledge gives the illusion of exhausting the possibilities of world-making.
37 Nietzsche, *Late Notebooks*, 37, and *Nachlaß 1884–1885, Kritische Studienausgabe*, vol. 11, 608.
38 Nietzsche, *Beyond Good and Evil*, 122.
39 Søren Kierkegaard, *Fear and Trembling and Repetition*, ed. and trans. Howard V. and Edna H. Hong (Princeton: Princeton UP, 1983). See page 131 for the conception of repetition as recollecting forward, and especially 179 for a moment when Constantine Constanatius paces back and forth, repeating and reinscribing his movement as he denies the possibility of repetition.
40 Nietzsche, *Genealogy*, 35.
41 Ibid., 38.
42 Ibid., 48.
43 Nietzsche, *Beyond Good and Evil*, 120.
44 Nietzsche, *Late Notebooks*, 37, and *Nachlaß 1884–1885, Kritische Studienausgabe*, vol. 11, 608.
45 See Ramon Grosfoguel, "The Structure of Knowledge in Westernized Universities: Epistemic Racism/Sexism and the Four Genocides/Epistemicides of the Long 16th Century," *Human Architecture* 11.1 (2013): 72–90. See also Enrique Dussel, *The Philosophy of Liberation*, trans. Eduardo Mendieta, Camilo Pérez Bustillo, Yolanda Angulo, and Nelson Maldonado-Torres (Durham, NC: Duke UP, 2013).
46 Nietzsche, *Late Notebooks*, 39, and *Nachlaß 1884–1885, Kritische Studienausgabe*, vol. 11, 611.
47 Ibid., 38, and ibid., 611.
48 Heidegger's thoughts on technological thinking would be another route to understanding how a conflation of colonized people is seen as raw materials and their lands seen as sites of extraction.
49 Nietzsche, *Late Notebooks*, 90, where notebook entry 2 can be found (148).
50 Nietzsche, *The Gay Science*, Aphorism 83, 82–3.
51 See Sean Kirkpatrick, *The Ontology of Socratic Questioning in the Early Platonic Dialogs* (Albany: SUNY Press, 2012), 134. He explains that "horizon" is a noun

derived from the verbalization of the Greek *horus*, which means "boundary" or "boundary stone." The verb *horizein* originally signified the act of defining something and was used in this manner by Plato in his dialogues. In modern European languages, horizon eventually came to mean concretely the limits of one's vision, and figuratively it connotes the limits of one's possible understanding (see its use in hermeneutics). This conception in all its connotations was central for Nietzsche as a metaphor for the possibility of assimilating experience. So, by extension, Nietzsche's statement about shapes and rhythm speaks to the way we conceive of space and time as an aesthetic experience from which our sense of the world is created. In other words, we create the interpretative limits that allow us to see; our vision is made possible by its restriction, and these restrictions are our own doing, but we can imagine a beyond. This raises another question: How do these limits engender interpretation and how does the locality of our interpretation, our senses lodged in our bodies extend?

52 Nietzsche, *The Gay Science*, 84.
53 Ibid., 85.
54 Ibid., 84.
55 See Nietzsche, *Beyond Good and Evil*, Aphorism 2, 5–6. Nietzsche's notion of the "dangerous perhaps" emerges after a questioning of the concepts of truth and error as they relate to "knowledge."
56 Nietzsche, "On Truth and Lies in a Non-Moral Sense," 153.
57 See Édouard Glissant, *The Poetics of Relation* (Ann Arbor: University of Michigan Press, 2010), 5.
58 I am indebted to the writings of George Lamming for this phrasing.
59 See Walter D. Mignolo and Catherine Walsh, *On Decoloniality: Concepts, Analytics, Praxis* (Durham, NC: Duke University Press, 2018), 4: "Coloniality is constitutive not derivative of modernity. That is to say, there is no modernity without coloniality."
60 Ngugi Wa Thiong'o, *Birth of A Dream Weaver: A Writer's Awakening* (New York: The New Press, 2016), 20.
61 Lamming, *The Pleasure of Exile*, 15.
62 Glissant, *Poetics of Relation*, 117.
63 Ibid., 39.
64 Nietzsche, *Late Notebooks*, 38.
65 Glissant, *Poetics of Relation*, 111.
66 Ibid.

Part II

Migration and Difference

5

Feminism as World Literature

Robin Truth Goodman

Feminism has always been a worldly endeavor. Virginia Woolf, for example, imagined a hypothetical woman saying in 1938, "In fact, as a woman, I have no country. As a woman I want no country. As a woman my country is the whole world."[1] Yet, the relationship of women to the world remains undertheorized as, at the same time and assumedly in contraposition, feminism has had a stake in the home: "Homes are the real places of the women,"[2] Woolf goes on, advocating that women should lure men home from worldly endeavors in war. Simone de Beauvoir, as well, wrote of women's gender role as "imminent" in its hominess and grounded in the naturalized physicality of her own body, especially in her reproductive, care, and familial capacities. Unlike Woolf, though, Beauvoir thought that woman's relation to the home, as a defense against the world, reduced her to dependency and obstructed her liberty: "The home becomes the center of the world and even its only reality: ... refuge, retreat, grotto, womb, it gives shelter from outside dangers; it is this confused outer world that becomes unreal. ... Few tasks are more like the torture of Sisyphus than housework, with its endless repetition."[3] Women's seemingly integral relation to the home and to nature has made feminism seem unworldly historically. Because of their seeming unworldliness, women have been the target readers for the novel form, as Nancy Armstrong taught us, that developed in response to a rising leisure class of bourgeois women who needed to be educated into "ensuring a happy household."[4] Given this history, how could Woolf—or I—identify the world or its literature as a feminist thing?

World Literature and the Problem of Feminism

This essay argues that social reproduction is currently "worlded" in practices of migration, translation, and new technologies that are remapping social ecologies and their imaginaries, sometimes in line with feminism and sometimes antagonistic to it, or even detrimental. The field of world literature, which is getting increasing critical attention, however, seems to skirt (so to speak) away from considering feminism. Debra Castillo has noted that the category of world literature often gestures to the "dark lady," that is, "the token woman in an otherwise all-male academic circle,"[5] and also that some scholars have been resistant to applying certain First-World categories—like feminism—to non-First-World contexts. A prior volume in this series, *American Literature as World Literature,* has in it one feminist critic writing on nonfeminist topics and one other critic writing on a feminist novelist.[6] David Damrosch's Wiley-Blackwell field-defining textbook/reader has no feminist contributions, even though there are a small number of feminist contributors. Such omission is far from coincidental and not necessarily simply following the pathways of familiar exclusions. Whereas world literature has concerned itself with both geographical range and global relations of inequality in the literary sphere (in its affinities with world systems theory), it has also, as did postcolonial and subaltern studies, situated women as outside of global circulation because of their relation to the home: Partha Chatterjee, for example, made the much contested claim that "nationalism's success [is] in situating the 'women's question' in an 'inner' domain of sovereignty far removed from the arena of political contest,"[7] where women invoke "tradition" against the onslaught of imperializing modernity. As well, Fredric Jameson alleges that "third-world texts," even when they "are seemingly private and invested with a properly libidinal dynamic,"[8] are allegories of the nation, thereby burying domestic space underneath a heavier and more world-oriented meaning-sphere of public and political embattlement in its nationalist form. With feminism wary of the world and world literature unworlded by feminism, it might seem odd to insist with Woolf that feminism is and has to be a world literature, and yet that is my task.

World literature criticism generally identifies world literature in contrast to femininity, as femininity conflates with interiority, stability, nature, and particularity. World literature has been defined, in opposition to this femininity, as literary works that transcend local markets and generate sales as well as critical interest beyond the borders of their nations of origin, like trade agreements. For example, David Damrosch situates world literature as "works that achieve an effective life outside their country of origin"[9] or "works in translation."[10] Franco Moretti notes that "the destiny of a culture … is intersected and altered by another culture (from the core) that 'completely ignores it,'"[11] implying that the politics of economic power between core and periphery is simply reflected in the value differentials of national literary productions. Pascale Casanova's "world republic of letters" likewise posits a specific "market" for the "literary economy," which is to say, "a space in which the sole value recognized by all participants—literary value—circulates and is traded."[12] Gisèle Sapiro looks to "statistics of flows," "asymmetries of exchanges between centers and peripheries," and "the factors that may hinder or trigger the circulation of symbolic goods."[13] Such descriptions relate world literature to production, exchange, and circulation, following Karl Marx and Friedrich Engels's attributions of the "cosmopolitan character to production and consumption" of literature: "In place of the old wants, satisfied by the productions of the country, we find new wants, requiring for their satisfaction the products of distant lands and climes. In place of the old local and national seclusion and self-sufficiency, we have intercourse in every direction."[14] Whereas in the earlier industrial stages referenced here, reproductive work was seen as removed from production and so removed from "world," preparing the next day and the next generation of work for free, under neoliberal capitalism, reproduction is an allure for capitalization, not an outside or a refuge but a dominant target of profit-making (some may call this biopolitics but there are other names, including exploitation). The privatization of schools, health care, housing, and pensions, for example; the vocationalization, technologization, and standardization of higher education; the proliferation of medications to keep you awake or make you sleep, to help you pay attention, lessen your obsessions, or change your moods; the internet-marketed boutique-clinics for cosmetic surgeries and gender reassignment;[15] and the commercialization of domestic work, food preparation, and childcare all testify to new areas of worldly market expansion in bodies, homes, and subjects, or what Cinzia Arruzza, Tithi Bhattacharya, and Nancy Fraser have called "the crucible of lived experience."[16]

The importance of reproduction in today's economies challenges the private/public, inner/outer, nature/culture, rooted-tradition/circulating-commodity split on which world literature discourse relies. Some critics of world literature do remark on the importance of narratives of subject formation for literature's ability to think outside of geopolitical add-ons of meaning, context, and national origin. Leerom Medovoi, for example, discusses the post-9/11 novel in its "retreats into domesticity,"[17] whereas Bruce Robbins situates the world novel as "behind national borders, behind the door of the family home."[18] Literature's historical relationship to particularity, the personal and the private, and the formation of subjectivity makes it into a kind of test tube where capital's struggle to absorb privacy and social reproduction can be seen at play. The question, then, that feminist world literature faces is how to grapple with the exploitive capitalization of domestic life and reproductive economies under neoliberalism, and what kind of alternative arrangements are available for thinking about what Hannah Arendt calls "the quest for worldliness," that is, the desire "to belong to something outside" ourselves where we are "denizen of the world-to-come."[19]

In keeping, Pheng Cheah notices the philosophical impact of the world in literature when he says, "The world market is not the true world."[20] If the world is simply a series of geographical add-ons, a line of inclusions, then literary works only have value through commercial success or by easing into already-existent circuits of exchange and can have no effective or creative determination on their own. Instead, says Cheah, "what defines a world is not merely geographical extension but rational-purposive human relationality, the connections and intercourse that unite people and places for the determinate end of production to satisfy human needs."[21] In other words, for Cheah, "the world" is not spatial extension or space measured by the quantity of objects produced, accumulated, or circulated within it but rather the temporality that brings human beings together to meet rational, or normative, human ends. Though Cheah does not explicitly link "world" to reproductive economies, his descriptions of "worlding" favor attendance to human needs to provide the context of human connection: "Production is a social, cooperative activity because the production of others is required to satisfy one's needs."[22] The time of reproduction and socialization clears an opening toward something new, the possibility of a different time that breaks from current practices of oppressive and unequal globalization in the expansion of world markets across space. This world for Cheah has a literary structure in as much as literature invokes "a web of normative intersubjective relations"[23] that, not yet existent, is emergent. In this sense, feminist theory has been engaged in the worldly imagination and, actually, cannot avoid such engagement. The rest of this essay looks at some social reproductive practices in which feminist theory identifies the emergent production of subjects and socialities as "worlding" processes, focusing on migration, translation, and new technologies.

Reproduction and Catastrophe

Tendencies within the field of feminist theory have already begun the work of thinking about social reproduction's "worlding" and literature's relation to it. Such tendencies, however, often rely on the nature/culture divide that has—often to the detriment of feminism—instrumentalized women and their work for their closeness to nature and their analogy to pre-alienated life-forms. Donna Haraway, for example, attributes the problems of neoliberal globalization—for example, economic polarization, ecological disaster, corporate dominance—to overpopulation: "Human numbers are almost certain to reach more than 11 billion people by 2100," she writes, "a 9-billion-person increase over 150 years from 1950 to 2100,"[24] imposing "vastly unequal burdens … on the earth by the rich compared to the poor—and even worse consequences for nonhumans almost everywhere."[25] What she calls "world," in contrast, is "eschewing futurism," or, rather, living with the slogan "Make Kin Not Babies!,"[26] a strategy of creating interspecial and interorganic affiliative networks not rooted in familial, blood, or generational ties but in mutual responsibility and survival. As she insists that there are too many babies, she is less forthcoming about how it would be decided who should make babies and who should not (the history of this has not been promising), and she offers no explanation of why, if population is exploding at the world's seams, we should not make war or extermination policies instead of kin *or* babies in order to kill off the extras. Such a transformation of what it means to think about reproduction in the twenty-first century, Haraway continues, participates in feminist theory's project of "unraveling the supposed natural necessity of ties between sex and gender, race and sex, race and nation, class and race, gender and morphology, sex and reproduction, and reproduction and composing persons."[27] Haraway's call, however, does the opposite of what she claims: by excluding baby-making from reproductive futurity, Haraway re-naturalizes "making babies" in opposition to "making kin," positioning babies as a fallen foil to the collaborative culture of association and kin-making. Instead of such borrowing from the population-control impetus of a long-ago disreputed eugenics, feminism's focus on reproduction as worlding must foreground all the world's webs of intersubjective interconnectedness as instances of producing future subjects and socialities, disregarding the nature-culture divide as its primary value marker.

Haraway's apocalyptic vision of the world—that we as a species have just had too many babies and need to stop if we are to go on living—is just one in a feminism (starting with Beauvoir) that has come to distrust "natural" reproduction as a problem. In such views, natural reproduction repeats social conventions of gender with all of the other hierarchies of race and class that these conventions reinforce. Helen Hester has followed Haraway in impugning biological reproduction as advancing "the idea that this stratum is immutable or fixed simply because it is biological."[28] For Hester, representing the future through the imperative to bear children means being obedient to restrictive conventions of heterosexual gender expression in the future as well as their associated inequalities. This type of heterosexual futurism, where "the Child" comes to stand in for an ethical purity in transcendence, says Hester, frames political messaging, particularly environmentalist messaging where nonreproductive sexualities or alternative social practices are stigmatized as pollutants. Hester, Laboria Cuboniks, and other feminists are calling for a version of imagining the world's future that neither upholds the romanticized innocence of biological reproduction as its transcendent hope nor treats it as an equally romanticized planetary collapse.

Feminist "worlding" is, then, about exposing production and circulation as inside social reproduction, its nature. Anna Tsing gives an account of worlding as social reproduction in an ethnography of a global mushroom—matsutake—that grows where "life is without the promise of stability,"[29] in "*disturbance-based ecologies,*"[30] "human-disturbed forests," "blasted landscapes," and "the ruin that has become our collective home."[31] Tsing explores, as "world making,"[32] vulnerable, precarious life forms reproduced in geographical regions that are devastated by human activity, where "contamination changes world-making projects"[33] and where "multiple futures pop in and out of possibility"[34] in response to modernization (e.g., capitalist development and expansion, global wars, mass exterminations, and the increasing concentration of wealth).

Neither a return to naturalized essentialisms nor an idealist vision of a future without bodies, migration, translation, and new technologies, as feminist, force the recognition of social reproduction as production's "worlding" at the edge of survival. As Hester concludes, "any framing of the issue [reproduction or population] that lets capitalism off the hook is obviously insufficient and myopic."[35]

Migration

The worlding of migration may best be discerned in the political posturing to build walls against it in order to "protect" the homeland. Though capital easily crosses borders as finance, for example, as points of information or trade, or as manufacturing that takes place at different sites on a global assembly line, the movement of laboring people across borders has created much more vituperative, racist, nativist, and other hateful responses. As Avtar Brah points out, migration is a feminist issue because "women have become emblematic figures of contemporary regimes of accumulation,"[36] but also because diasporic people have a "homing desire which is not the same thing as desire for a 'homeland.'"[37] In other words, migration as dislocation, diaspora, and dispossession makes visible the instabilities of homes as sites of social reproduction: homes are transformed from being distant memories and origins of identity into being objects of desire, with increased elusiveness alongside increased realness. As Effie Yiannopoulou adds, the migrant makes us see "that homes are not given but 'enacted' in relation to the differential dynamics of migratory movement that might have been willingly undertaken, forced, or forbidden."[38] In other words, migration reveals the intense realness of and passionate investments in home as a matter of ideological lament, showing that home is lost as soon as it can be imagined. In the age of advanced capitalism in which we live, this ideological positioning of migration as the sign of a home under threat turns us all into migrants.

The politics of migration tends to blame women and represent their reproducing bodies as problems, blaming those pregnant and protective bodies as what makes their homes unlivable. The political rhetoric surrounding migration tends to focus on suffering women and children fleeing from violence or on families separated by state enforcement; such narratives are less likely to focus on the historical trajectories that preceded migrants' appearances at borders. Victimized, suffering, wounded bodies and disordered social relations thus stand in for the geopolitics of domination. What might be most discordant and even frightening in the migrant is the way she exposes capital's violence as inhabiting and alienating even the most intimate and sentimentalized social relations (like in the family) without directly exposing capital as the culprit.

At the same time, the emphasis on women and children in the politics of migration, Yiannouplou goes on, reminds us that processes of "worlding" are embodied.[39] Pictures show children crying as they are wrenched away from the embrace of parents, while the narratives tell, for example, of bones found in the desert, groups not finding the food and drink left for them by activists and dying of hunger, dehydration, drowning, fever, and overexposure to the sun, or surviving to be corralled into overcrowded detention camps. Such desperation foregrounds not only the suffering body but also the body turned asunder and coming apart if not for the active intervention of others who take responsibility and care—a body defined as an open and precarious appeal—a summons or a call—for care. As Judith Butler reminds us,

> if we are beings who can be deprived of place, livelihood, shelter, food, and protection, if we can lose our citizenship, our homes, and our rights, then we are fundamentally dependent on those powers that alternately sustain or deprive us, and that hold a certain power over our very survival. ... And so we are already outside of ourselves before any possibility of being dispossessed of our rights, land, and modes of belonging. In other words, we are inter-dependent beings whose pleasure and suffering depend from the start on a sustained social world, a sustaining environment.[40]

Butler's analysis goes back and forth between situating dispossession as part of a human condition or as a phenomenological response to an historical experience, but in either case, the migrant is synecdochal for types of precarity and alienation that lay the groundwork for a worldly politics of responsibility and sustainability. The destruction and longing for home are thus met by new social relations of reproduction formed around a foundational recognition of social obligation and interrelatedness on geopolitical, worldly grounds.

Butler's examination asks us to see ourselves first as worldly because of our vulnerability and as dispossessed because we are worldly. Opening the human condition itself to constant crisis, this double-edgedness brings up questions not only about differential rights to security and access to care—who gets to cross borders and how easily—but also about differential obligation, including differential prices for conferring obligation on others. Aihwa Ong, for example, addresses the situation of migrant care workers in Singapore, Malaysia, and Hong Kong, where the high-tech economy has produced an import market for domestic help from the Philippines and China. In these examples, NGOs train young women to adopt gendered personality traits like obedience, adaptability, moral indebtedness, sacrifice, and solicitude in order to fit employment market norms in the destination culture: "Nongovernmental agencies, or NGOs, play a crucial role in training and indoctrinating would-be migrants, focusing in particular on self-managing techniques that instill proper attitude and conduct abroad .... [T]hey should be 'friendly but not familiar' with overseas employers."[41] In such scenarios, there is no gender identity before migration—gender identity is an after-image of displacement, a response to markets and to the circulation of production hubs; while the "family" as a unit for social reproduction and the satisfaction of needs—revealing its limits as a presumably organic organizational concept—is made possible only by labor pools mobilized to answer to the demands of newly capital-intensive cities. If "the world" "is a matter of disclosing and announcing through stories the experiences of a given people as a collective actor that is part of a shared world being destroyed by globalization,"[42] as Cheah intimates, then the experience of migration as it pushes alternative affiliations of reproduction, responsibility, and care into visibility for purposes of survival releases the world's "not yet," the world-in-progress (in-process): what the world could become.

Translation

In feminist interpretations of migration, then, the world is a process of making identities and subjectivities to respond to the globalization of dispossession. Though the process entails moving across space and time and, in particular, moving into the space and time of otherness, what is significant for feminism has to do with revealing that the process of creating and caring for subjects is an opening toward the other, even a demand. Uprooted, the migrant gives visible form to human vulnerability as well as revealing human interdependencies. In this sense, the migrant is in translation, surviving-on in the care of the other. Rather than copying and burying an original, deconstruction teaches us that translation changes language by opening it up to and surviving in the care of the other: "It [the text] lives more and better,"[43] says Algerian-born Jacques Derrida; translation "exhibits an incompletion, the impossibility of finishing, of totalizing, of saturating, of completing something on the order of edification, architectural construction, system and architectonics"[44]—the text, insufficient on its own, is indebted to the other (language). "Far from knowing first what 'life' or 'family' mean whenever we use these familiar values to talk about language and translation,"

Derrida continues, "it is rather starting from the notion of a language and its 'sur-vival' in translation that we could have access to the notion of what life and family mean."[45] In other words, translation reverses the genealogy that sees the translated text as the offspring of the original; instead, the translated text ultimately creates its source text, making it come to life in its connection to the other. For Derrida, there is no text that is not already in translation because every text's incompleteness reveals the responsibility of the other. Having lost its home language, the translation augments the language of the text in its reproduction. Feminist theory reads this translated text as a construction of social reproduction in migration, responsible for the life of the other.

Translation's emphasis on reproduction gives feminism a particular interest in it, especially in that translation assumes that difference underlies and marks reproduction. If Cheah is right that the structure of the world is literary, then translation plays a major role in world formation, as it assumes that literary meaning comes to life in the care of the other, that a literary text is accessible as meaningful once it is reproduced as other, and that literary texts create meaning because they illuminate that textual meaning requires a relation to the other. Translation makes reproduction a central consideration to what makes a world. A French feminist writer like Algerian-born Hélène Cixous, for example, would contend that every women's text by definition is in translation. "A woman's body," she writes, "with its thousand and one thresholds of ardor—once, by smashing yokes and censors, she lets it articulate the profusion of meanings that run through it in every direction—will make the old single-grooved mother tongue reverberate with more than one language."[46] As Cixous's own translator Peggy Kamuf has noted, Cixous's texts are "untranslatable" because "there are many others [languages] crossing and cross-fertilizing with it."[47] For Cixous, translation is akin to a women's language that bursts out of restrictions of conventional meaning and social practices by multiplying and, as such, challenges the norms of reproduction: "It's up to you to break the old circuits. It will be up to man and woman to render obsolete the former relationship and all its consequences, to consider the launching of a brand-new subject, alive, with defamiliarization."[48] Feminist theory thus notices the rich and mobile worlds of language that symbolic conventions try to lock out by imposing walls of restricted meaning on nature and culture alike in order to fix words in place along with the hierarchical social orders and constructions of power that they affirm.

Traditionally, the study of literature has been tied to nation, as literature has been corralled into defining national sensibility and enriching the national language, as Raymond Williams, among others, has explained.[49] Feminists counter by emphasizing translation's tendencies against binding language to predetermined cultural spaces. In this, feminism has identified translation as building toward a commons. As Emily Apter contends,

> one reason why literary studies falls short as anti-capitalist critique is because it insufficiently questions what it means to "have" a literature or to lay claim to aesthetic property. Literary communities are gated: according to Western law and international statute, authors *have* texts ..., and nations *own* literary patrimony

as cultural inheritance. Translation ... emerges as a form of creative property that belongs fully to no one. As a model of deowned literature, it stands against the swell of corporate privatization.[50]

Apter is concerned with "untranslatables" or failures in translation, which she sees as the core of world literature. Untranslatability—which includes both sex and gender—reveals the limits of reference, repetition, naturalization, and possession inferred in naming, as *"something new can be fully installed in the place of something else."*[51] For Apter, the non-correspondences and non-reconciliations that translation makes apparent in meaning-constellations are political in the sense that they "resist subsumption,"[52] meaning that sex, gender, and other untranslatables are terms that are disobedient to historical determination, sedimentation, and categorization through the name. Such a formulation suggests that language as such travels, landing within a particular meaning-context and then moving on, thereby acquiring agency outside of the intentions of its users; language resists hegemonic purposing, ownership, and containment by walls or other means.

Technology

New technology studies have interpreted the world as one, in the words of the collective Laboria Cuboniks, "that swarms with technological mediation."[53] Gender and sexuality are particularly salient in that they elicit a materialized semiotics, that is, a system of translation and retranslation between words and organisms via world technological circuits. Such technologies run by mixing up industrial, semiotic, corporeal, fictional, and political product, alienating bodies from symbolic designations of any sort. Hormones, for example, as Paul Preciado reads them, are biomedia or tele-cinematic communications like telephone messages or long-distance calling, that is, global transmitters of industrially manufacturable code that can be used to manipulate identities and populations through their cell structures, chemical makeup, sensory reactions, or genetic factoring.[54] In the form of drugs, surgeries, and pornographic messaging, gender and sexuality are made on global assembly lines, packaged, promoted, transported, exported, exchanged, and mass-marketed.

Feminist understanding of technology as inside gender and sexuality is somewhat indebted to Shulamith Firestone's early work on this issue in *The Dialectic of Sex*. Famously, Firestone predicted that the family would dissolve along with the illusion of control offered in its private institutions and psychoanalytic therapies, and in its place would be organized the production of babies in test-tube laboratories, liberating women from what she calls "the tyranny of reproduction":[55] "*Pregnancy is barbaric,*"[56] she exclaims; childbirth "isn't good for you."[57] The solution is to denaturalize and socialize reproduction, allowing science to work "by and for the people."[58] Firestone did not foresee that such measures were already controlled by giant conglomerates and powerful lobbies like the pharmaceutical industry that would develop and strengthen intellectual property rights in order to control and capitalize on gender constitution.

Firestone's feminist descendants do recognize the manipulation of hormones, sensibilities, and body forms through pharmaceuticals, pollutants, work regimes, and the porno culture industry as gender's "*economy of invention*":[59] "Hormones are sexopolitical fictions," writes Preciado, integrated in "global networks through which capital circulates."[60] "In the context of pharmacopornographic capitalism," they continue, "sexual desire and illness are produced and cultivated on the same basis: without the technical, pharmaceutical, and mediatic supports capable of materializing them, they don't exist. ... The postmodern body is becoming collectively desirable through its pharmacological management and audiovisual advancement."[61] An addict of testosterone, Preciado has asserted some control over her subjective invention by making the drug work on her terms, refusing to translate the gender norms of pharmacopornographic production and their global technologies into the limits of bodily experience. For Preciado, the fact that the body *is* the world—migratory and multilingual at once, exposed to multiple mediations and inputs—is what gives it the indeterminacy, plasticity, and fiction of its gender:

> I travel among three languages that I think of neither as mine nor as foreign to me. I personify a dyke-transgender condition made up of numerous biocodes, certain of which are normative and others spaces of resistance and still others potential places for the invention of subjectivity. In any case, these are artificial environments, synthetic islands of subjectivization that overlay the dominant sexo-urban tissue.[62]

At the core of Preciado's critique is the birth control pill and the porn industry, which, at the end of global production lines, release gender into the body, reproducing the body as gender. The social reproduction of subjects is, then, not carried out by female laborers, either naturalized or responding to needs in global markets and production centers. Rather, for Preciado, the Mother is the Machine while children are the chemical processes that the Machine uses to extract productive energies for its continual regeneration and growth.

Conclusion

Gayatri Spivak famously linked "worlding" to the role of literature in creating the individualist feminist subject in the nineteenth century. For Spivak, "worlding" paralleled what Marx called "commodity fetishism." That is, it produced an entity called "Third World" while concealing the process of its production where the colonized entered into a relation to the world as other. Just as the relations of production were alienated and hidden in the commodity, the history of imperialism is buried in the entity called "Third World." The important discursive moment for the feminist subject within this process, Spivak says, is "represented in two registers: childrearing and soul-making. The first is domestic-society-through-sexual-reproduction cathected as 'companionate love'; the second is the imperialist project cathected as civil-society-through-social-mission."[63] In Spivak's view, the shifting perspective between these two registers creates an individualist feminist subject that excludes the native female subject, erasing "a specific consideration of the political economy of the 'worlding' of the 'native,'"[64] or social reproduction. In other words, the expansion of imperialist power through "adding on" of geopolitical territory moves the feminist subject away from homemaking into the broader social world of modernity.

Spivak's influential thesis here has elicited a generation of responses. She has specifically spoken out against a world literature project on the basis of this "information retrieval" aspect where the "worlding" of literary histories that envisions "Third World as distant cultures, exploited but with rich intact literary heritages waiting to be recovered, interpreted, and curricularized ...; delivering the emergence of a 'South' that provides proof of transnational cultural exchange" while invisibly reproducing the "axioms of imperialism."[65] In this account, world literature is a form of positivism, of quantification through adding on. For Spivak, feminism has "worlded" in the wrong way. Yet, Spivak is opposing world to reproduction: "childrearing" is opposed to the "soul-making" that extends into the world as "social-mission," or capitalist expansion, independent of the biological.

Under neoliberalism, domestic society is "worlded" in its most intimate inner core. Practices of social reproduction are deeply integrated in capital's mobilities, imperialist processes, and resistances to these histories at the level of the everyday. In the legacy of Woolf, one might think of Margaret Atwood's *Oryx and Crake*, where gamers and genomes combine to make new biotech species, capital-saturated and sensible organisms, pigs with human-like intellect, for example, allying with blue avatar-like penis-waving creatures whose children eventually learn to write. One might also think of Arhundhati Roy's *The Ministry of Utmost Happiness*. A novel about the fight for a sovereign Kashmir, full of scenes of brutal torture and cruelty, populated with multilingualism and mistranslations, *The Ministry* also tells of a community of misfits and Hijra living in a graveyard, on the border of *Duniya*—or the "real world"— who find, at a political protest, a child abandoned by a militant, kidnap her, hide her from the police, and care for her. Roy twists together stories of multiple competing trajectories of globalization, from terror to advertisement (e.g., "Honda's newest luxury car"[66]), disaster (9/11, Bhopal Union Carbide Corporation), nuclear buildup, war, nationalism, guerrilla resistance, militarism, security, religion, and romance all undergirding the coming-to-be of a sovereignty, a world "to come"[67] formed from these social relations barely discernable on the edges of world catastrophe. While Warren Anderson, the American CEO of the Union Carbide Corporation, repeatedly waves "Hi Mom!" toward the TV news cameras in Delhi—in an attempt to impose the control of transnational capital onto the multiple languages and cultures of the region in the guise of familiar familial hierarchies— the transsexual main character Anjum explains, "Hum doosri Duniya se aaye hain" as she is photographed for the English-language press at the political rally. A response to the protestors' chant, the phrase translates as "We've come from there ... from the other world"—yet, "they had no idea what 'Duniya' [world] meant in Anjum's lexicon."[68] Like Kashmir, existing on the border between languages and unsettling the interests that vie for control, the orphaned baby is transferred between parents, histories, factions, origins, territories, and authorities to be finally embraced in this other yet-to-be-translated world of genderfuck.

On the edge of a total political breakdown and nuclear confrontation, the baby's arrival—like a global mushroom—brings into view a set of social relations that seem to come out of nowhere, in response to crisis: "She of the six fathers and three mothers (who were stitched together by threads of light)," concludes Roy, "'al Salaam,' she gurgled."[69] The baby is taken into the care of Hijras and other misfits and outcasts living in the graveyard guest house, in the midst of an ongoing war. The baby and Kashmir can be seen as occupying the same conceptual space—a negative space in the text, fully literary, which breaks the present, but which could appear as hope, or at least as difference. Whereas for Spivak, the world literary text is problematically the testing ground for the feminist individualist on a civilizing mission, for Roy, as it exposes the precarity of life caused by global exploitation and dispossession, the world literary text tries out narratives that outline yet-to-be-realized institutional arrangements in collective living—outside the family, national, or corporate line— responding to the emergency. Whereas the nineteenth-century novel that Spivak addresses might have had some role in supporting the nineteenth-century individualist adventure to control the world, the world literary text shows a subject borne of the socialization of experience, recombination, and responsibility in the midst of the ruins, reproducing a misfit-world beside the geographic one, that is, a home-in-opposition that we can call feminist.

Notes

1 Virginia Woolf, *Three Guineas* (San Diego: Harcourt, 1938), 109.
2 Ibid., 51.
3 Simone de Beauvoir, *The Second Sex*, trans. H. M. Parshley (New York: Vintage Books, 1980): 450–1.
4 Nancy Armstrong, *Desire and Domestic Fiction: A Political History of the Novel* (Oxford: Oxford UP, 1987), 70.
5 Debra A. Castillo, "Gender and Sexuality in World Literature," in *The Routledge Companion to World Literature*, ed. Theo D'haen, David Damrosch, and Djelal Kadir (New York: Routledge, 2011), 395.
6 This volume was edited by the same person, Jeffrey R. Di Leo. My benefactor and longtime friend, I would not necessarily fault him for the poor feminist presence, but rather I would say this was representative of the field.
7 Partha Chatterjee, "The Nation and Its Women," in *The Subaltern Studies Reader 1986–1995*, ed. Ranjit Guha (Minneapolis: University of Minnesota Press, 1997), 241.
8 Fredric Jameson, "Third-World Literature in the Era of Multinational Capitalism," *Social Text* 15 (Autumn 1986): 69.
9 David Damrosch, "Frames for World Literature," in *Grenzen der Literatur*, ed. Simone Winko, Fotis Jannidis, and Gerhard Lauer (Berlin: Walter de Gruyter, 2009), 497.
10 Ibid.
11 Franco Moretti, "Conjectures on World Literature," *NLR* 1 (2000): 56.

12 Pascale Casanova, *The World Republic of Letters*, trans. M. B. DeBevoise (Cambridge: Harvard UP, 2004), 13.
13 Gisèle Sapiro, "How Do Literary Works Cross Borders (or Not)? A Sociological Approach to World Literature," *Journal of World Literature* 1 (2016): 82.
14 Karl Marx and Friedrich Engels, "Manifesto of the Communist Party," in *The Marx-Engels Reader, Second Edition*, ed. Robert Tucker (New York: W. W. Norton, 1978), 476.
15 "The Suporn Clinic is a pink-and-white four-story villa on the main highway through Chonburi, a provincial city on the eastern Gulf coast of Thailand, one hour outside Bangkok …. [P]atients reported that they pay for more than his surgical skill in creating sensate vaginas and clitorises; they are paying for the entire care package" (Aren Z. Aizura, *Mobile Subjects: Transnational Imaginaries of Gender Reassignment* [Durham, NC: Duke UP, 2018], 174–5).
16 Cinzia Arruzza, Tithi Bhattacharya, and Nancy Fraser, "Notes for a Feminist Manifesto," *New Left Review* 114 (2018): 118.
17 Leerom Medovoi. "'Terminal Crisis?' From the Worlding of American Literature to World-System Literature," *American Literary History* 23.3 (Fall 2011): 643.
18 Bruce Robbins, "The Worlding of the American Novel," in *The Cambridge History of the American Novel*, ed. Leonard Cassuto (Cambridge: Cambridge UP, 2011), 1095.
19 Hannah Arendt, *Love and Saint Augustine*, ed. Joanna Vecchiarelli Scott and Judith Chelius Stark (Chicago: University of Chicago Press, 1996), 19.
20 Pheng Cheah, *What Is a World? On Postcolonial Literature as World Literature* (Durham: Duke UP, 2016), 65.
21 Ibid.
22 Ibid., 74.
23 Ibid., 154.
24 Donna Haraway, *Staying with the Trouble: Making Kin in the Chthulucene* (Durham: Duke UP, 2016), 4.
25 Ibid.
26 Ibid., 102.
27 Ibid.
28 Helen Hester, *Xenofeminism* (Malden, MA: Polity Press, 2018), 20–1.
29 Anna Lowenhaupt Tsing, *The Mushroom at the End of the World: On the Possibility of Life in Capitalist Ruins* (Princeton: Princeton UP, 2015), 2.
30 Ibid., 5. Emphasis in original.
31 Ibid., 3.
32 Ibid., 22.
33 Ibid., 27.
34 Ibid., viii.
35 Hester, *Xenofeminism*, 56.
36 Avtar Brah, "Diaspora, Border and Transnational Identities," in *Feminist Postcolonial Theory: A Reader*, ed. Reina Lewis and Sara Mills (New York: Routledge, 2003), 614.
37 Ibid., 614–15.
38 Effie Yiannopoulou, "Migration," in *The Bloomsbury Handbook of 21st-Century Feminist Theory*, ed. Robin Truth Goodman (New York: Bloomsbury, 2019), 425.
39 Ibid., 423.
40 Judith Butler, *Dispossession: The Performative in the Political, Conversations with Athena Athanasiou* (Malden, MA: Polity Press, 2013), 4.

41 Aihwa Ong, "A Bio-Cartograph: Maids, Neo-Slavery, and NGOs," in *Migrations and Mobilities: Citizenship, Borders, and Gender*, ed. Seyla Benhabib and Judith Resnick (New York: New York UP, 2009), 162.
42 Cheah, *What Is a World?*, 211.
43 Jacques Derrida, "Des Tours de Babel," trans. Joseph F. Graham, in *Difference in Translation*, ed. Joseph F. Graham (Ithaca: Cornell UP, 1985), 179.
44 Ibid., 165.
45 Ibid., 178.
46 Hélène Cixous, "The Laugh of the Medusa," in *Feminisms: An Anthology of Literary Theory and Criticism*, ed. Robyn R. Warhol and Diane Price (New Brunswick: Rutgers UP, 1991), 342.
47 Peggy Kamuf, "Hélène Cixous: Writing for her Life," in *Literature and the Development of Feminist Theory*, ed. Robin Truth Goodman (Cambridge: Cambridge UP, 2016), 129.
48 Cixous, "The Laugh of the Medusa," 346.
49 The idea of a "national literature" "drew on all the positive forces of cultural nationalism and its real achievements. It brought with it a sense of the 'greatness' or 'glory' of the native language" (Raymond Williams, "Literature," in *Marxism and Literature* [Oxford: Oxford UP, 1977], 51).
50 Emily Apter, *Against World Literature: On the Politics of Untranslatability* (New York: Verso, 2013), 15.
51 Ibid., 158. Emphasis in original.
52 Ibid.
53 Laboria Cuboniks, "Xenofeminism: A Politics for Alienation," http://www.laboriacuboniks.net/#firstPage (accessed January 24, 2019).
54 Beatriz Preciado, *Testo Junkie: Sex, Drugs, and Biopolitics in the Pharmacopornographic Era*, trans. Bruce Benderson (New York: Feminist Press, 2013), 160–1.
55 Shulamith Firestone, *The Dialectic of Sex: The Case for Feminist Revolution* (New York: Farrar, Straus, and Giroux, 1970), 201.
56 Ibid., 180. Emphasis in original.
57 Ibid., 181.
58 Ibid., 179.
59 Preciado, *Testo Junkie*, 53. Emphasis in original.
60 Ibid., 191.
61 Ibid., 53.
62 Ibid., 93–4.
63 Gayarti Chakravorty Spivak, *A Critique of Postcolonial Reason: Toward a History of the Vanishing Present* (Cambridge: Harvard UP, 1999), 116.
64 Ibid., 118.
65 Ibid., 114.
66 Arundhati Roy, *The Ministry of Utmost Happiness* (New York: Vintage Books, 2017), 116.
67 Ibid., 444.
68 Ibid., 114.
69 Ibid., 433.

6

Astonishing Worlding: Montaigne and the New World

Zahi Zalloua

In *The Passions of the Soul*, René Descartes takes stock of philosophy's epistemic ways, blaming its failure to attain a "better state" on an unhealthy excess of wonder: "Astonishment [*étonnement*] is an excess of wonder [*admiration*] which can never be anything but bad."[1] Against a pathologized mode of thinking, a healthy philosophy ought to be about successful translation: the translation of the new into a mastered and well-digested familiar. If Descartes announces modernity's epistemic enlightenment, the Renaissance author Michel de Montaigne (1533-92)—to whom Descartes was in no small part responding—refuses to see astonishment as something to be categorically dismissed. Quite the contrary, Montaigne's essayistic mode of writing indulges in the "uselessness" of astonishment, in its resistance to yield a *positive* body of knowledge, disclosing his skepticism concerning philosophy's returns on its cognitive investments. Indeed, Montaigne, in his *Essays*, yearns for and thrives on astonishment, the endless, multiple, and joyful pursuit of his subject matter (including his self and others). This essay turns to Montaigne's writing on the New World, exploring the essayist's rehabilitative if ambivalent figuration of the Cannibal of the New World. Though the designation of "Cannibal" became coterminous with the brutal exploitation, enslavement, and massacre of millions of Indians in what Tzvetan Todorov has described as "the greatest genocide in human history,"[2] Montaigne arguably retains the term for its astonishing value, for its capacity to shock—the Cannibal is, after all, the image of the radical other *par excellence*. At the same time, Montaigne is all too aware that the radical alterity of the Cannibal has been synonymous with the latter's subjugation and mistreatment. As we shall see, Montaigne's *essaying* of the Cannibal constitutes an act of worlding—an act that gestures toward an alternative reception and configuration of the radical other, toward a heterology—an ethics and politics of alterity—that troubles the boundaries between the human and his others. Central to this troubling is Montaigne's critical engagement with philosophy's classic question concerning what is "proper to man?":[3] *What are the essential and distinguishing features of (European) man?*

Desiring Difference

Lacking any humanity in the eyes of the European colonizers, the Indian as Cannibal meant his silencing and exclusion from the civilized world of men, without any hope of humanistic protection.[4] In "Of Cannibals," Montaigne blames European curiosity for the New World (mis)encounter, writing, "I am afraid we have eyes bigger than our stomachs, and more curiosity than capacity."[5] On one level, Montaigne's observation can be read as a philosophical intervention and correction of public judgment. This reading would reinforce a cognitive bias. The bodies of his contemporaries (figured by their "stomachs") should follow their minds (figured by "capacity"). Simply stated, demystification—the critical practice of philosophy—works to nullify Europe's cultural fantasies about the radical other. On another level, an eye for the affective register points to those fantasies' affective pull: how we're moved to action in ways that exceed and run counter to our given rational makeup. The example of the New World reveals the dangers of "bad affects": well-circulated fantastic tales of the New World produced affective intensities for their European audience, ultimately to the detriment of the cultural other. To counter the ill effects of that type of curiosity, Montaigne does not only propose a proto-Cartesian cognitive critique. He also develops his own personal form of curiosity, which hybridizes the cognitive and affective registers, and ultimately exceeds that of his French successor by refusing to contain and translate difference back into the knowable and masterable. In the first line of his last essay from Book III, "Of Experience," Montaigne makes curiosity constitutive of man: "There is no desire more natural than the desire of knowledge."[6] Later in the same chapter, Montaigne continues his rehabilitation of curiosity, in his characteristically oblique manner, through his evocation of the "generous mind [*esprit genereux*]":

> It is a sign of contraction of the mind when it is content, or of weariness. A generous mind desires difference; it never stops within itself; it is always aspiring and going beyond its strength, with impulses beyond its powers of achievement. If it does not advance and press forward and stand at bay and clash, it is only half alive.[7]

A generous mind eschews the dictates of self-immunization and forgoes the integrity of the self. To paraphrase Jacques Derrida, without curiosity, with absolute self-protection, nothing would ever be experienced. Without affect, with pure *stasis* or *ataraxia* (a Stoical ethos of indifference), there would be no interpretation, no life.[8] We would no longer be open to the future, to the outside world, or available for an encounter with difference.[9] Without curiosity, worlding as such would be impossible.

Curiosity entails a simultaneous sense of vulnerability and generosity. Curiosity entails a risk and an opportunity, an opportunity as a risk, and vice versa. The other as such astonishes and can appear only as a frightening otherness, as a paradox, an enigma that disturbs my enjoyment of comfort, resists my interpretive structure, escapes my expectations, frustrates my will to mastery. In Derrida's colorful language: "Monsters cannot be announced. One cannot say: 'Here are our monsters,' without immediately turning them into pets."[10] Indeed, even the perception of "a monster in a monster" initiates the process of epistemic domestication: "one begins ... compare it to the norms, to analyze it, consequently to master whatever could be terrifying in this figure."[11] Structures pacify and normalize, invariably turning raw affect into meaningful emotion, monsters into pets.

In "Of Cripples," Montaigne dramatizes this point by bringing the "monster" even closer to home. While pondering the notion that "we become habituated to anything strange by use and time,"[12] Montaigne discovers that this is not the case with him, since "the more I frequent myself and know myself, the more my deformity *astonishes me, and the less I understand myself.*"[13] Astonishment, in its immanence, discloses a divided Montaigne, a Montaigne haunted by a constitutive alterity—be it language, the unconscious, or the trace of others. Indeed, self-knowledge produces more and more opacity. The subject lacks transparency ("Our thoughts are always elsewhere"[14]), is disturbingly multiple ("Myself now and myself a while ago are indeed two"[15]), and is defined by its ontological and hermeneutic slipperiness: "Every minute I seem to be slipping away from myself."[16] It is beyond comprehension, beyond mastery and control: "But we are, I know not how, double within ourselves, with the result that we do not believe what we believe, and we cannot rid ourselves of what we condemn."[17]

Essaying creates a moment of *aphanisis*. For Jacques Lacan, *aphanisis* is constitutive of the subject and a perpetual source of alienation: "when the subject appears somewhere as meaning, he is manifested elsewhere as 'fading,' as disappearance."[18] Whenever the subject uses language and substitutes meaning for being, *aphanisis* happens. Catherine Belsey traces Lacan's account of *aphanisis*, offering a helpful gloss of its psychoanalytic significance and meaning:

> Aphanisis (disappearance) was a term first used by Ernest Jones, who argued that the subject's ultimate fear was that desire would disappear. Lacan appropriates the term to discuss the disappearance, or sometimes the "fading," of the speaking subject itself, as it loses its purchase on meaning. I can disappear from what I am saying, and in the process make apparent the provisional character of subjectivity.[19]

For Lacan, the lesson of Montaigne lies in the philosopher's keen disclosure of the provisional character of the subject.[20] Essaying *gives* Montaigne an unstable, precarious, and monstrous presence: "I have seen no more evident monstrosity and miracle in the world than myself."[21] What emerges from the writing process is a less than transparent and coherent subject; it is a subject whose thinking does not coincide with his being: "This is a record of various and changeable occurrences, and of irresolute and, when it so befalls, contradictory ideas: whether I am different myself, or whether I take hold of my subjects in different circumstances and aspects."[22] So cognizant of his own unknowingness, of his unruliness and foreignness to himself, Montaigne never assumes that the Cannibal is any more self-evident or homogeneous. Montaigne's epistemic motto "What do I know?"[23] blocks the impulse to translate the Cannibal, to render the indigenous other ready for cultural consumption.

In this light, Montaigne's concern for those who have bigger eyes than their stomachs must be qualified. It is not a wholesale indictment of curiosity. Desiring difference—heterology as such—is not the problem; at least, it is not *a priori* a problem. Desiring difference becomes a problem only when the desired object functions as a phantasmatic screen, onto which Europeans project their innermost fears and desires, onto which they project what is *improper* about man, turning the Cannibal into a being deemed irrevocably inhuman, excessively barbaric and cruel, and thus killable with impunity. In "Of Cannibals," Montaigne questions the superiority of his fellow Christian Europeans, their (self-appointed) privileged place in the Chain of Beings (*scala naturae*), ranked below God and angels but above all else at the summit of humanity, higher than Jews and Muslims, and far higher than "Africans, Asians, and native Americans"—whose humanity was not self-evident but disputed, who were "lower or nonexistent on the Chain."[24] Montaigne destabilizes this logic that hierarchizes and ontologizes the order of beings, this logic that would wall off Europeans (the standard of humanity) from Cannibals, locating the latter on the other side of civilization. As we shall see, Montaigne locates the "true" Cannibals—those rightly charged of savagery, of inflicting excessive cruelty on others—not out there in the New World, as reported by travelers like Jean de Léry and André Thevet, but in the midst of French life, in the midst of a France divided by a horrific civil war.

Navigating between Sameness and Difference

"Of Cannibals" begins with Montaigne's recounting of the story of King Pyrrhus's enlightened reflection on the substantive "barbarian." While observing and admiring the strategic deployment of a Roman army, Pyrrhus puts into question the logic of calling "barbarian" whoever is not Greek (etymologically derived from the Greek *barbaros*, a foreigner). After this brief anecdote, Montaigne generalizes while alluding to his own project of demystifying *doxa*: "We should beware of clinging to vulgar opinions, and judge things by reason's way, not by popular say."[25] Exemplifying this critical insight, Montaigne reflects on the so-called barbarism of the Tupinamba of Brazil and then proceeds to relativize and contextualize its meaning, to reveal the semantic elasticity of this morally charged term: "There is nothing barbarous and savage in that nation ... except that each man calls barbarism whatever is not his own practice."[26]

Far from considering them barbarians *in the negative sense of the term*, Montaigne paints these cannibals in the utmost positive light:

> It seems to me that what we actually see in these nations surpasses not only all the pictures in which poets have idealized the golden age and all their inventions in imagining a happy state of man, but also the conceptions and the very desire of philosophy.[27]

The Tupinambas exceed the conceptual framework of the Western mind, standing unmatched in their excellence. Even the idea of a Golden Age and the "desire of philosophy" of the Old World fail to do justice to the natives of this New World. With such a laudable portrait of the Cannibal, Montaigne has contributed to, if not created, the myth of the Noble Savage (*le bon sauvage*)—an image of the natural self that will find great resonance in the works of Jean-Jacques Rousseau and later Romantics.

The Cannibals live in a "state of nature," a utopian place where food abounds, bearing "no resemblance to ours."[28] Their wildness refers to their proximity to Nature, to their authentic mode of existence:

> Those people are wild, just as we call the fruits that Nature has produced by herself and in the normal course; whereas really it is those that we have changed artificially and led astray from the common order, that we should rather call wild. ... These nations, then, seem to me barbarous in this sense, that they have been fashioned very little by the human mind, and are still very close to their original naturalness. The laws of nature still rule them, very little corrupted by ours.[29]

The words "wild" and "barbarous" now signify what is properly *natural* and thus are freed from their negative connotations, cleansed from the vulgar opinions of Montaigne's contemporary Europeans, that is, of the tyranny of *popular say*. Montaigne repeatedly argues for the cultural superiority of the Brazilian natives over the Europeans whose artificiality is emblematic of their social and moral corruption. The Cannibals live *as if* they were still in the Garden of Eden, untouched by original sin, in a mythical place of plenitude prior to the violent emergence of Culture, while the Europeans clearly exhibit their condition of spiritual fallness and moral corruption. Their *barbarous* and *savage* mode of existence—epitomized by their cannibalistic practices—even finds a certain degree of *legitimization* in the practice of important ancient figures: "Chrysippus and Zeno, heads of the Stoic sect, thought there was nothing wrong in using our carcasses for any purpose in case of need, and getting nourishment from them."[30] Montaigne also cites as a precedent—and thus as another "historical" justification for cannibalism—the Gauls: "just as our ancestors, when besieged by Caesar in the city of Alésia, resolved to relieve their famine by eating old men, women, and other people useless for fighting."[31] Yet the last example deployed by Montaigne is quite paradoxical, since it is not at all convincing given the presumed aim of the chapter: to familiarize the Europeans with the anthropophagic custom of the Tupinambas, to reveal that their cannibalism is *not* motivated by a biological need to eat others but rather functions as a performance, as a symbolic act of social communion, where each member of the tribe takes a limb of the dead prisoner's body: "This done, they roast him and eat him in common."[32] Indeed, to overcome this common Western misconception, Montaigne draws attention to the fact that the intentionality behind the cannibalistic act lies elsewhere, that it is generated by a desire for vengeance: "This is not, as people think, for nourishment, as of old the Scythians used to do; *it is to betoken an extreme revenge*."[33] In this light, even the first example in retrospect strikes the reader as lacking cogency, since the Stoic leaders had excused cannibalism for presumably the "wrong reasons"—only because it satisfied a physical hunger, a biological need ("in case of need"; "getting nourishment").

Moreover, Montaigne's defense of the Cannibals is not without qualification. He holds that they are guilty of barbarism in the *negative sense of the term*:

I am not sorry that we notice the barbarous horror of such acts.³⁴

Their warfare is ... as excusable and beautiful as this *human disease* can be.³⁵

We may well call these people barbarians, in respect to the rules of reason, but not in respect to ourselves, who surpass them in every kind of barbarity.³⁶

In "Of Moderation," the essay just preceding "Of Cannibals," Montaigne expresses a more damning critique, recording his strong distaste for the "horrible cruelty"³⁷ practiced by the indigenous population of the New World, who "burn the victims alive, and take them out of the brazier half roasted to tear their heart and entrails out. Others, even women, are flayed alive, and with their bloody skins they dress and disguise others."³⁸ Sameness and difference between the Native Americans and the Europeans are by no means mutually exclusive. What they both share is an inhuman impulse for excessive cruelty. Europeans all too easily identify it in the indigenous other, while simultaneously disavowing it at home.

In a move that could have only astonished his humanist readers, Montaigne counters this Eurocentric blindness by *accusing* his countrymen of cannibalism—of an even worse kind:

> I think there is more barbarity in *eating a man alive* than in eating him dead; and in tearing by tortures and the rack a body still full of feeling, in roasting a man bit by bit, in having them bitten and mangled by dogs and swine ... than *roasting and eating him* after he is dead.³⁹

Although Montaigne diffuses somewhat his accusation, since we realize by the end of the sentence that his fellow Frenchmen don't actually eat the flesh of others but give it to dogs and pigs, he remains unwavering in his indictment. The force of his claim that there is *more* barbarity in torturing and burning living human beings—"on the pretext of piety and religion"⁴⁰—than in the cannibalism of the Indians who eat them *after* they are dead, after their ritual murder, is unaltered. Montaigne repeats this insight in "Of Cruelty": "Savages do not shock me as much by roasting and eating the bodies of the dead as those who torment them and persecute them living."⁴¹ Despite the moral turpitude of the anthropophagic act, it seems clear that Montaigne considers the "natural" barbarity of the Cannibals more excusable, or at least less intolerable, than the "civilized" barbarity of the Europeans. The term "Cannibal" therefore no longer refers solely or primarily to those primitives who eat human flesh but also—or especially—to Montaigne's civilized countrymen who inflict the most horrific forms of torture.

Montaigne's critical discourse on the New World restages philosophy's timeless question of *what is proper to man?*—revealing that it only masquerades as a universal question, that it is in fact Eurocentric, aiming at solidifying European man's sense of superiority, legitimatizing his status as the arbiter of human values. The Cannibal serves to justify Europe's exclusive claim to humanity and civilization, its idea/ideal of the subject immune from all the ills and barbarity Europeans witness in the New World. Against his contemporaries' ideological answers, Montaigne gives a most anti-humanist answer to what is *proper* to man: it is the penchant for inhuman, excessive cruelty. We might say that (the excess of) cruelty is "absolutely immanent [to] the very core of subjectivity itself."[42] It is part of our ontological makeup from the Old World to the New World. This is not to naturalize or justify cruelty; rather, it is to enjoin us to confront it, to fight it, and to resist gentrifying the *in*human, as is typical in humanist discourse and its rhetoric of *perfectio hominis*.[43] Demonizing the non-European for exhibiting cruelty (a sign of the other's animality, uncivilized culture) while ignoring both colonialist savagery and cruelty's crushing presence at home can only augment and fuel its destructiveness. Montaigne voices his unconditional objection to cruelty with his self-reflexive and ironic comment: "Among other vices, I *cruelly* hate *cruelty*, both by nature and by judgment, as the extreme of all vices."[44] Montaigne criticizes "cruelty" (it is unconditionally deemed the greatest vice) while signaling or better yet gesturing to its insurmountability with the paradoxical adverb "cruelly." "Cruelly" names here Montaigne's affective commitment to "putting cruelty *first*"[45] in his ethical orientation. This ineradicable vice, this unshakable otherness, is reminiscent of the monstrosity that Montaigne "discovers" within.

Useless Philosophy

If Montaigne's act of worlding astonishes his contemporaries with his accusation of cannibalism—compelling them to see themselves as agents of cruelty and to reassess their claim to sovereignty and superiority (to consider their "sovereignty [as] constituted through colonialism"[46])—the astonishment is arguably prolonged when Montaigne positions the Cannibals as speaking subjects, as ruthless *critics* of French society. Three Indians in Rouen share with Montaigne what they found most "amazing [*plus admirable*]," a term related to "admiration" (wonder). They mention three criticisms, of which Montaigne states he only remembers two. First, they are puzzled that a child could be invested with so much power over adults: "They said … they thought it very strange that so many grown men, bearded, strong, and armed, who were around the King (it is likely that they were talking about the Swiss of his guard) should submit to obey a child, and that one of them was not chosen to command instead."[47] Second, they are dismayed by the current reality of France's socioeconomic inequalities, anticipating the virtual eruption of a revolutionary egalitarian ethos: "they thought it strange that these needy halves could endure such an injustice, and did not take the others by the throat, or set fire to their houses."[48]

Turning the tables on his countrymen, it is the European who is now perceived as a strange oddity, revealing that both the experience and meaning of alterity are relative, non-substantial, and relational. If, by the end of the essay, it is the European and his political world that provoke amazement for the Native Americans, Montaigne turns their wonder into France's astonishment. Refusing to settle on his portrait of the radical other, Montaigne ironizes his message, rendering it "useless" and non-actionable; he disrupts yet again the unfolding of his argument, seemingly undermining his apology of the Cannibals in the final line of his piece: "All this is not too bad—but what's the use? They don't wear breeches."⁴⁹ Is Montaigne performing a "pirouette," reversing his (critical) position and returning to his (ethnocentric) senses? We seem to be back where we started: Europeans belong to their civilized world and non-Europeans to their barbaric one. But isn't the narcissistic blow, the damage to France's self-image already too significant? A return predicated on a "cosmetic" difference (about what they wear) hardly undoes the insinuated sameness between the Europeans and the Cannibals—the astonishing recognition of an inhuman core in *both* us and them.

Notes

1. René Descartes, *Meditations, Objections, and Replies*, ed. Roger Ariew and Donald Cress (Indianapolis: Hackett, 2006), 58.
2. Tzvetan Todorov, *The Conquest of America: The Question of the Other* (New York: Harper & Row, 1987), 5.
3. John O'Brien, "'Le Propre de l'Homme': Reading Montaigne's 'Des Cannibales' in Context," *Forum for Modern Language Studies* 53.2 (2016): 220–34.
4. The Dominican friar Bartolomé de Las Casas is an exception to this dehumanizing trend, seeing in the Native Americans the great possibility of spiritual transformation. Las Casas describes the indigenous population as ready-made for conversion: "They are very clean in their persons, with alert, intelligent minds, docile and open to doctrine, very apt to receive our holy Catholic faith, to be endowed with virtuous customs, and to behave in a godly fashion" (Las Casas, *The Devastation of the Indies: A Brief Account*, trans. Herma Briffault [Baltimore: Johns Hopkins UP, 1992], 28–9). To be assimilated to the Christian faith—through exposure to Spanish Catholic evangelization—is thus tantamount to an ontological upgrade. Las Cases rejected the view that the Indians were ontologically fixed in their baseness and inferiority (as many, drawing on Aristotle's ontology, felt) but, on the contrary, an alter ego and thus worthy of conversion. If Las Casas upholds the fantasy of sameness (via conversion) in his rehabilitation of the Cannibals, Montaigne complicates this rhetoric of sameness by disclosing the unsettling aspects that ties Europeans and Indians together.
5. Michel de Montaigne, *The Complete Essays of Montaigne*, trans. Donald Frame (Stanford: Stanford UP, 1957), 150. Montaigne devotes another essay on the New World, "Of Coaches," which takes as its object not the *primitivism* of the Tupinamba of Brazil but the conquest of the Aztecs of Mexico and the Incas of Peru, and the destruction of their marvelous *civilizations*. Montaigne noticeably suspends all references to the existing and available reports of cannibalism among these peoples.
6. Ibid., 815.
7. Ibid., 817–18; translation modified.
8. "Without autoimmunity, with absolute immunity, nothing would ever happen or arrive; we would no longer wait, await, or expect, no longer expect one another, or expect any event" (Jacques Derrida, *Rogues: Two Essays on Reason*, trans. Pascale-Anne Brault and Michael Naas [Stanford: Stanford UP, 2005], 152).
9. It is also true that Montaigne warns in the last pages of his essay "Of Experience" against the desire to "go outside ourselves" (857); yet here the essayist is objecting to a care of the self that is exclusively a care of the soul/mind at the expense of one's embodied existence. While Montaigne apparently spares Christian mystics from his

objections ("those venerable souls, exalted by ardent piety and religion to constant and conscientious meditation on divine things" [856]), there is no suggested criterion enabling one to discriminate between these "venerable souls" and those individuals dangerously engaging in similar practices, claiming to have similar mystical religious experiences. The latters' care of the self is a kind of caring that would paradoxically do violence to their "human" self (conceived by Montaigne as *both* mind and body): "That is madness: instead of changing into angels, they change into beasts; instead of raising themselves, they lower themselves" (856).

10 Jacques Derrida, "Some Statements and Truisms about Neologisms, Newisms, Postisms, Parasitisms, and Other Small Seismisms," in *The States of "Theory,"* ed. David Carroll (New York: Columbia UP, 1989), 80.
11 Jacques Derrida, *Points…: Interviews, 1974–1994*, ed. Elisabeth Weber, trans. Peggy Kamuf (Stanford: Stanford UP, 1992), 386.
12 Montaigne, *Essays*, 787.
13 Ibid. Emphasis added.
14 Ibid., 939.
15 Ibid., 736.
16 Ibid., 61.
17 Ibid., 469.
18 Jacques Lacan, *The Four Fundamental Concepts of Psychoanalysis*, ed. Jacques-Alain Miller, trans. Alan Sheridan (New York: W. W. Norton, 1998), 218.
19 Catherine Belsey, *Shakespeare in Theory and Practice* (Oxford: Oxford UP, 2008), 26.
20 I explore Montaigne's *aphanisis* in more details in my *Theory's Autoimmunity: Skepticism, Literature, and Philosophy* (Evanston: Northwestern UP, 2018).
21 Montaigne, *Essays*, 787.
22 Ibid., 611.
23 Ibid., 393.
24 Eric Nellis, *Shaping the New World: African Slavery in the Americas, 1500–1888* (Toronto: University of Toronto Press, 2013), 9.
25 Montaigne, *Essays*, 150.
26 Ibid., 152.
27 Ibid., 153. The character of Gonzalo, in Shakespeare's *The Tempest*, will draw upon this utopian image from Montaigne in his description of Prospero's enchanted island.
28 Ibid., 153.
29 Ibid.
30 Ibid., 155.
31 Ibid.
32 Ibid.
33 Ibid. Emphasis added.
34 Ibid.
35 Ibid., 156. Emphasis added.
36 Ibid., 155–6.
37 Ibid., 149.
38 Ibid.
39 Ibid., 155. Emphases added.
40 Ibid.
41 Ibid., 314.

42 Slavoj Žižek, *The Parallax View* (Cambridge: MIT Press, 2006), 22.
43 The desire to perfect the human is the desire for ontologically evacuate all excesses from him or her, to actualize a state of completion (from the Latin *perfectio* meaning "completion"). Montaigne acknowledges the ontological incompleteness of our being; or as Slavoj Žižek puts it, "there is an inhuman core in all of us, or, that we are 'not-all human'" (Slavoj Žižek, *In Defense of Lost Causes* [New York: Verso, 2008], 17).
44 Montaigne, *Essays*, 313. Emphasis added.
45 Judith Shklar, *Ordinary Vices* (Cambridge: Harvard UP, 1984), 8. Shklar reads Montaigne as announcing liberalism, whereas I see liberalism as covering over Montaigne's psychoanalytic insight of the inhuman core of humanity.
46 Antony Anghie, *Imperialism, Sovereignty, and the Making of International Law* (Cambridge: Cambridge UP, 2005), 38.
47 Montaigne, *Essays*, 159.
48 Ibid.
49 Ibid.

7

Literature of the World, Unite!

Peter Hitchcock

Following David Damrosch's advice that a good way to proceed with world literature is to take hints from a favorite author,[1] we begin with the writers of the *Communist Manifesto*. On the face of it, any consonance of communism and world literature would seem like a bizarre dream from another age, a "dream world and catastrophe," to borrow from Susan Buck-Morss,[2] that offers little more than a niggling nostalgia for a geo-cultural *Weltanschauung* that surely died with the fall of the Berlin Wall, or Chernobyl, or Lenin's stroke, or the 1848 revolutions, or even Goethe in 1832. Yet the scandal of such imbrication, never more than a promise in the *Communist Manifesto*, is very much an unsettled spirit, like some spectral presence of transformation compulsively conjured by communism's doubting adversary ("Speak to it, Horatio!"), capitalism, with all the verifiable forevers of a business cycle. In literary studies, no one is surprised by the worldliness and worlding of literature, although many would understandably balk at the inference or influence of political economy (perhaps beginning with Jacques Derrida's difference between world and globe[3]). Among political economists, the place of the literary is respected (and respectfully marginal)—poets are allowed to be legislators of the world so long as that recognition remains "unacknowledged" as a material force. Dragons can melt swords but they are a poor substitute for the imaginative reach of, say, the Federal Reserve. Perhaps only philosophy would have the temerity and truculence to interpret this rash imbroglio otherwise.

It is common knowledge that Karl Marx and Friedrich Engels use several versions of "literature" in assessing the impress of world literature in understanding the conditions of revolution. These include the specific genre of the manifesto, technical pamphlets, politically interested creative writing, and literature of a "purely literary aspect." The *Communist Manifesto* acknowledges that such literature might travel without the social conditions of its genesis, and here we begin to register the peculiarities of arraying at least three historical projects that can be articulated autonomously from one another. This is not because the economic, social, and cultural cannot be mutually implied—this, after all, is a mainstay of materialist critique. It is, rather, because the philosophical force of world as concept is highly differentiated in each case, so that any collective reciprocity or antagonism would necessitate a mediating notion of world irreducible to each instance yet expressible in relation. Globalization can be articulated precisely in this way, both across disciplinary concerns and in terms of its modes, as expansion, interconnectedness, intensification, velocity, and consciousness. Here we are interested principally in the antinomies of revolutionary worlding in a world whose crises ostensibly lie elsewhere than in the utopian *Welt* of worker unity. Initially, one might usefully confront the more modest scale of critical cosmopolitanism in the material conditions of Marx and Engels's *Manifesto*. Why? The advent of globalization, with specific integuments now gathered under the term "neoliberalism," throws into relief the conceptual contradictions of world as an abstract solution to the limits of provincialism, parochialism, and nationalism as currently construed, yet one is always surprised, even after the financial crisis of 2007–8, how much of this dialectic is symptomatic in an intervention that capitalist globalization claims to have sublated in advance. The reemergence or reinvention of "world literature" is not simply an effect of this sublation, or the false consciousness of a socioeconomic system structured in dominance, but is itself active in rethinking the perquisites of world literature as a longue durée and through the impasse it signals. World literature would simply be a relic of Enlightenment or industrial first principles if indeed the concept of world was consonant with its earlier manifestations and philosophical rationalizations, but its inconsistencies and contingencies suggest a more troubled arc that globalization finds inescapable even as, or precisely because, it represents a comparatively minor discourse in the hegemonic worlding of contemporary global transaction.

We can think of this first in terms of the logic of world that structures the *Manifesto*'s confrontation with capital, then figure the limits of such critique (separable from any claims to limits in critique per se) into the worlding of literature today as a materialist challenge. The tension of these Marxist moments (neither events nor elegies) is about the living on of particular components of materialist analysis in a philosophy of literature that pivots on concepts of world as such. Marx and Engels had already explored the expansion of commerce as a form of worlding in *The German Ideology*,[4] and Marx's distinction between political and human emancipation in "On the Jewish Question" is another way to think contradiction at different scales.[5] A major prompt, however, was an adaptation of Goethe's sense of world in the concept of *Weltliteratur*. Goethe's reported comment to Johann Peter Eckermann in 1827 sets the stage for a host of hermeneutical possibilities: "National literature is no longer of importance, it is the time for world literature, and all must aid in bringing it about."[6] What does Goethe mean by this? In announcing a "world literature" Goethe is thinking more of an extension of national literature than an articulation that would in theory negate the very possibility of literature as a ground for nation and national identity. Yet, while much of Goethe's conception could be read as a European-based para-national project (somewhat apposite with a form of cultural imperialism), he also reads the worlding of literature as a collocation of writing in multiple forms and languages, a multiplicity that is itself the substance of a new subject and subjectivity. World at this level is a condition of difference and particularity but cannot be reduced to the nation without obfuscating what cultural exchange does to the politics of scale. One should not be naïve about the Eurocentric genealogy of Goethe's appeal, but it is the implications of the idea of world that piques Marx's interest in particular. What if, for instance, the worlding of world literature was a more ambiguous arena of consciousness-making than the subjectivation of commodity lore? Goethe does not see the world as an object but rather as an emergence in which literature truly lives its difference as an imaginary challenge. World narration does not simply escape its nation (one could use Goethe's own writing to support the point) but in principle would render superfluous its constituency.

It is possible to read the drama of Goethe's conception of world in Georg Wilhelm Friedrich Hegel and Immanuel Kant's differences on the relationship of the universal and particular, with perhaps an emphasis on Hegelian mediation or refraction over reflection or externality.[7] For Marx, the emergence at stake is dialectically bound to a conception of human fulfillment, a kind of concrete particularity in human species-being itself. One telling term in this regard in the *Manifesto* is *Gemeingut*, or common property, a state in which the primary belongingness of nation and national literature falls away. What is understood as "the cosmopolitan character to production and consumption in every country,"[8] a bourgeois predilection to be sure, prepares the ground for cultural exchange that undoes class particularity structured in dominance, as if to show that class cosmopolitanism meets its own negation at a world scale. This is counterintuitive, or at the very least ambivalent, since one could quite easily imagine a scaling up of bourgeois cosmopolitanism that would strengthen rather than contradict the globalization of capitalist ideals. Part of the point is that worlding finds not just commodity relations but also class formations that can magnify as much as mollify opposition. As a structural antinomy of scale, the commoning of property exists in the clash of particularity and the limits of local expression as dynamics of the world per se. World literature, like world history in *The German Ideology*, is a struggle over the limits of world in socioeconomic and sociocultural extension. Even if the class characteristics of such worlding imply a specific hegemony, the historical motion of the concept itself interrogates the specificities of class in formation. In the *Manifesto*, the unity of the working class, the globality of proletarianization, is not the reaffirmation of class but the precondition of its abolition. The question for both philosophy and cultural politics is whether the world of world literature is consanguine with the worlding of history that Marx and Engels interpellate in the *Manifesto*. Would the full emergence of world literature and the absolute subsumption of national literatures be possible only in the disappearance of its modifier (as class determines socialization), when (commodity) exchange is no longer the measure of its value across the globe? If the endgame of the *Manifesto* is a communism that produces the fully human, is the aim of world literature a world in which it can just be literature?

There are several problems with this putative allegorization of the concept of world across class and culture (an impossibility arrayed against "impossibilism"). Historically, the content and nature of class relations have mutated, and, however rousing the flourish at the end of the *Manifesto* about workers uniting, the "worker of the world(s)" as I have referred to the phenomenon elsewhere[9] hardly corresponds to the clarion call of communism in anything but a problematic way. If the supremacy of the proletariat, as Marx and Engels describe it, will cause "national differences and antagonisms between peoples" to vanish still faster than a certain world of unity would seem to be less possible in the absence of this catalyst. Indeed, if anything, the abstract universality of capitalist valorization would appear more evident, as a hegemon admitting little or no alternatives to its reach. Whatever the provocation of world literature for the *Manifesto*'s formulations, its communist variant has no world defying present/presence in contemporary theorization. How then, to explain the renewed attention to world literature in recent decades? Is it indicative in other registers?

The problem of "world" for the social and the cultural is that it must be made rather than simply discovered. How is agency constituted toward such an end? What is its form and process? Does it indeed compose a history that is coterminous with its object, the world itself? Is world-making always already differentiated so that at every level of abstraction unity is unique, not universal, a world apart in scale and logic? Of course, as noted, philosophy is to a great extent founded on reconciling or mediating the universal and the particular, but in a world of post-structuralism and post-analytic philosophy, the world itself is less freighted by this classic tension or is highly resistant to such prescriptions. Gilles Deleuze, for instance, deployed conceptual peripeteia and an incredulity toward essence to (re)found a metaphysics articulated through immanence over externality in which something like the world is an abstraction to be explained in its singularity.[10] Richard Rorty, by contrast, develops anti-foundationalism along a different tack by emphasizing a pragmatism primed to question power and knowledge without renouncing claims to objectivity or the pesky presence of some form of human subjectivity.[11] The contingency of world in such a schema is not the negation of praxis but the contingency that is its very possibility. These examples accentuate that world, worlding, and worldliness constitute and refract situated and historically specific knowledges, just as world philosophy has defamiliarized and provincialized European or "Enlightened" first principles. To a certain extent, however one defines post-philosophy, philosophy has posted the world as a central axis of regimes of truth. No longer a universal or universalist horizon, the world as concept is a vernacular of the philosophical, a doxa in determination, a referential tic, a citational convenience, rather than an epistemological ground. Or perhaps not.

The invocation of the world as a concept being more-than-every-day is paradoxically more pivotal now precisely because the ideational sutures of the Enlightenment have been defamiliarized within modernity's reach. Among the classic antinomies of modernity (including "Civilization and colonization?" as Aimé Césaire put it[12]), the prominence of an agonistic worldliness or cosmopolitanism, in a world that has canceled in advance all such dubious world historical projects, is simultaneously an economic, political, and cultural conundrum. With the fall of the Berlin Wall symbolizing the collapse of "actually existing socialism" thirty years ago and the "mission accomplished" polemics of Fukuyama on the end of history[13] providing an albeit revisionist imprimatur, the world famously imagined by Marx and Engels in the *Communist Manifesto* (strictly speaking, it is not *Welt* but "*aller länder*") has not united under the sign of workers but instead, within a discourse both polysemous and sutured, has emerged in the shadow of labor's other, capital, as a preeminent way to cognize the world. Deleuze and Rorty hardly confirm this world beyond world, yet, whether radical or liberal, the sustained decentering of Enlightenment thinking is not outside the production of globalization as both a completion of its project and as an announcement that Hegel's owl of Minerva can henceforth be imagined perhaps as some banal commodity, available for purchase on Amazon. Such is the phantasmagoria of world at dusk.

Fortunately, history remains at work in philosophy in numerous ways, as reborn, for instance, in Alain Badiou's rather hasty reading of the "Arab Spring,"[14] or as delayed in its disappearance in the further gyrations of Fukuyama. Similarly, for all the "flat world" economics of Thomas Friedman's critique,[15] the world of globalization seems only multiple and uneven, and interpellates troubled histories as fast as it wants to forget them (certainly the case with the aforementioned paths of colonialism). On the one hand, the genuflections of world are indeed not inconsistent with the wavering of capital as a global dominant; on the other, an invocation of history does not in itself make a philosophy of resistance to the worldly pretensions of capitalism. To think of Marxism in this wild conjunction is both obvious (given its critique of capitalism) and a baleful anachronism of modernity, as if confirming the limits of world as an analytic and heuristic.

Like the *Manifesto*, concepts of world literature attempt to see beyond the horizon, even if for the most part anthologies of world literature are mere extensions of the status quo, a kind of Western traditions plus, with a creeping Eurocentrism as a normative measure. Critics of world literature not only deconstruct the dubious inclusivity of the additive or accretionist model but also draw attention to the commodification instincts of the field, signaling that globalization has yet one more ally in the saturation of cultural exchange (the work of Pascale Casanova, Damrosch, and Emily Apter offer variations on this critique).[16] Aamir Mufti's *Forget English!* (whose rousing title has the sound of a manifesto) is very clear that the world of world literature is deeply problematic: "The ability to think 'the world' itself, whether in a literary-critical thinking or other discourses and practices, is hardly distributed equally across the world."[17] Apter's *Against World Literature* both questions the centrality of English and adds further nuance on the thorny questions of translations and translatability (although much more can be said on the politics and poetics of literary translation, as Lawrence Venuti has made clear[18]). Rebecca Walkowitz's *Born Translated* is a provocative rejoinder to such debates, not least because Walkowitz considers translation as internal to specific contemporary anglophone novels, which is a polemical dialogic of literary markets today.[19] For his part, Mufti sees world literature as an expression of institutional logic and priorities over and above some Goethean realization of literary excellence on a world scale. Rather than explicate each contribution on its own terms, it may be possible to mediate these interventions through "world" as an arena of struggle itself.

For instance, in their commentary on Walkowitz's innovative approach, Birgit Neumann and Gabriele Rippl note that "born translated" novels take up an alternative ontological stance before the world stage:

> These ontologies, one might argue, make creative use of literature's inevitable subsumption under the logic of capitalist globalisation; they confirm the logic of the market only to claim literature's difference from it. Hence, hovering between the translatable and the untranslatable, between the subordination to a market

and an unruly difference from it, the worlds of world literature generate a complexity and openness that transgresses the world construed through capitalist globalisation. The frequently disruptive polyvalency and affective intensity of mediating processes, we argue, defy containment in systems of economic exchange and circulatory movement.[20]

To some extent, this is a rationalization of the commodity conundrum since the line between the unruly and the subordinated cannot be adjudicated exclusively by the otherwise well-meaning and creative consciousness of the cosmopolitan author or critic. The "hovering," let us say, is overdetermined. Nevertheless, the ideas that being in the world can and should be polycentric and pluriversal places the philosophical disposition of world literature front and center in framing the logics and locutions of contemporary change.

Walkowitz suggests that because English-language writing is both a medium of expression and specifically mediates the global circulation of the literary in its hegemonic role in translation, it is very much part of what and how globalization represents. Reading Jamaica Kincaid and Mohsin Hamid, for instance, Walkowitz finds that globalization is internal to their novels as event and as story. Walkowitz thinks of this tense relationship to "enlargement" as a scale of extension (principally to that of the nation but also in terms of a European *Weltanschauung*). While "unimaginable enlargement" is rather baggy theoretically, it does at least indicate that scale is at stake in a global imaginary, even as that might be thought of as an intensification of ontological possibility in the sense that Neumann and Rippl infer.

What is more interesting is the processes of world-making at stake, keeping in mind that this cancels through both aesthetic activity and the abstractions of the world market. In the *Manifesto*, Marx and Engels celebrate the revolutionary capacities of the bourgeoisie—its technological prowess (in what was then the Industrial Revolution) was a marvel of transformative activity, all in the cause of accumulation and value extraction. The *Manifesto* also details the massive contradictions this engenders, not least between the classes who otherwise hold the structural components of the economic regime in place. Economic systems are historical and as such are "born" both transforming and transformable. It is the very dynamism of capitalism that accentuates the antinomies of its historical demands. If "all that is solid melts into air" before it, capitalism yet shapes the very forces that challenge the density of its presence. If it is global, the thinking goes, its "gravediggers" will also walk the world stage. It is clear, however, that much depends upon the precise contours of the world constructed, rather than an abstract world to which all roads teleologically lead. Here, the nature of the manifesto as genre works against the complex dynamic of world-making the *Communist Manifesto* otherwise addresses. The unity of the proletariat, for example, is presented as a demand, as an imperative that elides the nuance Marx brings elsewhere to his distinctions between foundational and moving contradictions. Globality might be emergent in the 1840s, but emergency decrees spontaneous consciousness. The Goethean lesson in the *Manifesto* about world literature is that it signifies a process of becoming, the becoming of common property, but the political exigency short-circuits the conditions of cultural exchange and must assume a completed historical development in the absence of its concrete particularity. Manifestos are about desire: practicality is for handbooks.

Yet, if world-making is often discontinuous with the conditions of the world as such, the story of world literature is not beyond claiming worlds beyond the real of cultural exchange. Pundits of world literature in the present sometimes sound like a key figure of the *Manifesto*: "the sorcerer who is no longer able to control the powers of the nether world whom he has called up by his spells."[21] This very volume is a symptom of such wild magic. True, critics of world literature can sound like magicians merely of a different stripe, particularly when the transhistorical trumps the transnational as a condition of possibility. The distinctiveness of the project, however, is much more than globality by design, or a worlding that is simply a socioeconomic reflex (which is precisely the conceptual difficulty of its invocation in the *Manifesto*). Pheng Cheah's casting of world literature in *What Is a World?* maintains a meticulous "ethicopolitical horizon" that is highly suspicious of all this talk of systems of exchange and circulation as too much capitalist unconscious and not enough normative claim-making. As a philosophical intervention, Cheah's argument moves like Derrida's from phenomenology as worlding to ethics, a postcolonial space (given the literature discussed as world literature) in which the gift, for instance, is never innocent (on this subject, we share an interest in the work of Nuruddin Farah, the Somali novelist[22]). The advantage of Cheah's claims for world literature rests chiefly in beginning with "world" as concept rather than as a spatial reality, and, just like here, this can produce initially alarming anachronisms (cf. "world spirit"). His book, by contrast, is a veritable anti-manifesto, a "to-come," as Cheah puts it, "devoid of determinate promises." In fact, I would argue, this is the communist claim to world literature lost to generic compulsions, yet perhaps one lest beholden to "irreducible openness" as its own reward. Thus, while I would agree that "for Marx, the world is a normative category that exceeds the world market,"[23] world revolution, as its subsumption, is not only normative, but it is also how the world is made anew.

The proof of Cheah's argument, and many others in and around world literature, is that globalization really is a different world, a world of economic calculation, geopolitical maneuvers, rational exploitation, and high-speed transactions (the Amazon of literature rather than the world of the literary). If literature enables us to encounter absolute otherness, globalization has never found an "other" it could not commodify absolutely. If literature resolutely challenges its own boundaries, then globalization resolves to break borders (or harden them) by the millisecond. Literature is a passionately complex pact between writer and reader; globalization is the metric that can sell that as advertising space. If world literature specializations, institutes, research labs, and departments are inculcations of the market, or "sponsored content," few doubt what alienating concept of global integration is responsible for the banalization of the worlding at stake, and in English. Of course, this is a caricature of the difference in worlds (like, "Just MOOC it"), but, as I have tried to suggest so far, it is a logical element of the *Manifesto* that such difference must be thought simultaneously—it is the way in which, to borrow from the Marx's *Eighteenth Brumaire*, "the content exceeds the phrase."[24]

To think the world in this way does not accord with Goethe's extension of a nation paradigm to international exchange in any formal way, but its allegorical presence in the *Manifesto* speaks to the conditions of the "Spring of Nations" that took place the year of the *Manifesto*'s publication, in which the revolutionary phrasing squashed the content by following the past, not negating it. The logic of the *Manifesto* offers world literature to a future elided by the 1848 revolutions, but mostly for good historical reasons (the triumph of reactionaries was not outside this process). Thinking the irreconcilable in this way is obviously a key to dialectical materialism (with the psychoanalytic aura of "fail again, fail better" that Slavoj Zizek invokes[25]) and here suggests a troubled and troubling consanguinity between world literature and the critique of globalization. There are at least three paths that knot, philosophically, within the *Manifesto*'s challenge that sign a futurity for literature its present world undoes in a ruse of flattening. I mention these as indications of the *Manifesto*'s content reaching beyond the subsequent theorization or phrasing often deemed Marxist philosophy within actually existing socialism, yet without wishing away the historical processes involved. The first of these is the Trotsky commentary on combined and uneven development redeployed by the Warwick Research Collective (WReC) in its analysis of world literature.[26] On one level, the approach forwards a basic strategy for reading anomalous history against a will to homogeneity. This not only indicates an unevenness between globalization and world literature as referents, but also a certain disjunction within the literary concerns proposed—global literature as an extension of postcolonial literature; world literature as an extension of comparative literature. The collective reads such rearticulation as comparable to an earlier event of disciplinary crisis around the place of English Studies (a genealogy that weaves its way to the present), but the pivot of the polemic rests at a second level, namely, the disquieting simultaneity of combined and uneven development as a socioeconomic expression of the archaic in and alongside the new with world literature and modernism. If *Combined and Uneven Development* inevitably registers the twilight of comparative and postcolonial literary methods in its approach, the difficulty of its dialectics is in demystifying the tangled lineaments of the world system, one in which the oddly parochial concerns of world literature are an unquiet measure of contradictions at a world scale.

WReC does rather more with the Trotsky intervention on economic disjunction than it does on the weight of the *Welt* that finds Goethe in the *Manifesto*. The fractured dimensionality of the latter offers an alternative trajectory that is further complicated by the *Weltanschauung* at stake in interpretation. For instance, Martin Puchner's *Poetry of the Revolution* forwards a critique of the *Manifesto* (and manifestos in general) that positions the revolutionary spirit of the *Communist Manifesto* in the genre of the manifesto itself. While this depends to a degree on a misreading of Marx's Eleventh Thesis on Feuerbach, Puchner nevertheless provides a strong argument for the *Manifesto*'s literary prescience and its dissemination and influence as an exemplary world literature. Of particular note is the emphasis on subsequent avant-gardism, which is distinct in Lenin from the adumbration of vanguardism, with the proviso that radical aesthetics has often struggled to do more than shock the bourgeoisie. If anything, the familiar tussle of art and revolution is in step with WReC's exegesis, yet Puchner's use of uneven development also notes its limits, an uneven unevenness, that fails to register adequately the influence of manifestos in other spaces and places. Few Marxists would disagree with the major premises, that the superstructure is not some passive space of infrastructural determination, or that the *Manifesto* establishes a powerful literary genre. Even the sneaking suspicion that the *Manifesto* participates in the bourgeois world literature it invokes does not grate, since the troubled process of subsumption is a central thesis of the document as a whole. The bridge to our third element, the rational kernel, lies in Puchner's further extrapolation from Goethe: "The translator is a prophet [as Puchner notes, Goethe's assumption about the Koran is its own mistranslation], but also a businessman. In fact, the marketplace and translation depend on one another" and that, as a transaction, "world literature traffics not in sameness but in difference."[27] Crucially, as Puchner points out, what Goethe deploys to extend and defend the nation Marx and Engels invoke to undermine its autonomy. The global market, they assert, will produce a universal interdependence very much in the image of capital circulation, and therefore a cosmopolitanism with concrete contradictions. For the literary critic, it is a relatively easy leap from this to the idea that translation, or the literary, are forms of equivalence, but "world money," as Marx terms it, has a specific meaning in the alchemy of the value form and the form of the commodity. Thus, translation is an important part of worlding under capital, but it is an instance of equivalence, not the essence of capital as relation. It is this logic that is immanent to the worlding of literature the *Manifesto* interpellates. How?

While the writers of the *Manifesto* believed the revolution to be imminent, it is the specter of failure that haunts its original impress. Marx's revenge was to theorize the failure of the revolutions in 1848 through a long-term critique of political economy. *Capital* does not exhort labor to lose its chains but elaborates the ways in which capital as relation produces that possibility.[28] To a certain extent, we could argue that the notion of world literature in the early document persists in the later one, both as an example of a work that circulates globally beyond its country of origin and as a text that attempts to interlink diverse subjectivities in time and space. In the *Manifesto*, the keyword in the reference to world literature is *Verkehr*, which is rendered as "intercourse" in the standard English translation but encompasses traffic, transport, circulation, communication, and contact. Indeed, the latter, adapting the work of Mary Louise Pratt,[29] offers intercourse more specifically as a "contact zone," one that is not just a geographical reference but is more importantly a conceptual space, a philosophical condition of exchange. What Marx in particular is thinking about is how productive forces are generalized and, again with the merit of scandal, world literature exists as a developmental symptom. Unalloyed *Verkehr*, of course, can easily turn the generalized into the generalization, but this owes less to that tendency to make world literature anthologies baggier and more to the connotative exuberance of "world." The multivalence of *Verkehr* is further fragmented by the wanton vagaries of world, a flattener (very much in the sense of Thomas Friedman's diagnosis) that can render obscure the material force of circulation Marx has in mind. Part of the success of the *Manifesto* in its genre is *Verkehr* as generalizable; much of the limits of world literature persist in the floating and flaunting signification of "world." Yet the impasse in the latter keeps alive the specter of contradiction in the former and the struggle over what would constitute a "unity" in their otherwise rudimentary embrace. The dialectic here is not necessarily in the tension between materialism and idealism since *Verkehr* and *Welt* easily mediate both in their profusion. The rational kernel persists in the objective conditions that concretize the worlds of circulation as a whole. And this is now where the *Manifesto* meets globalization.

On the face of it, globalization permits the reification and commodification of literature as never before. When Marx and Engels note "In place of the old local and national seclusion and self-sufficiency, we have intercourse in every direction, universal inter-dependence of nations,"[30] surely this is an inkling of the demon of globalization rushing in from the future (alongside the specter that begins the *Manifesto*)? And, in another measure of prescience, is this not simultaneously comparative literature's world literature, "*el demonio de las comparaciones*," that Benedict Anderson refigures from José Rizal as "the specter of comparisons"?[31] The literary is preternaturally inclined to slip the homologies of commodity lore, but one would be forgiven for thinking that any nuance in its philosophy ultimately melts into the air of exchange value. Nevertheless, just as the expansion and intensification of commerce facilitates a consciousness of its negation, so would it be incautious to think that all of the business of world literature, the institutes, the publishing series, the prizes, or the Harvard University "Masterpieces of World Literature" (a MOOC, conceived by Damrosch and Puchner) simply confirm the right to commodify rather than stimulate alternatives to its embrace. In the twenty years since Franco Moretti discerned "conjectures" in world literature, the question of methodologies in the articulation of world literature has deepened, and Moretti's own, "distant reading" has been appreciably influential in such reconstellation. Leaving aside Moretti's contention that Marx did not see the literary world system as unequal (and yet used it in a polemic about inequality?), the philosophical sutures of distant reading, a condition of knowledge, are evolutionary in spirit, especially regarding the rise and dissemination of the novel. Here, the contact zone is modernity, and globalization (of the literary, etc.) is an evolutionary epiphenomenon. Pertinently, Moretti provides new interpretive metaphors for such systematicity: "Trees and branches are what nation states do; waves are what markets do … cultural history is made of trees and waves. … This, then, is the basis for the division of labor between national and world literature: national literature, for people who see trees; world literature, for people who see waves."[32] The metaphors are attached to scale and process and work incredibly well—rootedness for the local, flows for the transnational, and so on. Could we not say, however, that at the heart of a materialist critique is whether the distinctions above can be historically maintained and under what conditions the unevenness and inequality (tellingly in Moretti's polemic the term is "division of labor") is the ground for further interrelation?

Manfred B. Steger's "very short introduction" to globalization attempts a "very short definition": "Globalization is about growing worldwide interconnectivity,"[33] of which the volume and the Oxford University series (over five hundred titles in forty-five languages) are a very symptom. World literature shares this symptom and project, but each connection provides cultural questions (which languages, what translations, what forms and genres, etc.?). In a very short, introductory way, Marx and Engels's *Manifesto* encourages similar interconnectivity, but ultimately the logic of the genre eschews the reference points, if not the same temporal coordinates. Beyond the basic similarities, the scalar desire in all three (globalization, world literature, and communism) can only be contradictory, which, as noted, is the philosophical knot and more that Marxism seeks to fathom. The communism offered in the *Manifesto* is itself highly particularized (the original title, *Manifesto of the Communist Party*, provides a hint in that regard). The basic point is that the medium of the call to communism is in keeping with what the authors believe is the emerging world literature sanctioned by Goethe. That idea of world literature is a historical document, perhaps like the communist idea itself. Could world literature unite when the workers could not on a world scale?

One of the preferred ways in which globalization is measured economically is by comparing the market cap of mega transnational corporations (TNCs) with the flipside of their modernity, the gross domestic product (GDP) of individual nation states. As of May 2019, for instance, Apple had a market capitalization greater than each of 183 out of 199 countries for which the World Bank currently has available GDP data. Again, this is a particular version of globalization, one hinged on the neoliberal nostrums of the "free" market, yet this in itself accentuates the degree to which workers have unified on balance sheets in a way that they have not done or no longer do in parties for the most part, or extant communist states. The data signal not so much an eclipse of nations and their sovereignty but a reconfiguration of their role within globalization (free market enforcers, rent as profit facilitators, labor managers, class containers, etc.). The wealthiest, as Warren Buffett reminds us, know their class is winning and are quite willing to end all (other) forms of capitalism to secure the world in their image. If selling things will not do it, networking them might. If you cannot monopolize world literature, at least do your best to privatize the general intellect on which it based. If growth rates shrink, financialize the remaining fractions. Indeed, skip labor and its surplus value and emphasize M-M' instead. This is the world still to win.

To the extent that world literature offers to unify the globe it might seem closer to capitalist integration rather than communist possibility. This is the *Manifesto*'s initial acknowledgement, for world literature is invoked within the same process of political economy that Marx and Engels outline. The relevance of the *Manifesto* today chiefly rests there, in providing a picture of economic dynamism with cultural correlatives that continues to saturate species being. Alternatively, one could argue that, however expansive our definition of literature, both world literature and the politics of the *Manifesto* are simply out of step with the major modes of integration and opposition to the same in the world system. In a world where transgression is incorporated and oppression is monetized, even quoting the *Manifesto* is more like a lifestyle niche than a portent of great change. At the philosophical level, the *Manifesto* (and, indeed, the earlier *German Ideology*) confronts the mysticism, obscurantism, and idealism of German thought at the time by beginning its diagnosis and critique with the material reality of human beings as they collectively make that reality. It is from this basis that metaphysics, for instance, can be challenged. It is undeniable that the necessities of the genre tend to radically reduce the philosophical intricacy of thinking global change in the *Manifesto* but, as I have indicated, the generalizable is not without value, even if isolating individual elements of globalization certainly illuminates the structural logic in play. If the call for world literature to unite underlines rather than overcomes the limits to workers of the world doing the same, the lesson is salutary rather than a philosophical solution to the pitfalls of any "mondialisation" in Jean-Luc Nancy's terms.[34] The heuristic concerns the struggle of imagination and consciousness at work within and against the reification of *Verkehr* in contemporary capitalism. There must be, necessarily, better works of world literature than the *Communist Manifesto* (even if it can now be read as a graphic novel). There is certainly a hunger for manifestos that take seriously the radical genealogy that the 1848 pamphlet initiates. One thinks here of the *Chapo House Guide to Revolution*, *Feminism for the 99%*, *The Socialist Manifesto*, *#Accelerate Manifesto*, and occasional works by The Invisible Committee, among many others.[35] For its part, the unity the *Manifesto* calls for remains spectral and the common good it invokes is radically specific. Its philosophy is not its material force, but the connection it makes between crisis and worldliness, between contradictions on a world scale and the prospects of a consciousness that would want to transform the world itself. Therefore, it is a philosophy that not just participates in the world of world literature but also poses the question of its superadequation, even if, or precisely because, the phrasing today necessarily goes beyond the phrases of the requisite subject, literature, and world imagined.

Notes

1 David Damrosch, *How to Read World Literature* (London: Wiley, 2009), 125.
2 See Susan Buck-Morss, *Dream World and Catastrophe* (Cambridge: MIT Press, 2000).
3 See Jacques Derrida, "Globalization, Peace, and Cosmopolitanism," in *Negotiations: Interventions and Interviews, 1971–2001*, ed. E. Rottenberg (Stanford: Stanford UP, 2002), 371–86.
4 See Karl Marx and Friedrich Engels, *The German Ideology* (New York: Martino Fine Books, 2011).
5 See Karl Marx, "On The Jewish Question," *Marx-Engels Archive*, https://www.marxists.org/archive/marx/works/1844/jewish-question/.
6 Johann Wolfgang von Goethe, "Conversations with Eckermann on Weltliteratur," trans. John Oxenford, in *World Literature in Theory*, ed. David Damrosch (London: Wiley, 2014), 16.
7 Sean Gaston, *The Concept of World from Kant to Derrida* (London: Rowman & Littlefield, 2013).
8 Karl Marx and Friedrich Engels, *The Communist Manifesto*, introduction by Eric Hobsbawm (New York: Verso, 2012), 39.
9 See Peter Hitchcock, *Labor in Culture; or, Worker of the World(s)* (London: Palgrave, 2017).
10 See Gilles Deleuze and Félix Guattari, *What Is Philosophy?* (New York: Columbia UP, 1994).
11 See Richard Rorty, *Contingency, Irony, and Solidarity* (Cambridge: Cambridge UP, 1989).

12 See Aimé Césaire, *Discourse on Colonialism*, trans. J. Pinkham (New York: Monthly Review Press, 2000).
13 See Francis Fukuyama, *The End of History and the Last Man* (New York: Free Press, 1992).
14 See Alain Badiou, *The Rebirth of History* (London: Verso, 2012).
15 See Thomas Friedman, *The World Is Flat* (New York: Farrar, Straus and Giroux, 2005).
16 See Pascale Casanova, *The World Republic of Letters*, trans. M. B. DeBevoise (Cambridge: Harvard UP, 2004); David Damrosch, *What Is World Literature?* (Princeton: Princeton UP, 2003); and Emily Apter, *Against World Literature* (New York: Verso, 2013).
17 Aamir Mufti, *Forget English! Orientalisms and World Literatures* (Cambridge: Harvard UP, 2016), 10.
18 See Lawrence Venuti, *The Translator's Invisibility: A History of Translation* (New York: Routledge, [1995] 2008).
19 See Rebecca Walkowitz, *Born Translated: The Contemporary Novel in the Age of World Literature* (New York: Columbia UP, 2015).
20 Birgit Neumann and Gabriele Rippl, "Anglophone World Literatures: Introduction," *Anglia* 135.1 (2017): 12.
21 Marx and Engels, *Communist Manifesto*, 41.
22 Peter Hitchcock, *The Long Space: Transnationalism and Postcolonial Form* (Stanford: Stanford UP, 2010), 90–139.
23 Pheng Cheah, *What Is a World?: On Postcolonial Literature as World Literature* (Durham, NC: Duke UP, 2016), 2.
24 Karl Marx, *The Eighteenth Brumaire of Louis Napoleon*, trans. Saul K. Padover (New York: Create Space, 2015), 20.
25 See Slavoj Zizek, "How to Begin from the Beginning," *New Left Review* (May/June 2009): 43–55.
26 See Warwick Research Collective (WReC), *Combined and Uneven Development: Towards a New Theory of World Literature* (Liverpool: Liverpool UP, 2015).
27 See Martin Puchner, *Poetry of the Revolution: Marx, Manifestos, and the Avant Gardes* (Princeton: Princeton UP, 2006), 50.
28 See Karl Marx, *Capital (Three Volumes)*, trans. Ben Fowkes (London: Penguin, 1992).
29 See Mary Louise Pratt, *Imperial Eyes: Travel Writing and Transculturation* (London: Routledge, 2007).
30 Marx and Engels, *Communist Manifesto*, 39.
31 See Benedict Anderson, *The Spectre of Comparisons* (New York: Verso, 1998).
32 Franco Moretti, "Conjectures on World Literature," *New Left Review* 1 (2000): 62.
33 Manfred B. Steger, *Globalization: A Very Short Introduction* (Oxford: Oxford UP, 2017), 17.
34 Jean-Luc Nancy, *The Creation of the World: Or Globalization*, trans. Francois Raffoul and David Pettigrew (Binghamton: SUNY Press, 2007).
35 See Chapo Trap House, *The Chapo House Guide to Revolution* (New York: Touchstone, 2018); Cynzia Arruzza, Tithi Bhattacharya, and Nancy Fraser, *Feminism for the 99%* (New York: Verso, 2019); Bhaskar Sunkara, *The Socialist Manifesto* (New York: Basic Books, 2019); and Alex Williams and Nick Srnicek, *#Accelerate Manifesto* (Mexico City: Gato Negro Ediciones, 2013). The Invisible Committee have published three titles: *The Coming Insurrection* (Los Angeles: Semiotext(e), 2009), *To Our Friends* (Los Angeles: Semiotext(e), 2015), and *Now* (Los Angeles: Semiotext(e), 2017).

8

Transatlantic Thoreau: Henry S. Salt, Gandhi, and British Humanitarian Socialism

David M. Robinson

The American Poet-Naturalist

As Henry David Thoreau's reputation slowly emerged in the nineteenth century, he was recognized in the United States primarily as the poet of the New England landscape, the writer who had found the region's forests, mountains, and rivers a source of inexhaustible revelation. He ironically explained that "I have traveled a good deal in Concord," emphasizing constancy to a place rather than wide exploration as the source of wisdom.[1] Not a widely popular author in his day, his reputation rested principally on *Walden*, but in the early 1860s, near the end of his life, he was able to edit and publish his lecture materials into a series of essays for the prestigious *Atlantic Monthly*. In "Walking" and "Wild Apples," works based on his philosophical excursions over the countryside, he furthered his building persona of the "poet-naturalist," the knower and teacher of nature.[2]

Walter Harding noted that Thoreau's growing reputation as a master of informed and reflective outdoor observations "coincided with the end of the frontier and the great upsurge of interest in nature essays," but this identity "tended to emphasize Thoreau's nature writings at the expense of his social criticism."[3] Thoreau's identity as the poet-naturalist was also the product of the American publishing industry and its rapid expansion in the middle and late nineteenth century. Lawrence Buell traced the key role that Houghton Mifflin played in the advancement of Thoreau's recognition, describing "Thoreau's canonization as a marketing event."[4] Houghton kept *Walden* in print, brought out a series of seasonal selections from his *Journal*, and in 1906 published a fourteen-volume *Journal*, making him "the first American person of letters to have his diary published in full."[5] Houghton thereby nourished the American readership by building "the image of an emerging canon of literary nature writing with Thoreau at its head."[6] Thoreau was, in a sense, an American product, linked closely to a national cultural reverence for a previously unspoiled wilderness that was now slowly disappearing. The socially dissenting Thoreau, generally overlooked in the United States, came into focus instead in England, where Henry S. Salt and Edward Carpenter took Thoreau's portrait of a simple and natural life as a badly needed example for late Victorian Britain.

Salt, Carpenter, and British Transcendentalism

Both Salt and Carpenter were active proponents of the rapidly emerging British socialist movement in the 1880s. Salt had a well-to-do background and an Eton education, but his inclination to escape the narrow bounds of respectability grew during his continuing studies at King's College, Cambridge. It was there that Salt developed a strong friendship with James Leigh Joynes and met his sister Kate Joynes, who married Salt in 1879.[7] Salt and James Joynes embraced socialism at the staid King's, as Salt later explained: "I think we were brought together by our common impatience of the petty routine and respectability then dominant at King's; a system well calculated to make rebels and freethinkers." Resisting the Cambridge system together seemed to solidify their friendship and set them both on a path to nonconformity. "Our friendship was a mutual alliance against the Respectables, pursued with a youthful regardlessness of consequences which, looking back, I feel to have been highly beneficial. While reading very hard on our own lines, we were guilty of every species of 'bad form.'"[8]

After completing their academic work at Cambridge, both returned to teach at Eton, where James and Kate's father served as an assistant master. At Eton, they continued their development as radicals, adding vegetarianism to their list of offenses, and engaging in the socialist campaigns of the era. Joynes, greatly influenced by Henry George, was the most politically inclined of the two, and published *The Socialist Catechism* in 1884, a notable guide to socialist principles in the form of Christian dogma.[9] It was through Joynes that Salt met many of the influential young socialists and radicals, including William Jess Jupp, Henry Hyndman, George Bernard Shaw, and Edward Carpenter.[10] Carpenter, who formed a lifelong friendship with both Henry and Kate Salt, shared Henry's for literature and introduced him to Thoreau's *Walden*, a book that would restructure Salt's life.

Carpenter, an intense and discerning thinker, was an ardent socialist and a disciple of Walt Whitman. "From that time forward," he wrote of his first reading of Whitman's poetry, "a profound change set in within me."[11] Developing a theory of "homogenic attachment," his explanatory term for same-sex attraction and love, Carpenter became a leading theorist and advocate for the understanding and social acceptance of homosexuality, connecting this needed alteration of social norms with the range of radical issues emerging in late-nineteenth-century Britain.[12] Like Salt and Joynes, Carpenter was Cambridge educated and had brief stints in the ministry and a university extension lecturer. An inheritance from his father freed him to buy land and have a house built "in the style of the local farms" in Derbyshire in 1883.[13] Millthorpe, as he named it, was a central part of Carpenter's utopian attempt at realizing a more liberated and perfected society, "a prophetic vision of an ideal future," as Michael Robertson has shown.[14] Carpenter's essay on "Simplification of Life" extolled country living as a way of escaping restrictive conventional artificialities, focusing on household economy and the refusal of conventional luxuries as the key to a satisfying life "with as little labor and effort as may be."[15] He provided practical details on the cost of rural life, concluding that one could live well in the country on much less money than expected by prudent economizing and careful avoidance of splurges. "Moderation is the best general rule" for eating, he advised, cautioning that this rule must also "be varied by an occasional orgy."[16] Carpenter also pointed to one critical barrier to the achievement of just and satisfying life in modern society. The "whole matter hangs," he wrote, on "the question of women's work. Woman is a slave, and *must remain so* as long as our present domestic system is maintained." Such reform will meet resistance, even perhaps from many women, he acknowledged; the change "may have to come nevertheless."[17]

Carpenter's "Simplification of Life" began with an epigraph from *Walden* and developed as an expanded English version of Thoreau's condemnation of luxuries as barriers to meaningful living. However, Thoreau cannot claim credit for Carpenter's rural experiment. "Just about the very day I got into my new house and onto my plot of land—the realization of the plotting and scheming of some years—that book [*Walden*] fell into my hands, which took the bottom out of my little bucket."[18] After reading it, he confessed, "I felt that I had aimed at a natural life and completely failed." Even so, the book was of great value: "It helped, I must confess, to make me uncomfortable for some years."[19] Carpenter's testimony illustrates the dynamic interaction between his individualist social critique and the already simmering socialist unrest in Britain of the 1880s.

Carpenter and Salt were in this sense the transcendentalists of English socialism, with Salt the leading English proponent of Thoreau and Carpenter the greatest of Whitman's English disciples. Salt and Carpenter had absorbed the socially engaged romanticism that had rebounded across the Atlantic from the Emerson and his disciples, who themselves had been ignited by Coleridge and Carlyle.[20] In the hands of Thoreau and Whitman, romanticism was transformed into radical purpose. Salt and Carpenter welcomed transcendentalism as liberating critique of a corrupted and suffocating social order.[21] Salt's growing fascination with Thoreau, augmented by Carpenter's example, led him to leave his post at Eton in 1884 and move to a cottage in Tilford, Surrey, a liberating decision that launched a half-century of writing and activism. "Henry Salt was one of the first who tried to live out Carpenter's ideas about the simple life," Sheila Rowbotham noted.[22]

Thoreau among the Socialists

Soon after moving to Tilford, Salt published a sketch of Thoreau in *Justice*, the journal of the Social Democratic Federation, the first of the socialist organizations emerging in Britain. Salt later commented that socialism was "in its early and romantic stage, when the Social Democratic Federation was becoming a terror to the well-to-do."[23] Writing for a progressive readership, Salt introduced Thoreau as the most eloquent of "those American writers who have denounced the anomalies and tyranny of transatlantic government and society."[24] He "deserves to be attentively studied by every social reformer," Salt asserted, even though he was "not a professed Socialist." His importance arose from the "intensity of moral purpose and high literary power" of *Walden*, the "record of a very interesting experiment in practical life." Salt linked Thoreau to the principles and interest of socialists, finding in *Walden* the same sense of alienated restlessness that was driving his colleagues. He presented Thoreau's pragmatic approach to new beginnings at the pond as a symbol of a changed society. Thoreau's attention to the absolute necessities of life, with the "Socialist calculations" that support it, proved "how little labour is sufficient to support mankind." While he did not directly engage "the great social problem," in part because of his remote life in Concord, "on many points Thoreau's opinions will commend themselves to all Socialists."[25]

The next year, Salt published a more substantial essay on Thoreau for a broader audience, an article that would not only advance Thoreau's reputation but also contribute significantly to Salt's literary stature in England. "Henry David Thoreau" appeared in a November 1886 issue of *Temple Bar*, a monthly that vied with *Cornhill* in the thriving London magazine market.[26] Salt described Thoreau as "a young enthusiast who had declared open war against custom and society." This dissenter, "preaching a crusade against every sort of luxury and self-indulgence," is "one of the most remarkable and original characters that America has yet produced."[27] Salt's skillfully crafted portrait of this unique and fascinating American emphasized Thoreau's stubbornly principled resistance to thoughtless routine and praised his ethical insight. Salt's essay was, in many ways, an homage to the liberating principles that he himself had adopted.

Salt was an admirer of Thoreau's naturalist work, but in this essay he stressed Thoreau's rebellious nonconformity. He characterized Thoreau as neither a recluse nor a misty nature poet but an exacting social critic, who assailed the cultural norms that stood in the way of "the blessings of a simple and healthful life."[28] Like the ancient Stoics, Thoreau offered "ceaseless protest against all kinds of luxury and superfluous comforts," and most importantly, "he did not merely *talk* of Arcadian simplicity." Through his Walden experiment, he "carried his theories into practical effect."[29] He compared Thoreau to the outspoken John Ruskin, "a castigator of the faults of modern civilization and artificial society," and suggested that Thoreau "occupies in America a position very similar to that of Ruskin in England." Like Ruskin, he does not "yield homage to the supremacy of the nineteenth century," even showing the audacity to criticize "the Telegraph and Post Office."[30]

This portrayal of Thoreau's character and message was closely linked to Salt's emerging philosophical creed of Humanitarianism, the term he would use to define his values and commitments in the coming decades. While Thoreau exemplified these principles in many ways, Salt recognized that he must explain the "harsh and cynical expressions about mankind" that one can effortlessly find in *Walden*. "In heart he was at all times thoroughly kindly and sympathetic," Salt noted.[31] Thoreau's ringing support of abolitionism and his "enthusiastic admiration for the heroes of the anti-slavery agitation" were signs of his deep concerns for his brothers and sisters in humanity. "Thoreau could not be called a Socialist," but he had championed democratic and anti-colonial reform, condemning of "the iniquitous attack which the United States were then making on Mexico" and continuing in later essays to express his "detestation of the system of slavery."[32] Salt called particular attention to "Civil Disobedience" as a demonstration of "a vigorous protest," that confronted the government "in the person of its tax-collector."[33] Thoreau's nonviolent resistance to injustice, described in his narrative of his July 1846 night in jail, represented an innovative strategy of reformist activism, the "withdrawal of [one's] allegiance to the State."[34] With such an act, Thoreau identified the standing government, in whatever form, as the ultimate purveyor of evil and thus the force that must be resisted.

Thoreau's ethical stance on public questions was crucial to Salt. Thoreau's American biographers, he wrote, had "scarcely mentioned" his memorably expressed "humanitarian views."[35] His antislavery belief was part of a wider respect for all other beings. "Indeed he has a just claim to be considered one of the leaders of the great humanitarian movement of this century, his sympathy with the lower animals bring the most extraordinary features of his character."[36] As Emerson remembered, "snakes coiled round his leg; the fishes swam into his hand, and he took them out of the water; he pulled the woodchuck out of its hole by the tail, and took the foxes under his protection from the hunters."[37] This wizardly closeness to other living creatures, however exaggerated by Emerson, elicited deep reverence in Salt. Thoreau's enlightened respect and reverence for animals made him the "nearest in modern times to that sense of perfect brotherhood and sympathy with all innocent creatures" exhibited by St. Francis.[38] These principles of goodwill included not only vegetarianism but also the outlawing of all forms of animal abuse and the misuse of animals in both labor and sporting events. His conception of humanitarianism reached beyond the human to embrace a sense of kinship with other living creatures, a recognition and protective affirmation of their stature as conscious and feeling beings.

Thoreau was, however, neither a vegetarian nor a pacifist. He described fishing at the pond as an important source of food during his stay there. Frustrated by a woodchuck's damage to his bean-field, he actually cooked and ate the creature, as Salt himself notes. Salt responded deeply, however, to the meditative passages in which Thoreau looked ahead to a life based on a higher spirituality that would displace the human instinct to hunt. These moments, discussed in detail in the "Higher Laws" chapter of *Walden*, set Thoreau apart as a prophet of a future society regenerating itself through its embrace of the principle of kinship. Thoreau offered a considered assurance that men and women would inevitably rise to a higher state of understanding in which vegetarianism would replace the eating of meat. The principle of kinship would prevail. "I have no doubt that it is a part of the destiny of the human race, in its gradual improvement, to leave off eating animals, as surely as the savage tribes have left off eating each other when they came in contact with the more civilized."[39] Civilization is of course a term now under critique, but Edward Carpenter too was struggling with this problematic concept in the 1880s when he wrote *Civilisation: Its Cause and Cure*.[40] For Thoreau and Salt, as well as Carpenter, civilization was meant to describe a nonviolent society, free of class and economic oppression—a yet-to-be attained, but nevertheless possible, human future. Recognizing ironically the glacial pace of human ethical advance, Salt would eventually entitle his 1921 autobiography *Seventy Years among the Savages*.[41]

Vegetarianism and Animal Rights

In 1886, the year that Salt published his groundbreaking essay on Thoreau, he brought out *A Plea for Vegetarianism*, a collection of brief essays that bore witness to both the hardships and rewards of undertaking a vegetarian life. "A vegetarian," he wrote, "is still regarded, in ordinary society, as little better than a madman." One who takes up vegetarianism "will soon find that his friends and acquaintances look at him with strange and wondering eyes."[42] Vegetarianism produced a particularly strong social resistance because of numerous misconceptions about its impact on health and, more deeply, a lurking dread of having to confront the morally outrageous viciousness of eating animals. Salt explained that the "first and most obvious advantage of a vegetarian diet is its economy."[43] He moved from this pragmatic point, however, to the ethical argument that eating meat is undeniably "cruel towards animals" and thus "degrading to men" who perform their cruel acts only for their physical satisfaction. Such a practice "is revolting to all the higher instincts of the human mind."[44] Following the logic of his defense of vegetarianism, Salt became the foremost proponent of Animal Rights nineteenth-century Britain. He published *Animals' Rights: Considered in Relation to Social Progress* in 1892, a book recognized as a pivotal text on the ethical questions of the human treatment of animals. "Every time I re-read Salt's book—and I have now read it several times—I marvel at how he anticipates almost every point discussed in the contemporary debate over animal rights," Peter Singer wrote in 1980, in a preface to a republication by Singer of Salt's *Animals' Rights*.[45] Salt's book now seems contemporary because he held humans and other animals to be of the same natural origins. If men and women were worthy of rights, so were animals. "Our main principle is now clear," he argued. "If 'rights' exist at all—and both feeling and usage indubitably prove that they do exist—they cannot be consistently awarded to men and denied to animals, since the same sense of justice and compassion apply in both cases."[46]

Salt and Humanitarianism

As his work continued into the 1890s, Salt recognized that socialism in its purely economic sense was only part of a larger part of a critique of conventional society, or of civilization as he knew it. His most noteworthy political undertaking was his leadership in the establishment of the Humanitarian League in 1891, an organization that would advocate "an intelligible and consistent principle of humaneness—that it is iniquitous to inflict suffering, directly or indirectly, on any sentient being, except when self-defense or absolute necessity can be justly pleaded."[47] Salt and his colleagues conceived of the League as an umbrella for the range of reforms that pertained both to human and animal protections. It was intended "to proclaim a *general* principle of humaneness, as underlying the various disconnected efforts, and to show that though the several societies were necessarily working on separate lines, they were nevertheless inspired and united by a single bond of fellowship."[48] In his informative history of the Humanitarian League, Dan Weinbren described it as "a London-based radical pressure group," whose range of concerns included such issues as prison reform, humane diet and dress, animal welfare including opposition to inhumane sporting, and humanitarian issues in India, where the League had a branch in Bombay.[49]

Salt established the philosophical groundings of Humanitarianism as "nothing more and nothing less than the study and practice of humane principles—of compassion, love, gentleness, and universal benevolence."[50] While he argued that the principle of compassion was "intuitive," his use of the term differed significantly from that of Emerson and the transcendentalists, who had posited a religiously based innate connection to divinity.[51] Describing "two diverse and antagonistic impulses in the human mind, one prompting to injury and destruction, the other to gentleness and love," Salt posited an evolutionary development toward the greater impulse of gentleness and love. Thoreau's prophecy of the gradual ethical improvement of humanity had certainly affirmed Salt's belief in the slowly developing reach of compassion as the human future. "Civilization itself is a record of the partial extinction of the baser element and the gradual development of the nobler."[52] Thoreau had described human progress as the attainment of a "higher" and more "spiritual life," terms that avoid the supernatural but retain a religious residue.[53] Salt, however, insisted on a rational basis for humanitarianism. It is not as if humans will eventually transcend into a visionary embrace of universal compassion, he felt. "The instinct of compassion," he believed, "if not original in our nature, is an acquisition of such an early date as to be practically original."[54] The advances of science in his century were in fact allies of his cause, providing ever-clearer evidence of our shared place on the earth. "There is a tendency to forget," he wrote, "that it is to modern science that the ethic of humaneness owes its strongest corroboration."[55] Rather than see evolutionary science as destructive of human ethics, Salt welcomed it as incontrovertible proof of a universal earth-based kinship. A life was, in all cases, a life.

Salt feared most the danger that humane impulse could be derailed by "a partial and one-sided humanitarianism" that was not consistent in its application, resulting in the familiar act of declaring "our love for the beasts and bird in the meadow and woodland, and then returning home for them as they appear on our dinner tables."[56] Men and women are vulnerable to a "dull insensibility which is closely allied to cruelty" and must try to "cultivate the higher and more imaginative moral instincts," a task of both individual effort and organized educational planning.[57] "Morality being progressive," Salt explained, "there is no given point in our moral development where we can hold a perfectly logical and unassailable position; there are always indications of a further forward movement and an expansion of the whole moral horizon."[58] This statement concisely expresses Thoreau's purpose at Walden Pond. Salt's *Humanitarianism* was both a ringing defense of an ethics of compassion and a reformist call to arms.

With his focus still on universal compassion, Salt published *The Creed of Kinship* in 1935, four years before his death. He described the book as an explanation of the "single impulse" that allies all efforts of human reform. "The Creed of Kinship, I maintain, is itself a religion, and of all religions, the greatest."[59] Declaring that "'Civilization'" was presently in a "rude state" in comparison with a conceivable future of progress, he called for the abolition of "the extremes of Wealth and Poverty," the end of war, and the consideration of "the Rights of Animals" and their cruel mistreatment. He stressed "Free Thought" as the vehicle that will eventually lead to "a Creed of Kinship, a charter of human and sub-human relationships."[60] Unwavering in his criticism, Salt launched a blistering attack on modern complacency and self-congratulation. The question "*are* we living in a very late and civilized age?" must be answered with a resounding negative. "Thinkers who look further ahead," he maintained, understand that ages must pass "before a real civilization can be attained."[61]

Salt's Thoreau Biography and the British Thoreau Centenary

While deeply engaged as the voice of the Humanitarian League, Salt rose as a literary figure, and his biographical, critical, naturalist, and editorial work continued at a remarkable pace. His 1890 biography of Thoreau made an important contribution to Thoreau's gradual emergence from Emerson's shadow and established Thoreau's place in English literary circles. Grounding his biography in the 1886 *Temple Bar* essay's portrait of a caustic critic of America's greed and slavery-corrupted politics, Salt produced "the best early biography" of Thoreau, notable for its "sympathy, balance, and objectivity."[62] Salt made clear distinctions between Thoreau and Emerson, showing convincingly that "he was not a mere follower" of his friend and mentor."[63] Its 1890 publication linked Thoreau to other humanitarian causes and established Thoreau more completely as a voice of reform in Great Britain.

The careful scholarly reconstruction of the successive versions of this biography by George Hendrick, Willene Hendrick, and Fritz Oehlschlaeger provide a sense of the difficulties that the perfectionist Salt faced in bringing a comprehensive portrait of Thoreau to light. Having written most of the 1890 biography with resources from the British Museum Reading Room, Salt had also attempted to establish correspondence with Americans familiar with Thoreau. Much of the needed information arrived too late for the 1890 publication, making it clear to Salt that a new edition was needed. He developed a particularly useful correspondence with Dr. Samuel A. Jones, a physician and Thoreau devotee, which resulted in a much sharper sense of the contexts of Thoreau's life in Concord. Gathering this and other information, Salt published a second edition of his biography in 1896, a moment when the study of Emerson, Thoreau, and the transcendentalist movement was accelerating. Salt, who continued to see Thoreau as a vital modern thinker, felt a stake in the growing discourse on him and continued his correspondence with Jones and other American friends.[64] In light of this continually breaking information, he planned a revised third edition of his biography, completing it in 1908. However, Salt could find no publisher for this revised version and eventually sent the manuscript and other papers to the American scholar Raymond Adams in 1929. Salt's third edition was at last published in a well-annotated scholarly edition in 1993, bringing his work to the attention of Thoreau's still growing scholarly and public following.[65]

Salt's connection with Thoreau continued well past 1908, notably in the 1917 Thoreau Centenary in Great Britain. Organized by the Humanitarian League, prompted no doubt by Salt, this ambitious celebration is particularly notable as a literary and humanitarian event carried on in the face of war. The Centenary's "magnitude and significance,"[66] as Lonnie L. Willis commented, was a sign that the relevance of Thoreau's critique of the disarray of modern life was amplified for "the war-weary British people," with their "nostalgia for a time of simplicity and peace."[67] The Centenary included ceremonies and speeches at London's prominent Caxton Hall on July 12, but that event was preceded and followed by a stream of newspaper and magazine articles on Thoreau's life and ideas. "For a reader today," Willis wrote, "there is something incredible about not only the mass of material being put into print about Thoreau in the focused and relatively short period of the Centenary," which in fact "came to comprise most of the year 1917."[68]

Salt wrote a substantial essay on Thoreau for the Centenary that presented him as both an "Apostle of Simplicity" and a "Humane Naturalist."[69] These principles, however, made their impression through Thoreau's masterly and captivating style. Now more inclined to see Thoreau's achievement in literary and artistic terms, Salt observed that "it was as an artist that he first won unwilling homage from those who detested his views." His message, still far from wide acceptance, "makes too severe a demand on the conscience of his readers." This will be, Salt argued, the continuing challenge that Thoreau brings. "In Thoreau's Creed, the natural life is to be lived," he explained, and this brings his philosophy "to grips with conventional habit, as no writer has ever done."[70]

Willis added one particularly important observation to his history of the Centenary. While the Caxton Hall ceremonies in July generated a significant response all over Great Britain, making 1917 "the year of Thoreau in Britain," the Centenary also marked "a summit of interest in British readers" followed by "a diminishing of both popular and critical attention to his works."[71] Willis suggests, with some persuasive backing, that "the loss of working-class interests in [Thoreau's] ideas" accounts for this drop.[72] John Edwards's 1917 *Socialist Review* essay on Thoreau, which Willis cites, provides one view of England's 1880s reaction to Thoreau. "To those who were looking for imminent change in industry and social life 'Walden' came with refreshing force. How we reveled in the details of the building of the hut by the shores of Walden Pond in springtime!"[73] As Willis suggests, "Thoreau was 'beloved' of English Socialists because of the 'simple life' described in *Walden*."[74] These early Socialists were of course the generation of Salt and Carpenter, whose sense of future possibilities were, for the larger populace, damaged by the war. Willis's analysis of the fading of this sense of newness surrounding Thoreau makes the Centenary a high mark in Thoreau's early British reputation. Walter Harding also noted "a comparative lull in Thoreau activity" after the war, a drop in interest that was later offset by a "wide introduction of American literature into college curriculums."[75] As a result, "it was in the depression years of the thirties that Thoreau really came into his own." This growth in popularity and respect continued well through the forties as Thoreau gained recognition "as a social philosopher rather than just a nature writer."[76]

Thoreau, Salt, and Gandhi

One Thoreauvian principle was given a new kind of attention during the British Thoreau Centenary—passive resistance. "Thoreau was remembered as one who had been a conscientious objector and had put his life on the line," Willis noted. Thoreau's most important student of passive resistance was Mohandas Gandhi, who came to know of his work in London between 1888 and 1891, when he was studying law. Active in the Vegetarian Society, he became acquainted with Salt and was influenced, he later said, by Salt's *A Plea for Vegetarianism*, which gave him sound rational grounds for the vegetarian diet he had always practiced.[77] This was the book, as we previously noted, that began with a quotation from Thoreau. To see Gandhi in this way is to place him among the radical socialists of the 1880s and 1890s. As Martin Green has explained, Gandhi's discovery of London's Vegetarian Society began his entry into a period of prophetic social change. "Vegetarianism was then not just a diet option; it was at the center of a web of idealistic thinking and action." Gandhi's vegetarian connections brought him in contact with "other groups with comparable interest and other people ready to welcome a young Hindu."[78]

Gandhi would later read *Walden* and Salt's *Life of Henry David Thoreau*, and perhaps most importantly "Civil Disobedience," which was of great importance to him in South Africa. He was then, as he later wrote to Salt, in "the thick of [the] passive resistance movement."[79] His deepest engagement with Thoreau's ideas came when he translated excerpts from "Civil Disobedience" for *Indian Opinion*, which he edited in the early 1900s. Gandhi employed Thoreau's ideas as part of the grounding of his resistance to the discriminatory Asian Registration Act in 1907–8.[80] He later told the American journalist Webb Miller, "Until I had read that essay I never found a suitable English translation for my Indian word *Satyagraha*."[81] Gandhi's world-changing philosophy was of course fed by many sources and shaped by his own calculation and courage in enacting his principles. An important element of his philosophy, however, took form in 1846, on a July evening in the Concord jail.

Notes

1 Henry David Thoreau, *Walden*, ed. J. Lyndon Shanley (Princeton: Princeton UP, 1971), 4.
2 Thoreau's first biographer, though by critical consensus not the best, was Ellery Channing, *Thoreau, the Poet-Naturalist* (Boston: Roberts Brothers, 1873).
3 Walter Harding, *A Thoreau Handbook* (New York: New York UP, 1961), 181.
4 Lawrence Buell, *The Environmental Imagination* (Cambridge: Harvard UP, 1996), 340.
5 Ibid., 341.
6 Ibid., 347.
7 The authoritative biography of Salt is George Hendrick, *Henry Salt: Humanitarian Reformer and Man of Letters* (Urbana: University of Illinois Press, 1973). See also George Hendrick and Willene Hendrick's useful anthology, *The Savour of Salt: A Henry*

Salt Anthology (Fontwell, Sussex: Centaur Press, 1989). For further information on Salt, see the informative online archive of Salt materials: http://www.henrysalt.co.uk/.
8 "James Leigh Joynes: Some Reminiscences," Henrysalt.co (1897), http://www.henrysalt.co.uk/bibliography/essays/james-leigh-joynes-some-reminiscences.
9 See Hendrick, *Henry Salt*, 13–24; Stephen Winsten, *Salt and His Circle* (London: Hutchinson, 1951), 48–50; and J. L. Joynes, *The Socialist Catechism* (London: Modern Press, 1884).
10 Hendrick, *Henry Salt*, 27–36.
11 Edward Carpenter, *My Days and Dreams* (New York: Scribner, 1916).
12 Edward Carpenter, *The Intermediate Sex* (London: George Allen and Unwin, 1908), 39. Carpenter's works and career are receiving an important interpretive reassessment. See in particular Sheila Rowbotham, *Edward Carpenter: A Life of Liberty and Love* (London: Verso, 2008); Michael Robertson, *Worshipping Walt* (Princeton: Princeton UP, 2008); Kirsten Harris, *Walt Whitman and British Socialism* (New York: Routledge, 2016); and Michael Robertson, *The Last Utopians* (Princeton: Princeton UP, 2018). See Robertson, *The Last Utopians*, for a detailed analysis of Carpenter's work on homogenic attraction.
13 Rowbotham, *Edward Carpenter*, 75.
14 Robertson, *The Last Utopians*, 170.
15 Edward Carpenter, *England's Ideal, and Other Papers on Social Subjects* (London: Swan Sonnesschein, Lowrey, 1887), 79.
16 Ibid., 86.
17 Ibid.
18 Carpenter, *My Days and Dreams*, 114.
19 Ibid., 116.
20 For two important recent studies of the impact of Coleridge's impact on American transcendentalism, see David Greenham, *Emerson's Transatlantic Romanticism* (New York: Palgrave Macmillan, 2012), 70–101; and Samantha C. Harvey, *Transatlantic Transcendentalism* (Edinburgh: Edinburgh UP, 2013), 24–75. For the impact of Carlyle, see Barbara L. Packer, *The Transcendentalists* (Athens: University of Georgia Press, 2007), 32–45.
21 See Mark Bevir, "British Socialism and American Romanticism," *English Historical Review* 110.438 (1995): 878–901. Bevir provides an insightful analysis of the impact of the American transcendentalists on the rise of socialism in nineteenth-century Great Britain.
22 Rowbotham, *Edward Carpenter*, 96. The Salts stayed in Tilford until 1891 when Henry Salt's leadership of the Humanitarian League brought them to London. They remained strong friends of Carpenter, and the emotional ties between Kate Salt and Carpenter were deep enough to give her "a special place among his women friends" (Rowbotham, *Edward Carpenter*, 236).
23 Henry S. Salt, *Seventy Years among the Savages* (London: George Allen and Unwin, 1921), 79.
24 Henry S. Salt, "Henry D. Thoreau," *Justice* 96 (1885): 2.
25 Ibid., 2.
26 Henry S. Salt, "Henry D. Thoreau," *Temple Bar* 78 (1886): 369–83. On the origins of *Temple Bar*, see Peter Blake, "The Paradox of a Periodical: *Temple Bar* under the Editorship of George Augustus Sala (1860–1863)," *London Journal* 35.2 (2010): 185–209.

27 Salt, "Henry D. Thoreau" (1886), 369.
28 Ibid.
29 Ibid., 371.
30 Ibid., 374.
31 Ibid., 372.
32 Ibid., 375–6.
33 Ibid., 377.
34 Ibid.
35 Ibid., 375.
36 Ibid., 372.
37 Ralph Waldo Emerson, *Collected Works of Ralph Waldo Emerson: Uncollected Prose Writings*, vol. 10, ed. Ronald A. Bosco, Joel Myerson and Glen M. Johnson (Cambridge: Belknap Press of Harvard UP, 2013), 424.
38 Salt, "Henry D. Thoreau" (1886), 380.
39 Ibid., 376–7.
40 Edward Carpenter, *Civilisation: Its Cause and Cure* (London: Swan Sonnenschein, 1889).
41 Salt, *Seventy Years*.
42 Henry S. Salt, *A Plea for Vegetarianism, and Other Essays* (Manchester: The Vegetarian Society, 1886): 7.
43 Ibid., 11–12.
44 Ibid., 12.
45 Peter Singer, "Preface" to Henry S. Salt, *Animals' Rights: Considered in Relation to Social Progress*. (1892; reprint, Clarks Summit, PA: Society for Animal Rights, 1980), viii. This edition contains Peter Singer's preface and "An Updated Bibliography" by Charles R. Magel.
46 Salt, *Animals' Rights*, 24.
47 Hendrick and Hendrick, *Savour*, 43.
48 Salt, *Seventy Years*, 121.
49 Dan Weinbren, "Against *All* Cruelty: The Humanitarian League, 1891–1919," *History Workshop* 38 (1994): 86–8.
50 Henry S. Salt, *Humanitarianism: Its General Principles and Progress* (London: William Reeves, 1891): 3.
51 Ibid., 4.
52 Ibid., 5.
53 Thoreau, *Walden*, 210.
54 Salt, *Humanitarianism*, 15.
55 Salt, *Seventy Years*, 133.
56 Salt, *Humanitarianism*, 23.
57 Ibid.
58 Ibid., 24.
59 Henry S. Salt, *The Creed of Kinship* (London: Constable, 1935), v.
60 Ibid., viii.
61 Ibid., 102.
62 John T. Flanagan, "Henry Salt and His Life of Thoreau." *New England Quarterly* 28.2 (1955): 237.
63 Henry S. Salt, *Life of Henry David Thoreau* (Urbana: University of Illinois Press, 1993), xviii.

64 On Salt's continuing correspondence with Jones and other American Thoreau admirers, see Fritz Oelschlaeger and George Hendrick, *Toward the Making of Thoreau's Modern Reputation: Selected Correspondence of A. A. Jones, A. W. Hosmer, H. S. Salt, H. G. O. Blake, and Daniel Ricketson* (Urbana: University of Illinois Press, 1979).
65 See Salt, *Life of Thoreau*.
66 Lonnie L. Willis, "The Thoreau Centenary in Britain," *American Studies International* 37.2 (1999): 43.
67 Ibid., 44.
68 Ibid., 47.
69 Henry S. Salt, "David Henry Thoreau: A Centenary Essay," Henrysalt.co (1886), http://www.henrysalt.co.uk/bibliography/essays/david-henry-thoreau-a-centenary-essay.
70 Ibid.
71 Willis, "The Thoreau Centenary," 63.
72 Ibid., 63.
73 John Edwards, "Henry David Thoreau. Born at Concord, 12th July, 1817," *Socialist Review* 14 (1917): 241.
74 Willis, "The Thoreau Centenary," 64.
75 Harding, *Thoreau Handbook*, 183.
76 Ibid., 184.
77 Hendrick, *Henry Salt*, 166–8.
78 Martin Green, *Prophets of a New Age* (Edinburg: Axios Press, 2011), 56.
79 Hendrick, *Henry Salt*, 112.
80 George Hendrick, "The Influence of Thoreau's 'Civil Disobedience' on Gandhi's Satyagraha," *New England Quarterly* 29.4 (1956): 463–7.
81 Webb Miller, *I Found No Peace: The Journal of a Foreign Correspondent* (New York: Literary Guild, 1936), 139.

Part III

Philosophy, Religion, and the East

9

Nietzsche and World Iterature: The Eternal Recurrence of Dualism in *Thus Spake Zarathustra*

Jeffrey S. Librett

In the following, I approach the complex question of the relation between Friedrich Nietzsche and world literature in a narrowly specific manner with reference to *Thus Spake Zarathustra*.[1] I ask how this Nietzschean work positions itself, on the one hand, with respect to a previous particular body of world literature, and on the other hand, with respect to the notions of "self," "world," and "literature" as general conceptual figures. Concerning earlier literature I focus on the *Zend Avesta*, the ancient Persian texts through which the figure of Zoroaster, and the religion he founds, come down (and over) to the "Western" world.[2] For reasons of space and time, however, I limit myself here yet again to considering these ancient texts briefly only as they appear within the reception of ancient Persian religion as developed by Nietzsche's most important immediate predecessors and influences, and to situating Nietzsche's gesture with respect to these predecessors in the broadest terms. After having characterized initially the sense of Nietzsche's impersonation of Zoroaster as a gesture in response to the literary-philosophical reception of Zoroastrianism that immediately precedes him—a gesture that indeed, I argue, defines the overarching philosophical task of *Thus Spake Zarathustra*—I examine some key textual-conceptual elements and aspects of Nietzsche's approach to "self," "world," and "literature." I conclude by reflecting on the sense of *Thus Spake Zarathustra* as a work of world literature and on its implications for the reading of world literature in general.

Nietzsche's Response to the Orientalist Discourse: Dualism in Question

In this formidable text, Nietzsche the Classicist steps outside the Greek philology that still determined—if in Nietzsche's peculiar manner, much to (for example) Ulrich von Wilamowitz-Möllendorf's consternation and chagrin—the scholarly framework of his first book, *The Birth of Tragedy out of the Spirit of Music*. Going beyond the

Greco-Roman world, Nietzsche enters through his fictional impersonation of Zoroaster—and so in "Oriental" garb—into the discursive world of Orientalism in scholarship and literature, the "Oriental Renaissance," in Raymond Schwab's term.[3] It is therefore important for any reading of *Thus Spake Zarathustra*—especially a reading concerned with Nietzsche's place and placement of himself in world literature—to glimpse how Nietzsche intervenes in the Orientalist discourse of his day, in particular with reference to Zoroastrianism.[4] I begin by recalling the conventional view of Zoroastrianism—which takes it to constitute a metaphysically grounded moral dualism—predominant in the work of Nietzsche's German-language predecessors from the early nineteenth century.[5]

Subsequent to the translation of the *Zend-Avesta* by Abraham Hyacinthe Anquetil-Duperron (1731–1805) in 1771, the works of the ancient Persian spiritual leader, Zoroaster (also called Zarathustra, Zerdusht, and other variants in Western scholarship) became the subject of increasingly lively debate among European Orientalists. Retranslated into German in 1776 by Johann Friedrich Kleuker, Anquetil-Duperron's translation exercised an important influence on German Orientalist philology and cultural historiography. In the German scholarship of the early nineteenth century, including works on myth as well as philosophical and philosophico-historical treatises, Zoroaster appears predominantly under the heading of dualism, the dualism of light and darkness as the simultaneously moral and (meta)physical principles of good and evil represented by Ormuzd and Ahriman, respectively.[6]

The most important recent philological scholarship on Zoroastrianism for Nietzsche seems to have been the third edition (1836) of Friedrich Creuzer's *The Symbolism and Mythology of Ancient Peoples and in Particular the Greeks*, first published from 1810 to 1812 (second edition, 1819–23).[7] Here Nietzsche found both an emphasis on the dualistic character of the moral opposition between light and darkness, and an attempt to argue that these two principles were reconciled in Zoroaster's thought, and indeed originated there out of the unitary principle of infinite time.

> The fundamental idea ... is that of a *dualism* of *light* and *darkness* and of a *struggle* between both, which will end with the defeat of darkness. These two highest principles are now thought as two *beings*, *Ormuzd*, the purest light and the good, *Ahriman*, darkness and evil, who was also originally good, but then immediately filled with envy, and hence his darkening and his adoption of an inimical relationship to Ormuzd.[8]

This struggle between the two principles is in Creuzer's view grounded, however, in infinite time, an idea that is perhaps one of the distant inspirations of Nietzsche's "eternal recurrence of the same": "But the Persian doctrine certainly did not rest content with this dualism in the absence of another higher principle, as indeed many previously have opined, but rather without doubt they too recognized an *original principle* of this duality, *time without borders*, Zeruane Akerene, the creator of Ormuzd and Ahriman."[9] So Zoroastrianism appears, in the scholarly tradition Creuzer summarizes, as a metaphysical moral dualism of the struggle between light and darkness, and

Creuzer—in this at odds with some of his contemporaries and in line with others—sees this dualism as unified by a third principle.

While the present context does not allow us to reconstruct in any detail the scholarly and philosophical reception of Zoroastrianism that preceded Nietzsche's work, before we enter into the discussion of Nietzsche's critical response to moral dualism in his treatments of "self," "world," and "literature," it is important to mention one further source on Zoroastrian dualism that was doubtless particularly crucial for Nietzsche, namely Arthur Schopenhauer. In the essay "On Religion" (§179 on "The Old and New Testaments") from *Parerga and Paralipomena* (1851), Schopenhauer first sets up an opposition between Judaism, as a "realism and optimism," and Brahmanism and Buddhism, as "idealism and pessimism."[10] From this starting point, he goes on to argue—basing himself on previous scholarship such as J. G. Rhode's *Die heilige Sage und das gesammte Religionssystem der alten Baktrer, Meder und Perser, oder des Zendvolks* (1820)—that Judaism arises out of Zoroastrianism. In turn, he sees Christianity as arising fundamentally out of the pessimism and idealism of Indic religion, and so as compromising itself utterly by attempting to prop itself onto a Jewish origin that is philosophically opposed to its fundamental insights. Radically opposed to Christianity in everything except the myth of the fall from grace (which gives Judaism a bit of pessimism, albeit a bit that is ultimately contained and effaced by optimism), Judaism takes on the ancient Persian dualism, appropriating Ormuzd under the name of Jehovah, and reconstruing Ahriman as Satan. By giving Satan a "subordinate position," Judaism is able to constitute itself as an optimism, while maintaining a grain of the pessimistic truth of things in the figure of Satan, as the story of the fall indicates. For Schopenhauer, then, Zoroastrian dualism broaches an actual fall away from the good truth of pessimism, and Judaism consummates this fall by turning moral dualism into an optimism insofar as it elevates the principle of light above the principle of darkness. In contrast, for thinkers as diverse as Creuzer and Goethe, who are not pushing a pessimistic program, the primacy of light over darkness already appears crucial to the ancient Persian religion. We now have to consider what Nietzsche does with this reading of Zoroastrianism as the original moral dualism of light and darkness, good and evil, and how he responds in particular to Schopenhauer's version, which, given the importance of Schopenhauer's philosophy to Nietzsche's thought in general, is the crucial perspective to consider here.

In relation to Schopenhauer's construal of the Zend religion, Nietzsche's position can be seen as an inversion and displacement. As we've seen, Schopenhauer views Zoroastrianism as initiating a fall away from the truth of pessimism into the falsity of optimism. Dualism of light and darkness is a first mistake, according to Schopenhauer, leading to the particularly naive privileging of light in optimistic worldviews, Judaism above all. Nietzsche's gesture is evidently quite different from Schopenhauer's, even as he takes his distance from the "learned" scholarly modality that Schopenhauer uses as the foundation of his analysis.[11] For Nietzsche, the original dualism of Zoroaster signals a historically demonstrable human tendency to fall into *pessimism*, not into optimism, and of course Nietzsche has few positive things to say about ancient Indian religion and culture. For the latter represents in his work almost always a falling movement subject to what he calls in *Thus Spake Zarathustra* the "spirit of gravity," another (ironic) name for which is Zarathustra's "devil." In the idealist period, as the writings of Friedrich Schelling show very explicitly, and which Nietzsche follows on this specific point, gravity is conceived as the opposite of light, and so the movement of gravity is related to the principle of darkness itself.[12] Although Nietzsche cannot be said to be an "optimist" in any simple terms (despite the fact that he strives toward an affirmative stance), he rejects Schopenhauer's pessimism and, along with it, Schopenhauer's interpretation of Zoroastrian dualism as conducive to optimism.

While rejecting Schopenhauer's interpretation and negative evaluation of this dualism as leading to optimism, however, Nietzsche does, on the one hand, share with Schopenhauer the critique of dualism, to the degree that Nietzsche criticizes the manifold dualistic moralities of good and evil, especially the Christian one (although we shall have to look more closely at *how* Nietzsche criticizes them and try to gauge the sense of his critique). On the other hand, Nietzsche precisely speaks through or as Zarathustra, and so in this sense he seems to identify himself with dualism at its origin. How are we to understand this at least partial identification? Of course, Zarathustra remains marked in Nietzsche's text as a historical fiction and so retains some distance from Nietzsche himself, but, nonetheless, by making Zarathustra manifestly the mouthpiece of so many of his own views and experiences, Nietzsche as the author nominally identifies himself with Zarathustra and with Zarathustra's origination of moral dualism. Nietzsche thus in some sense repeats or replays that origination here. And yet he repeats this origination precisely as its negation or undoing. From this perspective, Nietzsche performs in this text the origination of dualism *as* its ending, the announcement of its origination *as* the announcement of its end.[13] Dualism, in other words, both re-originates here and presents itself as its own opposite: the negation of dualism. The implication is that there is no duality between dualism and its opposite (say, a moral or an amoral monism). Dualism is its own undoing, and the undoing of dualism participates in dualism. And yet there remains a duality, for manifestly, the speeches of Zarathustra in Nietzsche's text continue to struggle *against* moral dualism, largely by inverting it, affirming the evil as good (see e.g. "Of the Three Evils"), the good as evil (see e.g. "Of the Professorial Chairs of Virtue," "Of the Bumpkins," and "Of the Despisers of the Body") and both as forms of life, the one life of things in becoming, a life that, from Zarathustra's perspective, is to be affirmed. If dualistic moralism is bad, even if it is not evil in a Christian moral sense, this presupposes that there is a good outside of it, and hence that dualism of values remains. It survives its own undoing. Thus, the text appears, in a first approximation, to *complicate* dualism, even moral dualism, rather than simply either to throw it overboard or to capitulate to its necessity.

But as we shall have to see, the text doesn't simply complicate moral dualism in its internal structure or its relation with its negation. Beyond this, it *multiplies* dualism ad infinitum such that the critique of moral dualism at once appears as a hyperbolic dualism: the latter becomes the means to the former. That is, in *Thus Spake Zarathustra*, Nietzsche invokes and "deconstructs" dualistic conceptualities in a host of domains to show both how apparently nonmoral dualities overdetermine, condition, and contextualize strictly moral dualisms and how, conversely, such nonmoral dualities find themselves drawn into the orbit of the sphere of values due to the arbitrariness of any decision that is made upon their undecidable appearances in any given instance or situation. In what follows, I will focus on the way in which Nietzsche mobilizes binary or dual values from epistemic, ontological-temporal, and ethical conceptualities in the determination (and indetermination) of self, world, and literature.

The Self in *Thus Spake Zarathustra*: Dualities at Play

There is perhaps no better illustration of Nietzsche's repetition of dualism as its exacerbated suspension than the section "Of Old and New Tablets," because Nietzsche's text is replacing the old Zoroastrian dualism with a new one, the old law or set of imperatives and interdictions with another one. The Mosaic allusion is also striking here, especially since in the Old Testament the second set of tablets (produced as replacement of the first set after Moses has smashed the original tablets out of chagrin over the Israelites' idolatry) does not diverge in its contents from the first one. Which ironizes Zarathustra's desire for radical novelty as it underscores the sense in which opposition is repetition. I will focus here only on the very beginning of this very rich section, and only as it concerns the (in)determination of the self, that is, the source of creative value-positing.[14]

The manner in which Nietzsche introduces this section is telling, concerning the content of the polemical arguments in the subsections that comprise "Of Old and New Tablets." For in the introductory paragraph, he opens up a number of *ambiguities*, four of which we will examine, although the list is not an exhaustive one. These ambiguities operate in terms of, and thereby highlight, binary oppositions the indeterminate play of whose mutually (de)constituting opposed terms places in question the stability of the subject who is to be the source of creative value-positions. Before delineating their specifics, it is necessary to note that all of these ambiguities are treated also in many other ways throughout the text of *Thus Spake Zarathustra* and elsewhere in Nietzsche's writings, and that all of them constitute important elements of his writings on the situation of the human being in the world. Further, it is necessary to clarify in general terms that all of them operate in terms of, or invoke, conceptual dualities that tend to be aligned with moral judgments. Indeed, they are themselves not just binary *conceptual* aspects of the self but *already value-dualisms*, since in each case the ambiguity can only ever be resolved by an arbitrary decision, an act of will. In addition, as we'll see, all of the undecidable dualities here reinforce each other. Finally, as we'll see below, all of the dualities invoked and thrown into question here, in the characterization of the self or ego (as represented by the self of Zarathustra himself), will also be applied to the interrogations of world and of literature that Nietzsche elaborates in *Thus Spake Zarathustra*. Let me first cite the passage in which they occur and then consider the main specific ambiguities at stake here:

> Here I sit and wait, old broken tablets around me and also new half-inscribed tablets. When does my hour arrive?
> —the hour of my going down, going under: for one more time I want to go to the humans.

> This is what I'm awaiting now: for first the signs must arrive that it is *my* hour,— namely the laughing lion with the swarm of doves.
>
> In the meantime, I (will) speak, as one who has time, to myself. No one tells me anything new: so I (will) tell myself myself.[15]

First, we encounter here an ontological and temporal ambiguity about Zarathustra's own self-presence or self-absence (and self-deferral) in time. Zarathustra says he has time here, but he is not yet in his own proper moment ("*meine Stunde*"). Does this mean that Zarathustra is in time or that he is outside of time? Is he "between" (*zwischen*) his time and the time of another (or another's time, or another time)? In any event, Zarathustra is situated in a problematic relationship with his own time and therefore with himself. His own time is not (yet) his own, as he waits for the others. The text thus raises questions about what it might mean to be present or absent to the site of one's temporal inscription (especially since one can here evidently be both at once) and how the pastness and futurity of the time of waiting are related to the time of presence or absence.[16]

Second, we are interrogated by a psychological or psychosocial ambiguity about whether aloneness—a major motif throughout the text—can ever coincide with self-sameness, whether one can ever be a subject without addressing oneself as another and finding oneself as another, and conversely whether while addressing others one perhaps remains bound up within oneself. He repeatedly says that he will speak (or is speaking) to himself ("*zu mir selber*" and "*mir mich selber*"). But indeed he is evidently not just speaking to himself, but to readers, and even within the text to his "brothers," whom he repeatedly addresses as such in the subsequent subsections of this section. The "myself" spoken to is not (merely) himself but (also) the others, and the others may well be then avatars of himself. The borders between self and others are here placed in question even as they are maintained.

Third, we find ourselves confronted with a simultaneously epistemic and ontological ambiguity about whether personal identity is *reality* or *appearance*, given or construct. Zarathustra's relation to himself is suspended between *being* himself and *appearing* as himself, since when he says "*rede ich als Einer, der Zeit hat, zu mir selber*," "to speak as one who has time" can mean either "because I have time" or "as if I were someone who had time." There remains some question as to whether Zarathustra is truly or really himself or merely an appearance of himself, and one that he is himself perhaps constructing, or fashioning (as he manifestly is).[17]

And finally, we encounter a displacement of this epistemic-ontological concern about self as reality or appearance into an ambiguity about whether the self is purely a matter of subjectivity or whether it has an objective status. Zarathustra says that he will "tell myself myself." That is, the *content* of what he has to say is nothing other than himself. On the one hand, this could mean that he speaks of nothing outside of himself, the subject of narration, and therefore makes a purely subjective utterance. On the other hand, it could mean that he speaks of something objectively existent, namely, himself.

The very difficulty and subtlety of the positing of new values by the strong, solitary, creative individual self, which is the point of much of what follows in "Of Old and New Tablets" (and in all of *Thus Spake Zarathustra*), pertains to precisely these ambiguities, collapsing and separating binaries, especially the duality of subjectivity and objectivity. The ambiguity of subjective-objective, or the suspension and maintenance of this duality, is thus crucial to the central thrust of the book, the insistence that one should create one's own values in line with one's own desire.

For on the one hand, these values do not (yet) exist, so their origin is to be nothing but subjective and singular, and on the other hand, once they do exist, they immediately become instances of the false stability that enables weak subjects, those who lack the courage to be creative, to depend on them as if they were objective and stable, and to avoid the truth of the fact that "everything is in flux."[18] In other words, values must be neither subjective nor objective, and both (if they are to be posited and exist).[19] To posit new values requires having the strength to believe in one's own momentary desires (it's a matter of the "great longing"[20]), but to posit such values as actual *values* is to posit them as objectively valid for others as well. Hence the importance, for example, of the motif of "commanding."[21] Those who are creative command the others, and they want to rule, a desire Zarathustra calls "the giving virtue."[22] One cannot create values without creating them implicitly for others as well, that is, universalizing and objectivizing one's own sense of what is desirable as such, to which is opposed, in a duality, that which is not desirable, should be forbidden or destroyed, and so on. The "creative ones" are those who can maintain themselves on this infinitesimally wide edge or ledge between the affirmation of a purely subjective and singular desire, on the one hand, and the belief in the objectivity of what this desire posits as desirable and admirable, on the other hand. The Zoroastrian figure of the "arrow" is one figure through which Nietzsche concretizes this peculiar intermediary status or position, as is also the figure of the human being as a "bridge" between an animal and the over-human (*Übermensch*).[23] It is thus not that Nietzsche is actually telling us that one fine day the over-human will arrive, but rather that the human (since he often speaks of the human, and not only in disparaging ways) is always "underway" toward the over-human, striving to become something that he is not yet and yet also is. We return to this point below when considering the question of literature.

We have thus far considered how the subject of value is (in)determined by the conceptual value-dualities of presence and absence, temporality and eternity, unitariness and multiplicity, appearance and reality, and subjective and objective. We now turn to consider the functioning of these same oppositions, as well as the aesthetic and ethical oppositions of pleasure/pain and affirmation/negation, in the (de)constitution of world. What is the world for Nietzsche's Zarathustra?

The World: Three Doubled Perspectives

Before examining Nietzsche's conceptual figuration of world in (the period of) *Thus Spake Zarathustra*, it is useful to consider momentarily its philosophico-historical provenience. The background of his approach to the world even in the later texts is predominantly Schopenhauerian, as Nietzsche elaborates in many places, in his earlier career more positively, and later on, much more negatively in terms of his rejection of Schopenhauer's world-denying orientation. As is well known, at the outset of his publishing career, with *The Birth of Tragedy*, in 1871, Nietzsche still adhered much more closely (although not without divergences, notably concerning the aesthetic dimension) to the Schopenhauerian schema, in terms of which the "world" appears in two modalities.[24] This first of these modalities is the "will," that is, the inner core of things, the *Ding An Sich*, a groundless and interminably insatiable longing that is itself the ground of all appearances. The second of these modalities, in radical contrast, is "representation" (*Vorstellung*), also characterized as the *principium individuationis*, which constitutes the realm of appearances themselves that result from the ineluctable subordination of the will to the principle of sufficient reason. For Schopenhauer—who fails to recognize the degree to which, on this point, he simply inverts and so repeats the "Zoroastrian" dualism he rejects—the ethical stance is achieved by the "saint" who negates the will, which appears in the human being as the will to live. The ethically achieved human being is the one in and through whom the will qua will to live negates itself, instead of affirming itself, that is, the ascetic, who escapes suffering by suspending all desire, putting an end to the world within himself. In *The Birth of Tragedy*, the world as will appears as the Dionysian principle, while the world as representation appears as the Apollonian principle, with certain displacements into which we cannot enter here.

By the time we get to *Thus Spake Zarathustra*, however, which appeared some twelve to fourteen years later, these notions have undergone extensive critical elaboration and displacement—for Nietzsche has taken his distance increasingly from Schopenhauer (and from Wagner's appropriation of Schopenhauer)—but they remain "present" in altered forms in Nietzsche's thinking. Nietzsche now argues that the will is a will to power, not a will to live; that the world as will is to be affirmed rather than denied (a reversal that involves a rejection of Schopenhauerian eudaimonism and thus a rejection of happiness and pleasure as the telos of philosophical thought and of appropriate human striving); and that one should, in the name of this affirmation, overcome the duality of appearances and essences, that one should think and experience the two poles of Schopenhauer's "world"-concept in their unity (as indeed already in *The Birth of Tragedy*, tragedy itself was said from the very start to arise out of the unification of Dionysian will and Apollonian representation).[25]

How do these displacements appear in Nietzsche's mobilization of the motif of "world" in *Thus Spake Zarathustra*? While Nietzsche does not offer any succinct definitions of "world" in *Thus Spake Zarathustra* in the style of philosophical systematization, he uses or inscribes the term in numerous contexts that provide useful indications of how "world" is being conceptualized and figured in this text, some of which indications we shall consider here.[26] Above all, Zarathustra emphatically and programmatically insists on the value of the affirmation of the world: *worldliness* is to be affirmed, as life, as will, as subjective perspectivism, as embodiment, as temporal flux, as the play of forces, and so on. Nietzsche develops this imperative of world-affirmation in part by way of the sustained (dualistic) polemic against those who "deny" the world, "*Welt-verleumder*,"²⁷ including those who would propose an ascetic renunciation of the world, or a withdrawal from the world in terms of an admonition to "leave the world to the world,"²⁸ as against those who are "tired" of the world, "*die Welt-müde(n)*,"²⁹ and those who posit a "beyond" of the world, the "*Hinterweltler*,"³⁰ whether in the form of a life after death or in the form of some "essence" of the world or "thing in itself" that would be behind and within appearances. World appears here as something like the "reality" of the "here and now," as opposed to the "ideality" of an elsewhere that would be better or more profound than what presents itself in the mode of appearance, although Nietzsche also complicates the self-sameness of the presence of this present world, as we'll see. In any case, for Nietzsche, at this point, to affirm this world is the "good," Nietzschean "virtue," whereas to negate it is an "evil," albeit not in a moral sense but rather in the sense of a weakness or lack of courage, a lack of nobility of spirit, and so on. The reversal of the world-negating dualistic moralities that make the world itself a place of evil thus gives rise to an alternative dualism of the good and evil of affirmation and negation. But *where* is this positive world situated, and how is it further characterized?

Here we encounter the mobilization of the epistemic and ontological duality of subject and object for the (in)determination of the world. The world occupies, in terms of this opposition, (at least) two positions in *Thus Spake Zarathustra*, each of which ensures that we cannot master it in either expression or theoretical contemplation. Indeed, it is the nonmasterable character of the world—that we "suffer" from it (i.e., "leiden" in passivity)—that for Nietzsche constitutes the reason why human beings tend to want to deny it, or transcend it. I consider these two positions as they appear in "The One Who Is Becoming Healthy," where Zarathustra speaks with his animals, while recovering from his disgust at the thought of the eternal recurrence of the same insofar as this thought implies that even the weakest, most inadequate humans will return forever and that in this sense progress beyond moral dualism will never be final or complete. The immediate context is Zarathustra's pleasure taken in the fact that his animals have been speaking to him, which is helping him recover from the disgust. In this context, Zarathustra speaks of what conversation means, and how it relates to the question of world, suggesting that such conversation about the world can never access or express the world it attempts to represent. This gives rise to the (in)determination of two positions (or aspects and statuses) of the world.

On the one hand, the world is situated radically within each individual; it is a subjective experience. For what can we know of the world other than our experience? "To each soul belongs a different world; for each soul, every other soul is a beyond-the-world."³¹ The radical aloneness or loneliness (*Einsamkeit*) of which Zarathustra often speaks appears here as the determination of "world" itself as solipsistic (see "The Homecoming"). The insistence that each individual subject/body make its own set of values and assume radical responsibility for itself follows, as an amoral and asocial ethical postulate, from this solipsism. This subjective aspect of the world is not a bad thing, for Zarathustra here, even though the way in which we are linked to others and to the "world" of "things" outside us—that is, through language—remains illusory. While marking the illusoriness of the bridge that language seems to constitute between the different worlds of individual experience, and between any given world of experience and the things "outside" of that experience, Zarathustra notes the pleasantness of this illusion of connectedness, and the possibility of enjoying it. Just before the passage cited above, in which he states that each soul has a distinct world, Zarathustra says, "Where there is jabbering, there the world lies before me like a garden./How lovely it is, that words and sounds are there: are not words and sounds rainbows and illusory bridges between what is eternally separated?"[32] The beauty of the rainbow is that of a bridge in the sky that is not really there, and a bridge caused by the interpenetration of rain and sun, of the spirit of sadness (or gravity) and the rising light of joy. Lest one think that the lovely bridge is not pure illusion, Zarathustra continues, after speaking of the separateness of soul-worlds, "Between even the most similar, illusion lies [in the sense of speaking falsely] most beautifully: for the smallest rift is the hardest to bridge-over."[33] It's lovely, he says, that we forget that there is no "outside myself,"[34] as sounds allow us to do.

But language provides not only a false sense of communication between the separate inner worlds of individuals. In addition, it provides in general a false sense of referential connection between the subject and the things around him or her. "Are not names and sounds given to things, so that the human being can enjoy (or enliven himself through) things? Speech is such a beautiful madness: through speech, the human being dances over all things."[35] Through language, we deny our separateness from other people and from the world around us, which is nonetheless no world for us and which does not enter into our world. And this is a good thing, because it renders bearable the separateness of our solipsism. From this one perspective at least, the (true) world is only within the individual, and the appearance of a world outside and of a connection with the world(s) outside, the worlds of others and of things, is an illusory one, even if this illusion is a "good" one.

On the other hand, we exist as radically inscribed in an objectively existent world that exceeds us in every direction. The individual is part of a larger world, the world totality. Here, the polarities of truth and illusion are reversed: the truth of the world is that it is the totality of beings, whereas we tend to fall prey to the illusion that we are separate from this totality. Appropriately, it is when the animals respond to what Zarathustra has just been saying about solipsism, appearing to extend his thought and to agree with him, that they state the exact opposite aspect of things, namely, that the individual is part of a world totality that itself does not appear as such within concrete subjective experience. To his suggestion that humans dance over the things in language, they respond,

> O Zarathustra ... to those who think like us [apparently including Zarathustra in this "us"], all things themselves dance: they come and reach their hands out to each other and laugh and fly away—and come back. /All goes, All comes back; eternally rolls the wheel of Being. All dies, all blossoms forth again, eternally runs the year of Being. /All breaks, All is reassembled; eternally the same house of Being builds itself. All departs, All greets itself again; eternally the ring of Being remains true to itself. /In every Now, Being begins; around every Here, the ball of There rolls. The middle is everywhere. Crooked is the path of eternity.[36]

This statement of the eternal recurrence of the same, and of the circularity of time, of Being as a process of the totality of things coming and going again forever, provides a depiction of the world such as it is not directly experienced by the individual but exceeds and transcends him or her. For we are not immediately aware of our lives as repetitions, nor of our connectedness with all things. The appearance of world as the linear trajectory of a soul's life that is isolated within itself and occurs only once (the world of a life as situated within the subjective individual) is now opposed, in a binary duality, to the true essence of the world as an infinitely repeating process of the totality of Being and beings.

Thus, up to this point we see two models of world simultaneously in play in *Thus Spake Zarathustra*, complementary, perhaps, but also mutually incompatible. In either case, the world functions as something like the site and surround of the subject, the delimiting context within which the subject (the human—who is always also and most fundamentally a living body) exists.[37] This surrounding can be seen to be determined either from within (the world as "my" world) or from without (the world as the circular process of the totality of being), but there is no final perspective from which it can be glimpsed in a mastering gaze that would still it for all time. Thus, world as such remains beyond the reach of both theoretical reason and concrete experience, both of which nonetheless belong to it and continue to grasp after it, in accordance with the will to truth.

The unity of this bipolar world being both theoretically and intuitively inaccessible, the world remains a mystery. And at this point, the ethical duality of affirmative and negative desire enters upon the scene of the world's (in)determination.[38] Hence, Zarathustra sings (and does not say)—in "The Other Dance Song" and in "The Night Wanderer's Song" again (and here twice, once spaced by intermittent elaborations and once condensed)—the song in which he develops the notional feeling that "the world is deep, and deeper than the day thought."[39] The daylight of reason, knowledge, and conscious experience cannot plumb the depths of "world." But whatever it is, from an epistemic-ontological point of view—the context of our existence and/or that existence itself in the solipsism of its experience, being in itself or for itself (in Hegelian terminology)—the world appears *affectively*, presents itself to (aesthetic) *feeling* and to (ethical) *desire*, in primarily two ways. "Deep is its pain—Pleasure (and/or desire)—deeper still than the heart's suffering: Pain speaks: Pass away! But all pleasure wills (or wants) eternity—wills deep, deep eternity!"[40] Thus, affectively and ethically, there are two possible stances toward the world, two ways in which it appears. When it appears as suffering, we want it to disappear (and ourselves to disappear with it), and when it appears as pleasure or desire, we want it to last forever.[41]

We have here the two possibilities that Schopenhauer also offered, with the major difference that Nietzsche here, in the form of Zarathustra, tries to choose—and invites us to choose—affirmation over negation, even as he is aware that affirmation has negative, aggressive potential. This Nietzschean affirmation culminates in the affirmation of the eternal recurrence of the same but also implies or contains the affirmation of the appearance of the world as a world of solitary experience and responsibility. The affirmation appears in the section on "The Seven Seals" (the section that follows "The

Other Dance Song" and concludes the third Part of *Thus Spake Zarathustra*) most explicitly and simply, as I've indicated in a footnote above, in the refrain that concludes each of the seven subsections of that section, "For I love you, oh eternity!"[42] The desire for eternity is contextualized in its very hopefulness as a hopefulness doubled by desperation here, through the fact that Nietzsche's worldliness is one that denies any afterlife and affirms that what happens now happens forever, in a forever that is limited to the forever (conceived as repetition) of this very now, that hence a finite now is all we have and do not have. Accordingly, for example, he speaks of the world as "this finite world" in the section, "Of the Three Evils."[43] The desire for eternity, however, is nonetheless the affective manner in which "world" presents itself, as haunted always by the present danger of the pained desire (for the world) to disappear, otherwise known as Zarathustra's "devil"—the spirit of gravity and of weight (*Schwere*).[44]

But finally, as we have indirectly glimpsed but not yet thematized explicitly, the "world" has not just an ontological-epistemological determination (as inside or outside the subject, as subjective or objective, as accessible to immediate experience or not), nor is its conceptual figure exhausted by the addition of a dual affective perspective (as a negativity of the will arising out of suffering or a positivity of the will arising out of pleasurable desire or desirous pleasure). The world possesses further a *temporal* (in)determination. The question is not just: *Where* is the world and how is it to be known? nor: How do we *relate*, in terms of affective and desiring faculties, to the world? but also: *When* is the world? *When* can the world be said to take place? And what is the modality of its presence? Clearly, the fact that the world is more desired than known already implies that this temporal (in)determination will involve complexity and dispersion, because it's not simply present to the subject as an object of knowledge. The question of the world's time is put with some urgency in *Thus Spake Zarathustra*, as appears in key passages, of which I'll consider one in the "Song of the Night Wanderer." In this complex passage, Zarathustra sings of the tone of the midnight bell and of his lyre, both of them coming up out of the past and out of the (spatial) distance, and of the music's speech having become ripe, with a ripeness he likens to golden autumn, afternoons, and his hermit's heart. He then says, "Now ... the world itself became ripe, the grape is browning,"[45] and that "now it wants to die, to die from happiness."[46] The question of how to read this "now" in conjunction with the past tense of this "became" is complicated further by subsequent developments within the passage, in which Zarathustra tells us that the scent of eternity is rising, a scent of "drunken midnight's dying happiness"[47] and that this is the voice singing of the depth of the world. He then cries out, however, despite and because of the arrival of this ripeness of the world, that he is too pure for the day and wants not to be touched,[48] and so to be left alone with this perfection or fullness: "Did not my world just become perfect?"[49] Then he tells the world, identifying it with day, that he is too pure for it: "Oh world, you want *me*? Am I worldly to you? Am I spiritual to you? Am I divine? But day and world, you are too dull."[50] Zarathustra is moving here therefore between the arrival and the loss of full presence as presence of the world. On the one hand, there is a sense of *fullness*, but this fullness is already marked at its very appearance by the pastness of its becoming—"the world itself became ripe" (*die Welt selber ward reif*) and "did not my world just become perfect?" (Ward *meine Welt nicht eben vollkommen?*)" (my emphasis)—and it is also immediately threatened in its present stability by the grasping of day (for which, we recall, the world is too deep). On the other hand, Zarathustra registers here an explicit sense of loss: "Gone! Gone! O youth! O midday! O afternoon!"[51] We see thus that the possibility of the full presence of world is temporally conditioned, indeed thereby also suspended: the presence of the world is entirely fleeting, temporally dispersed from the very start. Hence the (very Faustian) desire for an eternity of the *Augenblick*, which presents itself precisely as a *desire* (i.e., as that which pleasure/desire wants or wills— "*Lust will ... Ewigkeit*"). Here—in the penultimate section of the fourth and final part of *Thus Spake Zarathustra*—the interpenetrations of happiness and loss, fulfillment and desire, the desire to die and the desire to live become even more complex than in the earlier version that appeared as "The Other Dance Song." And the subjective and objective models of the world—as "the" world and as "my" world also—come into immediate proximity of each other, the latter ("my world") as the repetition of or gloss on the former ("the world"), its incompatible synonym. In the context of (collapsing) dualities, the pathos of the desire for eternity is heightened by the emphasis on temporality as the fleetingness of the present in finite human experience.

The complex temporal structure of the "presence" of world-perfection, the fleetingness of the present as temporal dispersion, which appears in this repetition of "The Other Dance Song" in a song at midnight, gains further clarity if we reflect on the status of midnight here. The song invites us to do this, strikingly, when Zarathustra equates midnight with midday (or noon). The passage where this occurs also equates pain with pleasure (the two sources of life-denial and life-affirmation, respectively), cursing with blessing (thus, denial with affirmation themselves), night with sun, and wise man with fool, thus cancelling out on one level the fundamental dualities with which both Zoroaster and Schopenhauer, as well as Zarathustra himself, have been operating. Except that the cancellation is qualified to the degree that one term in each of these oppositions is said to be "also" the other, which implies that the opposition remains to some extent in force. In the crescendo of the "Song of the Night Wanderer" we've been considering, when Zarathustra says, "My world just became perfect," he finishes the sentence with "Midnight is also midday [noon]."[52] And he goes on: "Pain is also a pleasure/desire, curse is also a blessing, night is also a sun—go away or you will learn: a wise man is also a fool."[53] So as the narrative of *Thus Spake Zarathustra* approaches its conclusion, the gap between its perhaps most fundamental oppositions is closed—almost. Almost—because the metaphoric unification remains a metonymic juxtaposition of opposed terms. The duality repeats itself "also" as a unity, but remains a duality nonetheless. Concerning "presence," which is here the presence of the fullness of "the" (or "my") world, the operative opposition is midnight and midday. How do we have to understand this opposition, one of the most important leitmotifs—or light-motifs—of *Thus Spake Zarathustra*?

Evidently by following out the logic of the "moments" in question. Midnight is both the height of night (as the moment of the most radical absence of light and absence tout court) and the moment of turning from night into morning, the turning from the disappearance of light toward its re-arrival (recurrence, repetition, iteration), the turn from going to coming. Midday (noon) is the both the height of day (as the moment of the most radical presence of light, and presence tout court, the pan moment of the disappearance of shadows) and the moment of turning from morning into night, the turn from the rising of light to its falling away (under the influence of the "spirit of gravity"), the turn from coming to going. That the two moments are (not) equated, as the moments of absence and presence, in a (non)equation placed in serial quasi-identity with the (non)equations of pain and pleasure, curse and blessing, night and sun, wisdom and madness, helps us understand what it means for the world to be "present" in its perfection, perfectly present, and to understand thus "when" the world is present, the problematically elusive temporal modality of its presence. The present is already the past as a desired future repetition. Presence is already the transition to absence, absence already the beginning of presence. And in ethical terms, this means negativity is the start of positivity and the reverse. The temporal structure developed here ironizes, furthermore, the final, apparently triumphant and pathos-laden moments of the text, when Zarathustra emerges from his cave, "like a morning sun that comes out of dark mountains,"[54] just after saying "This is *my* morning, *my* day is beginning: *arise now, you great noon!*"[55] And finally, it reminds us that the affirmation of the world (and the negation of the moralistic dualities that arise out of and exacerbate its negation) remains a *project*, never definitively achieved, even if achieved fleetingly in disappearing moments, across the finitude of a lifetime whose non-revisable or non-redo-able character is guaranteed and summarized by the notion of its eternal repetition as it is.

The worldliness of the world appears here, then, strikingly, as the always of never and the never of always. The fleetingness of the *when* of the world exacerbates the dualistically perspectival indeterminacy of its *where*, as well as the radical ambivalence of its affective and desiring *experiential presentation* as positivity and negativity of the will.

Where Does Literature Lie?

What, then, of literature? In order to approach the question of the relation between "world" and "literature" in *Thus Spake Zarathustra*, I will briefly consider first what Nietzsche says about "literature" in this text, as *Dichtung* or "poetic writing," in the section "Of the Poets" (*Von den Dichtern*). Here, too, we see Zarathustra both establishing and suspending dualisms of value, in order in this case to develop a thoroughly aporetic relationship to literature. The (in)operative oppositions we have seen (in)determining both self and world above, including the epistemic-ontological one of subjective and objective, the ethical one of affirmation and negation, and the ontological temporal ones of presence and absence, pastness and futurity, are mobilized here again, in new ways, but still with a view to undecidability and reversibility. In particular, lying becomes centrally thematic here, as a simultaneously epistemic and ethical fault, hence also an aesthetic one, in opposition to the epistemic, ethical, and aesthetic virtue of honesty.[56] Indirectly alluding to the liar's paradox, Nietzsche develops a slightly more indeterminate version in which the poets stand in for the Cretans, while Zarathustra both echoes and subverts Platonistic objections to the poets.

The section is framed as a dialogue between Zarathustra and one of his disciples. After Zarathustra begins by stating his sense that, in light of the embodiedness of human beings, both "spirit" and "the permanent" have a purely figural status, the disciple comes back to a remark Zarathustra has made earlier, to the effect that "the poets lie to much."[57] When the disciple asks him to explain this remark, Zarathustra initially demurs, emphasizing the radical self-discontinuity of his own subjectivity. He asserts first of all that he can't be expected to recall the reasons why he came up with his "opinions"[58]—obviously a loaded word in a context that recalls Socratic-Platonic discourse—and second that, beyond this, his opinions are unstable and moreover, some of them belong to others rather than to himself.

The emphasis on this temporal and epistemic-ontological (and as it were spatial) self-discontinuity—consistent with the ambiguities concerning the self that we examined above—provides the appropriate background against which Zarathustra proceeds. Against this background, he goes on to suggest that the disciple should not "believe" in him, that indeed he is not a friend of "belief" per se. That is, he distances himself from religious idealizations and pushes the disciple to think for himself. But then, he nonetheless goes on to answer the disciple's question by asserting that, if someone felt that the poets lie too much, he would be right: "*We* lie too much."[59] He then gives the disciple the reasons why it is right to believe that the poets lie too much. What is the status of this answer, placed as it is against the backdrop of a refusal to answer?

The poet, Zarathustra—who may or may not be lying here, because the "poets lie too much," but not necessarily always—says that the poets lie too much. Given this structure, the discourse that follows, which contains Zarathustra's reasons for finding the poets dishonest, is doubly fraught: first, due to the fact that he seems to suggest that this discourse against the poets should not be credited because it is the discourse of a poet, and poets lie; and second, because we cannot exclude the possibility that this discourse *should* be credited, since he may not be lying in this instance. The Platonistic opposition to the poets as those who tell lies—which in Nietzsche's discourse of the 1880s is enunciated in the name of the value of *Redlichkeit* or "honesty," a (moral) value that is indeed upheld as a positive virtue (because it ultimately undermines moralism and idealism) insistently if not consistently throughout *Thus Spake Zarathustra*—is here at once asserted and (possibly) undermined by the self-characterization of Zarathustra as a poet, against the doubt-exacerbating background of his insistence on his own unreliability and ongoing subjective dispersion into the world around him, a world itself of vexed status.

Insofar as Zarathustra is manifestly asserting this opposition, he explains the various reasons for his opinion. The poets are deceptive and hence unsatisfactory because they accept conventional wisdom—such as, one should note, the conventional wisdom that the poets lie—and because they are narcissistic. They just want an audience, not really caring how worthy their audience is, and they imagine themselves in addition to have a privileged access to nature that they do not, in fact, have. Their naturalism supports their social conformity. They are, furthermore, superficial and impure, as their conventional, false naturalism implies, and they fake depth by confusing things that do not belong together.

But above all, perhaps, the poets are at fault because they are the ones who invent the gods: "For all gods are a poetic figure, a poetic sleight of hand [Dichter-Gleichnis, Dichter-Erschleichnis],"[60] he says, in a play on word-forms. Their lack of real virtue is responsible for the moralism that religious delusions support. And he goes on: "Truly, we are drawn on—namely, to the realm of the clouds: upon these we set our bright urchins and call them then gods and overmen;—/And they are indeed just light enough for these chairs!—all these gods and overmen."[61] As I have indicated above, the term *Übermensch* is used in (the first scene of Act I of) *Faust* for the eponymous hero by the Earth Spirit, and certainly Nietzsche is raising some questions here about Goethe's idealism, inconsistencies, and poetic seductiveness, just as he is mocking Goethe's "eternal feminine" with the language of "we are drawn on."[62]

But much more importantly, the appearance of the term, *Übermensch*, here cuts into the flesh—as Nietzsche says spirit does to life in general—of Nietzsche's own text and of Zarathustra's figurations of the *Übermensch*.[63] The opposition between the religious-moral dualisms of good/evil oriented toward divinity and the Zarathustran strong/weak dualism oriented toward the telos of the *Übermensch* is here placed radically in question, albeit under the sign of the reader's necessary uncertainty as to whether or not Zarathustra can be believed here and whether or not he is mixing up things that do not belong together, as he says the poets do. What it means for Zarathustra to be the teacher of the doctrine of the *Übermensch*—"I teach you the over-human!"[64]—becomes here quite uncertain, quite obscure, to say the least. Not to be believed, Zarathustra thus throws his disciple (and Nietzsche throws the reader) back upon his or her own resources for the determination of values in the dualistic oscillation of good and evil, on the one hand, and its uncertain beyond, on the other.

But as for literature, beyond its god-creating fictional function, it is not simply the case that Zarathustra opposes it. In certain respects, he simply states here that he is dissatisfied with all poetic writing hitherto. The generality of his opposition to poets is counterbalanced by its non-universality. While he has become "tired" of the poets, in some utterances Zarathustra indicates that he merely wants to see poets who are more pure, and deeper, and above all perhaps more in tune with an ardent passion for sound he evidently values highly: "What did they know of the ardent passion for sound!"[65] Zarathustra demands here that poets be less desirous of personal recognition, less self-centered, less easily contented with conventional beliefs, and more focused notably on the sensuous dimension of their art.

In short, Zarathustra's repetition of the philosophical dissatisfaction with literature also contains the assertion of a certain passion for literature as value, with a hopeful view to its future possibilities as tropes upon the past: "I am from today and before, he said then; but something is in me, that is from tomorrow and the day after tomorrow and once upon a time."[66] The self-negating literary negation of literature in its reality doubles here as its self-affirmation under the sign of possibility. But the futurity of possibility turns out—here as elsewhere—to be the reiteration of a past (*Einstmals*: once upon a time, long ago), as appears, for example, in the fact that there is no literature without a literary tradition.[67]

From Literature to World Iterature

We have thus far seen that, repeating what the Western scholarly tradition in Orientalism passes on to him as the Zoroastrian origination of moral dualism, but repeating this dualism as its self-overcoming, Nietzsche writes *Thus Spake Zarathustra* as an emphatic work of *worldliness*, as opposed to otherworldliness or non-worldliness. In doing so, he associates non-worldliness, or world-denial, with moralistic dualisms whose hypocritical character resides in their denial of their reversibility. More ambitiously, as Nietzsche contests such dualisms, he works tirelessly to expose through critical reflection also the pervasiveness and apparent ineluctability of dualisms that resemble moral ones in all imaginable (and even ostensibly or intentionally positive) world-constructs—dualisms such as self and other, subject and object, affirmation and negation, presence and absence. As part of his critical reflection on the problematic dualities (de)constitutive of our various available world-notions, he develops moreover an extensive reflection on the ways in which these same dualities (de)constitute our available notions of self as ego, including the self he envisions as a strong value-positing one, beginning with Zarathustra himself. Which does not prevent Nietzsche from reiterating through Zarathustra the affirmations of world-affirmation as a highest value, if only because he is in favor of life as such, even as he does not know finally what this is or means.

In this context, as we have seen, Nietzsche's Zarathustra works to affirm a *literature of worldliness*, the very type of literature to which Zarathustra aspires in his speech, combining purity, depth, and the overcoming of narcissism with the passion of sensuality and the body. This literature remains a literature of the future, an object of imagination and desire, but also one marked as fond memory, at least in part because the binary structure of the values it is supposed to combine remains in force even as the structure manifests its reversibility.

Where does this leave Nietzsche's work in *Thus Spake Zarathustra* in relation to the discussion of world literature today?[68] I will approach this very general question in terms of two subordinate ones:

1) Is *Thus Spake Zarathustra* a work of world literature, and if so, in what sense? This question in turn has two subordinate dimensions. First, does *Thus Spake Zarathustra* characterize and offer itself as world literature in the sense of a literature for the world *outside* of the German-European culture in which it arises? And second, does Nietzsche's *Thus Spake Zarathustra*, regardless of Nietzsche's self-characterization of the work, finally belong to a world literature, insofar as the term implies a literature that steps out beyond, and exceeds the confines of, its own—in this case, the European—cultural self-enclosure? Or is it still merely, once again, European, all-too-European?[69]

2) Does this book tell us anything potentially useful about how to approach the task of reading the literatures of the world today?

1) We can approach the first question by considering the book's subtitle: *Thus Spake Zarathustra: A Book for All and None*. Without attempting to exhaust the possibilities for the interpretation of this subtitle (for which every reader of Nietzsche probably has his or her own reading—as they should, in Nietzsche's terms): in the context of the discussion above, it appears that the book is addressed to "none" insofar as it wishes to engage us at a level that exceeds all inscription in specific cultural value systems, but no one escapes such inscription entirely.[70] It is addressed to "all" insofar as all human beings presumably exist also in some sense outside the cultural languages that define the value systems they nonetheless inhabit.[71] Summarizing the readings of Nietzsche in world literature such as it was accessible in his day, Zarathustra says laconically, in "Of a Thousand and One Goals" (a title that alludes to the "Thousand and One Nights"): "Many lands saw Zarathustra and many peoples: thus he discovered the good and evil of many peoples. No greater power found Zarathustra on earth, than good and evil."[72] In light of these and similar remarks, which universalize the "good and evil" problem (taking it well beyond the confines of the Christian world), Nietzsche appears to be addressing himself through Zarathustra—insofar as he addresses the book to "all"—to a potentially global readership, specifically in the sense of all those who are interested in—and capable of—taking seriously the project of critically examining the historical foundations and the limitations of the value systems they confront at home and abroad, wherever home and abroad may be situated.

The difficulty of reaching such an audience is performed in many ways throughout the text, but perhaps above all by Zarathustra's shifting movements from the self-exile in his hermit's cave, to his address to the "people" in the Prologue, to his addresses to his "companions" (who appear initially as disciples, then later as friends and brothers, whom he leaves to return to his cave at the end of Part I and again at the end of Part II), to his dialogues with animals, to his interactions with the "Higher Humans" in Part IV (who ultimately disappoint him as interlocutors when they fall back into naive forms of religious faith). Complicating these shifts and oscillations is the fact that the very interplay between the spiritual leader and his disciples here openly echoes the relationship between Jesus and his disciples in the gospel (while Zarathustra's speeches imitate Christ's rhetorical style), yet the content of the book explicitly opposes key tenets in the teachings of Christ. Without retracing the play and full implications of these shifting movements and allusive ironies in detail, it suffices to recall them here to indicate the complexity and reflective richness in the performance of the difficulty of the address to the Other in *Thus Spake Zarathustra*. It's not easy to address oneself to the creative core of humanity that dwells outside of all cultural languages of value, in a "properly" worldly dimension. Nietzsche destines his book to an ideal global (because culturally un-situated) readership whose existence, along with that of the subject of enunciation, remains problematic.

One important limitation of this address, of course, is that in many regards it seems to exclude roughly one half of the human race—women. The tone and rhetoric of puerile misogyny often mark Nietzsche's discourse in general—including some of the most (in)famous passages in *Thus Spake Zarathustra*—as primarily an address to other men of the European nineteenth century. Although there is not space to thematize this at length in the current essay, it is nonetheless necessary to mark this much discussed aspect of his work in which Nietzsche gains relatively little critical perspective on the cultural values of his own place and time.[73] This limitation remains even if one grants, as one should, for example: that his provocations of bourgeois notions of propriety are meant to disrupt, in some respects, oppressively conventional ideas about gender; that his hostile remarks about women in general are matched in hostility by many of his remarks about humans in general and men specifically; that he ironizes the image of truth as a woman in philosophical discourse (in the Preface to *Beyond Good and Evil*) and thereby takes his distance from the discourse of women as possessions and from idealizations of women that are tantamount to debasements; that his remarks on women's incapacity for friendship are both explicitly historicist and counterbalanced by the suggestion that men, too, are largely incapable of friendship; that his depiction in *Thus Spake Zarathustra* of both life and wisdom as female figures whom Zarathustra loves (in the "The Dance Song") is in many ways positive, witty, and humane; and so on.[74]

Despite this significant limitation, one could say that *Thus Spake Zarathustra* belongs rightly to a world literature not just because it aims at a transcultural readership (even if it is particularly obsessed with the Northern Protestant value system), nor even because it has been read widely with interest on an international scale for a century and a half, nor further merely because in this work the author imitates earnestly and yet critically a position of prophetically exalted status outside of the European tradition, but also because he works with such insistent force and effectiveness to begin to break apart the European discourse and European culture here from within. It is as if he were working to break out of the European enclosure, or to dig a tunnel out from this enclosure into some other space, a space he calls "the future." Such a future is perhaps the one dawning, but still to come, in the cultural globalization in which specific cultures and civilizations are entering more and more into contact, communication, and contention, leading to the mutual relativization of their value systems.[75] In such a "future," still coming toward us, Nietzsche's insistence that one create one's own values is more pertinent, timely, and demanding than ever.

2) Given the implications of Nietzsche's address of *Thus Spake Zarathustra* to "all" and "none," what, if anything, does Nietzsche offer of a general nature, in *Thus Spake Zarathustra*, by way of guidance to a (scholarly) reader of world literature? Does he provide any useful indications about how such a reader should approach works of world literature in general? One can say first of all, and as is evident, that he offers and encourages us to adopt the perspective of skeptical curiosity about the moral dualisms constitutive of other (and all) cultures, including his "own." He proposes, then, that we approach world literature with an interest in how given cultures constitute "good" and "evil"—norms, ideals, and prohibitions—and how the given authors, works, fictional characters, and theories of world literature position themselves with respect to, experience, and act with regard to, these dualities of "good" and "evil," their translations and rough equivalents.

But is Nietzsche in a position to be friendly toward world literature, especially the literature of cultural "others"? And does he encourage us to be? What sort of openness or closure does he suggest is appropriate with respect to the "foreign" versus the "native" literatures a culturally inscribed reader (as each of us is, even if in multiple, heterogeneous forms) might encounter? After all, right-wing, nationalist, and aryanist appropriations of Nietzsche might make us wonder. We can usefully consider this question by recalling briefly in conclusion what he says about friends, enemies, neighbors, and those from farther off in *Thus Spake Zarathustra*.

In Zarathustra's speech concerning the question of friendship and enmity ("Of the Friend"), he gives us some critical indications. Reversing the Christian tenet that one should love one's enemy, he suggests, "In one's friend one should still honor the enemy. Can you get really close to your friend without going over to his side? In one's friend one should have one's best enemy. You should be closest to him with your heart when you resist him."[76] With respect to the "friendship" one may feel either toward one's "native" traditions (or those closest to them) or toward the more distant traditions (and texts and authors) with which one is inclined to develop a sympathetic identification, the suggestion is useful: resist narcissistic, that is, needy identification, both because one thereby imposes oneself on the other (conceptually or affectively, personally or impersonally) and also because one tends to find elsewhere—in one's friends—what one wishes to find in oneself. As Zarathustra puts it, "our belief in others betrays that which we would like to find believable in ourselves."[77] And one's love of "friends"—here, from whatever traditions—may simply function to distract one from "depths" within the self that one finds unbearable, including the division of the self, its fundamental inner disunity. "I and Me are always too enthusiastic in conversation: how could it be bearable if there were not a friend?"[78]

In a similar vein, Zarathustra says (in the section "Of Love of the Neighbor" ["*Von der Nächstenliebe*"—where *Nächstenliebe* means literally "love of the nearest one"]: "You can't stand being with yourselves, and do not love yourselves enough: now you want to seduce your neighbor into loving you, and to gild yourselves with his error."[79] Whether this suggestion is understood as having potential reference to relationships with familiar traditions, or to relationships with more distant traditions, or for that matter to relationships with one's colleagues or readers, the suggestion contains a useful warning for the scholar of world literature.

But the position is a somewhat tricky one, because while Zarathustra proposes self-love—affirmation of one's own solitary creativity—as opposed to the pseudo-altruistic love of neighbor, saying "your love of neighbor is your bad love of yourselves,"[80] he proposes in the same breath the choice of the farthest, the most distant and foreign: "Higher than the love of the neighbor is the love of the farthest away and of that which is coming in the future; higher still than the love of humans is the love of things and ghosts."[81] If things that haunt us, and things we are concerned about, are more worthy of love than people in the sense of "our neighbors," this is because when we love our neighbor we tend to use him or her either for self-confirmation or for flight and distraction from ourselves (as excessively present or as excessively absent to ourselves). "One goes to the neighbor because he is looking for himself, and the other, because he would like to lose himself. Your bad love of yourselves makes of your loneliness [or solitude] a prison."[82] This explains why love of the farthest coincides with self-affirmation—an apparent paradox—in the sense Zarathustra in turn affirms: "love of the farthest" seeks to engage, while sustaining its aloneness, with something or someone unheard-of, something truly other, something that does not remind one of oneself, hence something not yet given, something in the future—an untranslatable. Such, Zarathustra says, is the "creative friend," at a distance from the self-same, "who always has a finished world to give away."[83]

Insofar as we set about to read world literature, literature in and of the world at the limits of particular cultures and civilizations, if we follow Zarathustra (always a questionable undertaking), we should be seeking such worlds of friends, who remain our best enemies. "And as the world rolled out of itself and apart for him, so it rolls together again for him in rings as the becoming of the good through the evil, as the becoming of purposes out of what happens by chance." When translated into our context, this nearly untranslatable passage suggests that in reading the writer of world literature, indeed any writer as such, one should seek to be receptive to the gift of a world coming apart and coming together, and to glimpse how the good arises out of evil there as its binary other, and how purposiveness and meaning arise out of the arbitrary and the meaningless, and vice versa, (non)dualistically. One should seek to grasp there also how the world in question, the world of this singular other, but not an identity, comes together in its punctual presence as a singular iteration—the ring of the eternal recurrence—a world that presents itself only once and nonetheless repeats itself forever, insofar as it both stays where it is and can only *appear* as repeated and temporally dispersed.[84] World literature as the literature of the iteration of an always singular world, at the never-ending ending of all dualities of value, always giving out and leaving something to be affirmed and desired: world iterature.

Notes

1 Thanks to Ahmad Nadalizadeh for his invaluable research assistance on this project.
2 Friedrich Nietzsche, *Also sprach Zarathustra, Kritische Studienausgabe*, vol. 4, ed. Giorgio Colli and Mazzino Montinari (München: Deutsche Taschenbuch Verlag, 1988). Translations of this and other German language texts are my own. When referring to "Zarathustra" below I will mean "Nietzsche's figure of Zarathustra," and when referring to the Anglicized "Zoroaster," I will intend "the prophet himself (as filtered through his Western reception in general)."
3 Raymond Schwab, *La renaissance orientale* (Paris: Payot, 1950).
4 If, as I have argued in *Orientalism and the Figure of the Jew* (New York: Fordham UP, 2015), with reference to Erich Auerbach's work on *figura*, nineteenth-century Orientalism saw the Occident as the fulfillment of the prefigural Oriental overcoming of a pre-prefigural pagan materialism, Nietzsche resituates the relation of pre-prefiguration, prefiguration, and fulfillment in the trajectory from animal to human to trans- or meta-human (the latter remaining futural). As I show below, he also resituates fulfillment in the moment of fullness when "my world," or "the world,"

as also in the moment when "my values" and "the values," coincide, i.e., in pure affirmation, which is posited as desirable (i.e., Nietzsche affirms affirmation) but never reliably or stably achieved: it comes and goes. These displacements, considered further below, undo in principle the metaphysical superiority of the West that Orientalism maintains.

5   On Nietzsche's relation with Zoroastrianism as mediated by the classical tradition and the scholarship of his day, notably Friedrich Creuzer, see François Dastur, "Who is Nietzsche's Zarathustra? A Note on the Iranian-Persian Background," *Comparative and Continental Philosophy* 1.1 (2009): 39–54; Daryoush Ashouri, "Nietzsche and Persia," *Encyclopedia Iranica* (2010), http://www.iranicaonline.org/articles/nietzsche-and-persia; David Aiken, "Nietzsche and his Zarathustra: A Western Poet's Transformation of an Eastern Priest and Prophet," *Zeitschrift für Religions- und Geistesgeschichte* 55.4 (2003): 335–53; Hamid Dabashi, *Persophilia: Persian Culture on the Global Scene* (Cambridge: Harvard UP, 2015), in which the relationship between Nietzsche's Zarathustra and Goethe's Hafez is emphasized, and the importance of the figure of Sarastro in Mozart's *Magic Flute* highlighted; Jenny Rose, *Zoroastrianism: an Introduction* (London: I.B. Tauris, 2011). For a useful examination of the romantic precursors of Nietzsche concerning the doctrine of eternal recurrence, which develops in particular the importance of Creuzer, and of Creuzer's rapprochement of Heraclitus and Zoroastrianism, for the elaboration of a cyclical view of the unification of dualistic opposites, see Robert A. Yelle, "The Rebirth of Myth?: Nietzsche's Eternal Recurrence and its Romantic Antecedents," *Numen* 47.2 (2000): 175–202.

6   One of the important predecessors of Creuzer who articulated the view of Zoroastrianism as a strict dualism was Friedrich Schlegel, in "Über die Sprache und Weisheit der Indier," in *Kritische Friedrich-Schlegel-Ausgabe*, ed. Ernst Behler and Ursula Struc-Oppenberg, vol. VIII, Studien zur Philosophie und Theologie (Paderborn: Ferdinand Schöningh, 1975. See especially Book II, Chapter 4, "Die Lehre von zwei Prinzipien" (229–41). The dualistic view is notably not so strongly emphasized in Goethe's *West-Östlicher Divan* (1819), however, where Goethe characterizes the religion of Zoroaster as worship of the sun, and of fire as reflection or fragment of the sun, and as an admirable concern with purity and honesty. In this respect, Nietzsche—who is much more intensely and critically interested in the interplay of light and darkness as one of good and evil—is not following Goethe, although by elevating a figure from ancient Persian culture as his own mouthpiece (and himself as mouthpiece of that figure), he is indeed following Goethe's Persianist example (even if Goethe focused largely on *medieval* Persian poets, especially Hafez), an example that involves the rejection of the Indomania (and neo-Catholicism) of the romantics from Friedrich Schlegel onward. The other allusions to Goethe in *Thus Spake Zarathustra*, however, are more closely linked to his *Faust* project than to his *Divan* project, notably the very term *Übermensch* (a term that the Earth Spirit applies to Faust himself in the "Night" scene of Act One of *Faust* I), as well as the language of that opening, "Da steh ich ich nun," which Nietzsche echoes in the song of the Wanderer and Shadow in the section "Amongst the Daughters of the Desert" in Part IV of *Thus Spake Zarathustra*. I return to the question of Goethe's *Übermensch* in the discussion of Zarathustra's view of poetic writing (or literature). On Goethe's *West-Östlicher Divan* as a seminal work in the world literature discussion, see Jeffrey Einboden, "The Genesis of *Weltliteratur*: Goethe's West-Östlicher Divan and Kerygmatic Pluralism," *Literature and Theology* 19.3 (2005): 238–50.

7 Friedrich Creuzer, *Symbolik und Mythologie der alten Völker besonders der Griechen* (Leipzig: Carl Wihelm Leske, 1821).
8 Ibid., 695.
9 Ibid., 697.
10 Arthur Schopenhauer, *Parerga und Paralipomena II*, in *Werke in fünf Bänden*, ed. Ludger Lütkehaus (Frankfurt am Main: Haffmans Verlag bei Zweitausendeins, 2006), 332-9.
11 On Nietzsche's distance from learned philology in *Thus Spake Zarathustra*, see "Of the Learned," 160-2.
12 See e.g. Friedrich W. J. Schelling, "Über das Verhältnis des Realen und Idealen in der Natur oder Entwickelung der ersten Grundsätze der Naturphilosophie an den Principien der Schwere und des Lichts," in *Ausgewählte Schriften*, ed. Manfred Frank, vol. III (Frankfurt am Main: Suhrkamp, 1985), 589-610.
13 Aiken, in his informative and judicious article, "Nietzsche and his Zarathustra," explores the question of Nietzsche's critique of dualism in relation to Zoroastrian dualism but does not pinpoint this paradoxical structure that constitutes in my view the central element of Nietzsche's response to dualism.
14 I consider the "self" as "subject" or "ego" here, one of the perspectives Nietzsche adopts in *Thus Spake Zarathustra*. For the perspective from which the "self" appears as distinct from the "ego" and as underlying it in the form of the "body," see "Of the Despisers of the Body." See Kristina Mendicino on "Of Old and New Tablets" in *Announcements: On Novelty* (Albany: SUNY Press, 2020), where she focuses on the paradoxically simultaneous insistence on novelty and repetition in Nietzsche's discourse, and on his mode of speech, rather than the contents of that speech, as the crucial dimension of his innovation. My approach here focuses on Zarathustra's mode of speech as the contestation, in language and from out of language, of a language of duality that encompasses the duality of duality and its other.
15 Nietzsche, *Also sprach Zarathustra*, 246.
16 To consider briefly the sense of the absence of the signs of Zarathustra's hour here: since the time announced by the signs of the lion with the doves would evidently be a time when the wild wisdom of warlike power is allied with quiet peacefulness, such that the duality of fierce aggression and peaceful love is overcome, as would be the case in the punctual "beyond" of good and evil, evidently the time of the overcoming of the duality of good and evil has not yet arrived. Given the course of the text, moreover, we have good reason to think that this time will never come, except insofar as it also goes, to come again another day, in line with the contradictory processuality and the repetitionality or iteratedness of the present in Nietzsche. The duality does not sublate itself into a unity. The unity remains an eternal desideratum, eternally present in its absence and absent in its presence. The duality of the unity and difference of good and evil remains. For Zarathustra both pushes for the reality of the "beyond" and maintains their difference (a difference still evident in the notions of "virtue," of "honesty," of "courage," etc., which Zarathustra values positively, and which imply the existence of their opposites as bad).
17 The ambiguity of "as" here would bear comparison with, and could—in terms of the relationship between fiction and interpretation—also shed useful light on, Martin Heidegger's distinction between the hermeneutic and the apophantic "as," as applicable to understanding and interpretation, respectively, in *Sein und Zeit* (Tübingen: Niemeyer Verlag, 1979), 148-60.

18 Nietzsche, *Also sprach Zarathustra*, 252.
19 Indeed, the various arguments Nietzsche uses to ground (and objectify) the "eternal recurrence of the same," Zarathustra's "most abyssal thought," are opposed to, and tend to obscure, the sense in which this thought is not just a theory about objective reality (which it also is) but—in contradiction to this—a desideratum, the object of a subjective desire and a pure groundless affirmation, as appears in "The Other Dance Song," and even more clearly in "The Seven Seals," in the refrain "For I love you, eternity!" and in the expression "Wohlan! Nocheinmall!" ("Let's go, then! One more time!), repeatedly used to characterize the affirmation of eternal return. The same ambiguities of subjective-objective and absent-present that affect all creatively posited values also affect the "eternal recurrence of the same," which is the epitome of all self-affirmation, the value of values.
20 Nietzsche, *Also sprach Zarathustra*, 268.
21 As one example: "When you are sublimely above praise and blame, and your will wants (or wills) to command all things, as the will of a lover: there is the beginning of your virtue" (99).
22 In "Of the Giving Virtue," 97–102.
23 The term *Übermensch* is an untranslatable term. See the admirable analysis of the role of the untranslatable in world literatures in Emily Apter, *Against World Literature: On the Politics of Untranslatability* (London: Verso, 2013), where she builds on the work of Barbara Cassin in *Dictionary of Untranslatables: A Philosophical Lexicon* (Oxford: Oxford UP, 2017).
24 For Nietzsche's early divergence from Schopenhauer on the topic of the aesthetic, notably the lyric, a divergence that still however makes use of Schopenhauerian concepts, see "Die Geburt der Tragödie aus dem Geiste der Musik," *Kritische Studienausgabe Vol I*, ed. Giorgio Colli and Mazzino Montinari (München: Deutsche Taschenbuch Verlag, 1988), 46–8.
25 The rejection of eudaimonistic ethics is condensed simply in the expressed privilege of the "work" over "happiness," which Zarathustra states repeatedly in various phrasings, e.g., in the last lines of the book: "Do I aspire then to *happiness*? I aspire to my *work*!" (Friedrich Nietzsche, *Also sprach Zarathustra*, 408).
26 Cf. Claudia Crawford, "A Genealogy of Worlds according to Nietzsche," *Philosophy and Rhetoric* 27.3 (1994): 202–17. Crawford tracks, in *The Will to Power* and "On Truth and Lying in an Extramoral Sense," Nietzsche's fragmentarily perspectival deconstructions of the "world" concept as it has been traditionally constructed in terms of reality versus truth and appearance versus reality. She formalizes usefully his questioning of these dualities as tools for the ostensible mastery of a "world" that remains ineffable and yet radically immanent, pointing us toward the task of worldly affirmation whose necessity announces itself in the name of an inevitable fictionality of the real.
27 Nietzsche, *Also sprach Zarathustra*, 257 et passim.
28 Ibid., 257.
29 Ibid., 259 et passim.
30 Ibid., 35–8 et passim.
31 Ibid., 272.
32 Ibid.
33 Ibid.
34 Ibid.

35 Ibid.
36 Ibid., 273.
37 See "Of the Despisers of the Body," 39–41.
38 The function of desire and will as explicitly "ethical" instances goes back, in the tradition Nietzsche inherits, at least to Kant, who calls the ethical will a "faculty of desire" (*Begehrungsvermögen*).
39 Nietzsche, *Also sprach Zarathustra*, 286.
40 Ibid., 286 and 398–404.
41 Note that the German word, "Lust," signifying both pleasure and desire, finds itself caught within this duality of satisfaction and non-satisfaction, presence and absence, fullness and lack, here as in Freud, which to some extent reintroduces the duality of pleasure and pain within pleasure itself. This reappearance of pleasure and pain within pleasure itself perhaps indeed explains why pleasure/desire is "deeper" than pain.
42 Nietzsche, *Also sprach Zarathustra*, 287–91.
43 Ibid., 235. In that context, he emphasizes the material physicality of the world as "number and force."
44 The fact that, in the dream at the start of Part II, he sees himself as a "devil" in the mirror indicates not only that he fears his doctrine will be misunderstood simply as a satanism but also that the "spirit of gravity" cannot be separated from the levity of Zarathustran dance.
45 Nietzsche, *Also sprach Zarathustra*, 400.
46 Ibid.
47 Ibid.
48 Ibid.
49 Ibid.
50 Ibid.
51 Ibid., 401.
52 Ibid., 402.
53 Ibid.
54 Ibid., 408.
55 Ibid.
56 Lying is an epistemic as well as ethical fault because the poets lie only because they don't know enough, as Zarathustra will say; and it is therefore also an aesthetic one because the aesthetic realm, at least since Kant, constitutes the realm where epistemic and ethical values (or "faculties") interpenetrate.
57 Nietzsche, *Also sprach Zarathustra*, 163. Zarathustra had said this earlier in "On the Happy Isles" (110). The point about the "permanent" is an allusion to Goethe's passage in *Faust*, II, V (the Mountain Gorges scene) that inverts it. In a very literal translation, Goethe writes, "All that is transient/is only a figure; the inadequate/becomes here event;/the indescribable,/here it occurs; The eternal feminine/draws us onward." In the context we are considering, as elsewhere in *Thus Spake Zarathustra*, Nietzsche sheds derision on this passage, including on the image of the pull of the eternal feminine, which he generalizes and displaces, rephrasing it as the pull of the gods, considered to be the false creations of the narcissistic and dreamy poets. Allusions to *Faust* abound, of course, in *Thus Spake Zarathustra*, where Nietzsche is struggling with the figure of Goethe in more than one respect.
58 Nietzsche, *Also sprach Zarathustra*, 163.

59 Ibid., 164.
60 Ibid.
61 Ibid.
62 Again, the allusion is to Goethe's "das Ewig-Weiblich zieht uns hinan" in *Faust*, and Zarathustra has just said, "And we even desire the things that old women tell us at night. We call this the 'eternal feminine' in ourselves" (164). I return to the vexed question of Nietzsche's misogyny briefly below.
63 "Spirit is the life that itself cuts into life: through its own torture it increases its own knowledge—did you know that?" (134).
64 Nietzsche, *Also sprach Zarathustra*, 14.
65 Ibid., 165.
66 Ibid.
67 In twists and turns of the poetic argument that we cannot follow but only point to here, when the poets reflect upon themselves, it turns out that they are actually "penitents of spirit" (166), i.e.—according to the earlier section "Of the Sublime Ones" (150–2)—those whose commitment to heroic seriousness and ascetic "contempt for the earth" (151) makes them ugly and humourless, and prevents them from accessing beauty, grace (152), or benevolence. The analysis of the "penitent of spirit" is extended in Part IV of *Thus Spake Zarathustra* when the figure returns in "The Magician" (318ff).
68 On the origins and sense of Goethe's concept of world literature, and its various interpretations within debates on world literature today, see John Pizer, "Johann Wolfgang Goethe: Origins and Relevance of Weltliteratur," in *Routledge Companion to World Literature*, ed. Theo D'haen, David Damrosch, and Djelal Kadir (New York: Routledge, 2012), 3–11; and for an essay that emphasizes the later Goethe's distance from Enlightenment traditions in favor of anthropology and historicism à la Herder, see Stephen Klemm, "Historicism, Anthropology, and Goethe's Idea of World Literature," *Seminar: A Journal of Germanic Studies* 54.2 (2018): 148–66.
69 While not all definitions of world literature would require that a given work step beyond its own cultural presuppositions (either in the intentions of its address or in the reality of its insights and formal scope, assuming the latter is even ever possible in significant degree), these questions seem important to the attempt to gauge Nietzsche's (or any given author's) relationship to world literature, because if the works remain intentionally or in fact provincial, then their import for a world readership would largely be restricted to something like information about a given subject in a given culture. And if there is no such thing as universal works of art, there might be some that are more translatable than others, despite and perhaps because of a certain untranslatability, even a certain relatively explicit insistence on untranslatability, such as we find in Nietzsche's insistence on the singularity of the creative, hence on the very limits of cultural languages with respect to aesthetic expression.
70 Cf. Martin Heidegger's gloss on the subtitle at the outset of "Wer ist Nietzsches Zarathustra," in *Vorträge und Aufsätze*, 4th ed. (Pfullingen: Neske Verlag, 1978), 97–122. Not surprisingly, and in this not necessarily at odds with the spirit of Nietzsche's own thought in its dimension of "think for yourself," although perhaps a bit too "sublimely," he bends Nietzsche's language from the outset in the direction of his own thought, e.g., by reading the "for all" as meaning "for each human as human, for each one in so far as he becomes for himself worthy of thought in his essence," and "for none" as for none of those who are merely "curious" and read Nietzsche only partially

71 In a psychoanalytic perspective, the level on which the human being exists outside of cultural languages is that of the unconscious. On this point, see the works of the Freudian School of Quebec, notably Jean-Pierre Boisvert, ed., *Mondialisation, défis pour l'humain* (Quebec: GIFRIC, 2016), in which hallucinatory jouissance is understood as the creative force that both gives rise to systems of values and is caught up in their deadening enclosure within given cultures and civilizations. See my summary of the current position of this school on the subject of culture in "The Subject in the Age of World-formation (Mondialisation): Advances in Lacanian Theory from the Québec Group," in *Innovations in Psychoanalysis: Originality, Development, Progress*, ed. Aner Govrin and Jon Mills (New York: Routledge, 2020), 75–99.

and do not "put themselves onto the path of thinking that here seeks its word" (97). The reasonable attempt to salvage Nietzsche from tendentious misreadings in 1953 itself tends from the start toward the Heideggerian thesis that the essence of the human lies in his existence, thus moving Nietzsche toward the question of Being.

72 Nietzsche, *Also sprach Zarathustra*, 74. Toward the end of the section, Nietzsche has Zarathustra repeat these lines but with the difference that at the end he replaces "good and evil" with "the works of the lovers/the loving ones: 'good' and 'evil' is their name" (76). When Zarathustra makes the fundamental values of any culture into the "works of the loving ones" in an Orientalist context, he is implicitly displacing the basic schema of nineteenth-century German Orientalism, according to which the East plays the role of the prefiguration to the West's fulfillment, which means (in terms of the Pauline model for the Jewish-Christian relation that underlies this Orientalist schema) that the East figures as the dead letter of "works" while the West appears as the living spirit of faith, hope, and "love." When Nietzsche speaks of the fundamental value systems of all cultures as the works that arise out of the love of the "creative" spirits—"Liebende waren es stets und Schaffende, die schufen Gut und Böse" (76)—he effectively collapses this distinction between love and works, and he also transfers it onto a "transcendental" level: the combined force of love and works becomes the condition of the possibility of *all* value systems, including the value system within which the dualistic opposition between works and love structures the Jewish-Christian and the East-West opposition in nineteenth-century German (and Christian) Orientalism. Moreover, in preferring his "works" to his "happiness," a point I have noted above, Zarathustra places himself on the side of "works" and against "faith," thus distancing himself from both (Lutheran) Christianity and its Orientalist Occidental repetition.

73 For an important collection of essays on this theme, see Peter J. Burgard, ed., *Nietzsche and the Feminine* (Charlottesville: University of Virginia Press, 1994).

74 It is worth pointing out further that one of the motifs to be analyzed in an extended thematization of Nietzsche's approach to women in *Thus Spake Zarathustra* would have to be the figure of *pregnancy*, of which Zarathustra says that, on the one hand, the solution to the riddle of woman is "pregnancy" (84) and that, on the other hand, Zarathustra uses frequently the metaphor of "pregnancy" for creative potential that is in the process of preparing to express itself (21, 111, 123, 156, 158, 195, 204, 287, 362), something he obviously affirms. These usages give maternity an interesting and important status, which however doesn't cancel the puerile sexism noted above.

75 See the essays in Boisvert, *Mondialisation, défis pour l'humain*, especially Willy Apollon, "Citoyen du monde, ...mais de quelle nationalité?" (205–74).

76 Nietzsche, *Also sprach Zarathustra*, 71.
77 Ibid.
78 Ibid.
79 Ibid., 77.
80 Ibid.
81 Ibid.
82 Ibid., 78.
83 Ibid.
84 For the affirmation of singularity as a "supplementary" contribution to the world literature discourse, see Gayatri Spivak's remarks in "Comparative Literature/World Literature: A Discussion with Gayatri Chakravorty Spivak and David Damrosch," *Comparative Literature Studies* 48.4 (2011): 455–85, and especially 466, 473–4.

10

Asian Philosophy, National Literatures, and World Literature Anthologies

Junjie Luo

Philosophy and literature enjoy a close relationship, and philosophers have a long tradition of commenting on literature. Aristotle's *Poetics*, for example, is one of the earliest, and the most influential, pieces of literary criticism. Major contemporary philosophers such as David Lewis and John Searle engage in literary criticism.[1] The philosophy of literature has become an important topic in the field of philosophy.[2] However, as Jim Marshall has argued, the line of demarcation between philosophy and literature is blurring in certain texts.[3] Richard Rorty has even proclaimed "the literary status of philosophy" as he seeks to subsume the once authoritative and truth-seeking philosophy under the more unstable and imprecise literary culture.[4] The interconnectedness identified between philosophy and literature allows for the examination of philosophical texts from literary perspectives.

Marshall uses the examples of writers such as Simone de Beauvoir and Jean-Paul Sartre to demonstrate that philosophy and literature cannot always be distinguished in the French tradition.[5] It should be noted that de Beauvoir and Sartre write primarily in French. In the reference section of Marshall's article, he often lists both the English translations of de Beauvoir's and Sartre's works and the French originals.[6] In discussing the relationship between philosophy and literature, the issue of translation is important given that philosophical and literary texts are written in a variety of languages.

Translation connects philosophical texts to world literature. David Damrosch defines world literature as "writing that gains in translation."[7] The eligibility of a text to be considered world literature depends on whether its translation can reach a wider audience and engage in dialogues with other national traditions.[8] Damrosch's definition of world literature is liberating in the sense that it does not confine world literature to a specific type of writing but focuses on the mode of transmission and interaction. To establish their relationship with world literature, Asian philosophical texts rely particularly on their mode of transmission. Without translation, these texts would not be able to "speak" to Western traditions, which until fairly recently had dominated the discussion of world literature. English-language world literature anthologies offer an important venue where the translations of Asian philosophical works can speak as part of world literature.

To offer a definition of Asian philosophy is as difficult as defining what philosophy is. In *Classic Asian Philosophy: A Guide to the Essential Texts* (hereafter, *Classic Asian Philosophy*), Joel Kupperman discusses works such as *Bhagavad Gita* and Confucius's *Analects*, which he considers to be "foundational Asian philosophical texts."[9] Instead of defining Asian philosophy, this essay focuses on how these major Asian philosophical works can be read as part of world literature. Out of the ten chapters of *Classic Asian Philosophy*, seven focus on Chinese or Indian philosophical texts, and two additional chapters also discuss Chinese and Indian philosophy extensively.[10] As a result, I will focus on Chinese and Indian traditions in this essay. While this type of simplification inevitably reduces the complexity and diversity of Asian philosophy, I hope that this essay can serve as a starting point for exploring the relationships between Asian philosophical texts and world literature.

I narrow my discussion of world literature to an examination of English-language world literature anthologies because the excerpts from *Bhagavad Gita* and *The Analects* often appear in these collections. A world literature anthology represents an imagined system of world literature by selecting and organizing texts. Why do the anthologies include these texts? What position do these Asian philosophical writings occupy in the system that these anthologies envision? In examining the world literature anthologies published between the late nineteenth century and the early twenty-first century, this essay seeks to address these questions.

According to Sarah Lawall, the earliest world literature anthologies include *Alden's Cyclopedia of Universal Literature* (1885–91; hereafter, *Alden's Cyclopedia*), *A Library of World's Best Literature, Ancient and Modern* (1897; hereafter, *World's Best*), and *Masterpieces of the World's Literature, Ancient and Modern* (1898; hereafter, *Masterpieces*).[11] As I have pointed out elsewhere, *Alden's Cyclopedia* and *Masterpieces* include only one Chinese author—Confucius.[12] Both anthologies acknowledge that Confucius is an "ethical philosopher."[13] *Alden's Cyclopedia* identifies similarities between the ideas and legacies of Confucius and those of Jesus and Mohammed, and connects the time of Confucius's death to "the battle of Lake Regillus, the first authentic date in Roman history."[14] This contextualization of Confucius implies that Confucius is not only the foundational figure of Confucianism but also the beginning of the Chinese civilization.

World's Best makes it clear that Chinese philosophy, especially the Confucian philosophy, serves as the foundation of Chinese literature:

> The Five Classics and Four Books may be said to be the foundations on which all Chinese literature has been based. The period when Confucius and Mencius taught and wrote was one of great mental activity all over the world. While the wise men of China were proclaiming their system of philosophy, the seven sages of Greece …[15]

Given this central role assigned to Chinese philosophy, *World's Best* uses its included excerpts from Confucian philosophical writings to represent the entire body of Chinese literature.[16] Confucian philosophy, instead of Chinese drama, fiction, or even poetry, which is often considered to be the crowning achievement of Chinese literature, has become the sole representative of Chinese literature in these early anthologies.

Using philosophical writings to exemplify a national literature is not common in these anthologies. For example, *Masterpieces* anthologizes the works of approximately 220 American authors, and only five of them are classified as philosophers in the index.[17] In addition to Chinese literature, *Masterpieces* includes at least nine national literatures represented solely by one or two authors. Works by philosophers are not selected for the overwhelming majority of these national literatures.[18] The preface to *World's Best* states that this anthology is, in general, literature only. Philosophers are included only for the literary value of their writings or "because their influence upon literature itself has been so profound that the progress of the race could not be accounted for without them."[19] In this sense, presenting philosophical writings as the sole representative of Chinese literature is an exception in these world literature anthologies.

The case of Indian philosophy in these world literature anthologies is different. Unlike the Confucian philosophical writings that appear in every world literature anthology discussed above, the anthologized Indian works are diverse. *Alden's Cyclopedia* does not include any selections from Indian literature. Instead, an excerpt from Charles Morris's *The Aryan Race* appears in the anthology, and the excerpt introduces two Indian epics—the *Ramayana* and the *Mahabharata*.[20] The only Indian author represented in *Masterpieces* is Pilpay, who is credited as an author of early Indian fables.[21]

World's Best has a more extensive selection of Indian texts. It includes excerpts from *The Upanishads* and *The Dhammapada*, which are discussed in *Classic Asian Philosophy*. However, many Indian texts anthologized in *World's Best* are from other sources such as the Vedic hymns, the *Ramayana*, and Indian plays.[22] Compared to Confucian philosophical writings that serve as the only representative of Chinese literature in these early world literature anthologies, Indian philosophical texts do not occupy such a prominent position. Furthermore, unlike Confucian philosophical texts, philosophy is not regarded as the foundation of Indian literature in *World's Best*. Both *The Upanishads* and *The Dhammapada* are important works that belong to the earlier stages in the development of Indian literature,[23] but they are by no means presented as the sole representative of Indian literature in *World's Best*.

Nevertheless, Indian philosophy still plays a significant role in its national literature, according to *World's Best*. Philosophical works may not be of the utmost importance in Indian literature, but "most important of all this subsidiary literature are the many works on philosophy."[24] Philosophical musings are also present in other major types of Indian literature. For example, some hymns in the Rigveda Collection are "purely philosophical and mystical."[25] More importantly, Indian literature has been greatly influenced by the tendency of "constant philosophizing."[26] Philosophy is a staple of Indian literature in *World's Best*. The question is: Why is Chinese and Indian philosophy so important for their respective national literatures in these early world literature anthologies?

The issue of national literature presented in these early anthologies is worth noting. The entries are arranged alphabetically in all three anthologies discussed above. *Alden's Cyclopedia* offers no structure to categorize the authors and their works into different national traditions. This is a possible reason why Indian literature has no representative in this anthology. The idea of national literature emerges in *Masterpieces*. Its last volume provides an index, which divides the authors into different historical periods and then categorizes them based on their nationalities (see Figure 10.1). National literature features even more prominently in *World's Best*. Several entries are surveys of national literatures as well as selections from these national literary traditions. These entries include one on Chinese literature and another on Indian literature.[27] Furthermore, the last two volumes of this anthology provide an index and several pieces of index-like apparatus, which categorize the authors and their works based on their nationalities in a variety of ways and highlight the concept of national literature.[28]

The selections from Chinese and Indian literatures are, in general, scarce in these anthologies. The limited space devoted to the texts of the two national literatures may be one reason why philosophical writings are so important. One criterion that *World's Best* uses to include a certain work is that "at one time it expressed the thought and feeling of a nation."[29] These classical philosophical texts reflect the deep-rooted beliefs of their cultures and nations. Given that there is insufficient space to accommodate different types of Chinese or Indian literature, philosophy may have become a ready choice to represent these two national literatures.

The selection of classical philosophical texts captures the long history of Chinese and Indian literatures. However, it also creates the impression that there has been little progress made in these two national literatures. For example, with only Confucian philosophical works anthologized in these collections, Chinese literature appears not to have developed since these philosophical writings. Robert Douglas indeed contends that later Chinese literature, such as its fiction and drama, are inferior to earlier Chinese literature.[30] *World's Best* does survey the development of Indian literature from "Vedic literature" through "modern Sanskrit and dialectic literature."[31] Nevertheless, the most recent piece included in this anthology, an excerpt from *The Bible of the Dadu Panthis*, is a sixteenth-century literary work, and the second-most recent piece appeared during the twelfth century.[32] The rest of the anthologized Indian works were all produced prior to the sixth century. This still leaves the impression that the achievement of modern and contemporary Indian literature is much less significant than that of ancient Indian literature. Moreover, many anthologized texts were produced during what Edward Hopkins calls "the philosophical era … from about 500 B.C. to the end of the period of Sanskrit literature," which significantly influences Indian literature. Classical philosophical texts play an important role in speaking for Chinese and Indian literatures in these early anthologies, but these anthologies do not sufficiently show how the national literatures have progressed since their ancient beginnings.

The Chinese literary texts became more diverse in world literature anthologies published around the mid-twentieth century. Confucian philosophy no longer serves as the only representative of the Chinese literary tradition. For example, the revised edition of *Our Heritage of World Literature* (1942) includes both the selections from

Index of Authors, Chronological and National

I
BEFORE THE CHRISTIAN ERA.

Greek.	VOL.	PAGE
525–456 B. C., Æschylus	I	77
Seventh Century B. C., Æsop	I	90
563 (?)–478 (?) B. C., Anacreon	I	329
450 (?)–380 (?) B. C., Aristophanes	I	477
384–322 B. C., Aristotle	I	502
-240 B. C., Callimachus	5	2215
384–322 B. C., Demosthenes	7	3477
Circ. 200–250 B. C., Diogenes Laertius	7	3674
342–270 B. C., Epicurus	8	4273
480–406 B. C., Euripides	8	4311
535–475 B. C., Heraclitus	11	5029
484–420 B. C., Herodotus	11	5949
962–927 B. C., Homer	11	6004
520–440 B. C., Pindar	16	8949
429–347 B. C., Plato	16	8964
556–469 B. C., Simonides	18	10072
470–399 B. C., Socrates	18	10134
638–559 B. C., Solon	18	10140
496–405 B. C., Sophocles	18	10142
-272 B. C., Theocritus	19	10563
470–400 B. C., Thucydides	19	10607
650 B. C., Tyrtaeus	19	10733
600–B. C., Sappho	18	9734
431–341 B. C., Xenophon	20	11237

Latin.	VOL.	PAGE
87–54 B. C., Catullus, Caius Valerius	5	2432
100–44 B. C., Caesar, Caius Julius	4	2143
106–43 B. C., Cicero, Marcus Tullius	5	2687
65–8 B. C., Horace, Quintus Horatius Flaccus	12	6192
59 B. C.–17 A. D., Livy	13	7207
95–52 B. C., Lucretius	14	7334
43 B. C.–18 A. D., Ovid	16	8676
254–184 B. C., Plautus	16	8983
86–34 B. C., Sallust	18	9696
3 B. C.–65 A. D., Seneca, Lucius Annæus	18	9919
70–19 B. C., Virgil	20	10799

Chinese.

	VOL.	PAGE
549–447 B. C., Confucius	6	2938

Egyptian.

	VOL.	PAGE
Two Brothers, The	20	11307
Shipwrecked Sailor, The	20	11303

Indian.

	VOL.	PAGE
Pilpay	16	8932

II.
THE FIRST FIFTEEN CENTURIES.

Greek.		
Second Century, Alciphron	I	180
-147, Athenæus	2	629
Third Century, Bion	3	1240
-118, Epictetus	8	4262
120–200, Lucian	14	7322
Second Century, Pausanias	16	8791
49–120, Plutarch	17	9007

Latin.		
340 (?)–394, Ambrose, Saint	I	300

Latin—continued.		
431 (?)–482, Apollinaris, Caius Sallius Sidonius	I	397
Second Century, Apuleius, Lucius	I	403
1225 (?)–74, Aquinas, Thomas	I	409
354–430, Augustine, Saint	2	672
121–180, Aurelius, Marcus	2	682
475–524 (?), Boethius	3	1450
-1255, Celano, Thomas of	19	10577
40–120, Juvenal	13	6732
43–104, Martial, Marcus	14	7787

Figure 10.1 Index of authors, chronological and national
Peck, *Masterpieces*, 20: 11339. The image is downloaded from *Internet Archive*, https://archive.org/details/masterpiecesofwo20peckuoft /page/11338.

The Analects and classical Chinese poems.³³ I have argued elsewhere that the inclusion of classical Chinese poetry in these world literature anthologies may be related to its influence on modernist poetry.³⁴ The new Chinese literary material is not confined to poetry, however. In the third edition of *An Anthology of World Literature* (1951), a Chinese play, *The Sorrows of Han*, is the first literary text appearing in the section on China.³⁵ *The Sorrows of Han* was produced during the thirteenth or the fourteenth century. The remaining Chinese texts including selections from Chinese philosophical texts all significantly predate this play.³⁶ Placing *The Sorrows of Han* before earlier Chinese texts highlights the significance of this play in Chinese literature, given that *An Anthology of World Literature* usually arranges the texts of one national literature in a roughly chronological order. Chinese philosophical texts are still an important component of the Chinese literature chosen for these anthologies, but other types of Chinese literature have, by the mid-twentieth century, begun to share with philosophy the representative position in Chinese literature.

Indian philosophy still occupies a place in these mid-twentieth-century world literature anthologies. All three editions of *An Anthology of World Literature* and the revised edition of *Our Heritage of World Literature* include *Bhagavad Gita*, a philosophical text from the Indian epic, the *Mahabharata*. *An Anthology of World Literature* calls the *Bhagavat Gita* "India's philosophy at its best."³⁷ Moreover, similar to what Hopkins argues in *World's Best Literature*, Philo Buck, the editor of *An Anthology of World Literature*, also indicates that Vedic hymns express philosophical ideas.³⁸ The words "philosophy" and "philosophical" appear multiple times in the revised edition of *Our Heritage of World Literature*, indicating the important role that philosophy plays in Indian literature.³⁹

In terms of the treatment of Indian literature, what makes some of the mid-twentieth-century anthologies different from their earlier counterparts is the inclusion of modern Indian literature. The section on Indian literature ends with excerpts from the *Panchatantra* in the revised edition of *Our Heritage of World Literature* and with Kalidasa's *Sakoontala* in the first edition of *An Anthology of World Literature*.⁴⁰ Both the *Panchatantra* and *Sakoontala* are ancient works. The poems of Rabindranath Tagore (1861–1941) are added to the subsequent editions of *An Anthology of World Literature*.⁴¹ In this sense, these newer editions of Buck's anthology no longer confine Indian literature to its ancient beginnings or the philosophical era. Modern literary works have been introduced to represent Indian literature. The revised edition of *Our Heritage of World Literature* does not include any modern Indian literature, but it still praises India's achievements during the modern era, such as Tagore's writings.⁴²

While these mid-twentieth-century world literature anthologies include a more diverse body of Chinese literature and sample modern Indian literature, they all stress continuity or even a "changeless" quality in these two national literatures. For example, Buck contends that "the tradition of India" has such a strong influence on modern Indian poetry that Kalidasa can pass as the author of Tagore's *Gitanjali*.⁴³ As for Chinese literature, "of all great traditions, *save perhaps that of India*, there is a signal uniformity, from the beginning, in the spirit and philosophy of the Chinese literature."⁴⁴ In other words, "this signal uniformity" was thought to exist in both Indian and Chinese literature. With this identified uniformity, classical Chinese and Indian philosophical writings remain essential to representing the two national literatures, given that philosophy is associated with the beginnings of Chinese and Indian literatures in these anthologies.

Following the logic of Buck, *Gitanjali*, which expresses "a mystical belief that below the fleeing beauty of nature is the Spirit of the All" may not be substantially different from *The Hymn of Creation* whose "pantheism ... became later the orthodox of the Hindoo philosophy."[45] Some of these anthologies also point out the influence of early Chinese philosophy on Chinese poetry and drama.[46] Compared to their late-nineteenth-century predecessors, these mid-twentieth-century anthologies indeed expand the diversity or the chronological scope of Chinese and Indian literatures. However, they still put classical philosophy at the forefront of the two national literatures by emphasizing their uniformity and changelessness. Later Chinese and Indian literary works are, to various degrees, presented as expressions of these philosophical ideas.

Classical Chinese and Indian philosophical texts remain an indispensable part of contemporary world literature anthologies. The three best known of these anthologies are *The Norton Anthology of World Literature* (hereafter, *Norton*), *The Bedford Anthology of World Literature* (hereafter, *Bedford*), and *The Longman Anthology of World Literature* (hereafter, *Longman*). The first volumes of these three anthologies include the excerpts from some of the philosophical works that Kupperman extensively discusses in *Classic Asian Philosophy*, such as *The Analects*, *The Mencius*, *Dao De Jing*, *The Zhuangzi*, *The Upanishads*, and *Bhagavad Gita*.[47] These philosophical texts, together with other types of literary works, such as poetry in the case of Chinese literature and epics in the case of Indian literature, constitute the beginnings of the two national literatures.

In a different work, I have noted that unlike the mid-twentieth-century collections, these contemporary anthologies do not place Chinese works in a single section. Instead, they usually divide the Chinese material into several sections based on chronological order. These sections scatter throughout the anthology and are separated by sections focusing on other cultural and literary traditions.[48] The same is the case with Indian works collected in these contemporary anthologies. While philosophical texts feature prominently in the beginnings of Chinese and Indian literature, the uniformity and continuity identified by the mid-twentieth-century collections are undermined by this editorial arrangement.

Furthermore, while individual sections are exclusively devoted to anthologizing earlier Chinese or Indian texts, the more recent, especially modern and contemporary, Chinese and Indian works often appear in the same section together with literary texts that are produced during the same time frame but from other traditions. For example, the first volume of the third edition of *Norton* features a section entitled "India's Ancient Epics and Tales" and another section entitled "Early Chinese Literature and Thought." The former includes selections from the philosophical work, *Bhagavad Gita*; the latter, selections from *The Analects*, *Dao De Jing*, and the *Zhuangzi*.[49] Nevertheless, the last volume of the same anthology does not devote any independent section to these two national literatures or any national literature. The works of both an Indian writer, Premchand, and the works of a Chinese writer, Lao She, appear in a section titled "Modernity and Modernism, 1900–1945." *Bedford* and *Longman* arrange Chinese and Indian material in a similar manner. For example, the first volumes of *Bedford* and *Longman* feature individual sections on ancient Chinese and Indian literature, and philosophical texts remain an important component of these sections. However, the last volumes of both anthologies contain only one section, "The Twentieth Century," which anthologizes a variety of texts including those by Chinese and Indian authors.[50]

The disappearance of individual sections on national literatures in the last volumes of all three anthologies reveals the challenges in using countries or regions to categorize contemporary literature. Which national literature do a modern writer's works belong to? More relevant to the discussion of this essay is the question: What makes an author a Chinese author or an Indian author? For example, the last volumes of both *Norton* and *Longman* include works by Zhang Ailing (1920–1995). Zhang was born in China, but she immigrated to the United States in 1955.[51] Moreover, her novel, *The Rice-Sprout Song*, "was first written in English,"[52] and the story anthologized in *Longman*, "Stale Mates," was also written in English.[53] Does Zhang count as a Chinese or American writer? *Bedford* includes a piece by Anita Desai (1937–), who "currently divides her time between India and America."[54] Which national literature should Desai's works be categorized into? Even those who can be fairly clearly defined as Chinese or Indian writers have also had transnational experiences and/or are influenced by Western literature. For example, Lao She (1899–1966), a Chinese writer who is famous for his depiction of Beijing, taught "Chinese in London and Singapore."[55] *Bedford* anthologizes a short story by an Indian writer, R. K. Narayan (1906–2001), who "traveled abroad only rarely."[56] Nonetheless, English literature still exerts an influence on him—when he was young, he read fiction by "Dickens, Conan Doyle, Sir Walter Scott, Tagore, and H.G. Wells."[57]

The three anthologies' organization of modern and contemporary material indicates that the twentieth-century Chinese and Indian literatures are products of global literary movements and trends. These Chinese and Indian authors are, to various degrees, connected to Western cultures. This type of organization also suggests that the influence of national traditions, which classical philosophical texts help mold, may not be as significant as the "world republic of letters"—to quote the title of Pascale Casanova's famous book—on modern Chinese and Indian literature.[58] *Bedford*, *Longman*, and *Norton* present classical philosophical texts as shaping the beginnings of Chinese and Indian literature, but the three anthologies also show that despite these highly influential philosophical works, the boundaries between national literatures began to dissolve in the twentieth century, if not earlier.

This essay outlines the changing significance of the classical Chinese and Indian philosophical texts included in world literature anthologies. In the late-nineteenth-century collections, Confucian philosophical works are synonymous with Chinese literature, and philosophy is presented as a running thread of Indian literature. The mid-twentieth-century anthologies suggest uniformity in both Chinese and Indian literatures, and classical philosophical texts set the tone of the two national literary traditions. Classical philosophical writings remain a key component that helps define the beginnings of the two national literatures, but modern Chinese and Indian literary works are presented more as products of global cultural movements rather than continuations of their respective national traditions. In any case, philosophy plays a pivotal role in representing Chinese and Indian literatures in anthologies. During this process, these classical philosophical texts have also become an important part of world literature.

Notes

1. David Lewis, "Truth in Fiction," in *Philosophy of Literature, Contemporary and Classic Readings: An Anthology*, ed. Eileen John and Dominic McIver Lopes (Malden: Blackwell, 2004), 119–27; John Searle, "The Logical Status of Fictional Discourse," in *Philosophy of Literature*, 112–18.
2. For a list of recent books on this topic, see Jonathan Gilmore, "Philosophy of Literature," last modified July 24, 2013, http://www.oxfordbibliographies.com/view/document/obo-9780195396577/obo-9780195396577-0213.xml.
3. Jim Marshall, "Philosophy as Literature," *Educational Philosophy and Theory* 40.3 (2008): 387–9.
4. Michael Fischer, "Redefining Philosophy as Literature: Richard Rorty's 'Defense' of Literary Culture," *Soundings* 67.3 (1984): 312–14.
5. Marshall, "Philosophy as Literature," 388.
6. Ibid., 392–3.
7. David Damrosch, *What Is World Literature?* (Princeton: Princeton UP, 2003), 288.
8. Ibid., 289.
9. Joel Kupperman, *Classic Asian Philosophy*, 2nd ed. (Oxford: Oxford UP, 2006), v.
10. The titles of the seven chapters are "The Upanishads," "The Dhammapada," "The Bhagavad Gita," "Confucius," "Mencius," "Daodejing," and "The Zhuangzi." The titles of the two chapters related to Chinese and Indian philosophy are "*Zen Flesh, Zen Bones*" and "Classic Asian Philosophies as Guides to Life."
11. Sarah Lawall, "Anthologizing 'World Literature,'" in *On Anthologies: Politics and Pedagogy*, ed. Jeffrey R. Di Leo (Lincoln: University of Nebraska Press, 2004), 50.
12. Junjie Luo, *Traditional Chinese Fiction in the English-Speaking World: Transcultural and Translingual Encounter* (unpublished book manuscript), 121.
13. John B. Alden, ed., *Alden's Cyclopedia of Universal Literature, Presenting Biographical and Critical Notices, and Specimens from the Writings of Eminent Authors of All Ages and All Nations* (New York: J. B. Alden, 1885–91), 5: 150. Harry Peck, ed., *Masterpieces of the World's Literature, Ancient and Modern* (New York: American Literary Society, 1898–9), 6: 2938. The introduction to Confucius in *Masterpieces* is a condensed version of that in *Alden's Cyclopedia*.
14. Alden, *Alden's Cyclopedia*, 5: 151 and 161.
15. Robert K. Douglas, "The Literature of China," in *A Library of the World's Best Literature, Ancient and Modern*, 31 vols., ed. Charles Warner (New York: The International Society, 1896–9), 6: 3636.
16. It should be noted that the Confucian philosophical writings anthologized in *World's Best* are not solely from *The Analects*. They also include excerpts from such works as *Mencius* and *Doctrine of the Mean*, 6: 3643–8.
17. Peck, *Masterpieces*, 20: 11330–1, 11342, 11345–7.

18 The only two exceptions are Belgian literature represented by the work of Maurice Maeterlinck and Swiss literature represented by the works of Johann Rudolf Wyss and Henri Frédéric Amiel. However, it should be noted that *Masterpieces* classify Maurice Maeterlinck as both a philosopher and a dramatist. Henri Frédéric Amiel is classified solely as a philosopher, but Johann Rudolf Wyss, who is classified as an editor and compiler, a poet, and a writer of juvenile stories, is the other representative author of Swiss literature. In contrast, Confucius is classified solely as a philosopher, and he is the only author representing Chinese literature (Peck, *Masterpieces*, 20: 11323–48).
19 Charles Warner, ed., *A Library of the World's Best Literature, Ancient and Modern*, 31 vols. (New York: The International Society, 1896–9), 1: xiii.
20 Alden, *Alden's Cyclopedia*, 15: Charles Morris, *The Aryan Race*, 1–3.
21 Peck, *Masterpieces*, 16: 8032–48.
22 Warner, *World's Best Literature*, 14: 7939–67.
23 Edward W. Hopkins, "Indian Literature," in *World's Best Literature*, ed. Charles Warner, 14: 7905–20.
24 Ibid., 14: 7922.
25 Ibid., 14: 7911.
26 Ibid., 14: 7922.
27 Warner, *World's Best Literature*, 6: 3629–48 and 14: 7905–67.
28 The Publisher's Preface to the last volume of *World's Best Literature* explains how one such index-like apparatus, Conspectuses of All the Literatures, is connected to an essential purpose of this anthology—presenting different national literatures:

> But even larger and more adequate help than any Index can be has been designed and executed, to serve the various purposes of a comprehensive Guide to the whole body of matters covered by the Library. *These matters are, first of all, the various national literatures found in the whole of human history.* To serve as a general guide to these, CONSPECTUSES OF ALL THE LITERATURES have been prepared, on the plan of a chronological catalogue of the authors in each national literature, and a concise critical characterization of each author, sufficient to make the conspectus of any literature an outline history of that literature. Both the chronology and the characteristics of literatures are thus given, with proper indexical references to the Library, for any study or reading desired. (Ibid., 31: iv–v)

29 Ibid., 1: xi.
30 Douglas, "The Literature of China," 6: 3642. For a discussion of Douglas's attitude toward traditional Chinese fiction, see Luo, *Traditional Chinese Fiction*, 122.
31 Hopkins, "Indian Literature," 14: 7905–39.
32 Warner, *World's Best Literature*, 7965–6.
33 Stith Thompson and John Gassner, eds., *Our Heritage of World Literature*, revised ed. (New York: The Dryden Press, 1942), 475–9. The first edition of this volume does not even include Confucian philosophical writings.
34 Luo, *Traditional Chinese Fiction*, 125–7.
35 Philo M. Buck, ed., *An Anthology of World Literature*, 3rd ed. (New York: Macmillan, 1951), 352–64. The first two editions of *An Anthology of World Literature* (1934 and 1940) do not include Chinese literature. The third edition includes Chinese literature for the first time.

36 Buck also expands the scope of Chinese philosophical texts collected in the third edition of *An Anthology of World Literature*. In addition to the two Confucian classics—*The Analects* and *The Mencius*—it includes excerpts from *The Book of Tao*, the founding text of the Taoist philosophy. See Buck, *An Anthology of World Literature*, 362–4. For an extended discussion of the inclusion of *The Book of Tao*, see Luo, *Traditional Chinese Fiction*, 127–8.
37 Buck, *An Anthology of World Literature*, 310–11. Unless otherwise noted in this essay, the page numbers refer to the third edition of *An Anthology of World Literature*. In this case, the citation is identical in all three editions.
38 Ibid.
39 Thompson and Gassner, *Our Heritage of World Literature*, 457–9.
40 Ibid., 471–4; Philo M. Buck, ed., *An Anthology of World Literature*, 1st ed. (New York: Macmillan, 1934), 258–95.
41 Philo M. Buck, ed., *An Anthology of World Literature*, 2nd ed. (New York: Macmillan, 1940), 349–50; 350–2.
42 Stith Thompson and John Gassner, eds., *Our Heritage of World Literature*, 459.
43 Buck, *An Anthology of World Literature*, 311.
44 Ibid., 352.
45 Ibid., 311.
46 Ibid., 352; Thompson and Gassner, *Our Heritage of World Literature*, 459. For an elaboration on the influence of classic Chinese philosophy on Chinese poetry and drama, see Luo, *Traditional Chinese Fiction*, 127–8.
47 Martin Puchner, Suzanne Conklin Akbari, Wiebke Denecke, Barbara Fuchs, Caroline Levine, Pericles Lewis, and Emily Wilson, eds., *The Norton Anthology of World Literature*, 3rd ed. (New York: W. W. Norton, 2012), A: xi–xiii; Paul Davis, Gary Harrison, and David Johnson, eds., *The Bedford Anthology of World Literature* (Boston: St. Martins, 2004), 1: xxxiv–xxxviii; David Damrosch and David L. Pike, eds., *The Longman Anthology of World Literature*, 2nd ed. (New Tork: Pearson Longman, 2009), A: x, xii–xiii. I refer to the above editions when I discuss these anthologies.
48 Luo, *Traditional Chinese Fiction*, 135.
49 Puchner et al., *Norton*, A: xi–xiii.
50 Davis et al., *Bedford*, 6: v–xiv, xxv–xxxviii. It should be noted that there are several subsections in the section "The Twentieth Century" of both *Longman* and *Bedford*. The titles of these subsections, such as "The Art of the Manifesto" and "Modernist Memory," are thematic in *Longman*. See Damrosch and Pike, *Longman*, F: v, vii. Some of these titles in *Bedford* are also thematic, such as "The Literature of War, Conflict, and Resistance" and "Existentialism." See Davis et al., *Bedford*, 6: xxix, xxxii. However, some of them, such as "Colonialism: Europe and Africa" and "Crossing Cultures: The Example of India," reflect both the themes of the subsections and the geographical regions on which they focus. See Davis et al., *Bedford*, 6: xxv, xxxvi-xxxvii. On the one hand, this suggests that geographical boundaries still play a role in *Bedford*'s organization of contemporary world literature. On the other hand, if we take the subsection "Crossing Cultures: The Example of India" as an example, some of the authors anthologized in this part, such as Martin Luther King and Octavio Paz, are not typically considered to be Indian writers, which indicates the volatility of geographical boundaries in the discussion of contemporary world literature.
51 Damrosch and Pike, *Longman*, F: 693.
52 Puchner et al., *Norton*, F: 497.

53 Damrosch and Pike, *Longman*, F: 693.
54 Davis et al., *Bedford*, 6: 1194.
55 Puchner et al., *Norton*, F: 409.
56 Davis et al., *Bedford*, 6: 782.
57 Ibid., 6: 781–2.
58 Pascale Casanova, *The World Republic of Letters*, trans. M. B. DeBevoise (Cambridge: Harvard UP, 2004).

11

The Dharma of World Literature

Ranjan Ghosh

Visva Sahitya (World Literature) is "untimely": quite often, caught in italics. Italicization, for me, is an evocation of cultural boundarization, a re-marked optic distinction not simply inscribed into the text-flow but also signposted within the flow of our understanding. It is a redrawing of the consciousness of a usage that demands "outstanding" and hence, outsider attention, questioning the efficacy of translation, inscribing its distinctiveness within the narrative, bracketing its status from the rest of the text-flow. As a practice, philosophy, and desire, italicization is mostly about "closing the circle": circling in the concepts, cultural understanding, and ideologies, and discretion in acts of representation and narration. If visva sahitya is about negotiating the worlds of literature across nations and cultures, every world would come with its own italicization—specificities of cultural formation and particularities of language, expression, and establishment. Any commitment to question the italicization of reading sahitya would make for the opening of interesting spaces of negotiations. Where, then, do we locate the "de-italicization dialectic" that makes for transcendence and collapsing of borders of cultural, literary, and epistemological negotiation?

In Sanskrit, "sahitya" is derived from the word *sahita*, "united together." V. Raghavan argues,

> The concept of Sahitya had a grammatical origin. It became a poetic concept even as early as Rajasekhara [an eminent Sanskrit dramatist, poet, critic]; as far as we can see at present, the *Kavyamimamsa* [880–920 CE] is the earliest work to mention the name Sahitya and *Sahitya-vidya* as meaning Poetry and Poetics. Even after Rajasekhara, grammatical associations were clinging to the term up to Bhoja's time. Kuntaka [950–1050, Sanskrit poetician and literary theorist], about the time of Bhoja himself, was responsible for divesting Sahitya of grammatical associations and for defining it as a great quality of the relation between *Sabda* [word] and *Artha* [meaning] in Poetry. Sometime afterwards, Ruyyaka or Mankhuka wrote a work called *Sahitya-mimamsa*, which was the first work on Poetics to have the name Sahitya. Afterwards, Sahitya became more common and we have the notable example of the *Sahitya-darpana* of Visvanatha [a famous Sanskrit poet, scholar, rhetorician writing between 1378 and 1434].[1]

The word "sahitya" retains its Sanskrit origin but is now commonly understood as literature encompassing poems, plays, poetics, and other forms of creative writing. Bhavya Tiwari points out that

> in Bharata's drama treatise *Natyashastra*, one of the oldest theoretical works in Sanskrit reflecting on the nature and concept of art, the author emphasizes that art, unlike the four Vedas, is democratic and social in purpose; art integrates within itself music, dance, poetry, composition, and acting so as to appeal to everyone while instructing through pleasure. Thus, if we come back to Rabindranath Tagore's idea of "World Literature," both words, "Visva" and "Sahitya," highlight connections that transcend geographical and artistic boundaries.[2]

Sahitya comes with *sahit* and *vidya* (knowledge): *sahit* in the sense of "combination" and also coming together. Although *sahita* means "united together," this does not point to fusion or intermelding but connection, a kind of being-with. Coming together is about understanding the politics and performative of italicization and figuring ways to de-italicize: sahitya, understood and interpreted as both coming together and being together and informed with the motor of cosmopolitanism and migrancy, performs the de-italicization in critical-aesthetic thinking. On that ground, I choose not to italicize sahitya here. "Sahitya" is not simply a linguistic equivalent of the English word "literature": it is, for me, a performance, an event, and an experience in surplus, aesthetic formations and geo-cultural transcendence. So what kind of *sahit* does sahitya create? How does this *sahit* matter in helping sahitya matter meaningfully and creating world(s)? Where is sahitya's *visva* (world) and, what makes for "visva sahitya," the being of sahitya?

If being becomes "a real distress and a real liberation,"[3] how can the distress and liberation be effected and explored in the being of Visva Sahitya? The question that at once inspires and bemuses me is what constitutes such a "being" and whether the being is explicable and accessible to enunciation. Heidegger's history of being leads us to rethink the "obvious," and this "obviousness rethought" can be the premise to begin thinking about Visva Sahitya. If finding a text in a remote recess of a culture and rescripting its presence within the predominant circulation of the literary marketplace becomes an agenda that "world literature" is usually seen to promote, there is manifest profit in working through the obvious; this allows the unconcealment of truth to contribute to our thinking of the literary. How can visva sahitya work through the "obvious"? What would it be or be with? The obvious carries a "presence" with it, a kind of attainment that does not always pitch on the methodologies or protocols of reading. It has a pervading and pervasive history that most thinking on/around visva sahitya has failed to acknowledge. The obvious "is" and, again, "is not"; the obvious loses its potency, its world-forming possibilities, in its obviousness. So visva sahitya formations are not always conditioned and calculative and "obvious"; the obvious, rather, corresponds with the meditative, the truth of the unconditioned and the undogmatic. The obvious in visva sahitya is what I see as the real standoff with the status quo of reception and inheritance of understanding. What, then, can we interrogate in "sahitya" when there is a "world" prefixed to it? How does that open the world of literature, the being of sahitya?

The "event" of sahitya is a case in point. Following Sandra Lee Bartky, we see two formations: one is the "horizontal" being-event that "refers to the meaning of what has heretofore happened, to the way in which Being, which is historical 'in its essence,' has given birth to the epochs of metaphysics," and the other is the "vertical" being-event that "refers to the ways in which within any epoch beings (*das Seiende*) come to be the beings they are." So on that note of explanation, horizontal being-event is about the "varieties of world-disclosure" and the vertical being-event is committed to the "modes of world-disclosure."[4] The world of sahitya is "there"; so before we see a text as belonging to a culture, a particular background, a relational context, and a timescape, the world of sahitya precedes our reductive experience counterintuitively. This, for me, contributes to how we see visva sahitya, presenting and "presencing" its formation not in isolation or apartness but by living holistically; this is the "opening forth." If the pre-reflective and pre-discursive experiences are pressed into play, then the *dasein* of sahitya works around a "poetic" where mattering and presencing oppose the tyranny of the theoretical (the structured). So what kind of truth are we exposed to? This brings us to the "imperative" to understand the experience and truth of "uncoveredness"—the disclosures we effect and sahitya's own world-disclosures, its worldings; for instance, more than what Tagore as a creative writer says or represents, we vector toward what unconceals Tagore, the world of Tagore, the "obvious" Tagore, his being-in-the-world: this is not what Tagore does or can be theorized about and, hence, reduced to explanatory parts and his own constructivism but the Tagore as an existing being that has always been on attendance upon alethic potencies—the uncovering of Tagore beyond our worldly understanding of him within his obvious literary, cultural, and political and existential circulations. Tagore within the flow and directions of world literature is an italicized entity, "obviously" regional in comparison to global English. But visva of sahitya puts him under the anxiety of being de-italicized. We, thus, uncover Tagore (technized) as much as Tagore is always attending an unconcealment and "openedness." Would it then be wrong to say that the visva of sahitya determines visva sahitya? In fact, there is a visva with its modes and varieties that visva sahitya is a part of and emerges from. This is for me tantalizingly close to Heidegger's notion of the earth.

Knowing sahitya is often about knowing the limits of questioning sahitya, which does not mean knowing the points of exhaustion; rather, it becomes a reminder of our inability to question further. The aesthetic of visva sahitya can be found in sahitya-illumination—the truth establishing system, the bringing-forth as an activity that is both translational and transcultural. The world being of sahitya is to question the conditions of knowledge-generation; it tries to see literature as "existing," as a phenomenon whose truths await to be discovered and are not always imputed and constructed. The truths of such findings lead us to see the "fundamental" of visva sahitya where the fundamental is not merely about what "is there" but about what essentially survives our investigation. This brings us to question the finitude of sahitya as performance and act: if Heidegger has inspired us to question the very role and dynamic of metaphysics in our thinking and understanding of life, I prefer to extend this to our thinking of both the visva, sahitya, and the visva of sahitya. If every move, gesture, act, and performance comes with historicity, as has been the idealized narrative of expectation and fulfilment in Western cultures, we are missing some part of the world that sahitya ungrounds and something that visva sahitya, as I see it, has not been able to realize. If visva sahitya, through a technology of thinking, permits and promotes certain protocols and procedures of doing and performing, it can also make allowance for certain unmapped categories and experiences. Here visva sahitya confronts its own "poetic"; this is not merely the uncanny but a non-appropriative relation to the being of sahitya. Isn't there a way to understand sahitya nontheoretically? Admittedly, this builds an "across-factor" that escapes a method and obviates a method after one has built a connection with the text. Thinking with Heidegger, I call this the "unconditioned across," the across that is more fundamental than we could ever think out; it has its own tribunal of reason. I claim the power of the "ordinary" and the "obvious" in a text and extend the notion of the "across" through terms that are more fundamental, associative, pre-conditioned, pre-reflective, and, hence, less settled in the "said" than in the "saying." What I mean is that all understanding is not theory; some understandings "happen," not necessarily awaiting to be theoreticized and "technologized." Understandings can be potentials, "out-of-condition" thinking, and mere empathetic responses as well. This, however, need not be confused with the aesthetics of "excess" and lack, the surplus and suture. Working through Heidegger's idea of the world, we encounter a space that is "unintended" and present in an "unprominent way," somewhat outside the conscious formalization of understanding and thought. So what stares back at us is the articulative difference between visva sahitya and what is "out there" in the visva of sahitya: representation and constructivism need not always find their way in the ways of the visva of sahitya. Is visva sahitya both being-in-world and "attunement" (*Stimmung*)?

It is interesting to note, following on Heidegger's notion of the "being-complex," that a text written within *desh-kal-patra* (context-time-identity) is meaningful only within a relation with others (*sahit*): the being of a text is in the complex that it builds with others—"a formal or transcendental notion in that it refers to the structure of any possible experience of being-in-a-world."[5] Tagore points out in his essay "Visva Sahitya" (1907) that

> how man expresses his joy in literature, how and in what form the human soul chooses to manifest its diverse, variegated, multiple images of self-expression, that is the only thing worth considering in world literature. Literature must actually *enter the world*—whether it pleases to express itself in the form of the diseased, the accomplished, or the ascetic person—to know how far man can find his *kinship* in the world, and to what extent he can realize truth. It will not do to know it as an artificial construct; it is a world in itself. Its essence exceeds the individual's grasp. It is in continuous creation, like the material universe itself, but in the innermost core of that unfinished creation is a perfected ideal that remains unmoving.[6]

If sahitya *enters* (sensed out of the Old French *entrer* meaning "enter," "go in"; "enter upon," "assume"; "initiate") into the world, then it must be coming from a world of its own or worlds affiliated to the writer, his times, his context, tradition, and, finally, a world beyond his own comprehension and construal. Sahitya's entering then is about worlds coming together, initiated, assumed, and getting into negotiation and play, into forms of expression and aesthetic matterings. So here is the lifeworld that sahitya builds with the world-being: the patterns of disclosures, or the levels of unconcealment that the self and the other in their complex turnings and returnings construct and inhere: "in the world," writes Tagore, "we witness two things—the expression of work and the expression of emotion. But that which is being expressed through work we cannot witness in its *totality* or understand fully."[7] Not that such a lifeworld denies the essence of history or historical world-making; rather, world-making as forms of "entering"—the entrance, as ingress, that unfixes worlds of understanding and performs its own disclosive acts of expressions.

Visva sahitya finds its home in world-disclosures that qualify as a kind expenditure that hardly thinks of losses. It expends and enjoys its bankruptcy: therein lies the joy of expression, argues Tagore, something he ascribes as the plenitude of sahitya. Expenditure of this nature reendows the self, brings the self back to thinking about itself, where staying within is reaching out for the world(s) without. This expenditure is "living" in the sahitya-being—its truths (the historical and political), happenings (sociocultural), event as happening, and the disclosive power (meaning formation). So Visva Sahitya embeds in "incommensurabilities"—impediments and challenges to think out the *sambandha* between the self and the other and in the kinship with the world. Tagore points out that "indeed, to recognize the dharma that is natural to us, to know it as such, to realize its full powers, we need to encounter impediments in its way. It is only thus that it realizes itself consciously, and the more its consciousness deepens, the more profound its joy is. Everything follows a similar pattern."[8] Tagore argues the importance of the struggle of "failing" when one learns to ride the cycle, for the whole effort is not to learn the falling but the ride, the impediments before one finds a way, the incommensurabilities before one gets to build the relation, *sambandha*, with the cycle. It is an expansion of the circle, the desire to manifest one's self in the other, the pleasure of being a history with the world "when we see our own character manifest in many people, many nations, many eras, many incidents, many varieties, and many shapes. Then whether I understand it clearly or not, in my heart I accept that I am one with all men—to whatever degree I experience that unity, to that degree is my well-being and joy."[9] Sahitya has its own *dharma*, and the world that it generates and enters into have their *dharma* too.[10] In fact, it is the regime of *swadharma* that commits to configure experiences between the self (*swa*) and the other. And the challenges to the understanding of sahitya is both in the *sva* and the other:

> It wants to disseminate its emotions into the world. It is not complete in its self. It always wants to make its own truths the truths of the world. The house it inhabits is not merely a structure of bricks and mortar—it attempts to make it a home and

colours it in its own hues. This is the cosmopolitanization of love, understanding of the self, the image of the other, the networks of existence, our svadharma.[11]

Perhaps, we need to explain the "joy" that Tagore points out in relation to sahitya and visva, in the world that expresses itself as literature, in literature that forms and unforms the world. Where do we connect the joy and the world, joy as world-making, the joy as the manifestation of sahitya-being? The joy in visva sahitya comes from three identifiable sources that beg enumeration—travel, estrangement, and nexus. Pheng Cheah observes that

> the idea of world literature should, paradoxically, be conceived more narrowly as the literature of the world-maginings and stories of what it means to be part of a world that track and account for contemporary globalization as well as older historical narratives of worldhood. It is also a literature that seeks to be disseminated, read, and received around the world so as to change that world and the life of a given people within it. One can then speak of world literature in a more precise sense as the literature of the world (double genitive), a literature that is an active process of the world.[12]

This is sahitya in its encompassive solidarity—in comradeship as Tagore has redoubtedly emphasized. Sahitya is in being "comparative" where its plenitude, plan, and power is caught in trans (ferrying across, momentum across traditions and genres and sites) and nexus (relationality)—both scalar and planetary. Uniquely, Tagore brings us before World-Comparative Poetics. However, the problem of creating such a discursive-performative space is in the vexatious mix of imagination, a "totalizing" impulse and pattern, and a plan that finds difficulty in negotiating with the invisible factors that create both global and literary capital. The difficulty of enframing the "local" and the "global" in understanding the visva of sahitya complicates the nature of "joy" further. Our aesthetic mappings enable *rasa*-generation (emotion) and also *rasa* that was never predetermined or preconceived.[13] Here is the "more" in the disclosures of sahitya: always unworlded, worldized. The more has an undertow of joy. This is a joy that does not make us, as Rabindranath Tagore argues, "limited by the power of the intellect or the power of work," but makes us experience ourselves without any "cover or calculation in between."[14] Tagore observes,

> The son is dear not because we long for the son, but because we long for the *atma*, our true self. Property is dear not because we desire the property but because we desire the *atma*, or the self. This means that in whatever we experience ourselves *more* fully, we desire that. The son eliminates my shortcomings; I find myself all the *more* in my son. In him, I become *more* of myself. This is why he is my dearest kin; he is a manifestation of my self outside of me. It is the truth I experience so certainly within myself that makes me experience love; that very same truth I know in my son and therefore my love for him expands. That is why to be close to someone is to know what they love. It is thus that we understand where, in this

wide world, they have located themselves and how far they have spread their souls. Where my *affection* does not lie, my soul only skirts the rim of its own boundary.[15]

It is a profound desire that dwells in the joy emerging out of being local and global at the same time—the father (the global, as it were) finding himself in the son (our assumed local). This enables the son to become dear to the father. In turn, the father comes to know himself more in the affective momentum, leading him to reach out to the son. This is his desire to locate himself in his son. That desire, again, is developed paradoxically, through a reaching-in, in modes of inner immigration, leading the father to find himself. So finding oneself more in others is to become more of oneself. This is integral to the visva of sahitya. The dharma of the localglobal as a part of the sahitya-being then is the *sambandha*, the astute listening where the father (global) and son (local) address each other in a resonant relationality. In *sambandha*, the global finds itself in the local, enabling a knowledge that helps the global to discover its globality, as when the father finds more of himself in his son. Here lies the more that produces joy when one's own truths become the truths of the world. Compared to a house, a home in its affective and aesthetic configurations is more fluid, less constricted, and knows the art of accommodativeness where the father and the son can live and learn and make greater senses out of their living (*sambandha*) at different points of time. I would like to argue that the house of the local and the global built out of the bricks and mortar of ideology, principles, traditions, and cultural individualities becomes the home of the more of the global, where the local and the global, like the son and the father, exceed themselves in the joy of discovering and reaching out for each other. The flow of knowledge in such continued disequilibria is not between the local's reaching for the global and the global's reaching down to meet the local. Instead, it becomes a moment, a now, that is both achronic and cross-chronic.

The "more," thus, defies the calculative and formal categories of separating the global and the local; instead, the local-global assemblage is an affection (is Tagore's 1907 essay written in Bengali under the colonial sky a "local" production that only becomes "global" when translated into English and anthologized in a publication from an international press?) that leads one to experience the other outside oneself and eventually to know oneself better. Tagore's essay builds in its own *rasa* within the confines of a local rendering both in its particular context and experience but stays unworlded in its own *rasa* even if it is not translated into a dominant global language. This is because the event of sahitya as revealed through the essay has always formed its world-disclosures both vertically and horizontally. Tagore's essay is "localglobal": affirmative and active sahitya-being. Writing from a local context—*sthaan-patra-kaal*—is not ignoring the *rasa* that connects literary effort with the currents that circumambient all literary forms: I call this the "greater form" that the world disclosures are informed by. This form, this potential to accept the locality and yet transcend it through its *rasa* experience, brings us to question the national, cultural, and ethnic borders of sahitya, as also, the ideologies of feminism, race, and body studies. This is close to literature-monde that "signifies a literature open to the world or, in other words, a literature which speaks of the real and the lived rather than turning in on itself in a state of narcissistic self-consciousness."¹⁶ Speaking of Goethe and *literature-monde*, Typhaine Lesevot argues that

> despite his initial desire to break up the fixed canon of the classics by daring to suggest that it was possible to admire contemporary authors, Goethe's world literature remains an elitist concept which favors the literary production of certain nations over that of others (France over Germany), of certain periods over others (the ancient world over the modern), of certain genres (poetry rather than the novel) and of certain readers (those from the elite classes rather than from the lower classes).¹⁷

For Tagore, sahitya is certainly not hierarchical, for the idea of the "comparative-world" embosoms all reflections and reticulations related to the being of sahitya. So Tagore admits to "interference" in all forms of sahitya—interference in forms that are cultural, rhetoric, political, linguistic, epistemic, and national. Literary expression then builds its connection and also stays connected in ways that are too subtle to methodologize and express programmatically. The world of sahitya is worlding: not a cluster of texts predetermined through certain protocols and patterns but a meaning-making process, a transitivity, a kind of nonreduction that is poetic and aesthetic at the same time. Visva sahitya is inherently anachronistic.

Tagore notes,

> All I have wanted to say is that just as the world is not merely the sum of your plough field, plus my plough field, plus his plough field—because to know the world that way is only to know it with a yokel—like parochialism—similarly world literature is not merely the sum of your writings, plus my writing, plus his writings. We generally see literature in this limited, provincial manner. To free oneself of that regional narrowness and resolve to see the universal being in world literature, to apprehend such *totality* in every writer's work, and to see its interconnectedness with every man's attempt at self-expression—that is the objective we need to pledge ourselves to.¹⁸

It is interesting to observe the "estrangement" that world-comparative literature builds: writing and expression is one's own and yet the greater currents take one's work outside of what one intended to establish and formalize. The very idea of visva sahitya is a mode of estrangement—attachment to *sthaan-kaal-patra* is the italicization and the de-italicization is the estrangement from its origins of culture and context; it is an affect form that exceeds every text's being in the world. Estrangement and attachment are caught in simultaneous order. This is the text's lifeworld that is always an unintended victim of disclosive release. Pheng Cheah points out that "any given or present world, any world that we have received and that has been historically changed and that we self-consciously seek to transform through human activity, is riven by a force that we cannot anticipate but that enables the constitution of reality and any progressive transformation of the present world by human action."¹⁹ This force is, most often, responsible for the joy that Tagore talks about; it articulates the "plenitude" of sahitya beyond enframed anticipations and prenominations. Sahitya, in promoting sahit, paradoxically believes in losing sahit, for disjunctures are the realities for transcendence and world-forming. So "structurally detached from its putative origin and that permits and even solicits an infinite number of interpretations," Cheah notes,

> literature is an exemplary modality of the undecidability that opens a world. It is not merely a product of the human imagination or something that is derived from, represents, or duplicates material reality. Literature is the force of a passage, an experience, through which we are given and receive any determinable reality. The issue of receptibility is fundamental here. It does not refer to the reception of a piece of literature but to the structure of opening through which one receives a world and through which another world can appear.[20]

This, again, brings me to the being-event of sahitya. It also largely expresses the "totality" of sahitya—the totality formed through "interconnectedness": the sahit here as not mere combinations but disjunctures that await transcendence and where going-beyond is networkism and world-formation. Tagore argues that

> in this world, whatever we see, we see in a scattered way; we see it a little here and there, a little now and then; we see it mixed up with ten other things. But in literature those gaps, those adulterations do not exist. There all the light shines upon that which is being expressed. For that time being nothing else is allowed to be seen. Through many contrivances such a place is created that allows only that to be luminous. That is why one places nothing that cannot withstand such stark individuality and luminosity in the space of literature. Because, to place the undeserving in such a location is to humiliate it.[21]

Sahitya has this ability to bring things together—not leave in isolation—build connections among things that look apparently scattered, here and there; this is the power of the comparative, the power of visva sahiya as an "ethical project," the cosmopolitan force that creates its own *rasa* of "coming together." Bruce Robbins argues that

> set against "other times and eras," as it is here, being oneself also signifies occupying the present tense. And being a self-in-the-present-tense signifies two quite different things. On the one hand, it signifies the burden of a provinciality or partiality or self-interestedness from which one may need and even want to be released. On the other hand, however, it also signifies the opportunity for an action that will produce change, an opportunity that the past by definition cannot offer and from which we should fear to wander too far away. The study of world literature, however cosmopolitan, can never be the most efficient or momentous of actions, yet action remains a criterion that permits a discrimination of better and worse cosmopolitanisms.[22]

Visva sahitya needs to look into promoting good and effective cosmopolitanism and also "estrangement as interconnectedness" through informed and productive ways of understanding and judgment.

The estrangement is, in fact, translational: a work written within the confines of a nation, a community, builds its own *rasa* outside the intentions and commitments of the writer. If a work relates to the circulation of writing outside oneself, the *rasa* of the work is relational. All expressions are translational; "everything is translated," notes Bruno Latour, "we may be understood, that is, surrounded, diverted, betrayed, displaced, transmitted, but we are never understood *well*. If a message is transported, then it is transformed."[23] So the travel in world literature through translation is also the travel through transformation; for me, besides worldiness, there is a world outside the text that sponsors the worlding, the ambiguity of its reception and reading, the politics of its global and transcultural flow, the power politics of language and dissemination. The world in visva sahitya is powerfully subjective and extra-subjective too: the extra-subjectivism coming from one's helpless submission to invisible forces of textual transmission, the inability of the subject to control the forces that determine the future of a work—the text's own world-disclosures. So the world of visva sahitya builds its resources and expanse through a new order of production both through its writers and the writing, as every writing becomes its own rewriting—a kind of co-occurrence and co-performance—through its transference and transmission in the global circulation of literary and market capital. Here I would like to see estrangement as attachment: attachment as mesh, as nexus.

Caught in symmetrical-assymetrical translation, geo-critical spatialization, itinerancy, and transcultural semiosis, visva sahitya then spells out a *totality*. Tagore sees this totality in an inexhaustible plenitude—the "universal being" of sahitya—that expends itself to regenerate; he sees this in the connectedness that visva sahitya constructs and sponsors; he finds it in the "comradeship" that visva sahitya builds working through the disjuctures and differences among literature across cultures and nations. Works across cultures and continents are "compatriots," which means ploughing a land here is connecting, albeit unaware, with the ploughing elsewhere—the "joy" and inevitability of connect. So this totality is not totalitarian; it speaks of a formation that does not allow interpretive conquering but has its own ways of manifestation and reordering. Totality forms additively with the worlds of a variety of literatures emerging from a variety of cultures, times, and places. But this aggregatory formation challenges itself every time one tries to conceptualize its existence. It is where "desire is mobilized and set into circulation, and where our "projections" about others are negotiated."[24] Totality then is in the *across* and lubricates the idea of space and place in the visva of sahitya. The world of sahitya disfavors canonicity and elitism, which is strategically and preferentially inclusive of works across national/regional literatures: it also refuses to be daunted by the immensity that informs the "quantitative approach" to reading world literature; it sets itself up as a "happening" across cultures and times, questioning the fluid roots and rootings of a work. The totality, thus, declares immanental reading, a literary semiosis; it ensures that Visva sahitya remains as an unfinished project.

Notes

1. V. Raghavan, "Sahitya," in *An Introduction to Indian Poetics*, ed. V. Raghavan and Nagendra (Bombay: Macmillan, 1970), 82.
2. Bhavya Tiwari, "Rabindranath Tagore's Comparative World Literature," in *The Routledge Companion to World Literature*, ed. Theo D'haen, David Damrosch, and Djelal Kadir (London: Routledge, 2012), 5.
3. See Ranjan Ghosh, "Jugalbandi," *Comparative Literature Studies* 55.4 (2018): 954.
4. Sandra Lee Bartky, "Heidegger and the Modes of World-Disclosure," *Philosophy and Phenomenological Research* 40.2 (1979): 212–36.
5. Ibid., 214.
6. See Rabindranath Tagore, "Visva Sahitya," trans. Rijula Das and Makarand R. Paranjape, *Journal of Contemporary Thought* 34 (2011): 289. Emphases added.
7. Ibid., 284.
8. Ibid., 289.
9. Ibid., 281.
10. Generally speaking, dharma is about law, order, principle, and conduct. It is being used here to signify a kind of philosophy of thinking, a principle of doing, and order of thought.
11. Tagore, "Visva Sahitya," 282.
12. Pheng Cheah, "What Is a World? On World Literature as World-Making Activity," *Daedalus* 137.3 (Summer 2008): 33.
13. *Rasa* is difficult to express in Western critical terminology. While it is being used here like "emotion," it can be translated as "essence," "taste," "mood," or "flavor," though none of these renderings is completely adequate.
14. Tagore, "Visva Sahitya," 213.
15. Ibid., 214.
16. See Michel Le Bris and Jean Rouaud, eds., *Pour une litterature-monde* (Paris: Gallimard, 2007), 25. Quoted in Typhaine Leservot, "From *Weltliteratur* to World Literature to *Litterature-monde*: The History of a Controversial Concept," in *Postcolonialism and Litterature-monde*, ed. Alec G. Hargreaves, Charles Forsdick, and David Murphy (Liverpool: Liverpool UP, 2010), 36–48.
17. Leservot, "From *Weltliteratur* to World Literature to *Litterature-monde*," 41.
18. Tagore, "Visva Sahitya," 288. Emphasis added.
19. Cheah, "What Is a World?," 35.
20. Ibid., 35.
21. Tagore, "Visva Sahitya," 287.
22. Bruce Robbins, "Uses of World Literature," in *Routledge Companion to World Literature*, ed. Theo D'haen, David Damrosch, and Djelal Kadir (London: Routledge, 2012), 383–92.
23. Bruno Latour, *The Pasteurization of France*, trans. Alan Sheridan (Cambridge: Harvard UP, 1993), 181.
24. Sanja Bahun, "Politics of World Literature," in *Routledge Companion to World Literature*, ed. Theo D'haen, David Damrosch, and Djelal Kadir (London: Routledge, 2012), 373.

12

Olive-Red in Orhan Pamuk and Anton Shammas: Deconstruction's Eastward Dissemination

Henry Sussman

Verily and truly, I've been everywhere and am everywhere ... I embellished Ushak carpets, wall ornamentation, the combs of fighting cocks, pomegranates, the fruits of fabled lands, the mouth of Satan, the subtle accent lines within picture borders, the curled embroidery on tents, flowers barely visible to the naked eye made for the artist's own pleasure ... the sour-cherry eyes of bird-statues made of sugar, the stockings of shepherds, the dawns described in legends ...

I hear the question upon your lips: What is it to be a color?

Color is the touch of the eye, music to the deaf, a word out of the darkness. Because I've listened to souls whispering—like the susurrus of the wind—from book to book and object to object for tens of thousands of years, allow me to say that my touch resembles the touch of angels. Part of me, the serious half, calls out to your vision while the mirthful half soars through the air with your glances.

I'm so fortunate to be red! I'm fiery. I'm strong. I know men take notice of me and that I cannot be resisted.[1]

Elaine had seen other things that day with her brother Elias, but didn't dare allow them across the threshold of her lips or even the threshold of her heart. She buried them inside herself and guarded them ... until she was about seventeen, she did not even allow herself to think of them. And when she finally did, she could not grasp their meaning. She would see images alternately rising and sinking into the oil slick that writhed and flickered on the surface of the saucer. She once saw a child dying. The child is her own son and also the son of another woman who is her kin ...

"Breathe deeply, Elaine, and look at the oil slick, look hard and concentrate on the slick," her brother says to her now. She does as he bids her, and tries once again to penetrate the sealed world behind the tiny oil slick. But she sees nothing except the saucer set on the embroidered tablecloth, nothing except the oil slick on the surface of the water...[2]

The Deconstructive Imaginary in Its Middle Eastern Drift

Jacques Derrida's elaboration of deconstruction's *weave* as a cohort or community, the dynamics of its *dissemination* or its spread, is almost simultaneous with his enunciation of its contrapuntal *bearing*. A philosophy "argued" more in the figures of poetics than through the historical tools of logic and philosophy; a systematic demolition burrowing into the *deep philology* of the conceptual mainstays buttressing the system in question; a general critical debunking that would implode an entire edifice by resolutely disclosing the multiplicity of its key terms, its claims to authority, hewing to a *specific context and occasion of inscription*. Such an intervention, collective in its very nature, does not proceed as a modular school of thought, legitimated by some purported turn in the *Zeitgeist* (or "new" paradigm shift), gathering authority with each major reformulation, to "take over" one new discipline or atelier of cultural improvisation after the next. This is enacted, in orderly, parliamentary fashion by the congresses of the respective disciplines and professions, and in the schools and departments of universities, maintaining their market share in the "battle of the faculties," the academic division of labor. Strategically grafted into the textual weave of fabrics, tissues, fibers, membranes, skin, cosmetic overlays, and even chemical compounds, as already adumbrated by Derrida in such groundbreaking contributions as "Plato's Pharmacy,"[3] and the early tribute to Stéphane Mallarmé, "The Double Session,"[4] deconstruction's spread, its outreach, its *influence*, will be far too diffuse and inchoate for that. Its growing sway will attain a very different *consistency* or tactile *feel*: something slippery, maybe even a bit uncomfortable. Deconstruction's dissemination, its outreach, is an oozing, not an earthquake but a mudslide, a slow sink. Something with very much the feel of a viscous film on the hand. Yet possessing the unbounded *spread* of a *color*.

When it comes to the pitched interactivity, say, of modernist and postmodern innovation, the ironclad figure of a *general Zeitgeist*, methodically bringing one cultural scene of experimentation and production after the next under its procrustean sway, simply will not work. The sympathetic vibrations and mutual reverberations are too indirect and understated. The metaphor we need for the mutual influence and nuancing by seemingly disparate and even antithetical cultural endeavors is more like breathing the same air, or catching a virus, or attending to common echoes and distortion-effects. I began thinking in such figures as it belatedly dawned on me, with the approach of a new millennium and upon encountering such works as *Gödel, Escher, Bach*,[5] *System and Structure*,[6] and *Chaos*,[7] that many of the same impulses and questions animating systems theorists and cyberneticists could have driven the decisive contributions of contemporary critical theory, from Lacanian psychoanalysis to deconstruction. The cybernetic figure of the "strange loop" may well emerge as a legitimate image for deconstruction's spread, whether from one discipline or profession to the next or from one linguistic or national arena of cultural production to another. As utterly inimical to the rigors of "high" theory as computer science and even electrical engineering may have seemed at the time, the set of commonalities emerged. Not only were the canons of Bach, and "impossible figures" common to M. C. Escher's drawings, Aesop's fables, and Alice's adventures, as purveyed by Douglas Hofstadter, situated in this interstitial zone, at once "no man's" and "everyone's." Jorge Luis Borges's fictions, Italo Calvino's parables, and postmodern meta-fiction, just to name a few instances, also recognizably bridged the seeming void between systems-speculation, even with some of its more tangible outcroppings, and contrapuntal deconstructive circumspect. Yet it is echoes, seepages, oil spills, and airborne viruses that define this almost inconceivable sharing among disparate sensibilities and projects of a particular moment, not a transference (*Übertragung*—"carrying over"), whether effected by a paradigm, or enabled by such constructs as epoch, arranged in linear order, canon, or aesthetic school.

It is under the aura of an asystematic, "chance-ful" modality of cultural diffusion (cf. Mallarmé, "Un coup de dès"), in accord with the demographics of a rhizomatic *non*-community among deconstructive readers and reading, that the two rich and deeply evocative passages appear at the head of this essay. They are, in sequence, by Orhan Pamuk, Nobel Prize–winning Turkish novelist, essayist, and curator, and by Anton Shammas, the Israeli Arab Christian poet, novelist, and scholar, whose Hebrew-language novel *Arabesques*, from which the extract derives, added amplitude, perspective, and diversity to modern Hebrew fiction. Both passages bespeak a dissemination eastward, a deconstructive practice and purview opening up, both within the Muslim framework of Turkey and within the daunting, breathtaking complexities of Middle Eastern sovereignty and politics.

But speaking *de rigeur* from a deconstructive (i.e., Derridean) point of view, an eastward diffusion or extension of a specialist's set of readerly and philosophical bearings incubated on Montparnasse is just as much an act of return as it is colonization, an incursion into new territory. Derrida minces no words about his Algerian beginnings, about the impact of growing up in Arab society, irrespective of his familial Jewish ethnicity.[8] Indeed, his complex knot of affiliations both sets him at odds with the deterministic and solipsistic thrusts of identity politics per se, and it distances him from any community, indeed, from the concept of community altogether. The arbitrariness hardwired into the very act of affiliation plays a decisive role in Derrida's theological writings; it facilitates his magisterial performance of "chunking" the endemic rivalry and competition prevailing between Judaism, Christianity, and Islam into a shared system, Abrahamic religion,[9] enabling his readers to productively philosophize on the vast historical and current redundancy and carnage perpetrated in the name of the respective faiths' purported self-interest.

> Let me get back to my saying "I am not one of the family." Clearly, I was playing on the formula that has multiple registers of resonance. I'm not one of the family means, in general, "I do not define myself on the basis of belonging to the family," or to civil society, or to the state; I do not define myself on the basis of elementary forms of kinship. But it also means, more figuratively, that I am not part of any group, that I do not identify myself with a linguistic community, a national community, a political party, or with any group or clique whatsoever, with any philosophical or literary school. "I am not one of the family" means: do not consider me "one of you," don't "count me in," I want to keep my freedom, always: this for me is the condition, not only being free and other, but also for entering into relation with the

singularity and alterity of others ... I am a Jew from Algeria, from a certain type of community, in which belonging to Algeria was problematic, belonging to France was problematic, etc. So all this predisposed me to not-belonging; but far beyond the particular idiosyncrasies of my own story, I wanted to indicate the sense in which an "I" doesn't have to be "one of the family."[10]

When it comes to Derrida, even the basic task of "self-ID"—spitting out "name, rank, and serial number"—entails complexity, and of a deconstructive magnitude. And in no instance does Derrida prioritize the multiple elements of his hybrid provenance and affiliation, nor does he privilege his Frenchness over being Algerian, his Jewishness over being Arab. And in this sense, the strong deconstructive disposition that we read in the works of Pamuk and Shammas is far from some odd turn eastward that both the critical bearing and its rhizomatic collectivity happened to take—this in its sporadic (as in *spores*) dissemination. Deconstruction's tending, its *Neigung*, toward the Muslim, the Arab, the Algerian, the Persian—deconstruction's always already pitching a tent in the Middle East and utterly thriving among the self-negating and self-effacing codes of hospitality and honor—is also its turning homeward back toward its base position of full-throttle critical engagement.

Pamuk's *My Name Is Red* and Shammas's *Arabesques: A Novel* were composed within the same interval of time (c. 1981–98) and were both published in English in 2001. Irrespective of when their authors became aware of Derrida and in what specific contexts Pamuk and Shammas initially encountered deconstruction, these texts, like the inebriating expansive universes common to Julio Cortázar's *Hopscotch*[11] and Hofstadter's *Gödel, Escher, Bach*, "breathed the same air" into which deconstruction emerged—and from this atmosphere extracted indispensable improvisational audacity. These two texts join *Hopscotch*, Ingeborg Bachmann's *Malina*, Thomas Pynchon's *Gravity's Rainbow*, and Thomas Bernhard's *Korrektur* as among the most innovative novels produced during this critic's lifetime, at least insofar as he is aware. And in the cases of the two novels, both the incredible burden and stakes of cultural transmission devolve into the *consistency* and application of *materials* critical in their impact upon civilization: *paint* (or *tint*), in the case of the dual histories of narrative and miniature painting at the apex of the Ottoman Empire posed in isomorphic parallel by Pamuk; and olive oil (along with stone) in the loose skein of multigenerational narratives both woven together and teased apart under the aesthetic aura and ethics of the *arabesque*.

Derrida's inaugural "master class" on the deconstruction of a canonical mainstay of Western metaphysics, his leisurely, playful, interdisciplinary, and multifaceted gloss, in *Of Grammatology* (1967), on Jean-Jacques Rousseau's *Essay on the Origins of Language*, pivots, as Rousseau's title implies, on a logically rigorous and etymologically dense debunking of concepts of *originality*. Derrida may not explicitly address the origin-concept until the final fifth or so of *Of Grammatology*, but its wide ramifications and repercussions within the edifice of Western metaphysics are broadly teased out, if this is possible, *even before* the grammatological exposé begins. Rousseau furnishes Derrida with a splendid occasion for pondering why it is that the linguistic postures and features aggregated under "writing"—that modality of communication and representation at once manifestly contrived, detached from the body, and unavoidably engendering more ambiguities than it purports to resolve—fares poorly in counter-distinction to modes of language elevated as more "natural," immanent, and intuitive. Even within what Derrida terms "speech," writing's ostensibly legitimate "rich cousin," the register of communication enjoying the approval of Western civilization's deeply engrained spirituality, there are paradoxes, aporias, at the origin, ones that Rousseau unavoidably highlights in the very act of glossing over:

> But can one speak of origins after that? Is the concept of the origin, or of the fundamental signified, anything but a function, indispensable but situated, inscribed, within the system of signification inaugurated by the interdict?[12]
>
> *To speak before knowing how to speak,* such is the limit toward which Rousseau obstinately guides his repetition of origin. This limit is indeed that of nonsupplementarity, but as there must already be language there, the supplement must announce itself without having been produced, lack and absence must have begun without beginning.[13]
>
> To speak before knowing how to speak, not to be able either to be silent or to speak, this limit of origin is indeed that of a pure presence, present enough to be living, to be felt in pleasure [*jouissance*] but pure enough to have remained unblemished by the work of difference, inarticulate enough for self-delight [*jouissance de soi*] not to be corrupted by interval, discontinuity, alterity.[14]

Well beyond Rousseau, it is this compulsive *riccorso* to clear-cut and pure originality that gives rise to so many distortion effects and blind spots on the part of philosophical speculation and critical exegesis, at least within a Western ambiance. Vast expectations regarding intellectual legitimacy, authority, truth, and systematic consistency are aroused under the delusion of access to a threshold of distinction between a definitive before and a definitive after, between a "primary" and a "secondary," between an "authentic" and a "derivative." To establish this threshold in his *Essay*, justifying the counter-languages of the South and the North, Rousseau imagines a primordial festival differentiating between the more and less immediately gratifying and aggrandizing modalities of language. Yet even in supplying a coherent mythopoetic basis for language's paradoxical bearings and iterations, Rousseau engages in a pronounced double-talk of his own on this matter; and Derrida, meticulous philosophical exegete that he is, *projects* the aporias entailed by Rousseau's recourse to the linguistic *utilities* of culture. In this process, Derrida enunciates a constellation of interrelated meta-tropes or philosophical figures, among them the *supplement, propriety, presence*, and *différance*, on which Rousseau and all teleological systems-makers implicitly rely, whether aware of this co-dependency or not.

The specific figuration of Rousseau's *Essay* furnishes Derrida with a cloud chamber or nuclear accelerator unleashing the intertwined constellation of meta-critical constructs by which deconstruction challenges the broader lineaments of Western metaphysics on multiple levels and in diverse "grains." Derrida's iteration does so through a sequence of deliberate stagings of where Rousseau's rhetoric and iterations revert into self-serving purism and devolve into "stops" imposed upon exegetical rigor and on the free-wheeling figurative improvisation facilitated by such close reading. Indeed, a critical constellation of distinctively deconstructive meta-tropes (or "infrastructures") coheres around Rousseau's regression to the linguistic origins, with Derrida in close pursuit. Among these number the *supplement*, a cypher of writing's presumed secondariness to speech (or voice), itself casting devastating aspersions upon any "natural language," upon the *propriety* common to moral certitude and possession (say, the ownership) of "truth" or "meaning." And if, in the universe of language, the supplement or the prosthesis of writing serves just as well as the divinely summoned and sanctioned Word, then irreversible damage has been wrought to the presumption and state of *immediacy*: the imminence and "self-presence" ascribed to exalted states of mind, interactions of sacred trust, and communications so intuitive as to seem transcendental. Indeed, if human culture cannot be other than a domain (if not "empire") of writing, then the downbeat of its core-medium of language is far more on the production of *différance*, distance, and discrepancy (*pace* Saussure) than on the establishment of equivalence.

It is no accident, then, that in the brief grammatological extracts displayed immediately above, broaching "a place before the origin" is implied in the very reversion *to* the origin: and, that the metaleptic paradox of "speaking before knowing how to speak" automatically engages the complex logic of the supplement, the enigma of infantile knowledge (as Freud understood better than anyone else), and the allure of pleasures sustained only in variance with themselves.

My Name Is Red: Contractual Negotiations

Although two very different works of fiction, with radically divergent formats, narrative strategies, cultural contexts, historical timeframes, and imagistic lexicons, Pamuk's *My Name Is Red* and Shammas's *Arabesques: A Novel* both set out with an irremediable separation and alienation from the origins that would otherwise furnish the protagonists' beings with redemptive meaning and resolution.

Both novels are infused and motivated by a pervasive sense of loss at the same time that their acute sensibilities of temporality and history preempt any sentimentality or tragedy from seeping into the transcript of inevitable dislocation and effacement. The loss to which both works attend is that of a *Lebensweise*, a distinctive, and in its time, composed (if not perfectly organic) *way of life*. Both novels embellish a rupture in time and culture mattering far more, and with much more telling impact upon storytelling, art, and even perception, than the demise of particular leaders, governments, cities, or even aesthetic schools.

In the case of *My Name Is Red*, we find ourselves in late-sixteenth-century Istanbul. Western techniques and ideologies of representation are in process of wreaking havoc on the conventions defining the tradition of Near and Middle Eastern miniature painting. The overall atelier of miniature illustration serves as a microcosm of an overall *déclassement* of the Ottoman as a world economy and power at the hands of newfound

Western technological capability and military might. This, just as the West's broader Modernity[15] is shifting into gear. At the same time, the diffusion of this exacting and multimedia art form has been vast, from the Bosporus to Afghanistan; from Uzbekistan to India. For all that Persian civilization and the interconnected Muslim states of the Middle East may find themselves in current disadvantage to Western powers, as personified by the Venetians, through such enterprises as carpet-weaving and pottery as well as book illumination, an integral and interactive culture exclusively grounded in no single social or geographical parameter: whether language, kinship, ethnicity, territorial boundaries, or even religion is well under way. The inherent radicality of such a hybrid, for lack of a better term, "cultural zone," then as now, is certainly not lost on Pamuk. Whether they read literature or not, current world leaders and students of politics would do well to attend to the staying power and sheer force implicit to cultural forms that Pamuk *curates* and explicates in this novel.

The wider historical phenomenon framing *My Name Is Red* is the transformations in perception and technique, not to mention the shifts in technology and commercial power, in the process of handcuffing the tradition of Near and Middle Eastern miniature painting during the sixteenth century. At the level of aesthetico-historical allegory, Pamuk marshals the very meticulousness that he ascribes to Seyyit Mirek, Bihzad, Sheikh Ali, Sheikh Muhammad of Isfahan, and the other masters of the art form in devising the narrative technology enabling a vast erudition, as much literary as art historical, to be eventful, dramatic, and exciting in its "delivery."

My Name Is Red is as momentous a tribute to the book-medium as has been generated, over in the Anglo-European sphere, at least since Marcel Proust's *Recherche*, James Joyce's *Ulysses*, and Walter Benjamin's *The Arcades Project*. In too many senses to enumerate, Pamuk's novel too is an illuminated text. Its erudition in a literature extending from Egypt through Persia has to match its art historical scholarship. Within the compass of *My Name Is Red*, literary erudition and visual culture are posed in a relationship of parallel indexing: this is the novel's DNA. This is a cybernetic feature. Art history is backed by an absorption into the materiality of the artifact perforce offering specificity in aesthetic provenance (location, dates, school) often bypassed in literary scholarship or critique. If we allow that *My Name Is Red*'s dual aesthetic focus is an *isomorphic* arrangement, the unfolding account of the illuminations' triumphs, masters, range, and succession of outcroppings plays the relatively more *quantifiable* partner to such pivotal narratives as Nizami's *Hüsrev and Shirin* and *Leyla and Mejnun*, *The Book of Kings*, Jami's *Seven Thrones*, El-Jefziyye's *Book of the Soul*, including their provenance and their broader cultural impact.

The "narrative delivery system" that Pamuk devises for the cultural *matériel* that he wishes to highlight is as intricate and demanding as the miniature's most persistent exemplars. He draws upon two major literary conventions in synthesizing a plotline that can rise to the challenge of making the Middle Eastern and Central Asian histories of art, literature, and the book around the seventeenth century compelling and exciting. The first is romantic: the itinerant art-trained regional administrator "Black" returns to Istanbul at a moment of crisis in the esteemed atelier of illustration that, twelve years before, he left behind. He discovers upon his return that he is free to reclaim

Shekure, love of his life and daughter of Enishte Effendi, master of that atelier (by the way, also his uncle), because she has been widowed. The rekindling of his love places him in direct competition over Shekure with Hasan, brother of Shekure's late warrior husband, and possibly with a colleague or two persisting from his former workshop. Shekure, by the same token, if she is to respond to his declarations and entreaties, in her roles as daughter, widow, and mother, must, in order to remarry, negotiate a minefield of conflicting emotions and "clear the field" of the conventional domestic constraints bearing upon a person of her status.

And in order to fully infuse the venerable history of book illumination in the Near and Middle East with heightened drama, Pamuk templates the unfolding debriefing concerning this art form to the genre of *detective fiction*. In this respect, he takes inspiration from Umberto Eco's *The Name of the Rose* (1980).[16] It will emerge that one or another member of Black's former atelier is a murderer, a brutal one at that, motivated by a lethal brew of extreme religious agnosticism laced with burning professional and romantic envy. An initial murder of Elegant Effendi, gold-leaf applicator in the atelier, multiplies on itself. And art historical expertise, the ability to discern the offending artist's personal *style of illustration* (still at a moment when the personal is systematically extruded from pictorial representation in Middle Eastern art), turns out to be the only foolproof avenue of detection. For pivotal stretches of the *dénouement*, the protagonists' archival efforts (competing atelier Master Osman in league with Black) to stylistically unmask the homicidal artist through visits to the royal treasury *are* tantamount to narrative development.

Pamuk achieves a strikingly *literary* treatment of archival and scholarly endeavor not only by contouring it in keeping with the generic parameters, respectively, of romance and crime fiction. Appealing to the signature cycles of self-engendering, "strange looping" fiction in Middle Eastern fiction, notably *The Arabian Nights* and Rumi's *Masnavi*, Pamuk improvises a relay, from one chapter to the next, of constantly changing narrators. Not only does this device fragment narrative "voice" and perspective; it also enforces an extreme implicit aesthetic assertion to the effect that *any element of the narrative*, whether the central characters or the most inconsequential, or even a gold coin, or a tree, or a detail from an illumination, say a dog, or the color red, can assume the narrator's role. The drama of romantic passion set against an expanding network of unresolved murders only becomes attenuated amid this phantasmagoria of evanescent and shifting narrative vignettes. In effect, Pamuk turns each chapter of *My Name Is Red* into a narrative miniature. Even while we begin to recall details strewn along the way and become familiar with the major characters' expository styles in addressing the most prominent question marks that the narrative raises, we cannot predict who will take over the storytelling, which "line of flight" the text will next pursue. The novel, for all its recapitulation of a foregone cultural history and its setting in an empire confronting an incremental, if not immanent decline, activates an open-ended matrix of narrative possibility and unpredictability. It thus affiliates itself with the experiment, entertained by other prominent masters of postmodern fiction, of wildly permutational narrative variation—even if it cannot quite claim the undecidability achieved by Cortázar in *Hopscotch*.

Not unlike the phenomenon of deconstruction itself, the meticulous practice of miniature illustration chronicled in *My Name Is Red* has diffused itself, by no strict logic of trade routes, over a sprawling "catchment area." The formidable body of conventions accruing to this practice, including, as set out by Pamuk, painting strictly by the eye and devoutly rendering each detail,[17] furnishes a strong example of what I have elsewhere characterized as aesthetic contracts:

> The aesthetic contract is in effect so long as its always provisional and tentative solutions are to problems whose relevance is agreed upon by some consensus. There are indeed what we call historical determinants to the problems that the aesthetic contract attempts to address or work through. A new order of government or a new system of production or technology may so alter living and thinking conditions so as to invalidate a particular aesthetic contract in effect. ... Like other time-specific documents, contracts go in and out of effect. Collectivities of writers and thinkers abandon certain projects, or the public evinces indifference toward them, not because of inherent flaws in these large experiments, but as the result of circumstantial changes, including changes in technological and socioeconomic paradigms, and wars. ... An existing aesthetic contract may no longer satisfy a community's interest in knowledge and experience to the same degree as an alternate exercise; or there may be durations when no paradigm for aesthetic invention satisfies these needs. The contract declines as well as rises; it can coexist with other prevailing aesthetic contracts as well. It guarantees public attention to certain stylistic and generic conventions. It protects artists from oblivion; it protects artists from each other, furnishing more or less explicit conditions of mutual recognition and sanction.[18]

These lines, although in a completely different text-display from Pamuk's exuberant narrative fabulation, apply to the kind of schools that both Near and Middle Eastern miniature painting and deconstruction exemplify. Over a long and storied run, miniaturist virtuosity, powered by its requisite material science and allied crafts (e.g., papermaking, formulating inks and colors), furnishes the canon of Persian and other regional fiction with precisely the visual supplement requisite to a virtual multi-medium. Pamuk's novel sets out just as this dominant medium, packing a double visual-textual punch, begins to feel under encroachment by Western painting, especially portraiture. Enishte Effendi, the eminence of the miniature medium who has proven most receptive to Western portraiture's allowances for the subjectivities of painted subject and painter as well as for the artist's painterly *style*, remains, within the confines of artistic Istanbul, an expendable quantity. It is no accident that his murder, to the accompaniment of brilliant aesthetic disputation with the same perpetrator who eliminated Elegant Effendi, takes place still within the novel's first third.

And indeed, as the person to whom the above contractual formulations *occurred*, I submit that deconstruction, too, furnished compelling answers to aesthetic, epistemological, and critical questions streaming from a varied host of contemporary stimulations. And may still. Chief among these provocations were a mid-century tradition of studies, across the academic gamut, that had extrapolated to the level of *structure* in brokering between claims of formalism and substantive demonstration in establishing authenticity (this may have afforded *breadth* but was not without its costs); twentieth-century phenomenology, with its *de rigeur* enlistment of poetic figuration in philosophical elucidation and the *autopoetic simultaneity* of inquiry with allegorical self-performance that it achieved; and not least, the emergence and proliferation of *media* grounded in the translation of what had been discrete art forms and their respective *displays* into electronic impulses. Let me submit as well, that my propositions regarding aesthetic contracts, for whatever they may be worth, could not *but* have arisen from my own apprenticeship in deconstruction's atelier.

Despite its creator's disclaimers, deconstruction, too, was and remains a *school*. At the same time that it hews tightly to the linguistic ur-medium that produces all kinds of "interference" (ambiguity, undecidability, polysemy) while establishing the very thresholds for articulation and culture, deconstruction facilitates an *outreach* of core-cultural aporias across a bewildering range of cultures and epochs, all the while that it *raises the philosophical power* of critical investigation and elucidation. (Cyberneticists would call this latter a "chunking" to a higher level of application and relevance, if you will, a "conceptual upgrade.") By the logic of aesthetic (or in deconstruction's case, *critical*) contracts, there may yet emerge a moment when the questions that deconstruction poses and the solutions it improvises have become *dépassé*; but to this critic, in view of what incited Derrida to devise it, this "replacement" cultural configuration has neither come about nor is in sight.

To whatever degree that *My Name Is Red* can be retrospectively charged with being launched or motivated by a deconstructive sensibility, it hijacks the twentieth-century experimental novel into a debate regarding baseline socio-aesthetic conditions at the highest philosophical level. Historically situated at a moment of decline, loss of traction, whether within an art form or within the systematic cultural conditions that back its *currency*, Pamuk's novel weighs the fate of culture's signature achievements as impinged upon by the contingencies of technique, technology, cultural literacy, and indifference.

Gum Arabic: Distilling Middle Eastern Complexity

The embroidery making Anton Shammas's *Arabesques* a particularly resonant companion to *My Name Is Red* may be telescoped into a timeframe both more foreshortened and closer at hand than the aesthetico-political deliberations transcribed in the latter novel. The context of the stresses and the strains, the rapprochements and the breakdowns in mutual understanding chronicled in *Arabesques*, has a pitched familiarity to the contemporary reader. We have become only too acclimatized to its political surround and the rare and habitually short-lived "outs" that its impasses seem to offer. And yet, as only very few of its literary contemporaries, *Arabesques* too rises into apotheoses of interconnectedness, literary tapestries of *Mitsein*, tolerance and coexistence—these are its eponymous *arabesques*—by which literature resoundingly establishes that there is something broader, more knowing, more forgiving, and ultimately more ethically commendable than the customary cycle of crimes, insults, recriminations, takeovers, and surrenders. These memorable "bubbles" in literary synthesis (they have the quality of the illusory but dimension-shifting "marbles" that Hofstadter "discovers" in stacks of envelopes),[19] comprise literature's *response*[20] to the politics of expansion, control, and endless revenge.

The "cloud chamber" of *Arabesques* is a conflation of diverse social and religious communities, with their respective traditions and histories, inhabiting the territory of the State of Israel as it was founded in 1948 but with significant outcroppings in modern-day Lebanon and in what belonged, prior to 1967, to Jordan. The novel's focal point may be an extended family of Israeli Arab Catholics, but regional Muslims and Jewish Israelis also figure crucially in the mix. In its "present" emanation—a mid-Western institute of international writers reveling in the time and wherewithal to focus on their work—Shammas's historical project of reconstructing a recalcitrant past in the name of achieving some moratorium enlists a recognizable cast of contemporary types and surrogates—Israeli, Polish, Swedish, Palestinian. Like so many of us, these characters contend with a barrage of duplicitous social codes and devise their "situational ethics" on the ground, in keeping with what they encounter. The past that "I-narrator" Anton must contend with as he brings a craft in storytelling that he inherited from his Uncle Yusef long ago in his home village,[21] to fruition, is at best a tattered tapestry, twisted around itself and beset with inconsistencies, indecipherable legends, and out-and-out gaps. Indeed, not too long in the novel, when Anton undertakes to visit his home village of Fassuta from Haifa where he now resides, Shammas empowers the novel's textual tapestry to speak on its own behalf:

> I had imagined that this Al-Asbah had made it possible for me to conclude the story the way it had ended in the previous chapter, and with this his role in the tapestry of the story had ended too. But here I am travelling along the road to Silwad holding onto the end of the thread he had spun and interwoven with the warp and woof of my life. Like a weaver I yank at the thread and find myself wondering about the opportunity that has presented itself to me as a result of the new turn of events, and before I have sufficiently considered my next steps, I comb out the unraveled thread and card it again, then turn to impart to it a completely different color and to weave it once more into the frayed tapestry, mending what had unraveled. What guarantee do I have that this act is not a proclamation of liberty on the part of the thread.[22]

Almost as soon as he can, Shammas wishes to leave no doubt that *Arabesques* is as much an allegory of writing as it is a story stitched together from other stories, a doubled saga of communal coherence, dispossession, and recalibration together with an account of the emergence of a writer's mission. Yet this particular account, of a chance encounter, in 1980, with Abdallah Al-Asbah, a former acquaintance of Anton's father, and someone who once had to quit the paternal barbershop in the middle of a shave, is always already intertwined with another saga, the most aggravated instance of deterritorialization in the novel, the staggered trajectory of Leylah Khoury. For it turns out that the elder Al-Asbah, a leader in the Arab Rebellion against the British in 1936, becomes father-in-law to the preternaturally blond Khoury, who early in life was farmed out to the Bitar family of Beirut as a servant, eventually converting to Islam in marriage and dwelling with her deaf-mute twin sons in the village of Silwad. In rendering an account of the jarring effect of disparate stories that "bleed" into one another in a text, the narrator, whether we prefer to think of him as "Anton" or "Shammas," projects us into the "here and now" of inscription; he makes us party to the give and take of the writerly choices that become liberated in the act of stringing words and figures. "I comb out the unraveled thread and card it again, then turn to impart to it a completely different color." In projecting a voice onto the process of writing itself, Shammas declares the independence and agency of the components of time, memory, and history to settle their own affairs. Fully in keeping with the "world," *pace* Heidegger, that the novel chronicles, does Shammas incorporate corresponding ruptures and inconsistencies into his own theoretical as well as narrative performance.

All of the communities implicated in *Arabesques* contend with loss, the effacement of tradition, the corruption of memory, and, in keeping with Franz Kafka's modernistic "fractured myths," the devolution of what were once vibrant communications and linguistic constructions into things, a materiality inarticulate even if crafted. The deterritorializations telescoped within the novel's compass belong no more to the Arab Christians than to the Muslims or to the Jews. Shammas is artful on this point. The impetus to appropriations, dispossession, internment, and forced emigration is no more the founding of the State of Israel than it is long-standing ethnic divisions, arbitrary, post–First World War political borders, and random patterns of migration and settlement by kinship. Nevertheless, the boundaries established by the State of Israel do end up, in multiple instances, "freezing" or blocking a prior "smooth space" of movement, kinship, and association that had previously prevailed in the region for generations. And the novel does chronicle a closely knit family's need to abandon Fassuta in 1948, in the wake of Israel's victorious War of Independence.

In registering the dislocation, confusion, and, in instances, of out-and-out disorientation undergone by its narrator and several of his relatives, whose immediate Arab Christian family originally hailed from Syria by way of a network of Galilean villages but then migrated to Haifa, *Arabesques* creates the double-helix of two narrative strands regularly circling around, repeating upon, and echoing one another. This may well exacerbate the dialectical tension between then and now, between before and after—more so than *My Name Is Red*'s proliferating vignettes proffered by a skein of mutually replaceable narrators. (The "contemporary" stratum of *Arabesques*, set mostly in and about the International Writing Workshop at the University of Iowa, does at times form itself into chapters divided into similar multi-narrator fragments.) Yet fiction, for Shammas as well as for Pamuk, is a zone in which tales and memories are interlocked one within another; they may not tally up perfectly in the end. The memory store that has been retrospectively composed leaves as many mysteries unresolved as dispatched. But a distinctive *feel*, a *tenor*—for social events, interpersonal relations, has nonetheless coalesced and been registered within the public transcript. This is a social fabric in which lines of tradition and filiation become summarily truncated; communal locations and addresses are arbitrarily shifted. No critic has better captured the enigma of *Arabesques* as a chronicle proliferating within itself but undermined by its gaps in continuity and coincidences or duplications that don't quite add up than Hannan Hever, who recognized early on the novel's transformative impact on the canon of Hebrew fiction.

Hever's prescient reception of the novel works outward from the complexities always already embedded in Shammas's identity and status as a Hebrew-language author, pursuing them with notable readerly acuity, into the author's artistic achievement.

> The identity of an Israeli Christian Arab does not line up in any simple way with the main political forces at work in Israel ... As an "Israeli Arab," Shammas is a member of a minority group, but as a Christian he falls outside the Islamic mainstream of the minority that ... tends more "naturally" to be identified with the Palestinians. On top of this, he writes in Hebrew, the language of the dominant Jewish culture, which is itself a minority within the predominantly Arab Middle East.[23]

Shammas himself has likened this position, in its complexity "to the image of a Russian babushka doll."[24]

For Pamuk in *My Name Is Red*, Islamic fundamentalism, whose unremitting drive for social control also encompasses aesthetic strictures, is a constant onus upon the characters: in their conjugal arrangements (as exemplified by Shekure's remarriage) and in their aesthetic striving. But its encroachment upon miniature painting feels distant; its impact is unpredictable and, more often than not, bizarre. Followers of one Nusret Hoja of Erzurum, the prevailing extremist evangelist of the novel's moment, may one evening decide to trash a dervish lodge frequented by miniaturist "Butterfly"—this in excoriation of its gay subculture and "encompassing" decadence. The sociopolitical contradictions and tensions faced, in *Arabesques*, by Shammas's surrogates (not only the "I-narrator" but also his cousin Michel Abbayad, "who himself had been named Anton Shammas, but soon after birth, was kidnapped from his natural mother Almaza ... to be raised in Beirut"[25]), are of a far more pressing and existentially damaging nature. And yet, by Hever's account, *Arabesques* is also "organized like a detective story."[26] Any sense it can derive from directing its quest for historical coherence and moratorium backward is tangled and unsatisfactory: "Shammas presents his family's ancestry as a hodgepodge of periods, religions, and nationalities."[27]

Pamuk and Shammas may well, then, be writing out of situations configured by very different timeframes, oppositional forces, and degrees of political exigency. Yet undoubtedly infused by the common air that they breathed (or "viruses" they contracted), they improvise within strikingly similar "aesthetic contracts" as they conjure universes of time, history, craft, love, and narrative under pressure from and in response to closed systems of political and cultural repression. Pamuk and Shammas both draw heavily, for example, on the fictive resources of magical realism and experimental meta-fiction as they synthesize the narrative infrastructure for their respective novels and as they sequence their characters' interactions. And yet these experiments, I would submit, comprise the fictive "theater" to deconstruction's polymorphous critical bearing. Thus, Hever's early "fresh look" at Shammas's bold position unavoidably characterizes its achievement in terms also most pertinent to Pamuk's fictive invocation of miniature painting:

> The interweaving of earlier and later events is a structural principle of the novel; Shammas exploits it chiefly as a means of realizing his cyclical conception of time. The numerous digressions, the twists and turns, the sudden predestined meetings all conform, in one way or another, to the Arabian iconography of the arabesque. The phenomenon stands out particularly in the "narrative" parts, which revolve mostly around the village of Fasuta. But a careful reading of the "narrator's portion" ... also reveals the figure of the arabesque. Even in such a straightforward matter as Shammas' travel journal, things are not as they seem: for one thing, the entries are not always in chronological order. The connections among events within each part are highly complex, as is the relationship between the two parts. The static arabesque frees the chronological flow of time in the plot from any necessary involvement with such notions as redemption or progress ...
>
> The traditional figure of the arabesque pervading the structure of the novel at every level, brings Shammas' representational mode close to a pure statement of formal relations. In the arabesque, Shammas has found a way to relate to the past without falling prey to its nondialectical universalism.[28]

Hever understands very well that *Arabesques*' epochal contribution to Hebrew literature consists every bit as much in its radical textual incompletion and anomaly, its involuted narrative development by nested elements, as in Anton Shammas's hitherto nonexistent (as in silent, pre-articulate) *position* as a literary "user" and hence fully documented *citizen* of the Hebrew language. Hever's early broad apprehension of the novel's radicality highlights its *recursions* of plot and circumstance (its "numerous digressions") as well as the imaginative power it generates by *looping* upon itself (its "twists and turns"). Though Hever is not the scholar to get misty over his latest laptop, his understanding of the amplitude that *Arabesques* brings to Hebrew letters is solidly pre-cybernetic: the novel's arabesques are, even if only fleetingly, dimension-expanding. They may be characterized, in the current parlance, as *strange loops*. They occupy the position of the Derridean *brisure* or hinge, by which the etymology-driven deconstructive exposé may derive from the menu of concepts prevailing in Western metaphysics but then, at least momentarily, veers *hors système*, outside the system.[29] The *arabesques* of the eponymous novel enable literary improvisation to implode the constructs of identity, sovereignty, and propriety (linguistic as well as territorial), making Shammas's voice, *pace* Gregor Samsa, barely recognizable, transforming Israeli statehood into a minefield of legal and ethical aporias. These impediments come into particularly sharp relief as both "real-life" people and literary surrogates negotiate its geographical and cultural sectors.

The deracination of the lines of filiation and tradition that, for one reason or another, converged in Fassuta at a certain epoch is made all the more poignant by the modesty and simplicity of the *Lebensweise*, the way of life, that prevailed there. This is not the ornate splendor, the painterly competition over small differences, and the political intrigue of the Ottoman court. Family and church affiliation reign supreme over the social fabric of Fassuta. To a surprising extent in the twentieth century, the community still lives off the land. Professional aspiration may not be the driving force in life. Those not engaged in agriculture, women and men, have sought out trades of service to the community and its local surround. The Christian Arabs of Fassuta are a far cry from peasants, as Fernand Braudel elaborates their decisive historical role.[30] Yet as members of communities defining themselves by their intimate internal affiliation and their unassuming social marginality, the people of Fassuta belong to a first generation of descendants who have been inflected by "full service" modernity.

The collective engagement with material culture is informed and impressive. The assumed degree of facility with such processes as extracting olive oil or husbanding rainwater in the local cistern is high. Culinary sophistication is a joyous feature of everyday life; one notes how many of the staples of the Fassuta diet have become the catchwords for Israeli cuisine as recognized internationally. *Matériel* is accorded utmost communal respect: the fruit of the olive tree, the grain milled into the flour for pita and the pulses transformed into such everyday delicacies as *mjaddara*; the hides converted by craft into custom shoes and sandals (this becomes Hanna Shammas's, Anton's father, trade, after he turns barbering into a weekend vocation). All kinds of carpentry skills support these core trades and the needs for physical comfort and storage. Mythically and practically, the community grounds itself in stone; stone-craft is both a historical and ongoing expression of its Being.

The embroidery of the arabesque places the material culture of the local Christian Arab culture, what Derrida would term its "local difference,"[31] at the service of the poetic synthesis, enabling Shammas's narrative, at every turn, to breach the ceilings lowered by sectarian thinking and violence. The narrative phantasmagorias through which, in turn, Shammas addresses Fassuta's geological substrate, its natural resources, and its intergenerational intertwining bridge the material culture of Arab Christian life to the material substrate of language. Indeed, as we shall further explore below, Pamuk and Shammas share a distinct virtuosity in the interjection of textually generated "narrative phantasmagorias." These particularly notable passages by both authors—and I have furnished strategic instances of this craft at the head of this essay—both *interrupt* the orderly unfolding of events and *open* dimension-expanding purviews of meta-fictive sensibility and critical allegory within storytelling. By labeling this sort of "strange looping" poetic consolidation and rises within fiction-power "narrative phantasmagorias," I am referring the practice back to nineteenth-century modernization—as chronicled, say, by Walter Benjamin in his work on the Second Empire[32]—and the spectacular increase of commodities, urban street life, and spectacles themselves as they transformed the rhythms and tenor of dwelling in places like Paris and London. Honoré de Balzac and Émile Zola[33] became masters at these frenetic "windows" casually installed into their novels and novellas. The phantasmagorical digressions pick up potent doses of the ambient frenzy—in capital, consumption, and sex—out on the streets surrounding their elaboration. The jazz-like improvisations on storytelling and both family and political histories that Shammas interjects within *Arabesques*' doubled narrative of communal displacement and incipient authorship may seem, in their nostalgic spareness, the very inverse of the cluttered, accelerated, chaotic extended vignettes that Balzac and Zola, seemingly from nowhere, import into the overheated panorama of nineteenth-century Paris.

No figure proves more fruitful than the box in *Arabesques* sounding the depths of the past for the tangles of things, movements, and snippets of anecdote that generate arresting narrative. The novel is literally a warehouse of boxes, of radically different shapes and dimensions, also serving as memory capsules or containers. There is the *smandra* or familial wardrobe, transported from the northern village of Rmeish;[34] the family bookcase, kept under lock and key when the narrator is young;[35] the "damascene wooden box inlaid with mother-of-pearl" given to Anton's mother, Elaine, upon her betrothal, later where family memorabilia are deposited;[36] the "rusty tin box full of bullets," accompanying a revolver discovered in a back lot, likely a holdover from the Arab Rebellion of 1936;[37] also, in an odd way, the cistern tucked beneath the western arch of the narrator's house, and site of a fleeting, partial early sexual initiation when Anton is coerced into cleaning it.[38] The "rusty tin box" may well be pressed back into action late in the novel, in the dénouement of the myth, propounded by the teacher, Rasheed Karrarah (a.k.a. Abdallah Al-Asbah), "about the golden treasures ... hidden away in the broad cave over which the [Fassuta] fortress was built."[39] The tin box, in its final emanation, contains forty gold pieces and *half* an amulet that will be necessary for releasing the treasure. (The other half hangs in a pendant around Surayyah Sa'id's neck. Shammas is as forthright in disclosing the profound superstition—of curses and written amulets—prevailing in the Arab Christian milieu of the Galilee as he is in underscoring the devoutness of religious adherence. Deep-seated superstition is a recurrent appurtenance within the literature, for example, in Mihail Sadoveanu's renditions of nineteenth-century agrarian Romanian life, furnishing a display case for peasant culture.)[40] Both the *smandara* and the bookcase are of an *olive-green* hue. This can be no accident given the intense torque, cultural as well as imagistic, placed by the novel on the oil of this fruit.

By contrast, Pamuk's elaboration of the serious consequences at stake in the divergence between "Venetian" and Near and Middle Eastern modes of pictorial representation;[41] the extended catalogue of masterworks of illumination through which Master Osman and Black scour in search of the "clipped" horses' nostrils that will establish the perpetrator:[42] though arising from a distant, centuries-prior scene of cultural production, these "asides" are very much of the same cloth as the heat, frenzy, and incendiary web of connections imported into fiction by the likes of Kafka, Joyce, and Alfred Döblin as well as by Benjamin's Second Empire "regulars." (Of all segments of *My Name Is Red*, the harried visual search through the royal archives comes closest to the most renowned Second Empire "phantasmagoria" of all: the panorama of historical things that Valentin, hapless narrator and protagonist of *Le Peau de chagrin*, discovers in the curiosity shop where his fate is set.)[43]

No key to the complex and multifaceted *occasion* of *Arabesques* is more compelling than the figure of olive oil, both in its material culture and its utterly central role to the persistence of a certain *Lebensweise*. As suggested at the head of this essay, its very *consistency* figures a modality of cultural diffusion and refinement in articulation. And in many crucial parallel respects, *color* would have to serve as an indispensable key in a novel of detection situated in the ateliers of sanctioned, official painting in sixteenth-century Istanbul. Color is a baseline condition of painting. The color red, in the extract reproduced at the beginning of this essay, "knows" that it is all-pervasive. Oils and paints are indistinct in their shape and meaning; their diffusion is haphazard and in significant aspects beyond control; in substance, they are vacuous and shaky. They require *containment* for their storage and deployment. Around the Mediterranean and in the Near East, the olive branch is the basic symbol of communal perdurance as well of peace. The displacements undergone by the likes of Anton, Michel-Michael Abyad, Laylah Khoury-Surayyah Sa'id, and Ameen Shammas bespeak this oil's loss of its potency as a guarantor of coexistence. Yet as conjured by Shammas at the beginning of the novel, the substance, in its viscous plasticity, is a temporal medium as well as a marker of demographic stability. Peering into the *mandal* and "reading" the oil slick, Elaine, who will marry Hanna the barber and become Anton's mother, divines future developments: the senseless destruction of three magnificent white horses and pregnancies in her own womb never coming to fruition.[44] What she is able to "see" in the oil slick is the demise of a community and a *Lebensweise*; and yet the same slippery substance is the medium for the community's persistence as narrative, the stain in which its involuted and indirect story will be inscribed. The narrative makes the association between oil slick and ink explicit, when Aunt Najeebeh, at "eccentric" Father Sim'an's suggestion, dissolves an ink inscription she had brought to him for interpretation, in water. "'This tastes like ink,' my grandmother said. 'I can understand that, but where does the taste of oil come from?'"[45] Literature emerges not from the olive oil of the present, with its powers to demarcate settlement and preserve vegetables and other comestibles, but from the olive oil of the past, which has stained memory, even in some instances by obliterating it. Father Sim'an loses his notebook to a cat, which in his pursuit of a mouse, nudges it into the open oil-crock below.[46]

The first epigraph to this essay, narrated by Pamuk's color red, is bisected by a profound philosophical question, one that also obsessed no less a literary personage than Goethe: "What is it to be a color?" The answer rendered by Pamuk's narrative is no less inventive and beautiful than we would expect it to be. Color is the substance of visual apprehension and sensibility. Without it, vision is a vacuous experience, akin to souls without their "whispering," to the winds without their "sursurrus."[47] Color is filling, fulfillment, the lifeblood of cultural fabrication. It is, as red elaborates it, the multisensory potentiality for tone, gradation, nuance, even articulation itself. Color thus becomes the chief visual gradient of language. Pamuk's allowing red to "bleed" into the immanence of souls and into the whisper of sound betrays a certain imperialistic grandeur in the sense of sight. Yet prior to this philosophical inquiry, the color red has prepared us for its expansionist ideology. Its range or "catchment area" is coterminous with human habitation; it adorns virtually *all* products of human fabrication, military banners, ambassadors' caftans, Ushak carpets, the outpouring of blood, "depicted" or actual, whether shed in aggression, passion, illness, or accident. The *extent* of color, the uncontrollable persistence of its outreach, even if its "strategies" are weak ones—pouring, seeping, dripping, are an essential part of their impact and performance. Red discerns itself in "blouses worn by stunning women with outstretched necks watching the street through open shutters, the sour-cherry eyes of bird-statues made of sugar, the stockings of shepherds."

The primary vehicle for Pamuk's treatment of Near and Middle Eastern miniature painting as a literature is, it so happens, *historical phantasmagorias of the international diffusion* of such highly refined arts as poetry and epic, illustration, calligraphy, carpet-weaving, and pottery. We will explore some of the most notable of these below. There is a powerful momentum, in Pamuk's evocations of the various art forms, toward *collation* and *curation* of the dominant masters and schools. Indeed, the narrative of *My Name Is Red* is more comfortable in reconstructing entire chains of artistic inspirations, influences, and migrations than with dwelling on any single masterpiece or master. The disquisitions of Enishte Effendi, reconstructing the then-current divide in pictorial rendition between East and West, or of Master Osman, reviewing the masterpieces housed in the royal treasury one last time, share this historical depth and grandeur of scope. The liquidity of red or any tint, for that matter, figures the *accumulative* impulse common to the acquisition of *objets d'art* and the retrospective "collection" (*pace* Benjamin)[48] performed by art historical accounting as well as by museums and individuals.[49] The passions that artwork evokes, in its producers, cognoscenti, and collectors, expand and intensify, a runaway blot of vivid color, blood red. This obsessive attachment to art furnishes the motive to the conundrum of double murder in the atelier endowing *My Name Is Red* with its genre and its form.

Oil and color; color and oil. These are the media by means of which military takeovers and martial law, borders imposed on the circulation of communities and ideas, as well on aesthetic and critical practice, expand and bubble into the resilience, suggestiveness, and *hope* that literature may venture. It was Kafka, of course, who arrived at the definitive disclaimer regarding hope, whether deriving from religion, material comfort, literature, or from any other source, particularly as it might pertain to *us*. And yet by innovative *delving* into language's concentrated liquidity at a shared moment in creativity, Pamuk and Shammas dramatize the diffusion of practices and concepts that will *respond* to the abuses of power; in the same gesture, they mobilize literature in its multilateral dissolution of prevailing assertions of brute force.

The Cunning Uncle: Storytelling as Deconstruction

In the foregoing, I have hopefully cobbled together a broad critical-theoretical context extrapolating the design parameters and highlighting the exceptional improvisations characteristic of both *My Name Is Red* and *Arabesques*. Before proceeding to the second and final phase—it will aim at accessing and annotating certain of the novels' virtuoso writerly performances—a few qualifications and disclaimers are in order. I am not submitting that Orhan Pamuk or Anton Shammas, in order to compose these novels, needed to be acolytes or disciples of Jacques Derrida. Rather, that a deconstructive bearing or sensibility was part and parcel of the broader cultural surround, or environment, out of which the novels emerged. (The "magical realism" coming to particular prominence in the Latin American "boom" and experimental Euro-US meta-fiction [or "surfiction"] could have also played part in this milieu, as could have speculative science fiction, whether by literary authors, say Borges and Calvino, or by cyberneticists.) Indeed, the embedded media of *My Name Is Red* and *Arabesques*—olive oil and paint—go so far as to *figure* the dissemination of a deconstructive *contretemps* and counterpoint, a bearing, a hold, philologically cutting against the grain by which culture's sanctities are hewn and perpetuated. But a novel, in itself, does not "deconstruct." A novel, rather, "is," having "come into Being." Its provenance and its scope are too wide to enable it to "discourse" or to explain. Its Being is the being of linguistic figuration, play, and complexity. A novel can, however, orchestrate the enlargement of the concepts and conditions brought under its representational purview; it can loosen, dissolve, and question ideologies instantiated in different ways within its compass. This is precisely what Pamuk and Shammas notably achieve in their respective novels. And this achievement, environmentally within the orbit of deconstruction, is all the more pitched—even in the liquidity, indirection, and incompletion of deconstruction's "transmission."

The figure of the *arabesque* is at once a *script* and a literary convention; in this indecision, it too, like color, hovers between substance and form. Viewed against the backdrop of the nineteenth-century narrative phantasmagoria—and beyond, in the rich traditions of Near and Middle Eastern literature—the arabesque is an outbreak, a dimension-shifting *bubble* of poetic condensation and figural power within a text, whether its *genre* be discourse or fiction. We know that Derrida, especially in keeping with his acceptance of the full gamut of ethno-religious fragments merging in his (social) *position*, would pose no objection were he charged with infusing arabesques within etymology-driven philosophical investigation. When recognition from the philosophy establishment mattered a great deal to him, Derrida paid dearly for his perverse practice of interrupting and deranging long arcs of meticulous textual elucidation with swatches of language play—often centering on the operative philosophical terms in question and unrepentant in their prolixity, their outrageousness, and their possible irrelevance. Readers of Derrida will know which of his asides into the unrestrained play of words I have in mind: the concatenations on *coup* in an odd place, at the foyer to "Plato's Pharmacy";[50] and on the signifier *glas* in the eponymous tract devoted equally to Georg Wilhelm Friedrich Hegel and Jean Genet.[51] Given the specifications that Derrida applied to his own intervention into philosophical discourse, these moments bubble up from the more "linear" (didactic) development of many of his inquiries. Yet the extract I would "post" in the context of *arabesques* by which both Pamuk as well as Shammas *up* the theoretical and political *ante* of their storytelling derives from Derrida's tribute, in "The Double Session," to Mallarmé. In view of what notorious weavers of narrative all three writers turn out to be (yes, there can be philosophical *narrative*), the passage is a patchwork of the materials appropriated into the fabric of Mallarmé's text. Derrida has already earmarked the systole/diastole in the background of such imagery: "The opposition between the closed and the open thus engenders certain beneficent figures in which both contradictory needs can be satisfied, successively or simultaneously: for example: the *fan*, the *book*, the *dancer*."[52] It takes nothing more formidable than the beat of a fan, in the idiom of deconstruction, to mark the syncopation between *ouverture* and closure engulfing conceptual systems. This is the sounding board to the patchwork of materials affording Mallarmé's poetry its distinctive *resonance*.

> The polysemy of "blanks" and "folds" both fans out and snaps shut, ceaselessly. But to read Mallarmé's *éventail* [fan] involves not only an inventory of its occurrences (there are hundreds, a very large but finite number if one sticks to the word itself, or an I finite number of diverse possibilities if one includes the many-faceted figure of wings, pages, sails, veils, plumes, scepters, etc., constituting and reconstituting itself in an endless breath of opening and/or closing; it involves not only the description of a phenomenological structure whose complexity is also a challenge; it is also to remark that the fan re-marks itself: no doubt it designates the empirical object ... but then, through a tropic twist (analogy, metaphor, metonymy), it turns to all the semic units that have been identified (wing, fold, plume, page, rustling, flight, dancer, veil, etc., each one finding itself folding and unfolding, opening/closing with the movement of a fan, etc.), it opens and closes each one, but it also inscribes above and beyond that movement the very movement and structure of the fan-as-text.[53]

Since weaving, stringing, diverting, patching, and seaming are the very processes endowing, in different ways, the works of Pamuk and Shammas with their expansive, dimension-shifting, and power-raising *aura*, what we have here, in Derrida's fabulation on fabrics, nothing less than *meta-arabesque*. For Derrida, masterful writing with the full resources of poetic figuration at its disposal became not merely an embellishment that might distinguish *some* philosophy; the synthesis of text astonishing both in its *impossibility* and its *inevitability* was inseparable from philosophical thinking. It *was* philosophy. History well remembers—situating his discourse in the chiasmus between logic and poetry did not go well with the discipline's true defenders.

It is precisely the degree to which Derrida, Pamuk, and Shammas succeeded in exploiting the writing process, as a nuclear accelerator for hitherto impossible articulation, as the generator for previously unthinkable poetico-conceptual hybrids, that their composition coincides within the shared framework of an *aesthetico-critical contract*. It is not terribly *material* whether the formats or formal occasions for their writing involved storytelling and narrative or philosophical disquisition and critique. What all three writers shared, most of all, were baseline poetic and figurative *specifications* for the textual weave and unscrolling of their works.

The novel's overarching narrative framework, the widest coherence that it establishes, comes to us by way of isomorphic parallelism. This megastructure links Anton's childhood and adolescence in Fassuta—the establishment there of significant others and resonant objects and animals that become the telling motifs in his creative vocabulary—to his later emergence as an émigré writer living both in Europe and Iowa. As in the structure of DNA, another isomorphic configuration, in some instances, these strands "hand off" to one another progressively; yet in others they communicate and duplicate one another, as when Michel Abyad who in youth emigrated to America and reemerges as the adult Michael, a researcher located in Beirut. What drives the novel forward within this overarching double helix are the constellations of significant others and "transitional objects"[54] (or auratic things), such as oil slick, the legendary subterranean boulder, the rooster, the "damascene wooden box inlaid with mother-of-pearl," that momentary coalesce and then disburse, only to reemerge in different permutations. The vividness with which the narrative can recollect these at best transitory things and situations bears testimony to the intense trauma of dislocation and to the poignancy of the once-coherent, if homespun, "holding environment"[55] of Fassuta. Shammas's virtuoso performance in *Arabesques* in large measure stems from his preternatural poetic gift in evoking and contextualizing these auratic things and moments, in letting them go once they have released, in context, their nuance and signification within the tapestry of a departed *Lebensweise*, and to summon them back when they yet enlarge upon the evolving transcript and establish further relatedness.

Any of a dozen of the major "transitional objects" of *Arabesques* creates its own narrative as it winds its way through the novelistic texture. The constellation of related objects that may make for vividness in one narrative situation may well "remix" the next time one or more of these telling objects appear. As merely one entrée into the "progressive jazz" that Shammas manages to perform in narrative, I am going to focus on the figure of Uncle Yusef's "red horse," which turns out not to be red at all.[56] The vicissitudes of this single carefully elaborated narrative "thing" will be emblematic of the weaving and the unweaving, the grafts and sutures, the half-references and partial meanings mobilized in the *ethos* as well as aesthetics of the *arabesque*:

> The new house was the lowest one on the southern slope of the village and only a single Ave Maria's distance from the new church ... I used to gaze at the end of the world through the south-facing window we called *bab es-sir*, literally "the door to the secret"—the name that is given in Arab architecture to the back exit for emergency use, a sort of low-silled window without a grille over it, through which in times of danger it is possible to escape.
>
> On the wide sill of that window I would sit and muse over the movements that break the stillness of the landscape as seen through the window. A flock of goats goes out to the pasture, like a shimmering black stain, getting farther and farther away, growing smaller and spreading out again and dwindling until it vanishes over the horizon, leaving a wake of dust. ... Furrow by hidden furrow he gets nearer to me. Despite the distance I interpret the motion of the farmer and his plow and his horse as sort of a self-assigned homework that I am doing for Uncle Yusef, who when he felt like it would take me down to the field and teach me the secrets of working the land, and the names of the parts that make up the wonderful plow. And even now as I sit at my desk in Jerusalem and write these things down

> I feel with one hand the chill of the windowsill and with the other hand I count the parts of the plow, as a prayer of sorts to the memory of Uncle Yusef, and as an act of reconciliation with the memory of his red horse.[57]

Particularly striking about this passage, and the qualities it lends to the novel as a whole, is the dynamic foyer, figured as a windowsill, it creates between past and present, between experience and interpretation. Evocative as it is of Proust's Combray and "Marcel's" voracious "reads" on the staircase, his visits to local steeples, and to Tante Léonie, it begins as an absorptive scene from Anton's childhood but is quickly re-transcribed into the grammar of the extended present. "Absent-minded window-gazing" over the agrarian panorama of Anton's youth enables the narrator to catalogue, from a wide-angle perch as it were, the elements of this once-viable *Lebenswelt*: peaceful farmers plowing furrow by furrow, women hoisting fodder gathered from tobacco shoots, the regional cash crop at the time. The elements of the recollected scene form a constellation of aspects all related to Uncle Yusef, who, by the end of this sequence, is remembered not merely as a guide into the mysteries of farming and plowing but also as Anton's chief model and inspiration as a storyteller. The unnamed farmer's horse is both an emanation of the three white horses whose slaughter shocks the outset of the novel and an echo of Uncle Yusef's red horse introduced at the end of the passage. The good uncle's flair as a raconteur even inflects his cataloguing the names and functions of the plow's parts. The amplitude of the panorama not only suggests the narrator's vibrant rootedness in his past; it opens a field for the full panoply of the novel's telling images, objects, and characters.

The perch from which the narrator first developed his powers of observation and discernment was the sill of a special window allowing for a hurried escape if need be (this becomes a self-fulfilling prophecy). It was situated on the house's southern exposure. The arch in the new house's western wall provides access to the underground cistern where the 10-year-old Anton not only dispatches a major adult task; in its dank obscurity, he gains an alluring foretaste of sex. The pitched cistern scene, in which Anton inhales Nawal's "fragrance, different from all the odors that had enfolded me," and, "cupping her two buttocks," experiences their "flinch with a shudder along the back that has arched itself into a taut bow,"[58] is eventually threaded into the novel's most detailed diasporic narrative, centering on Laylah Khoury-Surayyah Sa'id.[59] For it is this gorgeous woman, encountered in youth, who becomes the narrator's overarching lifetime vision of beauty, the enduring horizon of his longing. Via Surrayyah Sa'id, the allegory of olive oil as a talismanic material of sustenance, memory, and writing reaches its unfortunate apotheosis. Israeli Defense Forces soldiers spill two precious jars of it when they raid her modest home in Silwad. "And the twins stood on the side and, like a pair of mute turtledoves, watched the olive oil seep into the earth."[60]

If Hever is correct in discerning the development of a mystery story in the engine room of this novel, "Uncle Yusef" is the only possible solution to the conundrum, that is, at least if we pose the following as our key question: What is the rapport between the panoramic canvas of recollection and diaspora arising in Fassuta and the tangent bringing Anton first to Paris and then to Iowa City? The task attaching to the "good uncle" is precisely supplementing, to growing children, what cannot be supplied by paternity.

> His stories were plaited into one another, embracing and parting, twisting and twining in the infinite arabesque of memory. Many of his stories he told again and again, with seemingly minor changes, while other stories were granted only two or three tellings during the whole of his lifetime. All of them, however, glowed around him in a swirling current of illusion that linked beginnings to endings, the inner to the external, the reality to the tale.[61]

Storytelling, as here embodied in Uncle Yusef, is as much a vital social function as a literary endeavor. Over a lifetime in a more-or-less stable community, the storyteller distributes, allocates, the narratives in his repertoire. Part of his creative achievement consists in his *husbanding* the stories. There is both an economy and a strategy to the telling.[62] His literary achievement and what he knows of farming and cultivation are offshoots of the *same stock*. (Hence in the passage below, with a flick of the *kufiya*, Uncle Yusef turns from recalling an anecdote to pruning his plants.) With this craft he establishes and periodically renews the community's distinctive tales, those at the crux of its values and *Lebensweise*. Artfully "pleating" one episode into another, he enables one story, in Cognitive Science terms, to "trigger" or "activate" another. Continuing the physical task of the ambient *smandra* or storage space, the storyteller creates a virtual memory capsule in narrative that will not only hold the community in good stead through its customary departures; in dispossession and diaspora, the "arabesque of memory" will be everything of what the community retains of its past. In the figure of Uncle Yusef, narrative art merges into social persistence.

And this is so, even if a great deal of the fiction is sheer make-believe. Prepossessing as a model for the conduct of fiction as of human affairs, richly suggestive as his repertoire of tales and anecdotes may be, Uncle Yusef is fated to leave Anton in the lurch—by the very processes and dynamics intrinsic to writing. The beloved uncle's legacy counts only so much; but then, the receptive nephew has to take over—in his own time frame, in his own predicament, his own idiom, and through his own inventions.

> So here I am standing at the entrance of the cave, without a key, or rather with only a flawed key in hand. Uncle Yusef, in his great cunning, gives me a tiny key to use to find my way through the winding chambers of the arabesque, where I stand at the gate, ajar, behind which lies another story that will invent itself in a different way. Then, with his charming gesture of the right hand, he flips the left tail of his pure white *kufiya* behind his back and devotes all his attention to the pruning. But I know very well that he foresaw it all, down to the smallest detail. He knew that I was destined to retell his story one day. That's why he so graciously granted me the key that let me into all the corridors but kept the master key in his own hands.[63]

The contemporary author has been endowed with a precious key—to the past, to the narratives it has unearthed, and to the mission of storytelling. The key is by nature flawed. It will unlock the gateway to a subterranean treasure primarily existing in a community's superstition. It will release the treasure but only partially. On our first encounter with Uncle Yusef, he warned that "it is better for a story not to be told, for once it is, it is like a gate left ajar."[64] Now the dutiful but observant nephew, in claiming his legacy, addresses an expansive panorama of open gates, open-ended narratives awaiting their development under *his* stewardship. Such is the task of the storyteller under the communal ethos of storytelling; under the aura of the arabesque.

The Blind Master: Deconstruction into Literature

Pamuk is no less a practitioner and trader in the arabesque than Shammas. Both the historical trajectory pursued by miniature painting and its geographical catchment area may be grander than the displacements and self-recastings transpiring within a small and contested zone of the western Mediterranean. (The world of *Arabesques* is more constricted even with the tangents in Paris and Iowa City thrown in.) And both Pamuk and Shammas make their tributes to Proust and Kafka, very different enablers of their fictive innovations, explicit. In particular, there is a palpable Proustian overtone, reminiscent of the pages-long outcry when the narrator of the *Recherche* recounts the crazy-making experience of being—outside the gay universe—alternately embraced and castigated,[65] to the arabesques in *My Name Is Red*. These are extraordinary passages, in which the key motifs: murder in the atelier, the diaspora and demise of miniature painting, the fusion of slavish devotion and quasi-grandiose mastery in true artistry—to the point of self-inflicted blindness—are *enlarged* to the points both of reverie and of stunning theoretical crystallization.

A remarkable feature of *My Name Is Red* is how much of the decisive dialogue is placed in the hands of the victims, suspects, and perpetrator of its murder mystery. With the exception of the great lines regarding love, marriage, and domesticity accorded to Shekure, the notable utterances shy away from the protagonists and their immediate predicament. Master Osman and Enishte Effendi, masters of competing ateliers of miniaturism, run away with the show when the spotlight is trained upon them—even if, as in the latter case, they are a few minutes shy of being murdered.

> In the end, our methods will die out, our colors will fade. No one will care about our books and our paintings, and those who express interest will ask with a sneer, with no understanding whatsoever, why there's no perspective—or else they won't be able to find the manuscripts at all. Indifference, time, and disaster will destroy our art. … Women lighting their stoves, thieves, indifferent servants and children will thoughtlessly tear out the pages and pictures. They'll blacken people's eyes, wipe their runny noses on the pages, doodle in the margins with black ink. And religious censors will blacken out whatever is left. … Not only our own art, but every single work made in this world over the years will vanish in fires, be

destroyed by worms or be lost in neglect. ... The lute players that embellish Hafiz's enigmatic poems; the wall ornamentations that have ruined the eyes of thousands, nay tens of thousands of miniaturist apprentices; the small plaques hung above doors and on walls; the couplets secretly written between the embedded borders of illustrations; the humble signatures hidden at the bases of walls, in corners, in façade embellishments, under the soles of feet, beneath shrubbery and between rocks; the flower-covered quilts covering lovers ... The small charming blades of grass reproduced in thousands of pictures.[66]

Enishte Effendi, only a few moments more of this world, details the end of an art form upon which has been lavished great care and mastery, and the treasures of this great collective enterprise that will too pass away. This in the form of the *small* details, the accouterments to everyday life, the *petits objets*, in whose *minor* singularity resides the evanescence of communal life. There is an extraordinary *humility* involved in a decisive practitioner's disavowal of the long-term endurance of the art form that he has mastered, his attestation of the immanent dissolution of an aesthetic contract prevailing for centuries over a vast sociocultural domain and that guided the efforts of thousands.

Within the overall development of this evolving elucidation, it serves well to hazard an impact report on the above interjected window of text, which, by the way, was far from being cited in full. Pamuk's panoramic afterimage of an art form begins in desolation and degradation at the inevitable historical decline of miniature painting, and it ends in an agglomerative summation of the details epitomizing the entire school's originality and distinction. If the Proustian echo to this passage I have pointed out seems in any way excessive, it should be noted that the doom and gloom facing miniature painting with which the passage sets out bears striking tonal assonance with the unremitting catalogue of social insults to the "race of the *hommes-femmes*." I would submit that the cascading phantasmagoria of details distinctive to miniature painting as the passage strings itself along comprises the compensation, in the currency of "poetic prose," for the two inevitable losses toward which the narrative inexorably leads at this point: the conflated losses of Enishte Effendi as an unusually receptive and flexible "center" in the world of Ottoman miniature painting, and the *overall* decline and marginalization of miniature painting as a prevailing *medium*.

Within this environment of demise upon demise, or loss squared, the performance in fictive prose to which the narrative rises, "holding" a bravura "note" in masterful textual synthesis almost beyond comprehension, stands in general for what scholarship, art and cultural history, trenchant critique, and curating collections and exhibitions hold in store in the face of inevitable cultural decline and obliteration. *Writing brilliantly* is the answer, but it is also the by-product—of foreclosures in the aesthetic contract, of precipitous decline in the cognitive and critical faculties at moments of transformation. Hence, Pamuk makes certain that the forthcoming degradations to which miniature painting will be submitted are spelled out in the most concrete, corporeal terms: vermin and insects will devour the illuminated treasures; what snot and children's doodles doesn't obliterate from the pages, religious censorship will. The only redemption to this blanket cultural degeneration is the retrospective words themselves, the words detailing the details, blanketing them over the page. And in the unscrolling plenitude of the details that made miniature painting what it was, Pamuk extracts the full possible effect from juxtapositions, from abrupt reversals in mood, tone, and symbolism. The sheep presented by the "deceitful" sheepdog to the she-wolf, his consort, immediately precedes the lute players and the bird, flower, and leaf-border illuminations embellishing Hafiz's "enigmatic" poems. "Small plaques hung above doors and on walls," and even more miniscule touches, "couplets secretly written between the embedded borders of illustrations" and "humble signatures hidden at the bases of walls, in corners, in façade embellishments, under the soles of feet" are the setup to the most disquieting, because demonic, of the details: "severed infidel heads patiently awaiting Our Sultan's late grandfather"; also, "devils, with and without horns, with and without tails." And yet Pamuk cannily incorporates dodoes—they were still extant during the timeframe of the novel—into the concluding aviary catalogue with which he counteracts the details' devolution into the demonic.

In his arabesques of the motifs, styles, historical evolution, and geographical diffusion of the miniature—and the passage glossed immediately above hardly stands alone[67]—Pamuk places "poetic prose"[68] and the rhythmic impact of an unfettered accumulation of examples and variations at the service of the *visual*. It is only through visual inspiration and debriefing that the novel manages to complete its unique mission: to set a tale of love surmounting multiple sociocultural obstacles against the backdrop of aesthetic transformation and seismic historical shift.

Pamuk does not neglect to remind us that within the community of Islam, the sense of vision is charged with divine commandment and stricture. Indeed, along the vast spectrum of the three major Abrahamic religions, visual politics may reach its culmination in the culture of Islam. "Allah created the earthly realm so that, above all, it might be seen,"[69] atelier illustrator "Olive" reminds us as he discourses. (He emerges, over the novel, as "prime suspect" for the double murder.)

> Through our colors, paints, art, and love, we remember that Allah had commanded us, "to See"! To know is to remember that you've seen. To see is to know without remembering. Thus, painting is remembering the blackness. The great masters, who shared a love of painting and perceived that color and sight arose from darkness, longed to return to Allah's blackness by means of color. Artists without memory neither remember Allah nor his blackness. The great masters, in their work, seek that profound void within color and outside time. Let me explain to you what it means to remember this darkness, which was revealed in Herat by the great masters of old.[70]

This early passage serves as a focal point for the novel's motifs and plot twists. Simply as a phenomenon, vision is a supercharged domain in Islam. Its dialectical opposition to blindness is a fundament of spiritual as well as cognitive life, to which we will return. In view of this conflict at the deep roots of Muslim culture, painting is as much imbricated in the persistence of memory as in the phenomenon of perception. "To paint is to remember," muses Black as he surveys the Sultan's treasures.[71] And cultural persistence, Islam's most decisive "pillar" of all, is contingent on the stores of cultural memory that painting supplies. It is the *visual* manifold that furnishes the retroactive trail toward blackness—the Judeo-Christian-Muslim *origin* of the universe (all three components of Abrahamic religion subscribe to this myth). Indeed, the *revelation* of the substrate of blackness to color at Herat strongly echoes the extended revelation of the verses of the Quran to Mohammed—exactly one millennium before the timeframe of our novel.

"Black," then, as the name for the novel's male protagonist, has more to it than a casual workshop nickname. His claim on Shekure is primordial. In more senses than one, he is the "return of the repressed" in the novel. He stakes an even prior claim on Shekure's love and beauty[72]—she *crowns* the order of the visual—than was met by her legitimate marriage to her warrior husband. Black restores order and sanity to the atelier he left twelve years before, which has been riven and deranged by sectarian conflict and creative jealousy. His heroic missions fulfilled, he subsides into the maimed, slightly depressive civilian that was always his disposition.

The overarching conflict into which Pamuk inscribes the novel is even more primal than imperial or sectarian struggles or the obstacles faced by thwarted love. No less than the cosmic alternation between color and darkness inscribed into the Abrahamic religions' creation scene, it is both dialectical, as all conflicts are, and meta-dialectical, as in the Eastern dynamic of yin-yang (hence, perhaps, Pamuk's careful attention to the inroads of Chinese art and aesthetics into Near and Middle Eastern miniature painting).[73] Under the aura of yin-yang relations, as the polar opposites reach their fullest intensity, there is a flip, a digital switch at the extremes, as it were, *into* one another. In the theoretical disquisition on blindness and insight that the novel, in addition to its various stories of love and conflict and histories of art, delivers, blindness is not the negation or annihilation of vision but its ultimate intensification. This is a crucial proviso of the novel's "platform." Pamuk expends precious attention and language on the master minaturist's circular dance with blindness: the greater the virtuosity in the artist, the stronger the allure of this extreme state (and anti-state) of vision; the closer that blindness approaches, whether through ocular over-expenditure or self-blinding, the more the meta-visual faculty—painterly virtuosity in blindness—kicks into action. The novel's detailed investigation into vision hails not only from the same neighborhood, in Derrida's speculations on art, as his *Memoirs of the Blind*;[74] it also accesses, as suggested above, Paul de Man's densely woven allegories of reading and cultural critique in his *Blindness and Insight*.[75] As the color red continues the disquisition cited at the head of this essay:

> Once, in a Persian city, as I was being applied by the brush of an apprentice to the embroidery on the saddle cloth of a horse that a blind miniaturist had drawn by heart, I overheard two blind masters having an argument:
> "Because we've spent our entire lives ardently and faithfully working as painters, naturally we, who have now gone blind, know red and remember what kind of

color and what kind of feeling it is," said the one who'd made the horse drawing from memory. "But what if we'd been born blind? ...

"An excellent issue," the other said. "But do not forget that colors are known, not felt."

"My dear master, explain red to somebody who has never known red."

"If we touched it with the tip of a finger, it would feel like something between iron and copper. If we took it into our palm, it would burn. If we tasted it, it would be full-bodied, like salted meat. If we took it between our lips, it would fill our mouths. If we smelled it, it would have the scent of a horse. If it were a flower, it would smell like a daisy, and not a red rose."[76]

The paradoxical figure of the blind master is as adept in painting similes and metaphors as he is in rendering miniscule details on the page. In his parlance, the color "red" takes on the formidable question of aesthetic knowledge: a knowledge requisite for performative virtuosity, yet neither grounded in empirical savvy nor in intuitive detachment from the world. It is this aesthetic knowledge that could allow red to be accessed figuratively, as touch, taste, and smell—in the absence of sight. Consummation, in the vast atelier of Near and Middle Eastern miniature painting, is an informed virtuosity that continues when the stimulations emanating from sight, consumption, and lust have died down. The end or telos of art, at least under the Muslim ethos of vision, is something more muted and complex than transcendence.

Master Osman, united one last time with the treasures of manuscript illumination and a panoply of Near and Middle Eastern arts and crafts, under the pretext of identifying a rogue artist by tracking down a few stray strokes, also determines to leave his visual sensorium behind. The description of his self-blinding is not only a vignette of almost inconceivable self-mutilation but also a narrative of a certain aesthetic and motivational *letting go*. It is a letting go of the riotous world of the drive, aesthetic perfectionism, professional competition, and material rapacity in the name of an *informed blindness*, the knowledge that will serve for all occasions. Informed blindness, detachment from the stimuli and experiences out of which memory has been both distilled and fabricated, also irradiates *Arabesques*—in its own locally distinctive fashion. Master Osman's act speaks for itself.

> Lowering the magnifying lens, as if beholding a melancholy depiction of love with a matching sense of melancholy, I looked at the needle for a long time. I tried to imagine how Bihzad could have done it. I'd heard that one doesn't go blind immediately; the velvety darkness descends slowly, sometimes after days, sometimes after months, as with old men who go blind naturally. ...
>
> "How had Master Bihzad done it?" I asked myself one more time.
>
> Never once taking my eyes off the mirror, with the practiced movements of a woman applying kohl to her eyelids, my hand found the needle on its own. Without hesitation, as if making a hole at the end of an ostrich egg to be embellished, I bravely, calmly, and firmly pressed the needle into the pupil of my right eye. My innards sank, not because I felt what I was doing, but because I knew what I was

doing. I pushed the needle into my eye to the depth of a quarter the length of a finger, then removed it. ...

For a long while I didn't move. I stared at the world—at everything.

As I surmised, the colors of the world did not darken, but seemed to bleed ever so gently into each other. I could still more or less see.[77]

It is only in a domain of muted colors, cloudy sight, unclear influences, obscure origins, and nuanced positions that there can be *allowance* for the give, leeway, tolerance, and forgiveness engendering coexistence and ongoing, persistent multi-communal life. Both *Arabesques* and *My Name Is Red* are replete with the murky rooms, halftones, blurry solutions, and unanswered questions permitting *gradations* of faith, belief, tradition, influence, and propriety to continue unmolested. The palettes of both novels are filled with complex mixtures of tone, coloration, and ethnic mix. In the rich tapestry of late-sixteenth-century Istanbul, most of the gossip and bad news is conveyed by Esther, the Jewish clothes hawker. Not only does Laylah Khoury convert from Christianity to Islam in *Arabesques*, never fully resolving her dual identity, but Major Nimr is a Jewish neighbor from the Galilee villages and purported owner of the tobacco field. His familiarity with his non-Jewish neighbors persists even when he joins the Israeli military.

Complexity reigns in the literature of cultural articulation, dissemination, transformation, and nuance. The arabesque becomes the alchemy by which sociohistorical complexity morphs into narrative intricacy, synthesis, and interrelatedness—as literature strives toward a broader horizon of cultural possibility.

Notes

1 Orhan Pamuk, *My Name Is Red*, trans. Erdag M. Goknar (New York: Vintage Books, 2001), 185–6.
2 Anton Shammas, *Arabesques: A Novel*, trans. Vivian Eden (Berkeley: University of California Press, 2001), 18.
3 Jacques Derrida, "Plato's Pharmacy," in *Dissemination*, trans. Barbara Johnson (Chicago: University of Chicago Press, 1981), 61–171.
4 Jacques Derrida, "The Double Session," in *Dissemination*, 173–286.
5 Douglas R. Hofstadter, *Gödel, Escher, Bach: An Eternal Golden Braid* (New York: Vintage, 1979).
6 Anthony Wilden, *System and Structure* (London: Tavistock, 1972).
7 James Gleick, *Chaos: Making a New Science* (New York: Viking, 1987).
8 See, e.g., Jacques Derrida, "Taking a Stand for Algeria," in *Acts of Religion*, ed. Gil Anidjar (London: Routledge, 2001), 299–308.
9 See Henry Sussman, "The Fourth Abrahamic Religion?" in *The Task of the Critic* (New York: Fordham UP, 2005), 176–241.
10 Jacques Derrida and Maurizio Ferraris, *A Taste for the Secret*, trans. Giacomo Donis (Cambridge: Polity Press, 2001), 27–8.
11 Julio Cortázar, *Hopscotch*, trans. Gregory Rabassa (New York: Pantheon, 1966).

12 Jacques Derrida, *Of Grammatology* (Baltimore: Johns Hopkins UP, 1976), 266.
13 Ibid., 247.
14 Ibid., 249.
15 In seeking a rubric for the heightened individuation, fraught moral sensibility, and increased social investment in media coterminous with printing, guilds, Protestant theology, and aggravated capital accumulation, I have deployed this term ("broader Modernity")—also, in Foucauldian fashion, as a premise for new linguistic strategies. See Henry Sussman, *The Aesthetic Contract* (Stanford: Stanford UP, 1997), 2-4, 34-9, 79-100.
16 Umberto Eco, *The Name of the Rose*, trans. William Weaver (New York: Harcourt Brace Jovanovich, 1983).
17 Pamuk, *My Name*, 72.
18 Sussman, *The Aesthetic Contract*, 166-7.
19 Douglas Hofstadter, *I Am a Strange Loop* (New York: Basic Books, 2007), 92-5, 180, 188.
20 If literature comprises an enriched, amplified *response* to the politics of aggression and recrimination, this could only be in the sense in which Derrida, in his groundbreaking "Faith and Knowledge," under the purview of *religio*, elaborates the bearing of *responsibility*. See Jacques Derrida, "Faith and Knowledge," in *Acts of Religion*, 72-7.
21 Shammas, *Arabesques*, 228.
22 Ibid., 36.
23 Hannan Hever, *Producing the Modern Hebrew Canon: Nation Building and Minority Discourse* (New York: New York University Press, 2002), 176.
24 Ibid.
25 Ibid., 178.
26 Ibid.
27 Ibid., 183.
28 Ibid., 186.
29 Derrida, *Of Grammatology*, 65-6, 69, 265, 308.
30 Within Fernand Braudel and the *Annales* School's decisive intervention into conventional historiography, a "history from the ground up," rooted in material conditions, the peasantry is the decisive, previously invisible "secret sharer," exerting an indispensable influence. Peasants indeed become evident, even indelible, on the photographic proof-sheet when the historical viewfinder takes off from human material culture and the practices of trade, commerce, and technology ensuing from the basic rapport to what, from the *Umwelt*, has been extracted, consumed, and sold. For the figure of the peasant and her transformations and impact on early Modernity, see Fernand Braudel, *Capitalism and Civilization: 15th to 18th Century*, trans. Siân Reynolds (Berkeley: University of California Press, 1992), I, 49, 283; II, 255, 267-9; III, 55-8, 254-5, 265-7, 269.
31 Derrida, *Of Grammatology*, 251, 268.
32 See Walter Benjamin, *The Arcades Project*, trans. Howard Eiland and Kevin McLaughlin (Cambridge: Harvard UP, 1999), 10, 14, 17, 21-2, 26, 64, 116, 429.
33 Zola's *The Ladies' Paradise* may well be the juncture, in his vast multi-novel Rougon/Macquart cycle, where narrative most gives way to what might be called the commercial phantasmagoria of the pre-First World War Golden Age. See Émile Zola,

The Ladies' Paradise, trans Brian Nelson (Oxford: Oxford UP, 1995), 87–8, 108–9, 117, 234–6, 249–50, 390–1, 397–9.
34   Shammas, *Arabesques*, 7, 47.
35   Ibid., 7.
36   Ibid., 15.
37   Ibid., 41.
38   Ibid., 47–56.
39   Ibid., 192.
40   Note, e.g., the fusion of religious devoutness and out-and-out superstition in the character Vitoria, mystery-solving protagonist of Sadoveanu's *The Hatchet*. Against many odds, she solves her husband's murder at the hands of two avaricious fellow shepherds. Through Vitoria's unerring intuition, Sadoveanu transports the uncanny acuity of an Auguste Dupin out into the eastern Carpathians. See Mihail Sadoveanu, *The Hatchet and The Life of Stephan the Great*, trans. Eugenia Farca, East European Monographs (New York: Columbia UP, 1991).
41   Pamuk, *My Name*, 170–5.
42   Ibid., 297–306.
43   This exhibition of collectibles is described, in *Le Peau de chagrin*, as a diorama of historically auratic objects. Indeed, Valentin, the narrator, attributes encyclopedic inclusiveness to its "coverage." See Honoré de Balzac, *The Wild Ass' Skin*, trans. Herbert J. Hunt (New York: Penguin, 1977), 34–42. Apropos of this pivotal passage in the nineteenth-century Euro-imaginary, see *My Name*, 299, "Black" reporting:

> I saw swords, elephant tusks, caftans, silver candlesticks, and satin banners. I saw mother-of-pearl inlaid boxes, iron trunks, Chinese vases, belts, long-necked lutes, armor, silk cushions, model globes, boots, furs, rhinoceros horns, ornamented ostrich eggs, rifles, arrows, maces, and cabinets. ... A strange light, the likes of which I'd never seen, shone on the cloth, the boxes, the caftans of sultans, swords, the huge pink candles, the wound turbans, pillows embroidered with pearls, gold filigree saddles, diamond-handled scimitars, ruby-handled maces, quilted turbans, turban plumes, curious clocks, ewers, and daggers, ivory statues of horses and elephants, narghiles with diamond-studded tops, mother-or-pearl chests of drawers, horse aigrettes, strands of large prayer-beads, and helmets adorned with rubies and turquoise.

This opulence may be a far cry from the *smandra* and bookcase of Shammas's Fassuta, but it is not unrelated.
44   Shammas, *Arabesques*, 17–18.
45   Ibid., 69.
46   Ibid., 68.
47   Pamuk, *My Name*, 186.
48   See Benjamin's dialectical allegory of the collector in relation to the "allegorist," above all in Convolute H of *The Arcades Project*. Benjamin, *The Arcades Project*, 204–7, 211.
49   See Pamuk, *My Name*, 159–60. Curiously, the role played by collecting within the overall covetousness of Ottoman society toward masterfully crafted artworks and other treasures is filled in by chief perpetrator, "Olive."
50   Derrida, "Plato's Pharmacy," in *Dissemination*, 169–70.
51   Jacques Derrida, *Glas*, trans John P. Leavy Jr. and Richard Rand (Lincoln: University of Nebraska Press, 1990), 142, 144–50, 154–62, 234–7.

52 Derrida, *Dissemination*, 247.
53 Ibid., 251.
54 This is D. W. Winnicott's term, and it is a crucial element in his practice of psychoanalytical healing, particularly with children. See D. W. Winnicott, *Playing and Reality* (London: Routledge, 1971), 1–19, 47–54, 120–9.
55 Another term of Winnicott's, also elaborated in *Playing and Reality*. It denotes both the space of empathic "disillusionment" programmed for her growing infant by the "good enough mother" and the compass for play and open-ended improvisation that Winnicott would wish to infuse into the practice of psychoanalytic healing.
56 Shammas, *Arabesques*, 64.
57 Ibid., 63–4.
58 Ibid., 54–5.
59 Ibid., 248.
60 Ibid., 33.
61 Ibid., 226.
62 Much of what Walter Benjamin is getting at in his "The Storyteller," a major extrapolation of narrative technique in the shorter forms centering on Nicolai Leskov, inheres to Uncle Yusef. See Walter Benjamin, "The Storyteller: Observations on the Work of Nicolai Leskov," in *Selected Writings* (Cambridge: Harvard UP, 2003), III, 143–66.
63 Shammas, *Arabesques*, 227.
64 Ibid., 46.
65 For the extended ejaculation on the human inconstancy to which gays and lesbians are routinely subjected (in my English translation, a three-page plus extended sentence), in all likelihood the longest such utterance in the *Recherche*, see Marcel Proust, *Sodom and Gomorrah*, trans. John Sturrock (New York: Viking, 2004), 16–19.
66 Pamuk, *My Name*, 171–2.
67 Other extended art historical phantasmagorias concerning miniature painting's masters, conventions, and geographical extent are to be found at 48–50, 62–5, 119, 301–5, 313–17, and 331–2.
68 This may well be a term that Benjamin "pirates" from Baudelaire's "The Painter of Modern Life," in tribute to the latter's editor, Arsène Houssaye, as a soubriquet for the poetic compression and power Benjamin now considers requisite to critical elucidation. See Walter Benjamin, "On Some Motifs in Baudelaire," in *Selected Writings*, IV, 320.
69 Pamuk, *My Name*, 79.
70 Ibid., 76.
71 Ibid., 303.
72 This stages the even more fraught and attenuated tale of yearning and romantic waiting on the part of a male narrator—this in Orhan Pamuk's *The Museum of Innocence: A Novel*, trans. Maureen Freely (New York: Viking, 2009).
73 Pamuk, *My Name*, 309–11, 315, 322.
74 See Jacques Derrida, *Memoirs of the Blind: The Self-Portrait and Other Ruins*, trans. Pascale-Anne Brault and Michael Naas (Chicago: University of Chicago Press, 1993). Ascertaining Pamuk's possible exposure to Derrida's writings or any involvement in deconstruction is of far less significance than noting the conflation between blindness, portraiture (albeit concentrated on the genre of self-portraiture), and memory emerging in this Derridean venture into the history of art. This constellation

of interests emerges within the canvas of *My Name Is Red* in homologous form. It crystallizes in such a passage as the following:

> I hesitate between two paradoxes, two great "logics" of the invisible at the origin of drawing. Two thoughts of or about drawing thus take shape, and by correlation, two "blindnesses."
>
> —Give them names, for memory's sake.
>
> I shall name them the *transcendental* and the *sacrificial*. The first would be invisible condition of the possibility of drawing, draw*ing* itself, the drawing of drawing. It would never be thematic. It could not be posited or taken as the representable *object* of a drawing. The second, then, the sacrificial event, that which comes to or meets the eyes, the narrative, spectacle, or representation of the blind, would, in becoming the *theme* of the first, reflect, so to speak, this impossibility. It would represent this unrepresentable. Between the two, in their fold, the one repeating the other without being reduced to it, the *event* can give rise to the speech of narrative, to myth, prophecy or messianism, to the family romance or to the scene of everyday life, this providing drawing with its thematic objects or spectacles, its figures and heroes, its *pictures* or *depictions of the blind*. (Derrida, *Memoirs*, 41)

In Pamuk's parallel treatment of portraiture, although in a novelistic arena; spectacles, such as the riches overflowing in the Royal Treasury; events, such as the novel's dual murders or the hurried effort, in the Enishte Effendi atelier, to complete the illuminated Book of Death secretly commissioned by the Sultan; and domestic romance all come to figure in an environment in which blindness, and its depiction, serve both as the annihilation and consummation of sight.

75 See, in particular, Paul de Man, *Blindness and Insight*, intro. Wlad Godzich (Minneapolis: University of Minnesota Press, 1983), xix, xxi, 109–12, 139–41.
76 Pamuk, *My Name*, 187–8.
77 Shammas, *Arabesques*, 324–5.

Part IV

Philosophy versus World Literature

13

Existentialism as World Literature: De Beauvoir, Heidegger, and Tolstoy

Robert Doran

This volume on "philosophy as world literature" asks us to reconsider the relation between philosophy and literature even as it invites us to broaden the concept of literature. Certainly, the vexed and convoluted relation between "literature" (understood as imaginative fiction)[1] and "philosophy" (Continental or Anglo-Analytic) is challenging enough on its own. Considering it alongside the equally vexed and convoluted concept of "world literature" (*Weltliteratur*) is perhaps too much to ask for a modest essay, but the reader will no doubt gain a greater understanding of the term by reading all the essays in this volume.

If these twin tasks appear impossibly daunting, they are rendered somewhat wieldier by the subject of existentialism, an intellectual movement that traverses, even subverts, the boundary between philosophy and literature. Existentialist-themed novels and plays are generally more explicitly philosophical than their non-existentialist brethren, and existentialist philosophy tends to be more literary in nature, or at least more open to literary modes of expression, than other contemporaneous types. Whether this is more a function of the proclivities of individual writers or of existentialist thought itself is perhaps impossible to know, but the convergence between philosophy and literature in existentialism has been, from the first, one of its essential features. The Danish writer Søren Kierkegaard (1813–1855), widely credited as the "father" of existentialism, wrote unclassifiable works that hover between philosophy, autobiography, Biblical exegesis, and literature.

With respect to the concept of "world literature," existentialism is an intellectual movement that, while mostly European in sensibility, also reverberated globally, as evidenced by the Nobel Prize in Literature awarded to two of the most important figures in existentialist thought: Albert Camus (1957, accepted) and Jean-Paul Sartre (1964, refused). Its main philosophical progenitors—Kierkegaard, Friedrich Nietzsche, Karl Jaspers, Martin Heidegger, Sartre, Simone de Beauvoir, José Ortega y Gasset—cover a wide range of styles, languages, and cultural contexts. This is no less true of the literary engagements with existentialist ideas, from Fyodor Dostoevsky and Leo Tolstoy in Russia, and Rainer Maria Rilke and Franz Kafka in Germany, in the nineteenth century, to Sartre, Camus, and de Beauvoir in France, and the "black existentialists," Ralph Ellison and Richard Wright, in the United States, in the twentieth.

It would be near impossible in a short essay to undertake a survey of existentialist works, and such an effort would most probably not be very illuminating. Instead, I propose to take up some key issues that might elucidate the idea of "philosophy as world literature" from the perspective of existentialist writing. In particular, I shall focus on the philosophy-literature relation: first, as explored by the French novelist and philosopher Simone de Beauvoir, and second, as a sort of "case study" of how a German philosopher (Martin Heidegger) and a Russian fiction writer (Leo Tolstoy) treat the theme of death in an existentialist manner.

Philosophy versus Literature I: Simone de Beauvoir and the "Metaphysical Novel"

The line demarcating literature from philosophy has until fairly recently not been very clear. Literature has often been about ideas, and many canonical philosophical works have been written in literary form. Plato's philosophical dialogues and Lucretius' didactic poem *De rerum natura* (*On the Nature of Things*) are early examples of literary philosophy (or philosophical literature). When Plato (or Socrates) talked about the ancient "quarrel between philosophy and poetry"[2] and banishing (mimetic) poets from the ideal city,[3] he was referring to the tendency of his fellow Greeks to put too much stock in the Homeric myths as opposed to relying on their own reasoning capacity. Philosophy thus originated as a demythologizing exercise. If Plato cultivated mythical form (*mythos*, narrative) and the drama of the dialogue, it was to beat the competition at its own game.

Since the Renaissance, literature too has embraced a quasi-philosophical project of demystification, casting off the aura of myth and legend, as ingeniously demonstrated by Miguel de Cervantes's *Don Quixote*, the first modern novel. Prior to the nineteenth century, educated readers were not yet segregated into academic disciplines, and they often saw philosophy and imaginative literature as continuous (just as they saw "history" as a branch of rhetoric rather than the empirical or quasi-scientific endeavor it is seen as today). The inaugural work of modern philosophy, René Descartes's *Meditationes de prima philosophia* (*Meditations on First Philosophy*) was written with literary flair, and Enlightenment writers such as Voltaire, in his *contes philosophiques* (philosophical tales) *Zadig* and *Candide*, and Denis Diderot, in his satirical *Jacques le fataliste et son maître* (*Jacques the Fatalist and his Master*), used fiction to engage with philosophical themes and with philosophy itself. Georg Wilhelm Friedrich Hegel's *Phänomenologie des Geistes* (*Phenomenology of Spirit*) has been characterized as a *Bildungsroman*. It is only relatively recently, with the rise of Anglo-Analytic philosophy, that the gulf between philosophy and literature has significantly widened. Casting its lot with the physical sciences and with logic, analytic thought has, with the exception of ethics, generally devalued narrative and fiction as tools of thought—even as it embraces the "example," a rhetorical device.[4]

Existentialism stands in stark contrast to this development. It is notable that Sartre and de Beauvoir wrote philosophical and literary works in equal measure and with equal success. Sartre's first novel *La nausée* (*Nausea*, 1938) introduced themes that subsequently received a more traditional philosophical cast in his magisterial *L'Être et le néant* (*Being and Nothingness*, 1943). In turn, his roughly contemporaneous plays *Les mouches* (*The Flies*, 1943) and *Huit clos* (*No Exit*, 1944) developed ideas advanced in *Being and Nothingness* but also went beyond it. It would thus be wrong to describe Sartre's literary works as a mere "illustration" of his philosophy. As Gary Cox puts it in *Sartre and Fiction*:

> The abiding themes of Sartre's philosophical works are also the abiding themes of his fiction: self-identity, mortality, the existence of others, freedom, responsibility, bad faith and authenticity. Sartre's philosophy can be understood to some extent without reading his fiction, just as his fiction can be enjoyed without any knowledge of his philosophy, but to really appreciate the subtlety, profundity and humanity of Sartre's fiercely honest existential assessment of the human condition the two must be taken together.[5]

There is a kind of symbiosis between Sartre's philosophical texts and his literary writings, a symbiosis that can characterize existentialism as a whole—which is why it cannot be fully comprehended as fundamentally or even primarily a philosophical project. In his well-regarded reader, *Existentialism from Dostoevsky to Sartre* (1956), Walter Kaufmann includes both philosophical and literary texts in an effort to capture both the extent and the richness of existentialist thought.

To better understand how existentialism necessitates a reconsideration of the relation between philosophy and literature, I propose to examine de Beauvoir's brief but thought-provoking essay "Littérature et métaphysique" ("Literature and Metaphysics"), published in 1946 (originally delivered as a lecture entitled "The Novel and Metaphysics," in 1945). De Beauvoir is certainly not the first to discuss the idea of the philosophical novel; however, she is among the first to treat it as a *problem* rather than as mere polemic or simple object of analysis. Her attitude is of course a function of her dual identity as a novelist and philosopher; but she is also responding obliquely to some of the reactions generated by her earlier work. While Maurice Blanchot (who himself straddles the line between philosophy and literature) praises her first novel *L'invitée* (*She Came to Stay*), of 1943, he disparages her second, *Le Sang des autres* (*Blood of Others*), of 1945, as a *"roman à these"* (thesis novel).[6] That de Beauvoir felt the sting of such criticism is clear in "Literature and Metaphysics" but also in her 1954 novel *Les Mandarins* (*The Mandarins*), on which she comments, "In my estimation *Mandarins* is not a thesis novel. I describe certain manners of living the postwar period without proposing any solution to the problems that worry my protagonists."[7] "Literature and Metaphysics" can thus be regarded as an effort to more explicitly account for her practice as a novelist as well as a recognition that a course correction was in order, one that resulted in *The Mandarins*.

Despite the generality of the title, the main topic of "Literature and Metaphysics" is the philosophical novel, which de Beauvoir simultaneously judges and defends. At stake is the very concept or viability of philosophical literature. De Beauvoir begins by acknowledging that critics of the philosophical novel have a valid point in decrying this literature, if it is nothing more than a mere dramatization of philosophical concepts:

> The adversaries of philosophical literature argue, rightly, that the signification of a novel or a play, or a poem for that matter, cannot be translated into abstract concepts. Otherwise, why construct a fictional apparatus around ideas that one could express more economically and clearly in more direct language? The novel is justified only if it is a mode of communication irreducible to any other.[8]

That is to say, there is a right and a wrong way of writing a philosophical novel; its critics have merely identified the wrong way. It shall be her task, then, to describe the right way, but in so doing she will have to redefine what she means by "philosophy" and "metaphysics," thus simultaneously weakening and strengthening her argument.

In the above-quoted passage, de Beauvoir lays out her main contention: that the meaning of literary work cannot be *adequately* expressed in philosophical propositions (philosophical propositions can still be abstracted from a literary work, but these would merely be an impoverished reflection of the work, however compelling they are in themselves); or conversely that the mere translation of philosophical ideas into literary form—the thesis novel—results in a novel in name only. A true philosophical novel, it would seem, expresses something *other than* philosophy or perhaps *another conception of* philosophy. At the same time, however, this irreducible excess expressible only in literary discourse is philosophy *nonetheless*, for how else to justify the nomenclature of the "philosophical" or "metaphysical" novel?

De Beauvoir might also be said in the passage above to be criticizing a particular starting point, namely, going *from* philosophy *to* literature. If philosophy is a kind of plenitude, then it does not need literature; it expresses its ideas amply and fully. Why, then, should a philosopher write a novel? "One renounces the philosophical novel if one defines philosophy as a fully constituted, self-sufficient system."[9] If a philosopher does choose to express her- or himself in literary form, this choice might be said to indicate a lack in philosophical discourse itself, one that literature—and perhaps only literature—can address.

Clearly, de Beauvoir believes that something philosophical is to be gained by taking literature, or at least a *literary attitude*, as a point of departure: "In the real world, the meaning of an object is not a concept graspable by pure understanding. Its meaning is the object as it is disclosed to us in the overall relation we sustain with it, and which is action, emotion, and feeling."[10] Thus, literature (the novel) might in fact offer a *superior* insight into the meaning of objects in the world;[11] for it presents a more holistic sense of the phenomenal world than philosophy proper (i.e., logic, argument, proposition), taking into account, as it does, our individual subjectivity, our psychology, as well as history and culture.[12] In short, the novel embraces *contingency* and *concrete subjectivity*—what Heidegger calls "being-in-the-world."

Now, of course, it was this perceived deficiency in philosophy that phenomenology, and existentialist phenomenology in particular, proposed to remedy. Philosophical or "metaphysical" literature provides an antidote to traditional philosophy, just as the phenomenological and existentialist philosophy of Heidegger and Sartre provided a similar antidote. Thus, for de Beauvoir, "it would be absurd to imagine an Aristotelian, Spinozan or even Leibnizian novel, since neither subjectivity nor temporality have a place in these metaphysics."[13] In other words, a purely objective metaphysics that seeks to describe the nature of ultimate reality (as substance, monads, etc.) is not amenable to novelistic expression, which necessarily includes the subjective dimension. "For the writer, it is not a matter of exploiting on a literary plane truths established beforehand on the philosophical plane, but, rather, of manifesting an aspect of metaphysical experience that cannot otherwise be manifested: its subjective, singular, and dramatic character, as well as its ambiguity."[14] In short, de Beauvoir endeavors to redefine what "metaphysics" means in the context of the "metaphysical novel":

> Metaphysics is first of all not a system; one does not "do" metaphysics as ones "does" mathematics or physics. In reality "to do" metaphysics is "to be" metaphysical; it is to realize oneself in one's totality before the totality of the world. Every human event possesses a metaphysical signification beyond its psychological and social elements, since through each event, man is always entirely engaged in the world; and surely there is no one to whom this meaning has not been disclosed at some time in his life. In particular, it often happens that children, who are not yet anchored in their little corner of the universe, experience their "Being-in-the-world" as they experience their bodies. ... Through his joys, sorrows, resignations, revolts, fears, and hopes each man realizes a certain metaphysical situation that defines him far more essentially than any of his psychological attitudes.[15]

Readers might be forgiven for a bit of head scratching here, having been taught, since the post-structuralist revolution of the 1960s (in Jacques Derrida et al.) to view "metaphysics" as what continental philosophy had been striving to overcome, beginning with Nietzsche and Heidegger. Indeed, as the "being-in-the-world" reference makes clear, what de Beauvoir is referring to here might be better described as *ontology*, which in Heidegger is strictly *opposed* to metaphysics (in the sense of "timeless truth about ultimate reality"). To be sure, "metaphysics" did not have the same negative valence in the 1950s that it acquired post-1968, and the phrase "metaphysical novel" was in the air. Clearly, however, the "metaphysical novel" is nothing other than the existentialist novel.

In fact, what de Beauvoir is doing is not dissimilar to what Voltaire does, in his *contes philosophiques*, in reference to the systematic metaphysics of his predecessors Gottfried Wilhelm Leibniz and Descartes. Voltaire in effect redefined philosophy as an inquiry into human nature and society as opposed to one concerned with metaphysical abstractions (e.g., the immortality of the soul, the existence of God). This is what distinguished the eighteenth-century *philosophe*, the public intellectual, from the seventeenth-century rationalist philosophers. Both de Beauvoir and Voltaire endeavor to reorient philosophy toward the concrete conditions of human experience, the adoption of the literary attitude being, in their view, the most effective way to achieve such a transformation.

This said, de Beauvoir is hesitant, given her dual identity, to simply declare literature superior to philosophy. When she exalts literature over philosophy, it is usually to contrast it with an already surpassed conception of philosophy, a conception she herself does not adhere to or accept as that which defines her. Nevertheless, she states that "a metaphysical novel that is honestly read, and honestly written, provides a disclosure of existence in a way unequaled by any other mode of expression."[16] Indeed, it would seem that at times in the essay, de Beauvoir conceives of literature as a kind of therapy or perhaps a heuristic—not as thesis literature but as a literature of experience, literature *as* experience: "[the novel] allows one to undergo imaginary experiences that are as complete and disturbing as lived experiences."[17] The novel plays this imaginative, non-didactic role not only for the author but for the reader as well: "The reader ponders, doubts, and takes sides; and this hesitant development of his thought enriches him in a way that no teaching of doctrine could";[18] and "the novel is endowed with value and dignity only if it constitutes a living discovery for the author as for the reader."[19] The novel "must escape its author"; only then will it be a "truly great work" and "appear as an authentic adventure of the mind."[20] Given its greater scope for ambiguity, literature is "autonomous" in a way that philosophy is not.

To the extent, then, that de Beauvoir is contrasting authentic literature with inauthentic philosophy, it would seem that she is eliding the whole question of philosophy versus literature, with systematic philosophy on the one side and the "metaphysical novel" and existentialist philosophy on the other. In reality, she is perhaps performing the idea that there is no real dividing line between philosophy and literature in the type of writing labeled "existentialist." As she herself puts it, "it is not by chance if existentialist thought today attempts to express itself sometimes by theoretical treatises and sometimes by fiction; it is because it is an effort to reconcile the objective and the subjective, the absolute and the relative, the timeless and the historical."[21]

Philosophy versus Literature II: Martin Heidegger and Leo Tolstoy on Death

Heidegger's analysis of death in his magnum opus *Sein und Zeit* (*Being and Time*, 1927) was pivotal to making the concept a quintessentially existentialist theme. Indeed, to the extent that philosophy (qua metaphysics) had traditionally endeavored to discern the timeless, the immortal, and the eternal, the idea of death reveals, perhaps more effectively than any other topic, the existentialist emphasis on the concrete, responsible individual, or what Heidegger calls "mineness" (*Jemeinigkeit*).[22]

Given the lack of models in philosophical discourse for the discussion of death, it is not surprising that Heidegger would have been inspired by a literary treatment. This is evident from a footnote reference to Tolstoy (highly significant given the paucity of footnotes in *Being and Time*) in his chapter entitled "The Possible Being-a-Whole of Dasein and Being-toward-Death" (Division II, Chapter 1). It reads: "L. N. Tolstoi in his story 'The Death of Ivan Ilyich' has portrayed the phenomenon of the disruption and collapse of this 'one dies.'"²³ The footnote is attached to the following sentence in Heidegger's text: "Indeed, the dying of others is seen often as a social inconvenience, if not downright tactlessness, from which the public should be spared."²⁴ This sentence is in fact a succinct characterization of Tolstoy's novella: the title character faces an early death, while those around him express varying degrees of indifference or even impatience with his fate, less from callousness than from a desire to evade their own anxiety in the face of death—what Heidegger calls "fleeing" from existential *angst*. Hence the "social inconvenience" of death.

But Tolstoy's *The Death of Ivan Ilyich* (1886) had a broader impact on Heideggarian thought than this one isolated footnote might suggest. According to Walter Kaufman, Heidegger's discussion of death in *Being and Time* "is for the most part an unacknowledged commentary on [Tolstoy's] *The Death of Ivan Ilyich*."²⁵ Božidar Kante similarly observes that "right at the start of the novella we come across almost literally identical formulations regarding the view of death as we find in *Being and Time*."²⁶ Other critics, while acknowledging an influence, are less convinced of its depth: "One cannot identify Heidegger with Tolstoy," writes Robert Bernasconi, "at least on the basis of the minimal and highly selective reading that Kaufmann offered."²⁷ Agreeing with Bernasconi, William Irwin avers: "It is tempting to describe *The Death of Ivan Il'ich* as an excellent illustration of some major elements of *Being and Time*, but that would not be accurate."²⁸ Nevertheless, even Bernasconi concludes at the end of his essay that there is "a remarkable appropriateness to Heidegger's reference to 'The Death of lvan Ilych' because the final pages of Tolstoy's story struggle in their own way with a similar problem of reticence that faced Heidegger."²⁹

The nature of "influence" is notoriously difficult to pin down,³⁰ even more so when it concerns that of a literary work on a philosophical one. However, what is at issue here is not influence per se but rather *convergence*: namely, how Tolstoy contributes to the existentialist concept of death and how Heidegger contributes to an existentialist interpretation of Tolstoy. One leads to the other; one *questions* the other. With de Beauvoir it was a matter of how an author could express herself in a *complementary* fashion through literary *and* philosophical discourse; here it is a matter of literary and philosophical modes of expression converging on the same topic, from the perspectives of authors who define themselves by just *one* of these modes. The Tolstoy-Heidegger connection is thus larger than these two authors; it can be seen as emblematic of the literature-philosophy tension at the heart of existentialism.³¹

On its face, Tolstoy's tale would appear to illustrate the cardinal existentialist opposition between authenticity and inauthenticity: a journey from an existence defined by what Heidegger calls the inauthentic "they-self" (*das Man*) to the realization of an authentic "being-toward-death." But how much do Heidegger's concepts truly illuminate Tolstoy's tale—or vice versa?

Let us first examine the category of "inauthenticity." It is certainly undeniable that *The Death of Ivan Ilyich* recounts the life of an inveterate conformist. The second section of Tolstoy's novella details Ilyich's obsessive efforts to meet social expectations in every facet of his life, particularly work and marriage: "To lead a decent life approved of by society, one had to work out a certain attitude, as one did to one's work ... He demanded of marital life only those comforts of dinner at home, housekeeping, bed, which it could give him, and, above all, that decency of external forms which was defined by public opinion."[32] This description certainly coheres with Heidegger's "they-self"—a concept that draws on what Kierkegaard had called "the crowd" and Nietzsche "the herd"—namely, a leveling and tyrannical sociality (Heidegger uses the term "publicness") that has become ever more debilitating with the rise of mass culture in the nineteenth and twentieth centuries. Although Heidegger insists that his concept is value-neutral—it is an essential part of our "everydayness" and is what we all are "initially and for the most part"—in many passages, such as the following, he clearly uses this concept as a critical and historical marker to denounce the contemporary situation:

> In utilizing public transportation, in the use of information services such as the newspaper, every other is like the next. This being-with-one-another dissolves one's own Dasein completely into the kind of being of "the others" in such a way that the others, as distinguishable and explicit, disappear more and more. In this inconspicuousness and unascertainability, the they [*das Man*] unfolds its true dictatorship. We enjoy ourselves and have fun the way *they* enjoy themselves. We read, see, and judge literature and art the way *they* see and judge. But we also withdraw from the "great mass" the way *they* withdraw, we find "shocking" what *they* find shocking. The they, which is nothing definite and which all are, though not as a sum, prescribes the kind of being of everydayness.[33]

This idea of the "dictatorship" (*Diktatur*) of the they-self is clearly pejorative (ethical, ontic) and as such is in tension with the structural-ontological analysis of *das Man* that Heidegger ostensibly favors. But this passage also places Heidegger closer to Kierkegaard and Nietzsche: all three can be said to valorize true (authentic) individuality over the self-alienating absorption into the collective mindset.

However, as Zoltán Hajnády observes, "Ivan Ilyich is no everyman."[34] He is in fact a representative or epitome of the "post reform middle-class style clerk."[35] Perhaps "middle class" is a relative term, for Tolstoy writes that "[Ilyich] considered his duty all that was so considered by highly placed people,"[36] and "from the earliest age he had had this quality of being drawn, as a fly is to light, to the most highly placed people in society, of adopting their manners, their views of life."[37] Tolstoy later clarifies that this was a matter more of emulation than of being: "It was the same with all people who are not exactly rich, but who want to resemble the rich, and for that reason only resemble each other: demasks, ebony, flowers, carpets, and bronzes, dark and gleaming—all that people of a certain kind acquire in order to resemble all people of a certain kind."[38] Ilyich thus represents an upper middle class that strives, however futilely, to be like the *grande* or *haute bourgeoisie*.[39] In existentialist terms, Ilyich is clearly being *inauthentic*: he renounces his individuality in the mindless and slavish imitation of others. As Heidegger puts it, "Dasein [individual human consciousness] always understands itself in terms of its existence, in terms of its possibility to be itself or not be itself."[40] Thus, Ilyich has for most of his life "chosen" not to be himself; he has chosen not to choose.

Heidegger's they-self is certainly not a class concept; it applies to every *Dasein* indiscriminately. But Tolstoy's art does not allow him to make abstract statements about the human condition. As an author of realist fiction, he must portray particular characters in a particular sociohistorical (ontic) situation. Nevertheless, an author of imaginative literature can use synecdoche to represent types or even structures. Ilyich might then be seen synecdochally as representing the ontological category of they-selfness *as well as* thematizing an ethico-ontic judgment on the dangers of social conformism.

This is more explicit when it comes to the inauthentic attitude toward death that is at the heart of the novella, what Heidegger calls "the evasion of death which covers over [and] dominates everydayness."[41] In the following passage, Tolstoy's language prefigures Heidegger's with remarkable accuracy:

> "Three days of terrible suffering and then death. Why, that could come for me, too, right now, any minute," he thought, and he was momentarily afraid. But at once, he did not know how himself, the usual thought came to his aid, that this had happened to Ivan Ilyich and not to him [Pyotr Ivanovich], and that it should and could not happen to him, that in thinking so he had succumbed to a gloomy mood ... And having reasoned thus, Pyotr Ivanovich calmed down and began asking with interest about the details of Ivan Ilyich's end, as if death was an occurrence proper only to Ivan Ilyich, but not at all to him.[42]

This passage clearly inspired Heidegger's analysis of the everyday "evasion" of death, as in these sentences: "Dasein, fleeing *from* it [death], initially and for the most part covers over its ownmost being-toward-death"; "'Dying' is leveled down to an event which does concern Dasein, but which belongs to no one in particular ... With such ambiguity, Dasein puts itself in the position of losing itself in the they."[43] In other words, the everyday, pre-reflective awareness of death does not involve *mineness* ("ownmost being-toward-death"); it represents flight, denial, in sum: *self-deception* (what Sartre will call *la mauvaise foi*, "bad faith").[44] We refuse to own up to *our own* death; death is something that happens to other people; it is merely a datum. Tolstoy himself seemingly invokes the existentialist idea of self-deception, as when he observes concerning Ilyich's transformation toward the end of the novella: "In them he saw himself, all that he had lived by, and saw clearly that it was all not right, that it was all a terrible, vast deception concealing both life and death."[45]

Let us now turn to the end of Tolstoy's story and examine how it relates to the existentialist concept of authenticity; that is, does it describe *authentic* being-toward-death? It is certainly evident that, prompted by his approaching death, Ivan Ilyich has taken sudden stock of himself and has found that his life—a life of servile imitation—was lacking in the essential:

> It occurred to him that what had formerly appeared completely impossible to him, that he had not lived his life as he should have, might be true. It occurred to him that those barely noticeable impulses he had felt to fight against what highly placed people considered good, barely noticeable impulses which he had immediately

driven away—that they may have been the real thing, and all the rest might have been not right.[46]

That is, his ownmost potentiality of being had sometimes called out to him ("barely noticeable impulses") in the midst of his "fallen" state.[47] This is exactly what Heidegger in the next chapter describes as the "call of conscience": "Conscience calls the self of Dasein forth from its lostness in the they."[48] Facing up to death allows Ilyich to face up to life, as it were, to get in touch with the self that was covered over in the desperate attempt to conform to social ideals. "As the they-self, Dasein is *dispersed* in the they and must find itself."[49] Confronting death *authentically*, in the mode of what Heidegger calls "anticipation" (the opposite of "evasion"), Ilyich realizes that he must choose for himself and in so doing *choose himself* (create himself, be responsible for himself) rather than allowing others to choose for him. As Heidegger puts it, "understanding the call [of conscience], *Dasein listens to its ownmost possibility of existence. It has chosen itself.*"[50]

We can now understand the significance of Heidegger's footnote to Tolstoy, cited above: "L. N. Tolstoi in his story 'The Death of Ivan Ilyich' has portrayed the phenomenon of the disruption and collapse of this 'one dies.'" In other words, the story reveals the collapse of the illusion and deception of the tranquilizing, they-self attitude toward death (i.e., evasion): "He tried to go back to his former ways of thinking, which had screened him formerly from the thought of death. But—strange thing—all that had formerly screened, hidden, wiped out the consciousness of death now could no longer produce that effect."[51] Ilyich is roused from his they-self by *anxiety*—another key existentialist concept—in the face of death: "By his work in court he could not rid himself of *it*. And what was worst of all was that *it* drew him to itself not so that he would do something, but only so that he should look it straight in the eye, look at it and, doing nothing, suffer inexpressibly."[52] Tolstoy even uses the term "anguish" (the Russian equivalent of the German *angst*) to describe being-toward-death: "The dull anguish he experienced in a half-sleeping state only relieved him at first as something new, but then became as much or still more a torment than outright pain."[53] For Tolstoy, as for Heidegger, anxiety in the face of death is existentially positive; it is the key to the protagonist's *authentic* self-transformation. Anxiety *individuates* Ilyich, forces him to own up to his essential freedom.[54] As Hajnády observes, "the catastrophe of death raises [Ilyich] out of the sphere of impersonality, and makes him an individual. In the light of death's nearness he rejects the banality of everyday life—that life which, up until today, he frittered away on the attainment of false ideals."[55] I generally agree with this characterization, except that it is not mere "banality" that is at issue but the ontological integrity of *Dasein* as a truly free being than can/must choose itself.[56]

Bernasconi, on the other hand, notes that "it would appear that a Heideggerian reading of the story must stop short of the last moments of Ivan's life for good reason. It runs completely counter to the *existentialist* picture of man dying alone which has been drawn from Heidegger's discussion of death by critics from Sartre onwards."[57] No doubt the last moments of Ilyich's life—a mishmash of quasi-mystical visions of light and victory over death—are somewhat of a puzzle,[58] but this is largely irrelevant to an existentialist interpretation of Tolstoy. What is fundamental to Tolstoy's story is the *revelation of inauthenticity* in the face of death, the irony that we only begin to understand life when we are about to die. As Heidegger writes,

> What is characteristic about authentic, existentially projected being-toward-death can thus be summarized as follows: *anticipation* [of death] *reveals to Dasein its lostness in the they-self, and brings it face to face with the possibility to be itself ... to be itself in passionate, anxious freedom toward death, which is free of the illusions of the they, factical and certain of itself.*[59]

Indeed, this is also a good summation of the conclusion and meaning of Tolstoy's novella, thus demonstrating the great *convergence* of Heidegger and Tolstoy on the subject of death (and indicating a much closer relation between the philosopher and the novelist than Bernasconi would care to admit). Clearly, a Heideggerian reading of Tolstoy and a Tolstoyan reading of Heidegger are far richer for existentialist thought than a consideration of either in isolation.

Conclusion

As mentioned above, it is not surprising that Heidegger took inspiration from a literary treatment of death, given the paucity of philosophical reflection on the topic prior to the twentieth century. In fact, to the extent that philosophy is a discourse that enables the *evasion* of death—for example, the innumerable discussions of the "immortality of the soul" throughout the history of philosophy—it actively encourages *inauthenticity*. Modern literature, insofar as it is almost always concerned with individual human existence, is better able to understand and uncover authentic attitudes. This is what I think Heidegger, Sartre, Camus, and de Beauvoir all understood, in different but similar ways.

While existentialism is undoubtedly a philosophical movement, literature, as we have seen, is an inextricable part of its development and identity. The fact that existentialist ideas traveled freely across both linguistic/geographical and generic/discursive boundaries is indicative of a common historical condition in European thought and history. Existentialism was a cry of lament in the face of rapid and unprecedented techno-scientific advances that seemed to outstrip human control, unleashing unparalleled violence, destruction, and death in two successive world wars. As existentialist philosopher Karl Jaspers observes, "in 1914 the World War caused the great breach in our European existence. The paradisiacal life before the World War, naïve despite all its sublime spirituality, could never return: philosophy, with its seriousness, became more important than ever."[60] Existentialism also viewed the democratization of culture and politics with great suspicion, for, while it heralded a new era of widening political participation, it also brought ever more powerful and oppressive social forces to bear on the individual. Despite some valiant and belated attempts—in particular, Sartre's magisterial *Critique of Dialectical Reason* (1960)[61]—existentialism ultimately failed to square this circle, casting its lot with the forlorn individual and leaving the question of the political to later generations.

Notes

1 The concept of "literature" is relatively recent, its contemporary usage dating from around 1800. See in particular Germaine de Staël, *De la littérature considérée dans ses rapports avec les institutions sociales* (1800). And of course "literature" nowadays conveys a broad meaning that includes non-aesthetic works, e.g., "scientific literature."
2 Plato, "The Republic," in *The Collected Dialogues of Plato*, ed. Edith Hamilton and Huntington Cairns (Princeton: Princeton UP, 1961/1989), 832 (607b).
3 Ibid., 820 (595a5).
4 Even if philosophy departments invariably teach the "history of philosophy," many analytic thinkers nevertheless view it as equivalent to the history of physics or chemistry, i.e., as of mere historical interest.
5 Gary Cox, *Sartre and Fiction* (New York: Continuum, 2009), vii.
6 Simone de Beauvoir, "Literature and Metaphysics," in Simone de Beauvoir, *Philosophical Writings*, ed. Margaret A. Simons (Urbana: University of Illinois Press, 2004), 264.
7 Ibid., 266.
8 Ibid., 270.
9 Ibid., 272.
10 Ibid., 270.
11 This can certainly be said of Proust: "As Ribot's disciple, Proust bores us; he teaches us nothing; but, as an authentic novelist, Proust discovers truths for which no theoretician of his time proposed an abstract equivalent" (ibid., 273).
12 Thus, Sartre's first novel, *Nausea*, precedes by several years his breakthrough philosophical work, *Being and Nothingness*.
13 de Beauvoir, "Literature and Metaphysics," 274.
14 Ibid., 274–5. "Ambiguity" is of course a key term for de Beauvoir. See her philosophical essay *The Ethics of Ambiguity* [1947], trans. Bernard Frechtman (New York: Open Road Integrated Media, 2018).
15 de Beauvoir, "Literature and Metaphysics," 273.
16 Ibid., 276.
17 Ibid., 270.
18 Ibid.
19 Ibid., 271.
20 Ibid., 272.
21 Ibid., 274.
22 "Every Dasein itself must take dying upon itself in every instance. Insofar as it 'is,' death is essentially my own. And it indeed signifies a peculiar possibility of being in which it is absolutely a matter of the being of my own Dasein. In dying, it becomes evident that death is ontologically constituted by mineness and existence" (Martin Heidegger, *Being and Time*, trans. Joan Stambaugh, rev. and fwd. Dennis J. Schmidt [Albany: SUNY Press, 2010], 231).

23 Heidegger, *Being and Time*, 244, n. 12. The original German reads: "L. N. Tolstoi hat in seiner Erzählung 'Der Tod des Iwan Iljitsch' das Phänomen der Erschütterung und des Zusammenbruchs dieses 'man stirbt' dargestellt" (*Sein und Zeit* [Tübingen: Max Niemeyer Verlag, 1967], 254, n. 1). In his article "Literary Attestation in Philosophy: Heidegger's Footnote on Tolstoy's 'The Death of Ivan Ilyich'" (in *Philosophers' Poets*, ed. David Wood [London: Routledge, 1990], 7–36), Robert Bernasconi makes much of the Macquarrie and Robinson translation of this note in their 1962 edition of *Being and Time*.
24 Heidegger, *Being and Time*, 244.
25 Walter Kaufmann, "Existentialism and Death," *Chicago Review* 13.2 (1959): 81.
26 Božidar Kante, "The Death of Ivan Ilyich: Death and Authentic Life," in *Tolstoy and Spirituality*, ed. Predrag Cicovacki and Heidi Nada Grek (Boston: Academic Studies Press, 2018), 150.
27 Bernasconi, "Literary Attestation in Philosophy," 14–15.
28 William Irwin, "Death by Authenticity: Heidegger's Debt to Ivan Il'ich's Fall," *Tolstoy Studies Journal* 25 (2013): 15. See also: Alan Pratt, "A Note on Heidegger's Death Analytic: The Tolstoyian Correlative," *Analectica Husserliana* 38 (1992): 297–304; Natalien Repin, "Being Toward Death in Tolstoy's *The Death of Ivan Il'ich*: Tolstoy and Heidegger," *Canadian-American Slavic Studies* 36.1–2 (2002): 101–32; William V. Spanos, "Leo Tolstoy's 'The Death of Ivan Ilych': A Temporal Interpretation" [1980], in *A William V. Spanos Reader: Humanist Criticism and the Secular Imperative*, ed. Daniel T. O'Hara, Michelle Martin, and Donald Pease (Evanston: Northwestern UP, 2015), 171–223.
29 Bernasconi, "Literary Attestation in Philosophy," 31.
30 "Influence" is indeed a slippery concept, and Heidegger may have felt some "anxiety of influence" (Harold Bloom's phrase) with regard to Tolstoy, but no more than that he experienced with respect to Kierkegaard, from whom Heidegger borrows heavily in *Being and Time*, while barely acknowledging his debt in a few footnotes.
31 Indeed, Bernasconi writes that "the language to which Heidegger has recourse in the face of the difficulties threatening to overwhelm the quest for fundamental ontology gives a centrality to the question of the relation of philosophy and literature that readers of *Being and Time* seem not to have observed" ("Literary Attestation in Philosophy," 21). And later: "Just as the Greeks recognized that only the poetic could preserve praxis, so we need literary texts to show resoluteness and Being-towards-death" (ibid., 24).
32 Leo Tolstoy, *The Death of Ivan Ilyich*, trans. Richard Pevear and Larissa Volokhonsky (New York: Vintage Books, 2009/2012), 14.
33 Heidegger, *Being and Time*, 123.
34 Zoltán Hajnády, "Ivan Ilyich and Existence Compared to Death: Lev Tolstoy and Martin Heidegger," *Acta Litteraria Academiae Scientiarum Hungaricae* 27.1–2 (1985): 4.
35 Ibid., 4.
36 Tolstoy, *The Death of Ivan Ilyich*, 9.
37 Ibid., 10.
38 Ibid., 19.
39 "[Ilyich] was the son of an official who had made a career in Petersburg in various ministries and departments, of the sort that brings people to a position in which,

though it becomes clear that they are unfit to perform any sort of substantial duties, still, because of their long past service and rank, cannot be dismissed" (ibid., 9).
40 Heidegger, *Being and Time*, 11.
41 Ibid., 243.
42 Ibid., 7.
43 Ibid., 243. Emphasis in the original.
44 According to Geoffrey Clive, "in 'The Death of Ivan Ilyich,' Tolstoy confronts us with three inseparable dimensions of inauthenticity: first, the horrendous emptiness of society masquerading as respectability; second, the frightening power of a man to deceive himself; and third, our adamant desire to conceal from ourselves what we abstractly admit to be indubitable truths" (Clive, *The Broken Icon: Intuitive Existentialism in Classical Russian Fiction* [New York: Macmillan, 1970], 107).
45 Tolstoy, *The Death of Ivan Ilyich*, 50.
46 Ibid.
47 Heidegger in fact uses the term "falling" (*Verfallen*, also translated as "falling prey" or "entanglement") to describe the absorption and lostness in the they. See Heidegger, *Being and Time*, 169–73.
48 Ibid., 264.
49 Ibid., 125. Emphasis in the original.
50 Ibid., 276. Emphasis in the original.
51 Tolstoy, *The Death of Ivan Ilyich*, 33.
52 Ibid., 33–4. Emphases in the original.
53 Ibid., 35.
54 "Her clothes, her figure, the expression of her face, the sound of her voice—all told him one thing: 'Not right. All that you've lived and live by is a lie, a deception, concealing life and death from you'" (ibid., 51).
55 Hajnády, "Ivan Ilyich and Existence Compared to Death," 6.
56 As Sartre said famously, we are "condemned to be free."
57 Bernasconi, "Literary Attestation in Philosophy," 17.
58 Commentators have speculated that Tolstoy may have been obliquely referring to his own religious conversion in the 1870s.
59 Heidegger, *Being and Time*, 255. Emphasis in the original.
60 Walter Kaufmann, *Existentialism from Dostoevsky to Sartre* [1956] (New York: Penguin, 1975), 160.
61 See Robert Doran, "Ethics beyond Existentialism and Structuralism: Sartre's *Critique of Dialectical Reason* and the Debate with Lévi-Strauss," Chapter 1 of Doran, *The Ethics of Theory: Philosophy, History, Literature* (London: Bloomsbury, 2017), 19–34.

14

Jorge Luis Borges and Philosophy

Efraín Kristal

Notwithstanding his philosophical acumen, his lifelong interest in philosophical perplexities, his essays on philosophical conundrums, or the abundance of philosophers from both the continental and analytic traditions who find his writings genuinely inspiring or intriguing, Jorge Luis Borges was not and did not consider himself to be a philosopher.[1] He thought of himself, rather and appropriately, as a creative writer for whom philosophy was a precious source of literary ideas, although certainly not his main concern or exclusive source of inspiration.[2] This being said, one of Borges's most distinctive contributions to world literature does involve his dazzling ability to endow a short story, a poem, or an essay with philosophical dimensions. As Edgardo Gutiérrez put it succinctly, "Borges appreciated metaphysical and theological ideas for aesthetic rather than metaphysical or theological reasons. And this gave him freedoms not allowed to the professional philosopher, including the freedom to contradict himself."[3] In a similar vein, Guillermo Martinez shows that Borges was interested in mathematics, and in the philosophy of mathematics, but did not pretend to be a mathematician or a philosopher of mathematics. In Borges, mathematical insights, as Martinez points out, are transformed into literary tropes or "stylistic procedures."[4] With the characteristic humor and irony with which he sometimes made a point, Borges would occasionally say that he regretted the omission of philosophers in his *Antología de la literatura fantástica* (anthology of fantastic literature, 1940), one of his proudest achievements: "I acknowledge the unfortunate omission of the overlooked, greatest masters of the genre: Parmenides, Plato, John Scotus, Albert the Great, Spinoza, Leibniz, Kant, Francis Bradley."[5]

Borges held a view of philosophy as a "a set of doubts, of hesitations,"[6] and expressed disapproval for any definition of philosophy as the search for certainty: "How can philosophy be clear and distinct knowledge? Philosophy is the knowledge of a series of doubts and of contradictory explanations."[7] In this spirit, Borges referred to the "clear and distinct ideas" of René Descartes as "a fiction of rigor."[8]

Borges attributes his initiation into philosophical speculation to his father who exposed him to arguments that feel irrefutable even though they contravene experience and common sense, as when Zeno demonstrates that the movement of an arrow is impossible, or that the faster Achilles will never reach the slower tortoise, once the unhurried reptile gets a head start. Borges's father used a chessboard to teach his son "the paradoxes of Zeno, Achilles and the Tortoise, the arrows, the fact that movement was impossible because there was always a point in between, and so on. I remember him speaking of these things to me and I was very puzzled by them."[9] Another decisive philosophical source was Fritz Mauthner, whom Borges discovered as a high school student in Geneva, and who was also an inspiration for James Joyce and Samuel Beckett.[10] Borges read, reread, and carefully annotated his personal copy of Mauthner's two-volume philosophical dictionary (*Wörterbuch der Philosophie*). The dictionary of over 1,200 pages contains many essays on philosophical topics but only a limited number of entries devoted to individual philosophers, some of whom Mauthner respected, like Arthur Schopenhauer and Baruch Spinoza, and others whom Mauthner lambasted for what he considered to be their perverse impact on Western thought, most notably Aristotle.[11]

Mauthner's dictionary inspired many of Borges's literary ideas. It is a work of reference he often cites in essays in which he explores concepts such as eternity or circular time. Mauthner was highly critical of sacred or canonical books that are read as truth, especially if those "truths" are not based on experience but are imposed upon those who are not allowed to refute them. Mauthner's critical impulses came from one of his guiding ideas, the notion that language is powerless as an instrument to gain knowledge but powerful as an instrument for producing art: "I will underscore why language is an admirable means to produce art, but a miserable instrument to produce knowledge."[12] According to Mauthner's view of language, words can be carriers of strong emotions, memory, and collective experiences thanks to their connotations and associations, but they do not generate knowledge or understanding about the world. For that you need experiences and observations that will never even be fully captured with words: "In the end, it is impossible to hold on to the conceptual content of a word, and that is why knowledge of the world through language is not possible. On the other hand, it is possible to hold on to the emotional content of a word, and that is why art is possible with language, an art of language, meaning poetry."[13]

Borges mined Mauthner's dictionary for ideas and relied on it when he did not have access to some primary works Mauthner had discussed in the dictionary's entries. For example, when he wrote "John Wilkins' Analytical Language," an essay Michel Foucault famously cites as an inspiration for *The Order of Things*, Borges did not have access to the book in which Wilkins describes his "analytical language," a language in which letters associated to concepts are purported to play a similar role in facilitating conceptual thinking, as numbers in the decimal system are able to facilitate calculation. In the essay, Borges acknowledges that he could not read the book by the seventeenth-century English natural philosopher in Buenos Aires because the Argentine national library did not own a copy, and he regrets that the most recent edition of the *Encyclopedia Britannica* he consulted removed the entry on Wilkins that had appeared in previous editions.[14] But Borges did not need to read Wilkins to write about him because Mauthner's dictionary includes a critical account of Wilkins's analytic language, and Mauthner also mentions Wilkins in other works Borges consulted, including his three-volume *Contributions to a Critique of Language*

(*Beiträge zu einer Kritik der Sprache*). With Mauthner and other secondary sources Borges can describe Wilkins's method, explore its literary possibilities, and discuss its limitations to conclude that "there is no classification of the universe that is not arbitrary and conjectural,"[15] in a way that inspired Foucault.

In Mauthner, Borges encountered an admirer of Schopenhauer and Spinoza, two of his most recurrent philosophical references. Mauthner's dictionary was clearly a springboard to Borges's own take on Schopenhauer, but Borges also studied and quoted Paul Deussen, a commentator of Schopenhauer frequently mentioned by Mauthner, who also wrote about Buddhism and about the connections between Schopenhauer's philosophy and the philosophy of India. It is not a coincidence that Borges's book on Buddhism opens with a reference to Deussen.[16]

Borges was particularly taken by Schopenhauer's ideas regarding the self: "Schopenhauer reduces every person in the universe to incarnations or masks of a single person (predictably of a single collective Will), and declares that all the events of our lives, fateful as they may be, are pure inventions of our self, like the miseries of a dream."[17] Borges was inspired by those pages of Schopenhauer that blur the lines between dreaming and wakefulness, and he was fascinated by Schopenhauer's idea that history is the product of a collective dream, an idea he would use in many of his stories, essays, and poems: "Schopenhauer has written that history is an interminable and perplexing dream of human generations; in the dream there are recurring forms, perhaps nothing but form."[18] One of the many stories that rely on this idea is "Theme of the Traitor and the Hero," in which the central event of the story involving the assassination of a man remembered as a hero is prefigured by antecedents, such as the story of Julius Caesar, as it anticipates events in the future, such as the assassination of Abraham Lincoln.

In the early 1920s, when Borges returned to Buenos Aires from his formative years in Geneva and Spain, he befriended the Argentine writer and thinker Macedonio Fernández many of whose ideas converge with those of Schopenhauer, as far as Borges was concerned. Borges remembers his philosophical conversations with Fernandez as decisive to his intellectual formation, and he has called him "the most concise and admirable conversationalist I've ever encountered."[19] In those conversations, Fernández must have expanded on his view that "the world, being, reality, are but a dream without a dreamer, a single dream, and the dream of one and therefore the dream of no one, all the more real when it is entirely a dream."[20] Edwin Williamson has lucidly summarized the significance of the intellectual relationship between Borges and Fernández and its connection to Schopenhauer:

> The influence of Macedonio's ideas on Borges' writings was crucial, especially as regards to two fundamental themes that would not come to maturity until the 1940s—the "unreality" of the material world and the nonexistence of the "I," or individual subject. Borges would elaborate this latter idea into one of his most striking themes—the arbitrariness of personal identity, the notion that an individual could, in principle, be any other, an idea he had already come across in Schopenhauer.[21]

Schopenhauer's ideas feature prominently in Borges's first book of poems, *Fervor the Buenos Aires* (1923). In the book there is a constellation of poems in which the first-person poetic voice wanders through the outskirts of his city, which appear to be empty of other people as a metaphysical landscape of sorts, wondering if he might be experiencing a space that could also be a window into his soul. His wanderings give pride of place to the time of twilight and the time dawn—when day turns into night or night into day, and perceptions become fluid—a poetic setting ripe for metaphysical insights and revelations. These poems avoid broad daylight as much as they avoid total darkness to develop the metaphysical insight—in line with Borges's take on Schopenhauer and with his take on Bishop Berkeley whom he saw as an antecedent to Schopenhauer—that reality may be a dream of sorts. In one of the poems Borges makes explicit references to the philosophers by name:

> Curious about the shadow
> and intimidated by the threat of dawn
> I relived the tremendous conjecture
> of Schopenhauer and Berkeley
> that declares the world to
> be an endeavor of the mind,
> a dream of souls
> without a ground, without purpose, without volume.[22]

Schopenhauer was dear to Borges, but the Argentine fabulist was not interested in reconstructing his entire philosophical system or in Immanuel Kant, who was central to Schopenhauer's philosophical frame. Borges preferred the essayistic and aphoristic Schopenhauer of the *Parerga and Paralipomena* to the more systematic *The World as Will and Representation*. Borges was interested in a limited number of philosophical ideas in the writings of Schopenhauer that were particularly suggestive to him, and this was his approach to many other philosophers: one can think of Borges as a miner digging for philosophical nuggets that might inspire ideas for his essays, stories, and poems, while sometimes identifying the temperament of an individual who could have entertained those ideas. Borges's aim was never to flesh out every aspect of a philosophical system, and he was not averse to ideas he thought were impossible or contradictory.

It would be misleading to draw on Borges's short stories, poems, and essays as emanating from a coherent philosophical system because Borges was not committed to philosophical coherence for coherence's sake, even in the context of the same essay or short story, and his approach to philosophy in his literary works was playful: he was fond of philosophical paradoxes, of exploring a range of philosophical ideas that are mutually exclusive, and when he wrote the signature tales that made him famous in the 1940s (gathered in *Ficciones* and *The Aleph*), even in the most philosophical ones, he never expected his readers to take any of his philosophical conceits as a serious means of describing or understanding their own realities. His purpose was to generate perplexities or astonishment with the impossible, and even with the preposterous, as when he first published the short story "Pierre Menard, Author of the *Quixote*" in a literary journal, as if it were an essay and not the fiction its first readers discovered it was in the process of reading the tale. In that same story, the protagonist contrasts his work on a novel to the work of philosophers, in ways that resonate with Borges's own approach to philosophy in a literary work:

> My purpose is merely astonishing. ... The final term of a theological or metaphysical proof—the world around us, or God, or chance, or universal Forms—is no more final, no more uncommon, than my novel. The sole difference is that philosophers publish pleasant volumes containing the intermediate stages of their work, while I am resolved to suppress those stages of my own.[23]

The narrator of the story then offers a commentary, also in keeping with Borges's approach to philosophy, namely, that Menard's undertaking was to come up with an interesting impossibility.[24]

Some critics have called Borges a philosophical skeptic, when it might be even more accurate to say he was skeptical about philosophy as a discipline that can offer a true description of the world, even in the writings of those philosophers closest to his heart. At best they give him the *sensation* rather than the *conviction* he is being exposed to a description of things as they are:

> Except for Schopenhauer or Berkeley, no philosopher has ever given me the sensation that I was reading a true or even a probable description of the world. I've looked at metaphysics rather more as a branch of fantastic literature. For instance, I'm not sure whether I'm a Christian but I've read a great many books on theology for the sake of their theological problems—free will, punishment, and eternal happiness. All these problems have interested me as food for my imagination.[25]

Borges often drew on some philosophical ideas to consider impossibilities as elements he would feature in his fictions, sometimes as comforting wish fulfillments, and other times as wish fulfillments that become unbearable, in the way Robert Louis Stevenson wrote "be careful what you wish for" kinds of stories such as the "Imp in the Bottle," in which the last living owner of a bottle that can fulfill any wish will go to hell on their death.[26] In Borges's fictional world, the potential boons of a perfect memory, immortality, eternity, a library that contains every book that can ever be written, and the like can become unbearable banes. There are wish-fulfillment Borges stories in a more comforting mode, such as "The Secret Miracle," in which time comes to a standstill, allowing a character a year to finish a piece of writing in his mind, as he is facing a firing squad; and there are stories, such as "The Immortal," in which the gift of immortality becomes a dreadful burden.

Borges was fond of writing essays with philosophical arguments and ideas he found suggestive, even when he was sure they are flawed. He was particularly keen to explore absurdities that don't feel absurd because they appeal to his imagination. One of the most salient features of his approach to fiction is precisely the creation of impossibilities or incongruities that have the air of the credible, or even the compelling, as they might in a dream. Indeed, it is possible to trace Borges's entire trajectory as a short story writer from the earliest signature tales in which those absurdities or impossibilities are covered up by dizzying erudition and ingenious plot twists, to stories in which the conceits are laid bare without subterfuges.[27]

Borges's approach to the philosophical essay resonates with his penchant for exploring impossibilities that feel persuasive in his stories and poems: he enjoys blurring the lines between a philosophical demonstration and a fiction when he knowingly skips steps in a logical proof or plays with a double meaning of a word or concept to move an argument along, like a magical sleight of hand. He also inserts contradictory messages in his philosophical reflections, sometimes with thoughtful irony or humor, as when he uses the temporal word "new" in the title of the essay "A New Refutation of Time," to destabilize his refutation of time.

Borges was drawn to ambiguities that defy conventional logic, ambiguities in which a reader must accept more than one mutually exclusive possibility at the same time, or even a contradiction. He discussed this kind of ambiguity in one of his philosophical meditations inspired by an entry in Mauthner's philosophical dictionary, in which Mauthner argues that Aristotelian logic is an arbitrary linguistic convention rather than a method of reasoning that must be universally accepted: "Logical opposites can be synonymous words for art: their climate, their emotional temperature tends to be shared ... Fritz Mauthner proves this with splendid sarcasm."[28] In art it might be necessary to accept two contradictory possibilities, even if they do not have anything in common at all, even if they are logical opposites: "In real time, in history, whenever someone is confronted with several alternatives, they choose one and eliminate and loose the others. Such is not the case in the ambiguous time of art, which is similar to that of hope and oblivion. In that time Hamlet is sane and is mad."[29] Borges cultivates this kind of ambiguity in his own writings, as when the same text has multiple meanings in stories like "Pierre Menard, Author of the *Quixote*" or "Undr" and even in minor details, as in "The Circular Ruins" in which, unaccountably, a circular enclosure is adorned by a stone sculpture which represents, simultaneously, a tiger and a horse.[30]

Borges would sometimes report on the disappointment of some of his readers seeking to grasp the philosophical system informing his writings, as when he told Adolfo Bioy Casares about an encounter with a reader: "The other day a young woman wanted me to tell her which philosophical system was informing my short stories. When I told her there was none, although some of my stories draw on philosophical ideas that were helpful to me as a writer, I soon realized that I had plummeted in her estimation."[31]

The response of Borges's disappointed reader is in keeping with an influential view according to which Borges's fundamental literary achievements are philosophical. This view was articulated by Ana María Barrenechea in her seminal book, *Borges the Labyrinth Maker*.[32] Since its publication in the 1950s, the reception of Borges's oeuvre has been hampered by the assumption that his works can be read collectively as a self-contained literary universe underwritten by overarching philosophical gestures.

The philosophical gesture Barrenechea thought was informing Borges's work is the transformation of the real, or that which is assumed to be real, into the unreal: "Borges is an admirable writer pledged to destroy reality and convert Man into a shadow."[33] Some have seen Borges as a neo-skeptic, a precursor to postmodernism, and more recently as a thinker that can be properly grasped with the insights of French thinkers such as Jacques Lacan or Alain Badiou.[34] There have also been admirable efforts by literary critics with a sensibility to the salient philosophical topics on the surface of Borges's writings, such as Juan Nuño, who have attempted to identify literary themes that amount to a set of recurrent philosophical concerns, if not a philosophical system he calls "Borges' Philosophy."[35]

Many of the views that purport to offer a synthesis of Borges's oeuvre as a coherent philosophical system, or that single out a philosophical idea in a story or an essay for its philosophical implications, or that read a Borgesian situation as philosophical thought experiment are of considerable interest. They also show how rich Borges writings have been in stimulating the meditations of philosophers of different traditions, how readily and pliable some of his writings have been to provide examples that seem to corroborate a myriad of different philosophical views—but none do ultimate justice to the underlying pathos of Borges's philosophical impulses, and they do not take sufficiently into consideration that Borges was fond of exploring philosophical ideas for their literary possibilities, that the philosophical ideas he played with in one story or poem may be incompatible with those in another one; that Borges hardly ever glossed a philosophical idea without transforming or editing it; and that, as a spellbinding fabulist, he had many tricks up his sleeve to persuade his readers to consider ideas he found preposterous.

A good example of Borges's modus operandi is "Tlön, Uqbar, Orbis Tertius," arguably his most ambitious and far-reaching philosophical fiction. The tale exemplifies his panache for transforming philosophical systems into literary themes. It can be read as the translation of the world as we know it into another world that functions according to assumptions drawn from the speculations of idealist philosophers for whom the universe is composed of perceptions rather than an objective world independent of the senses.

The protagonist of "Tlön, Uqbar, Orbis Tertius" uncovers, with the help of others, an extravagant conspiracy involving many individuals, over several generations, who have been fathoming an alternative universe. The conspirators have produced a collective work, an encyclopedia, in which a universe called Tlön is understood according to some premises and assumptions conceived by the classic philosophers of British Idealism, and most notably Berkeley, with some important caveats, as there is no room in their design for a God who could bring the manifold of sensations coming from the five senses into coherent coordination in time and space, so that objects don't suddenly appear or disappear, and the shape of an object to the eye would correspond to the same shape to the touch. In the design of this world there is even less room for Spinoza's God who would guarantee both the autonomy of the material world and its coordination with the world of the senses:

Spinoza ascribes to his inexhaustible divinity the attributes of extension and thought; no one in Tlön would understand the juxtaposition of the first one (which is typical only of certain states) and the second—which is a perfect synonym of the cosmos. In other words, they do not conceive that the spatial persists in time or the necessary continuity of objects. The perception of a cloud of smoke on the horizon and then of the burning field and then of the half-extinguished cigarette that produced the blaze is considered an example of free association.[36]

The engineers of Tlön shunned Spinoza's brand of rationalism and embraced a version of Berkeley's view according to which "to be is to be perceived."

Borges sometimes spoke of this story as grounded on "the idea of reality transformed by a book,"[37] an idea that has resonances with Mauthner. Mauthner was skeptical of books and of any culture based on books rather than on experience, but he cautioned that books that do not provide any real knowledge about the world can nonetheless have a transformative impact on the world, and sometimes a nefarious one. Mauthner deployed these kinds of arguments against book-based religions or philosophical traditions based on books: "The philosophers of the school of Aristotle were 'readers,' men with eyes for books only. They thought that they *saw* what was to be found in Aristotle. What was not to be found there they *saw*, but were determined not to see it."[38] Mauthner thought that any procedure of this kind (any imposition of the works of Aristotle as sources of truth about the world) could affect reality, and Borges made a similar point in a discussion of "Tlön, Uqbar, Orbis Tertius" when he said that there are books that have such an impact in his own world: "In the final account we are the work of the Bible and of the Platonic Dialogues."[39]

Borges's story moves beyond Mauthner's view that a book can transform a reality when it is canonized or imposed as a source of truths. His story moves from the outlandish when Tlön is just an elaborate thought experiment by the writers of the encyclopedia, to the fantastic, when the universe, down to its physical laws, begins to transform itself into Tlön according to the designs of the conspirators. In this brave new world, the five senses are no longer coordinated, nothing is necessarily identical to itself, and the mind generates sensory phenomena. It is enough to imagine an object for it to materialize, but the existence of objects is not continuous. Things appear and disappear according to the accidents of consciousness, memory, and the imagination.

To illustrate the nature of the world of Tlön, the narrator discusses the difficulties in translating a sentence from one of Tlön's two *Ursprachen*, one of Tlön's two conjectural languages (akin to our Indo-European) from which all other languages in Tlön can be derived: "There is no word corresponding to the word 'moon,' but there is a verb which in English would be 'to moon' or 'to moonate.' 'The moon rose above the river' is *hlör u fang axaxaxas mlö*, or literally: 'upward behind the onstreaming it mooned.'"[40] The last phrase of this quote is an instance of Borges at his most magical: it would be impossible to reconstruct Tlön's *Ursprache* from Borges's brief translation. That being said, the translation appears to offer access to the foreignness of an original into the target language. It also evinces an exquisite linguistic sensibility intended to evoke differentiated grammatical features the reader is in no position to fully tease out, even as it suggests a reality operating according to the notion that the physical world is made up of perceptions generated by the mind. Suspension of disbelief is required to accept the existence of a language that corresponds to a world constituted by independent events rather than by independent objects because Borges does not offer sufficient information to reconstruct such a world in the first place. But the narrator's explanation of Tlön's conjectural languages has the air of the credible, and one of the tricks up Borges's sleeve was Mauthner's philosophical dictionary. As Jacques Le Rider has shown, the description of the two main language trees in Tlön, one of which lacks nouns and the other in which the adjective is primordial, is based on Mauthner's entry on the *Verbales Welt* (the verbal world) for the former and the entry on the *Adjektivische Welt* (world of adjectives) for the latter.[41]

Borges cleverly conflates two different strands in his story: the work of a secret society that imagines a universe according to the principles of a philosophical view, akin to Bishop Berkeley's idealism but without Berkeley's God who would have underwritten the continuity of objects and coordinated the experiences of the five senses; and a universe working according to the same principles that slowly takes over our own. Borges is also superbly imaginative in presenting the transformation in a transition period, when the conspiracy is beginning to manifest visible effects, but before the obliteration of the world as we know it, that is to say, before the physical laws of our universe are entirely replaced by the physical laws of another universe, those of Tlön.

In Borges's story, the creation of an encyclopedia has a direct bearing on the radical transformation of the universe, but the change also requires the willing participation of many individuals all of whom have studied British idealism and shunned the rationalist tradition of Descartes, Spinoza, and Gottfried Wilhelm Leibniz. There is, however, another philosopher at play in this story because the idea that human beings can *will* the transformation of the physical universe is a wild fantasy inspired by Schopenhauer.

The transformation of the universe as we know it to the universe as conceived in the Encyclopedia draws on Schopenhauer's notion of the world as will and representation, the view that what we might experience as an objective world is actually the product of a collective will. Borges, however, does not and cannot offer a blueprint for a humanly willed transformation of the natural laws of the universe any more than he can flesh out the new natural laws his conspirators are imposing on the universe, because he is creating the spellbinding illusion of an impossible world. Any drawn-out explanation of the transformation would break the spell and undermine the fantasy Borges is creating, laying bare its extravagant premises involving an outrageous synthesis of ideas by Berkeley and Schopenhauer. Borges's tale feels persuasive because his characters take for granted the transformation his narrator sketches, not because his readers understand how it has taken place. Borges presents so persuasively both the conspiracy and the pathos of his protagonist as he struggles with the unbearable consequences of the transformation of his universe that his readers willingly accept the preposterous premises of this clever, extraordinary tale.

Borges is not invested in the coherence or the truth of the philosophical ideas with which he plays. In the footsteps of his admired Rudyard Kipling, he wrote many fictions informed by propositions in which he did not believe, in some cases by ideas he found ludicrous. Since Borges considered himself, first and foremost, a creator of fictions, his response to the philosophical or metaphysical reception of his own oeuvre has ranged from caustic bewilderment to playful acquiescence, and he often cautioned that he did not necessarily take seriously the philosophical ideas that sparked his imagination:

> I am fond of the circular form. That does not mean that I believe in circular time, in the hypothesis of Pythagoras, Hume, Nietzsche, or many others. The stoics also held that history repeats itself in exactly the same fashion. I do nothing but take advantage, to the best of my ability, of the literary possibilities of this hypothesis Nietzsche thought he had invented.[42]

Borges has also expressed delight with philosophers who pretended to take seriously mysteries that were not mysterious to them at all. In an essay about paradoxes in pre-Socratic philosophy, Borges said, "These Greek philosophers were only playing with perplexity and with mystery."[43] Borges would agree with Bertrand Russell's view that "to learn to conceive the universe according to each of these systems is an imaginative delight and an antidote to dogmatism."[44] Another feature in Russell's *A History of Western Philosophy*, with echoes in many of Borges's own reflections on philosophers, is to make commentaries about their temper, personality, and humanity of individuals who can countenance this or that philosophical view.

In Borges's own account, some ideas of the pre-Socratics are quaint trivialities, such as the thought that the moon is nothing but concentrated clouds; others are suggestively incomplete or incomprehensible, and yet fascinating, such as Heraclitus' fragment according to which every time we return to a river, the river is not the same. Borges argued that these incomplete propositions that have come down to us mostly in fragments can become fodder for brilliant insights that makes us see them in new light. Of all the pre-Socratics, the most complete, and most suggestive for Borges, is Zeno of Elea, thanks to his paradoxes.[45]

Many of Borges's philosophical essays can be read as explorations of ideas that will inspire some of his literary conceits, and many of them are in the form of a survey of possibilities. This is the case with one of his essays on the eternal return, in which he explores three conceptions. The first conception, which Borges associates to Plato's *Timaeus*, is astrological in as much as the heavenly bodies, which affect the history of humanity, align according to recurrent patterns, and "if planetary movements are cyclical, universal history will also be cyclical."[46] According to the second view, which Borges associates to Friedrich Nietzsche, a finite number of objects is not susceptible to an infinite number of combinations, so that in an eternal duration, the finite number of occurrences will repeat themselves an infinite number of times.[47] In the third possibility, Borges surveys, which he attributes to Heraclitus and Schopenhauer, events recur in similar but not identical cycles. Readers of Borges's stories will immediately recognize that the second possibility involves a variation of the thought process Borges will deploy in "The Library of Babel" in which a finite number of letters used in a book of a finite number of pages will eventually produce every possible book that can ever be written, and that the third possibility informs the "The Circular Ruins" and other stories that involve an ongoing process of repetition with variations.

Borges would sometimes offer an ostensibly more prosaic explanation for his interest philosophical speculation, seeing it as a consolation for painful experiences that are all too human: "The denial of temporal succession, the denial of the self, the denial of the astronomical universe are apparent expressions of despair, as well as secret consolations."[48] The pangs of an unrequited lover, which are present in Borges's poetry, may be the rock bottom of his emotional range, even when couched in irony, as in his famed couplet in which his lyrical voice puts on the mask of the philosopher Heraclitus to lament his misfortunes in love:

I, who have been many men, have never been
The one in whose arms swooned Matilde Urbach.[49]

Occasionally, Borges made confessional statements in which he reflected on the limited solace that philosophy was able to provide for his personal tribulations:

Sometimes, far from any philosophical idea, I wonder why the destiny of an individual named Borges who lived in the twentieth century in a city named Buenos Aires, in the southern hemisphere, is of any interest to myself, why his fate, which is nothing in this universe, interests me so. But it is difficult to console oneself in this way.[50]

Borges confessed that some of his philosophical speculations were subterfuges that helped him cope with the miseries of life, but he was always proud of the way he used philosophical ideas as one of his literary inspirations. His final statement about the significance of philosophy in his career was made in one of the very last interviews he ever gave:

It is a very common human ambition that all things have an explanation, or to think that one can understand them. Take for example the different conceptions regarding the origin of the universe. Since I can't imagine an infinite time, or the beginning of time, any thought process is sterile, since in any case it is inconceivable. I have not gotten anywhere with these matters. I am a mere man of letters, that is all. I am not sure I have thought about anything in my life. I am a *weaver of dreams*.[51]

Notes

1 The impressive list of major philosophers who have been inspired by Borges range from Michel Foucault and Remo Bodei in the continental tradition to Nelson Goodman and David Lewis in the analytic tradition.
2 Borges drew literary inspiration from major and minor figures of world literature, Argentine literature, history and popular culture, historical works, etc.
3 Edgardo Gutiérrez, *Borges y los senderos de la filosofía* (Buenos Aires: Altamira, 2001), 12.
4 Guillermo Martínez, *Borges and Mathematics*, trans. Andrea G. Labinger (West Lafayette: Purdue UP, 2012), 5.
5 Jorge Luis Borges, *Obras completas*, 3 vols. (Barcelona: Emecé, 1989), vol. 1, 280–1.
6 Interview in Osvaldo Ferrari, *Reencuentros: Diálogos inéditos* (Buenos Aires: Sudamericana, 1999), 203.
7 Ibid.
8 Osvaldo Ferrari, *En diálogo II* (Buenos Aires: Sudamericana, 1998), 164.
9 In Richard Burgin, *Conversations with Jorge Luis Borges* (New York: Holt, Rinehart and Winston, 1969), 9.
10 A pioneer and specialist on the seminal importance of Mauthner for Borges is Silvia G. Dapía: see *Die Rezeption der Sprachkritik Fritz Mauthners im Werk von Jorge Luis Borges* (Cologne: Forum Ibero-Americanum, 1993). Another important book by Dapía on Borges and philosophy is her *Jorge Luis Borges, Post-Analytic Philosophy and Representation* (New York: Routledge, 2016). This book mentions Mauthner at relevant junctures. On the significance of Mauthner on Joyce, Beckett, Borges and other twentieth-century literary figures, see Jacques Le Rider, *Une biographie intellectuelle* (Paris: Bartillat, 2012), 431–63. I thank Ronan Mcdonald and Baylee Brits for letting me know in conversation of a growing critical literature on Beckett's readings of Mauthner, backed up by recent scholarship on Beckett's notebooks.
11 Fritz Mauthner, *Wörterbuch der Philosophie* (Zurich: Diogenes, 1980).
12 Fritz Mauthner, *Beiträge zu einer Kritik der Sprache, Erster Band* (Leipzig: Verlag von Felix Meiner, 1923), 93.
13 Ibid., 97.
14 See Jorge Luis Borges, *Selected Non-Fictions*, ed. Eliot Weinberger (New York: Viking, 1999), 229.
15 I modified the translation slightly by using the word "conjectural" instead of "speculative" for the Spanish "conjectural." Ibid., 231.
16 Jorge Luis Borges, *Qué es el budismo* (coauthored with Alicia Jurado), in *Obras completas en colaboración* (Buenos Aires: Emecé, 1991), 721.
17 Jorge Luis Borges, *Textos cautivos* (Barcelona: Tusquets, 1990), 295.
18 Borges, *Selected Non-Fictions*, 343.
19 Roberto Alifano, *Borges: Ultimas conversaciones* (Buenos Aires: Torres Agüero, 1988), 41.
20 Gutiérrez, *Borges*, 57.
21 Edwin Williamson, *Borges: A Life* (New York: Viking, 2004), 97.
22 My translation of "Amanecer." Borges, *Obras completas*, vol. 1, 38.
23 Jorge Luis Borges, *Collected Fictions*, trans. Andrew Hurley (New York: Penguin, 1999), 91.

24 "The undertaking was impossible from the outset, and of all the impossible ways of bringing it about, this was the least interesting one" (Borges, *Collected Fictions*, 91).
25 Interview with Rita Guibert in Burgin, *Conversations with Jorge Luis Borges*, 57.
26 In Stevenson's story the bottle must be sold by a willing buyer at a lower price than was paid by the previous owner, and if it is not sold before the owner dies, he or she will go to hell.
27 Edwin Williamson, ed., *The Cambridge Companion to Jorge Luis Borges* (Cambridge: Cambridge UP, 2013), 160–71.
28 Borges, *Selected Non-Fictions*, 39.
29 Ibid., 279. I made a slight stylistic modification to the published translation.
30 Borges, *Obras completas*, vol. 1, 451.
31 Adolfo Bioy Casares, *Borges* (Buenos Aires: Destino, 2006), 1959.
32 Ana María Barrenechea, *Borges the Labyrinth Maker*, trans. Roger Lima (New York: New York UP, 1965), 144.
33 Ibid., 144.
34 José Eduardo González writes that "postmodern culture has found in [Borges] a precursor and, for many critics he was already a quintessential postmodern author" ("Borges, Jose Luis," in *Encyclopedia of Postmodernism*, ed. Victor E. Taylor and Charles E. Winquist (London: Routledge, 2001), 42). An example of a book-length monograph on the topic of Borges and skepticism is Susanne Zepp's *Jorge Luis Borges un die Skepsis* (Stuttgart: Franz Steiner Verlag, 2003). According to Bruno Bosteels,

> it belongs to Jacques Lacan to have coined (or recast) the term "antiphilosophy" for this peculiar critical stance, somehow occupying a position both inside and outside, with regard to the claims to truth that have defined the discourse of philosophy since its inception in ancient Greece. In recent years, furthermore, the question of what constitutes antiphilosophy has also been taken up by Alain Badiou in an attempt to recapture the project of philosophy from the hands of its antiphilosophical rivals. Borges, I will argue in the following pages, can be situated profitably in the context of this debate: his work will then turn out to have been in large part the work of an antiphilosopher, one who is indeed ironically opposed to the universality claims of truth but one who is also forever in search of a radical gesture that would be able, if not fully to replace, then at least continuously to compete with the prestige of truth in philosophy. ("Borges as Antiphilosopher," in *Borges escritor del siglo XXI*, ed. Silvia N. Barei and Christina Karagerourgou-Bastea, special issue of *Vanderbilt e-Journal of Luso-Hispanic Studies* 3 (2006): n.p.)

35 Juan Nuño, *La filosofía de Borges* (Mexico City: Fondo de cultura económica, 1986).
36 Jorge Luis Borges, *Labyrinths*, trans. Donald A. Yates and James E. Irby (New York: New Directions, 1964), 9.
37 Antonio Carrizo, *Borges el memorioso: Conversaciones de Jorge Luis Borges con Antonio Carrizo* (Mexico City: Fondo de cultura económica, 1982), 222.
38 Fritz Mauthner, *Aristotle* (London: William Heinemann, 1907), 62.
39 Carrizo, *Borges el memorioso*, 222.
40 Borges, Labyrinths, 8.
41 Le Rider, *Une biographie intellectuelle*, 447.
42 André Camp, *Entretien avec Jorge Luis Borges* (Paris: HB éditions, 1999), 63.
43 Jorge Luis Borges, "Revista Multicolor de los Sábados," *Crítica* (12 May 1934): 5.

44 Bertrand Russell, *A History of Western Philosophy* (New York: Simon and Schuster, 1945), 38.
45 For a brilliant account of how Borges used Zeno's paradoxes, and how he used them to offer an interpretation of Kafka, see Sarah Roger, *Borges and Kafka: Sons and Writers* (Oxford: Oxford UP, 2017).
46 Borges, *Obras completas*, vol. 1, 393.
47 Ibid, 394.
48 Borges, *Obras completas*, vol. 2, 149.
49 Ibid., 231.
50 Jorge Luis Borges, *Borges en la Escuela Freudiana de Buenos Aires* (Buenos Aires: Agalma, 1993), 76.
51 Jorge Luis Borges, *Textos Recobrados: 1956–1986* (Buenos Aires: Sudamericana, 2011), 337.

15

Philosophy for the Masses: Haldeman-Julius, Durant, and *The Story of Philosophy*

Jeffrey R. Di Leo

One hundred years ago, a world reeling after "the war to end all wars" looked toward education as a way for history not to repeat itself—and humankind not to destroy itself. Mass education through what came to be called "humanized knowledge" was regarded as a means to stop the worldwide ascent of inhumanity. The period directly after the First World War of 1914–18 saw numerous publishers and authors engaged in what was widely viewed, following H. G. Wells, as a race between "education" and "catastrophe."[1] This essay is about Will Durant, one of the leading figures in this race and one of his contributions to it. But it is also about one of his publishers, Emanuel Haldeman-Julius, without whom Durant's project probably would not have been accomplished. As the new millennium deals with its own versions of "inhumanity" and "catastrophe," we might look to work done by Durant—as well as Haldeman-Julius—almost a century ago for guidance and insight. Let's turn now to his publisher, Haldeman-Julius, to understand better the unique genesis of Durant's project, before turning to it directly.

Publishing for the Masses

R. Alton Lee argues that in the 1920s, 1930s, and 1940s, "the literary and publishing Mecca of the United States" and "the international center for Western civilization"[2] was not located in New York City or even Chicago. Rather, it was in the small town of Girard located in the tristate region of southeastern Kansas. For it was at this unlikely location that the remarkable publisher, Emanuel Haldeman-Julius, built a publishing empire that produced the "Little Blue Books" that came to be distributed and read all over the world.

Haldeman-Julius's parents, David Zolajefski and Elizabeth Zamustin, were "poor Russian immigrants who were part of the great Jewish migration to the land of opportunity in the late nineteenth century."[3] David, his father, was a bookbinder by trade, and when he arrived in the United States from Russia, he found a job in Baltimore but soon thereafter relocated to Philadelphia where "bookbinders were more respected."⁴ When Haldeman-Julius was born in 1889, he was given the "American name" "Julius" rather than the hard to pronounce name "Zolajefski."⁵ He grew up very poor and though a precocious boy, he dropped out of school after the seventh grade to take a job in a toy factory to help support his family. An early recollection about his impoverished childhood was "seeing a book I could not afford to buy was worse than being hungry and looking at a bun in the bakery window."⁶

In his early years, while working a series of odd jobs, he read voraciously and began writing his own short essays for publications like the *New York Call*, a socialist daily, and the *International Socialist Review*. Writers for the *Call* included the "leading figures in the eastern wing of the Socialist Party" such as George R. Kirkpatrick, John Spargo, Charles Edward Russell, Morris Hillquit, and John Wanhope.⁷ His first story for the *Call* appeared in June 1911. It was on the "infamous" Triangle Shirtwaist Company fire. Later, he wrote Sunday features on art and sketches of everyday people for the *Call*.⁸

Given the fierce competition among the established writers at this socialist daily, Haldeman-Julius left his New York job at the *Call* for a position at a new newspaper, the *Milwaukee Leader*.⁹ It was started by Victor L. Berger, the first socialist elected to the US House of Representatives. At the *Milwaukee Leader*, Haldeman-Julius wrote "five to seven columns daily" for $18 a week.¹⁰ The poet Carl Sandburg, still unknown and in his thirties, worked at the desk next to Haldeman-Julius. From there, Haldeman-Julius moved on to work in turn for the socialist newspapers, the *Chicago World* and the *Los Angeles Citizen*. Then, he became editor of the *Social Democrat* and the *Western Democrat* but soon left both to return in early August 1914 to New York to work again for the *Call*. His journalistic odyssey around the country would end when Louis Kopelin, the editor who first hired him to work for the *Call*, who was now in Washington, DC, as national correspondent for the National Socialist Press, invited him in October 1915 to become Assistant Editor for the *Appeal to Reason*, the world's largest socialist newspaper with a circulation of over 750,000, which was located in Girard, Kansas.

In Girard, he met Marcet Haldeman, the daughter of a prominent local banker. Marcet, who was very independent and progressive, and regarded Jane Addams as her "aunt," got on well with Haldeman-Julius, and they married in July 1916. Marcet had left Girard but returned about the same time that Haldeman-Julius had arrived because her parent's will stipulated that upon their death, she was required to move back to Girard and live there for one year if she wished to receive her inheritance.

At the end of the First World War, subscriptions to the *New Appeal* started to go down. So, as a measure to increase publishing revenue, Haldeman-Julius published the first two numbers of the *New Appeal*'s "Pocket Series" in February 1919. By some accounts, the 1920s would be first time in US history where nearly the entire population could read and write, so the *New Appeal*'s series took off in part because of both a greatly expanding readership base and its relatively low price. "I thought it might be possible to put books in the reach of everyone rich or poor, though mostly poor—books that they would want, and which they could chose for the sake of the books alone," said Haldeman-Julius. "By that I mean that I dreamed of publishing in such quantities that I could sell them at a price which would put all books at the same cost level."¹¹

He regarded his mission in life now to be educating the masses through cheap classics. After he had published over two hundred titles, he changed the name from the "Appeal Pocket Series" to "Little Blue Books." Sixty-four pages or so in length with a trim size of 3½ inches by 5 inches, they were printed on poor quality, thin-wove paper, which was stapled twice in the center to a soft blue paper cover with black print.

According to R. Alton Lee, these Little Blue Books would come to "revolutionize the book-publishing industry."¹² Moreover, Lee contends that Haldeman-Julius "became the greatest publisher in world history" because he sold 500 million copies of the 2,580 titles that his press published.¹³ According to Lee, this "was second only to the U.S. Government Printing Office" in terms of quantity of publications.¹⁴ In addition to the Little Blue Books, Haldeman-Julius also published at different points in his publishing career in Girard a weekly, a quarterly, and a monthly, and often used them to raise funds for his little books. In 1923, he was already looking to print eighty thousand books per day in his southeastern Kansas facilities and relished being called "The Henry Ford of Literature."¹⁵

The books, which sold for as little as a nickel, were aimed at "Mr. Average Man." While some were simply reprints of the shorter classics of world literature including the plays of Shakespeare, many others, as was said of one of Haldeman-Julius's most famous authors, Bertrand Russell, were considered by some to be a "violation of the public health, safety, and the morals of the people."¹⁶ By 1929, the following titles were already in print and had sold very well: *Women's Sexual Life* (97,000 copies sold), *Homosexual Life* (54,500), *Modern Aspects of Birth Control* (73,000 copies sold in spite of the fact that it was *illegal* to publish or distribute contraceptive material), *Catholicism and Sex* (65,000), *Prostitution in the Modern World* (129,500), *Why I Believe in Companionate Marriage* (64,000 copies and written by Haldeman-Julius's wife, Marcet Haldeman-Julius), *Facts about Venereal Disease* (41,500), *Love Letters of a Portuguese Nun* (46,000), and *Sex Obsessions of Saints and Mystics* (35,000).¹⁷ But in addition to the sex, religion, marriage, and love books, there were also "How to" Little Blue Books on just about anything one could imagine, for example, *How to Play Golf* (17,000), *How to Psycho-Analyze Yourself* (43,000), and *How to Write Book Reviews* (8,000), as well as titles on many areas of common knowledge, for example, *Facts about Music* (37,000), *Latin Self-Taught* (10,500), and *Facts about Cancer* (15,000). And many of these sold well too.

But as the titles of some of these books indicate, there is another way too to measure the impact of these Little Blue Books aside from sales figures, namely, the commitment of Haldeman-Julius's publishing company to the publication of progressive, provocative, and controversial writing. One good example of this is his commitment to the publication of the writings of Bertrand Russell, particularly his more socially and politically controversial work such as *What Can a Free Man Worship?* (Little Blue Book, No. 677, 1925) and *Why I Am Not a Christian* (Little Blue Book, No. 1372, 1929).¹⁸ Of the former title, a decade after its publication in his series, Haldeman-Julius said,

It's one of the finest things I've ever read. This short masterpiece is an intellectual adventure that every intelligent person should want to experience by reading and studying it. I was so pleased with it when I first came on it some 10 years ago that I decided to give it a place in my library of Little Blue Books, where it has held an honored place ever since. It hasn't been a very popular number, but that doesn't hinder me from keeping the essay in print. Such a great, beautiful, profound study should always be available for minds capable of assimilating liberating ideas.[19]

But, in spite of his admiration for his writing style, it was not Russell, one of the most progressive and well-known philosophers in the world, that Haldeman-Julius asked to pen a series of introductions to the some of the classic philosophers in the Western tradition.[20] Rather, it was a relatively unknown young philosopher just a few years out of graduate school: William James Durant.[21]

Philosophy for Immigrants

Before he completed his doctorate in philosophy at Columbia University in 1917, and published it as his first book the same year, Durant attended seminary and taught at the Modern School in New York and lectured at other Modern Schools. After his PhD, he also taught extension courses at Columbia University and became Director of the Labor Temple School in New York City.

In his doctoral dissertation, entitled *Philosophy and the Social Problem*, Durant argued that philosophy had not grown because it avoided the actual problems of society. Durant describes its thesis as double-edged:

1) "Philosophy was ailing, and had forfeited public influence, because it had lost itself in the esoteric abstractions of logic and epistemology, and had turned, fainthearted, away from those problems of origin and destiny, nature and civilization, morality and government, religion and death" that had occupied philosophers from Plato to Friedrich Nietzsche; and
2) "The social problem—of narrowing the gap between our moral ideals of humanity and justice and the biological realities of human nature, economic greed, political corruption, and aggressive war—had elicited only superficial or impracticable proposals because it had been approached without a scientific study of needs and means, and without a philosophical grasp and reconciliation of desires and ends."[22]

Comments on the book were described by Durant as generally "merciful," but there were also those like M. C. Otto who described it as a "get-rich-quick-philosophy" and Felix Adler who said of Durant, "This young man thinks he has discovered everything."[23] The book sold only one hundred copies and the remaining nine hundred were given back to Durant by the publisher. Needless to say, it was not his first book that caught the attention of Haldeman-Julius but rather his public lectures in a New York City church.

The first time Haldeman-Julius heard Will Durant lecture was in 1922. Durant's wife, Ariel, knew Haldeman-Julius from Greenwich Village, when he was "an impoverished, ambitious, book-loving youth called Emanuel Julius," and had spoken with him at some point about Durant's lectures at the Labor Temple.[24] The Labor Temple was a Presbyterian church at Fourteenth Street and Second Avenue on the East Side of New York. In 1910, the church lost most of its congregation to immigration and as a result became a community church "theoretically dedicated to converting the immigrants to Presbyterian Christianity, but actually serving as a social and educational center for the pullulating neighborhood."[25]

In the fall of 1913, Durant was asked by Dr. Jonathan C. Day to give his first lecture at the Labor Temple. The topic he chose was the philosophy of Baruch Spinoza. His audience consisted of "five hundred new Americans plus a handful of surviving Presbyterian church members."[26] When he finished the lecture, a man in the audience complained to Dr. Day saying, "What do you mean by letting this young radical preach an anti-Christian philosophy in this Christian church?" Dr. Day replied "that as long as he remained in charge of Labor Temple it would be open for the study of any philosophy that did not preach violence against the government of the United States."[27] The following year, Durant gave twelve lectures at Labor Temple from January 3 to March 21, 1914, "on the history of philosophy from Socrates to Bergson."[28]

Thus began his lecture career at the Labor Temple, where from the fall of 1914 to February 1927 Durant gave lectures on thirty or forty Sundays and Wednesdays a season "on almost every major subject: forty lectures on biology, forty on psychology, forty on the history of art, forty on music in the nineteenth century, forty on the history of science, forty on sociology, and probably 160 on political and economic history."[29] During the 1917–18 season, for example, he delivered eighty lectures: forty on "Supermen: An Interpretation of History" and forty on psychology.[30] All of these lectures were designed by Durant to be "intelligible" to audiences of four hundred to seven hundred people, mostly immigrants, "with little formal education."[31]

Having heard about Durant's lectures from his old neighborhood friend, Ariel, and seeing a sign for an imminent lecture on Plato at the Labor Temple one Sunday afternoon in 1922, Haldeman-Julius dropped in to listen. He liked what he heard and was impressed by the size and composition of the audience but had to "hurry away without making himself known."[32] Instead, he wrote Durant a letter offering to publish his lecture on Plato. Durant responded that his schedule was too busy for him to write up the lecture for publication. Haldeman-Julius responded to Durant's refusal by sending him a check for $150 as prepayment for the lecture, and by the close of 1922 his lecture was published as Little Blue Book No. 159.

Then, in May 1923, Haldeman-Julius heard that Durant would be in Kansas City,[33] so he decided to drive there from his home in Girard, Kansas, to meet up with him. Haldeman-Julius liked Durant's book on Plato and nontechnical approach to philosophy, which he knew as a publisher would appeal to his audience, so he traveled to Kansas City intent on signing the philosopher to write for the *Haldeman-Julius Weekly*. It was a progressive newspaper he had just launched on December 9, 1922, with a blistering attack on the Ku Klux Klan, which he described as "something slimy which had crept out of the gutter. It represents organized hatred, bigotry, maliciousness, jealousy, and cruelty. It is living proof that America is not a civilized country."[34]

Haldeman-Julius prevailed, and Durant went on for the next three years to write a series of essays on philosophy for the progressive publisher located in America's heartland.[35] These essays were published by Haldeman-Julius as Little Blue Books. The series, launched in 1919, found in Durant an author that sold surprisingly well: as of 1928, Durant's Little Blue Book on the philosophy of Henri Bergson had sold 8,000 copies; Herbert Spencer, 19,000 copies; Voltaire, 24,000; Immanuel Kant, 24,000; Francis Bacon, 25,500; Arthur Schopenhauer, 26,500; Aristotle, 27,000, and Plato, 39,000. The best-selling one, though, was his essay on Nietzsche, which as of 1928, had sold 45,000 copies.[36]

In July 1925, Haldeman-Julius was in New York City for a vacation with his wife, Marcet. While there, he met with M. Lincoln Schuster of the publishing house Simon and Schuster. Like Haldeman-Julius, who became notorious and successful for publishing books on topics such as sex, birth control, prostitution, and freethinking, Schuster too gained notoriety and success in the early 1920s albeit for taking advantage of the country's crossword puzzle craze by founding a company in 1924 with Richard Simon to publish them.[37]

Over lunch, Schuster told Haldeman-Julius that unlike the publisher of the Little Blue Books, he was not interested in the mass production of books. Rather, Schuster just wanted to produce a few quality books and picked Haldeman-Julius's brain for book ideas. "How about a good, well-written history of philosophy," suggested Haldeman-Julius. "But who would write it?" asked Schuster. "There are not many Will Durant's," responded Haldeman-Julius.[38]

The more he thought about Schuster's question the more he became convinced that Will Durant should be the author, so he pitched the idea of publishing Durant's fifteen Little Blue Books on philosophy in one volume. Schuster thought this was a good idea, and a year later, *The Story of Philosophy: The Lives and Opinions of the Greater Philosophers* (1926) came out.

Initially, though, Durant was hesitant to publish his book with Simon and Schuster. Earlier, just after the publication Durant's final Little Blue Book on the history of philosophy, Haldeman-Julius told Durant "he intended to buy a large press and a bindery, and to issue clothbound books of which one would be *The Story of Philosophy*."[39] But Haldeman-Julius abandoned the idea and said that they should both "seek a publisher, and divide the royalty."[40]

While Durant was talking with Simon and Schuster, he had also worked out a deal to publish the book with The Macmillan Company, who had published his dissertation some years earlier.[41] When Haldeman-Julius suggested publishing with Simon and Schuster, Durant balked, saying, "Who were Simon and Schuster?" Continues Durant,

I had heard of them, but only in connection with crossword-puzzles books. Why shouldn't I enjoy the prestigious imprint of the most highly regarded publishing firm in America, perhaps in the world?[42]

To that, Haldeman-Julius, sagely countered, but that "was just the rub: it was an old firm, grown cautious and stodgy; our book would be lost in the hundreds or so volumes Macmillan would issue in 1926."[43] Simon and Schuster, continued Haldeman-Julius, "constituted a young enterprising duo; [the] volume would be their first serious publication; their own fortune would in some measure be bound up with [yours]; they would push the book with a youthful initiative and energy that could not be expected of an established firm."[44] And he was right.

The Story of Philosophy proved to be both a groundbreaking and best-selling book that made Durant financially independent.[45] This allowed him to leave teaching and lecturing to focus on writing the eleven-volume work, *The Story of Civilization* (1935–75),[46] of which the first six volumes would carry only his name, while the final five would carry the name of his wife, Ariel, as coauthor. The writing on this multivolume project would go on for the next four decades. The tenth volume, *Rousseau and Revolution* (1967), was awarded the Pulitzer Prize for General Nonfiction, and the Durants received the Presidential Medal of Freedom in 1977 from US President Gerald Ford for their work on the multivolume series.

Durant later expressed his appreciation to both Simon and Schuster ("Happy the day they came into our lives"[47]) and Haldeman-Julius, writing to the latter, "I owe you two great debts: first, you took the initial chance on me and had the unprecedented courage of putting philosophy into a magazine and into your booklets and second that you secured Simon and Schuster as publishers."[48] Moreover, if Haldeman-Julius had not introduced Durant to Schuster, who knows if either of these beloved "stories" would have ever been published: one that helped to popularize philosophy in the United States and the other that became the most successful historiographical series in history—and put Simon and Schuster on the publishing map.[49] In fact, Ariel Durant said, "Will had no intention of writing a *Story of Philosophy*; indeed, such a book would be only another example of what he was to call 'shredded history,' treating a single strand of the complex web called civilization."[50] But he did—and it opened the door that allowed him to explore in print the "complex web" of civilization for the next forty years.

Popular Philosophy and Its Critics

Unlike *Philosophy and the Social Problem*, which only sold one hundred copies and was not well advertised by The Macmillan Company, *The Story of Philosophy* was an immediate best seller largely through heavy advertising. Publishing in May 1926, by November it "was heading best-seller lists of non-fiction throughout the country from Boston to Los Angeles."[51] "My book," says Durant, "became a social necessity; every proper family felt obliged to display it on the table or the shelf."[52] By October

1927, the *New York Times* reported that *The Story of Philosophy* had sold close to two hundred thousand copies. But it also took a jab at Durant reporting that though Bertrand Russell's *Principia Mathematica* had probably sold about 120 copies since its publication in the early 1910s, "Mr. Russell believes in the common people and Mr. Durant does not."[53] And so too did many others in many different ways take jabs at the book.

In fact, in spite of their financial success, neither Durant "story" is without its critics and controversies. And Durant was well aware of this from the beginning. He entitled both of these projects "stories" to differentiate them from the work published by specialists in philosophy and history, but it was not enough to spare him from their wrath and scorn. In his opening address, "To the Reader," in the 1926 edition of *The Story of Philosophy*, Durant acknowledges the idiosyncratic nature of his project: "This book is not a complete history of philosophy. It is an attempt to humanize knowledge by centering the story of speculative thought around certain dominant personalities."[54] The philosophers he focuses on are Plato, Aristotle, Bacon, Spinoza, Voltaire, Kant, Schopenhauer, Spencer, Nietzsche, Bergson, Benedetto Croce, Russell, George Santayana, James, and John Dewey—albeit the latter six in much less detail than the others. He continues,

> Certain lesser figures have been omitted in order that those selected might have the space required to make them live. Hence the inadequate treatment of the half-legendary pre-Socratics, the Stoics and Epicureans, the Scholastics, and the epistemologists. The author believes that epistemology has kidnapped modern philosophy, and well nigh ruined it; he hopes for the time when the study of the knowledge-process will be recognized as the business of the science of psychology, and when philosophy will again be understood as the synthetic interpretation of all experience rather than the analytic description of the mode and process of experience itself.[55]

Another reason for some of the omissions is that Durant does not regard them as thinkers in the history of *philosophy*. So, for example, he says that Karl Marx is not in the book because Durant sees him as belonging to the history of economics and politics; Christ is not in the volume because he belongs to the history of religion; and the Scholastics are not in the volume because they belong to the history of theology.[56]

Moreover, Durant continues in his opening address his assault on analytic and professional philosophy by refusing to acknowledge the importance of the "parts of philosophy" to its study.[57] For him, the practice of philosophy as logic, aesthetics, ethics, social and political philosophy, and metaphysics (which includes ontology, philosophical psychology, and epistemology) "dismembered it" and led it to lose "its beauty and its joy."[58] "We shall seek it," continues Durant,

> not in its shrivelled [sic] abstractness and formality, but clothed in the living form of genius; we shall study not merely philosophies, but philosophers; we shall spend our time with the saints and martyrs of thought, letting their radiant spirit play

about us until perhaps we too, in some measure, shall partake of what Leonardo called "the noblest pleasure, the joy of understanding."[59]

In short, Durant summarizes the four major criticisms of *The Story of Philosophy* as follows:

> that the book had unforgivable omissions, that it paid too little attention to metaphysics and epistemology, ... that its effect would be to make the reader think that he had now sufficient acquaintance with the philosophers ... [and that] [i]t was disgracefully and unforgivably popular.[60]

Many of these criticisms came from established professional philosophers such as Paul Weiss and Morris Cohen. Even Dewey, who is well covered in Durant's volume and overall praises it, still attempts to "forgive" its popular aspects:

> While the book is one of popularization, it is also much more than that as popularization is usually conceived. The work is thoroughly scholarly. Dr. Durant has gone to the original writings and not to second-hand sources. He has selected the thinkers who are expounded with good judgment; his expositions are accurate as well as clear; his personal comments are always intelligent and useful. He has shown remarkable skill in selecting quotations that are typical, that give the flavor of the author, and that are readable. In fine he has humanized rather than merely popularized the story of philosophy.[61]

Of this last line, Dewey seems to propose that it is more acceptable to "humanize" the story of philosophy than it is to merely "popularize" it. The distinction is an interesting one, though probably it would not stand up well to closer scrutiny. But Dewey's point is clear and well taken: we need to be suspicious of popular philosophy.

When I first encountered Durant's "story" about philosophy, it was as someone who had never taken a college course in philosophy but had read works from a number of the philosophers discussed in his book. His style of writing was engaging and his outlines of the opinions of these philosophers were clear and easy to understand. So aside from the sin of omission, what was not to like about it?

Over the years, as I came to take more and more university courses in philosophy, both as an undergraduate and a graduate student, Durant's "story" became an increasingly inadequate one. I cannot recall any of my philosophy professors at any level speaking well of this book. In fact, I learned that it is best to dismiss it as mere "popular" philosophy that pales in comparison to the work of specialists in the various areas of philosophy.

A few months ago, a friend of mine, who had just "discovered" Durant's book, shared his excitement about it to me and asked me my opinion of it. While I gave him the obligatory professional philosopher dismissal of it, I found myself dissatisfied with the response. It was not that the book had changed in terms of its content (the version found in every Barnes & Noble philosophy section in America is still basically the same text as found in the first edition and the Little Blue Books). But rather it was that the market for "popular" philosophy has changed.

Whereas in 1926 philosophy in America had not yet become "popularized," today it is. Academic and trade publishers alike now have many options available for learning about philosophy, short of plowing through primary philosophical writings. They include a wide variety of dictionaries, handbooks, glossaries, textbooks, and anthologies. Major philosophy publishers like Oxford University Press and Routledge now even put out book series of "very short" introductions to major philosophers and ideas in philosophy, some of which like Peter Singer's *Hegel: A Very Short Introduction* (Oxford, 2001) are written by major contemporary philosophers.

There are also a variety of "illustrated" introductions to philosophy such as *Introducing Hegel—A Graphic Guide* (Icon Books, 2012) written by Lloyd Spenser and illustrated by Andrzej Krauze, a book that was formally published under the title *Hegel for Beginners* (Icon Books, 1992). Think too of books like *Star Trek and Philosophy* (Open Court, 2008) where twenty-one professional philosophers address philosophical issues in the television and movie series.[62] There is even another book called *The Story of Philosophy* that is now in its second edition (DK, 2016) written by Bryan Magee, who has taught philosophy at Oxford University (though even today, it does not sell as well as Durant's original). The list here is endless as is the market for these books. And many of these books like the ones above are written by professional philosophers—folks from the same group that today still sneers at Durant's "story."

Given the plethora of options for "popular" philosophy today, it seems untimely to dismiss summarily Durant's story—even if one is a professional philosopher. Why? Because to take it down is also to take down the immense market for and range of popular philosophy books today. Many of which, like my own book, *From Socrates to Cinema* (McGraw-Hill, 2007), are aimed at college students and general readers who are interested in philosophy but find many of its primary texts too daunting and much of its contemporary professional writing completely inaccessible. In *From Socrates to Cinema*, I address this challenge directly by using both short stories and films in conjunction with more traditional philosophical writing, to introduce the reader to philosophy.[63]

In 1953, over twenty-five years after the publication of the first edition of *The Story of Philosophy*, the 68-year-old Durant was asked by his publishers to write a new preface to the second edition. Taking his title from John Henry Newman's famous defense of his religious opinions, *Apologia Pro Vita Sua* (*Defense of One's Own Life*, 1864), Durant defended his philosophical opinions with the tongue-in-cheek title, "Apologia Pro Libro Suo," which literally means "a defense of one's own book."

He begins by reminding us that in the first quarter of the twentieth-century, "outlines" like his were all the rage.[64] "Human knowledge had become unmanageably vast; every science had begotten a dozen more, each subtler than the rest," and "millions of voices called for" help from writers and publishers to navigate it.[65] Durant ridicules "specialists" in science and philosophy, saying "the scientific specialist [was one] who knew 'more and more about less and less,' and the philosophical speculator [was one] who knew less and less about more and more." "The specialist," snarks Durant, "put on blinders in order to shut out from his vision all the world but one little spot, to which he glued his nose."⁶⁶

Much like today, where understanding science and philosophy involves mastery of a discipline-specific vocabulary, Durant bemoaned that in the mid-1920s, "every science, and every branch of philosophy, developed a technical terminology intelligible only to its exclusive devotees."⁶⁷ He saw a situation in science and philosophy where people educated in these areas "found themselves ever less capable of expressing to their educated fellow-men what it was that they had learned."⁶⁸

For Durant, the problem with this communication gap between specialists and nonspecialists is a *political* one. Without teachers to bridge this gap, he feared a rise of authoritarianism. Writes Durant,

> If knowledge became too great for communication, it would degenerate into scholasticism, and the weak acceptance of authority; mankind would slip into a new age of faith, worshipping at a respectful distance its new priests; and civilization, which had hoped to raise itself upon education disseminated far and wide, would be left precariously based upon technical erudition that had become the monopoly of an esoteric class monastically isolated from the world by the high birth rate of terminology.⁶⁹

In a way, his project in *The Story of Philosophy* is much like the one H. G. Wells set out to achieve in *The Outline of History* (1919–20), which was written to educate the masses about history in order to avoid "catastrophe"—or more simply put, to save the world.⁷⁰ Also, Durant rightly sees his own book as comparable to Wells's book, which he says was criticized for its "errors" and which historians "did not quite know what to do with." "History became popular" with the publication of *The Outline of History*, writes Durant, "and historians became alarmed." "Now it would be necessary for them to write as interestingly as H. G. Wells."⁷¹

Durant points out that his book was written at a time when there was a "flood" of "story" and "outline" books: "Outline followed outline, 'story' followed 'story'; science and art, religion and law, had their storiographers."⁷² But the market for these "story" and "outline" books was soon saturated, and the

> public appetite was quickly satiated; critics and professors complained of superficiality and haste, and an undertow of resentment set in, which reached every outline [and story] from the last to the first. As quickly as it had come, the fashion changed; *no one dared any longer say a word for the humanization of knowledge*; the denunciation of outlines was now the easy road to critical repute; it became the style to speak with a delicate superiority of any non-fiction book that could be understood. The snob movement in literature began.⁷³

Twenty-five years after the publication of his book, Durant does not shy away from the conditions of its production, nor does he deny that many of the criticisms of it are warranted. "The worst sin of all—though the critics do not seem to have noticed it—was the omission of Chinese and Hindu philosophy," or what we today might call "world" philosophy. "Even a 'story' of philosophy that begins with Socrates, and has nothing to say about Lao-tze and Confucius, Mencius and Chwang-tze, Buddha and Shankara, is provincially incomplete," he continues. He claims that his attempt to atone for the omission of Eastern philosophy was the publication in 1935 of *Our Oriental Heritage*, the first volume of his *The Story of Civilization*.[74]

"As for the word 'Story,' which has since been so abused with use," writes Durant, "it was chosen partly to indicate that the record would concern itself chiefly with the more vital philosophers, partly to convey the sense that the development of thought was a romance as stirring as any in history."[75] But in spite of all its flaws, the book allegedly raised interest in the philosophical classics. According to Durant, "sales of the philosophical classics increased some two hundred per cent. [sic] after the publication of the *Story*." He continues,

> Many publishers have issued new editions, particularly of Plato, Spinoza, Voltaire, Schopenhauer and Nietzsche. A high official of the New York Public Library, who asked to be unnamed, reports that: ever since the publication of *The Story of Philosophy* we have had a wide and increasing demand from the public for the philosophical classics, and our stock of them in branch libraries has been gradually increased ... Formally, current books about philosophy were purchased in small quantities for the system; but in the last two or three years a readable new book about philosophy is purchased very generally at the outset, in anticipation of a demand which eventually does develop, and quickly at that.[76]

Durant adds too that as of 1953, the book was already translated into German, French, Swedish, Danish, Jugo-Slavian, Chinese, Japanese, and Hungarian. Today, many other languages have been added to the list, and it still has a global readership. One can easily find, for example, online comments about it from enthusiastic lay readers from across the world in Arabic, Chinese, Russian, and a host of other languages.

Conclusion

Durant reminds us that we should not be "ashamed of teaching the people" even if we are "imperfect" at it by some standards. "We are all imperfect teachers, but we may be forgiven if we have advanced the matter a little, and have done our best."[77] He did his best spending eleven years researching the material in his book and three years writing it first as series of Little Blue Books aimed at lay readers and then publishing it as one volume at the request of M. Lincoln Schuster.

Today, close to one hundred years after Durant offered us a "story" about philosophy complete with humor and colorful characters, the book continues to be widely read by nonspecialists—and disparaged by specialists. However, the story of philosophy today does not end with John Dewey, and if anything, philosophy has become even more specialized and complex over the past century. Moreover, if the "humanization" of knowledge was already suspect in the 1950s as noted by Durant above, then twenty-first-century posthumanism presents a whole new set of challenges for the general dissemination of knowledge. But the world today is not unlike the world of Wells and Durant in that it flirts daily with "catastrophe" and has seen a rise in authoritarianism. Educated opinion seems to be in short supply, and the world stage is now open to bullies, tyrants, and dictators. In brief, our inhumanity is threating to eliminate its opposite, humanity.

In addition, in spite of the plethora of popular options to learn about philosophy, its popularity seems to be waning. Philosophy departments are being closed and the major struggles to attract students compared to vocational ones such as business, nursing, and engineering.

Some might find it naïve today to believe, along with Durant, Wells, and Haldeman-Julius, that the publication of accessible and popular books aimed at a mass audience can keep us from moving down the path of monstrosity and inhumanity. However, I don't.

Philosophy needs a "story" now more than ever. Durant's "enduring" "romance" served its audience well, but it is time for a new one—a story that transitions philosophy from the twentieth-century to the twenty-first and not the nineteenth-century to the twentieth like the original. Why not hope too that it is a "story" or a series of "short stories" that saves academic philosophy from obsolescence in the age of authoritarianism and vocational training? This would be an ironic and bittersweet victory for Durant after a century of dismissal of his own "story" by academic philosophers.

Notes

1 "Human history becomes more and more a race between education and catastrophe" (H. G. Wells, *The Outline of History* [New York: The Macmillan Company, 1921], 1100).
2 R. Alton Lee, *Publisher for the Masses, Emanuel Haldeman-Julius* (Lincoln: University of Nebraska Press, 2017), xi.
3 Ibid., 1.
4 Ibid., 5.
5 Ibid.
6 Ibid., 6.
7 Ibid., 41.
8 Ibid.
9 Ibid.
10 Ibid., 42.
11 Ibid., 96.
12 Ibid., 200.
13 Ibid., 202.
14 Ibid., 203.
15 Ibid., 111.
16 These are the words of New York Supreme Court Justice McGeehan, who revoked Lord Russell's appointment to the City University of New York (CUNY) in 1940.

McGeehan described Russell's appointment to CUNY as "an insult to the people of the City of New York" (Paul Edwards, "Appendix: How Bertrand Russell Was Prevented from Teaching at the College of the City of New York," in *Bertrand Russell: Why I am Not a Christian*, ed. Paul Edwards [New York: Simon and Schuster, 1957], 221). According to him, the CUNY Board "in effect established a chair of indecency" and "acted arbitrarily, capriciously, and in direct violation of the public health, safety, and the morals of the people and of the petitioner's rights" (ibid., 221). Russell's appointment to CUNY was announced on February 24, 1940, and Judge McGeehan's ruling revoking it was made on March 30, 1940.

17 Lee, *Publisher*, 205–20.
18 For an excellent survey of Russell's publishing relationship with Haldeman-Julius, see William F. Ryan, "Bertrand Russell and Haldeman-Julius: Making Readers Rational," *Russell* 29–32 (original series, 1978): 53–64.
19 Emanuel Haldeman-Julius, *Questions and Answers*, 6th series (Girard, KS: Haldeman-Julius Company, 1936), 93.
20 Eventually, Russell would write a history of philosophy, but it would not be until after the revocation of his appointment from CUNY in 1940. Written during the Second World War, *A History of Western Philosophy: And Its Connection with Political and Social Circumstances from the Earliest Times to the Present Day* was published in 1945 in the United States by Simon and Schuster and in the United Kingdom in 1946 by George Allen & Unwin. It began as a series of lectures he gave at the Barnes Foundation in Philadelphia during 1941 and 1942. He received a $3,000 advance from his publishers and wrote the book between 1943 and 1944 while living at Bryn Mawr College. Like H. G. Wells and Will Durant before him, his survey would provide him with financial security for the rest of his life. Also, when he won the Nobel Prize for Literature in 1950, the Nobel committee cited it as one of the books that helped him win the award. Still, in spite of its popularity, it was highly criticized in academic circles for its errors and overgeneralization.
21 According to Durant, who was born in 1885, there was no connection between his name and William James, who was a member of the Harvard University faculty from 1872 to 1907, and who upon his death in 1910 was pronounced in his *New York Times* obituary as "America's foremost philosophical writer, virtual founder of the modern school of psychology and exponent of pragmatism" (*New York Times*, August 27, 1910). As if to prove the lack of connection between America's foremost philosopher and his own name, Durant writes that his father "received no schooling, and never learned to read or write." "His education," continues Durant, "was almost entirely of character and by experience" (Will and Ariel Durant, *A Dual Autobiography* [New York: Simon and Schuster, 1977], 28).
22 Durant and Durant, *Autobiography*, 72.
23 Ibid., 73.
24 Ibid., 95.
25 Ibid., 58.
26 Ibid.
27 Ibid.
28 Ibid.
29 Ibid., 58–9.
30 Ibid., 78.
31 Ibid., 58.

32 Ibid., 95.
33 Ibid., 109. In February 1923, Durant took a leave of absence from the Labor Temple to help set up the "Kansas City Academy," which he hoped would be a "prelude to a university." "In the thirty-four days between February 15 and March 20," writes Ariel Durant, "Will gave forty lectures for the academy, on history, literature, philosophy, economics, and politics. On top of this, in Kansas City, he faced Clarence Darrow in another debate on 'Is Life Worth Living?'" (Durant and Durant, *Autobiography*, 96). Darrow would write in a letter to Samuel D. Schwartz on August 12, 1925, "Dr. Will Durant is one of the ablest debaters I ever met" (*In the Clutches of the Law: Clarence Darrow's Letters*, ed. Randall Tietjen [Berkeley: University of California Press, 2013], 309).
34 Quoted in Lee, *Publisher*, 108.
35 Lee, *Publisher*, 109.
36 Ibid., 219.
37 Ibid., 122.
38 Ibid.
39 Durant and Durant, *Autobiography*, 101.
40 Ibid., 101.
41 Macmillan published Durant's thesis only on the condition that he could guarantee the sale of a thousand copies. It only sold one hundred copies, and Macmillan "burdened with nine hundred unsold copies, appealed to [Durant] to come take them away," which he did, "stack[ing] them imposingly on a projecting cornice that ran around our living room" (Durant and Durant, *Autobiography*, 73). Durant seems to believe that the lack of sales were not because of the content of the book but rather because of poor advertising on the part of the publisher. Writes Durant, it only "received a brief listing among Macmillan's spring publications for 1917" (72).
42 Ibid., 101.
43 Ibid.
44 Ibid. At the time of deal, Max Schuster was 28 and Richard Schuster was 26.
45 The book was published in May 1926. The contract with Simon and Schuster granted Durant half of the 12.5 percent royalty and Haldeman-Julius the other half. Schuster suggested to Durant that he offer Haldeman-Julius $500 for his share, and Haldeman-Julius accepted. When the book became a financial success, Durant reports that Haldeman-Julius "never complained of this somewhat selfish transaction" but rather "rejoiced in the success of the book which owed its existence to him, and he entertained me with fraternal hospitality when, a year later [1927], my wandering lectures took me near his home in Girard, Kansas" (Durant and Durant, *Autobiography*, 103).
46 A Brooklyn newspaper interview with Durant from May 27, 1922, reveals that well before he was financially successful with Haldeman-Julius, Durant longed for the financial independence to write *The Story of Civilization*:

> It is his ambition ... to lay aside enough money so that when he reaches the age of forty he may dispense with giving lectures, ... and go on extended trips to France and England to engage in research work in preparation for a book that would show the interdependence, in history, of politics, economics, art, literature, and science. "These subjects," Dr. Durant said, "have been written separately. My ambition is to write a complete history of the world, showing all

these factors working in harmony, and giving as a result the kind of world we know" (Durant and Durant, *Autobiography*, 95).

47 Ibid., 101.
48 Ibid., 122.
49 Durant says that Macmillan seemed "relieved" to not have to publish the book (ibid., 101).
50 Ibid., 95.
51 Ibid., 103.
52 Ibid.
53 Ibid., 119. To which Durant responded, "I believe in the equal right of common people to access to the education that may make them uncommonly fit for uncommon tasks" (119).
54 Will Durant, *The Story of Philosophy: The Lives and Opinions of the Greater Philosophers*, 1st ed. (New York: Simon and Schuster, 1926), xiii.
55 Ibid., xiii.
56 Durant and Durant, *Autobiography*, 103. It should be noted that the government publishing office of Soviet Russia rejected *The Story of Philosophy* because there was no chapter on Marx (103).
57 Analytic philosophy found, in the conceptual analysis of G. E. Moore and logical atomism (and logical-analytic pluralism) of Bertrand Russell, a methodology that could mirror the exactitude and certainty of the sciences. Logical empiricism rejected metaphysics as unverifiable and focused instead on perfecting conceptual analysis. Moreover, analytic philosophers had a "linguistic turn" that involved the logical empiricism in addition to American pragmatism and ordinary language philosophy. Durant's work set itself in opposition to this approach to philosophy. Nevertheless, Durant also says, "I doubt philosophy when it is metaphysics" (Durant and Durant, *Autobiography*, 404), describing his own philosophical position to be "agnostic, with pantheistic overtones" (ibid., 403) as well as "socialist, but some cautions" (ibid., 402).
58 Durant, *The Story of Philosophy*, 1st ed., 4.
59 Ibid., 4.
60 Durant and Durant, *Autobiography*, 103.
61 Ibid., 102.
62 This title appears in the Open Court series "Popular Culture and Philosophy." As of 2019, it has published 125 titles, the latest of which are Lester C. Abesamis and Wayne Yuen, eds., *Rick and Morty and Philosophy* (2019); Rachel Robison-Greene, ed., *The Handmaid's Tale and Philosophy* (2019); and Randall E. Auxier and Megan Volpert, eds., *Tom Petty and Philosophy* (2019). The series began in 2000.
63 I do something similar in *Morality Matters: Race, Class and Gender in Applied Ethics* (New York: McGraw-Hill, 2002), albeit for applied ethics.
64 Will Durant, *The Story of Philosophy: The Lives and Opinions of the Greater Philosophers*, 2nd ed. (New York: Simon and Schuster, 1953), v.
65 Ibid.
66 Ibid.
67 Ibid., vi.
68 Ibid.
69 Ibid.

70 For an account of Wells's efforts to save the world through textbook writing, see Jeffrey R. Di Leo, "Catastrophic Education: Saving the World with H. G. Wells," *The Comparatist* 41 (2017): 152–75.
71 Durant, *The Story of Philosophy*, 2nd ed., vii.
72 Ibid.
73 Ibid., vii–viii. My emphasis.
74 Ibid., viii.
75 Ibid.
76 Ibid., x.
77 Ibid.

Contributors

Jeffrey R. Di Leo, *University of Houston-Victoria, USA*

Robert Doran, *University of Rochester, USA*

Ranjan Ghosh, *University of North Bengal, India*

Robin Truth Goodman, *Florida State University, USA*

Peter Hitchcock, *City University of New York, USA*

Efraín Kristal, *University of California, Los Angeles, USA*

Jeffrey S. Librett, *University of Oregon, USA*

Junjie Luo, *Gettysburg College, USA*

Paul Allen Miller, *University of South Carolina, USA*

Brian O'Keeffe, *Barnard College, USA*

David M. Robinson, *Oregon State University, USA*

Nicole Simek, *Whitman College, USA*

Michael Stern, *University of Oregon, USA*

Henry Sussman, *Rutgers University, USA*

Zahi Zalloua, *Whitman College, USA*

Index

absence 167 n.16
   and presence, equating 150, 153, 156–8
abstraction of object world, from subject 54, 55
abstract universalism 65
active forgetting. *See* willful ignorance
Adams, Raymond 136
Addams, Jane 262
Adler, Felix 264
aesthetic contracts and deconstruction 205–6
affirmation, Nietzschean 155, 158, 161
African memory, palimpsest of 71. *See also* Nietzsche, Friedrich
   civilizing mission of Africa and 72
   imperial will to ignorance and 77
   willful ignorance and 72
Against World Literature (Apter) 119
Agamben, Giorgio 34
Aiken, David 166 n.5, 167 n.13
Aizura, Aren Z. 103 n.15
Alden's Cyclopedia of Universal Literature 174
   on Confucius 174
   national literature idea in 176
Aleph, The (Borges) 250
alētheia 49, 50, 51
aloneness 150, 153, 165
Alpers, Edward A. 85 n.12
alterity 107, 111
   radical 12, 105
Althusser, Louis 52
Altieri, Charles 8
ambiguity, types of 150, 252
American Philosophical Association (APA) 18 n.15
Amiel, Henri Frédéric 182 n.18
Analects, The (Confucius) 174, 178, 179
analytic philosophy 1, 3–5, 8, 18 n.10, 19 n.16, 25, 276 n.57
Anderson, Warren 101

Anderson, Benedict 124
an de Vall, Renée 17 n.3
Anglo-American analytic philosophy 1, 2
Animals' Rights (Salt) 134
Anquetil-Duperron, Abraham Hyacinthe 146
Anthology of Fantastic Literature (Antología de la literatura fantástica) (Borges) 247
Anthology of World Literature, An 178, 183 nn.37–8
   on Indian literature 178
apagogic reasoning 32
aphanisis 107
Appeal to Reason (newspaper) 262
Apter, Emily 17 n.1, 98–9, 119, 168 n.23
arabesques 206, 220, 222
   aesthetics of 200, 217–18
   as alchemy 225
   local difference and 211
   of memory 219
   as outbreak 215
   static 210
Arabesques (Shammas) 199, 200, 202
   aesthetics of *arabesque* and rootedness in past in 217–18
   color significance in 213
   distilling middle eastern complexity in 206–14
   Hever on 209, 210
   isomorphic parallelism in 216–17
   narrative art in 219–20
   olive oil importance in 213
Arabian Nights, The 204
Arcades Project, The (Benjamin) 203, 227 n.48
"Archipelago, The" (Hölderlin) 29
Arendt, Hannah 93
argumentation, significance of 5, 7–8
Aristotle 248
Armstrong, Nancy 91

Arruzza, Cinzia 93
Aryan Race, The (Morris) 175
Ashouri, Daryoush 166 n.5
Asian philosophy 173–81
Askin, Ridvan 20 n.35
astonishment. *See also* Cannibal
   immanence of 107
   significance of 105
Atwood, Margaret 101
Auerbach, Erich 165 n.4
Austin, J. L. 18 n.10
authenticity, significance of 241–3
   dimensions of 246 n.44
avant-gardism 122
Azoulay, Jacques 68 n.18

Badiou, Alain 28, 31–4, 119, 253
   on Heidegger 31–2
Balzac, Honoré de 34, 211, 212, 227 n.43
barbarism. *See* Cannibal
Barrenechea, Ana María 252–3
Bartky, Sandra Lee 187
Batchelor, Kathryn 67 n.9
Baudrillard, Jean 9
Bayoumi, Moustafa 67 n.7
Beast and the Sovereign, The (Derrida) 23
beauty, notion of 54–5
Beckett, Samuel 248, 258 n.10
Beckman, Frida 20 n.35
Bedford Anthology of World Literature, The
   179, 180, 183 n.51
Being 48, 51, 52, 57 n.39, 171 n.70, 187, 211
   novel and 215
   as process of totality of things 155
being 11
   Visva Sahitya and 186
   world of 48
Being and Nothingness (*L'Etre et le néant*)
   (Sartre) 235, 244 n.12
Being and Time (*Sein und Zeit*) (Heidegger)
   238, 239, 245 n.30
being-in-the-world 236, 237
being-toward-death 241–2, 245 n.31
Bellow, Saul 200
Belsey, Catherine 107
Benjamin, Walter 34, 203, 211, 213,
   227 n.48, 228 nn.62, 68
Berger, Victor L. 262

Berkeley, Bishop 250, 253, 254, 255
Bernasconi, Robert 64–6
   on Fanon 69–70 n.33, 70 n.40
   on Heidegger 239, 242, 245 nn.23, 31
Bernhard, Thomas 200
Bevir, Mark 139 n.21
Beyond Good and Evil (Nietzsche)
   76, 78, 79
Bhabha, Homi K. 67 n.7
Bhagavad Gita (Indian philosophy) 174,
   178, 179
Bhattacharya, Tithi 93
Birth of Tragedy out of the Spirit of Music,
   The (Nietzsche) 145, 152
blackness and Abrahamic religions 223
Black Notebooks (Heidegger) 27
Black Skin, White Masks (*Peau noire,*
   masques blancs) (Fanon) 59, 61, 63,
   64, 66, 69 n.31
   addressing situated readers 64–5
   on language 62
Blair, Tony 9
Blanchot, Maurice 235
Blindness and Insight (de Man) 223
Blood of Others (*Le Sang des autres*)
   (de Beauvoir) 235
Bloom, Harold 6, 18 n.8
Boahen, Albert Adu 72, 84 n.9
Bodei, Remo 257 n.1
Boisvert, Jean-Pierre 171 n.71
Borges, Jorge Luis 86 n.36, 199, 259 n.34
   on ambiguities 252
   approach to philosophy 250–2
   Barrenechea on 252–3
   confessions of 257
   on exploring impossibilities 251–2
   Fernández's influence on 249
   Mauthner's influence on 248–9, 252,
      254, 255
   on pre-Socratics 256
   on reality 254
   Schopenhauer's influence on
      249–50, 255
   Zeno's paradoxes and 259 n.45
Borges the Labyrinth Maker
   (Barrenechea) 252
Born Translated (Walkowitz) 119
"born translated" novels 119–20

Index 283

Bosteels, Bruno 259 n.34
Bourdieu, Pierre 27
Brah, Avtar 95
Braudel, Fernand 211, 226 n.30
British transcendentalism 130-1
Buck, Philo 178, 183 n.37
Buck-Morss, Susan 115
Buddhism 249
Buell, Lawrence 129
Buffett, Warren 125
Burgard, Peter J. 171 n.73
Butler, Judith 96-7

Calvino, Italo 199
Camus, Albert 28, 57 n.32, 233
Candide (Voltaire) 234
Cannibal 105
   desiring difference and 106-8
   and sameness and difference, navigating between 108-11
   useless philosophy and 111-12
Capital (Marx) 123
Carlyle, Thomas 139 n.20
Carpenter, Edward 130-1, 133, 139 nn.12, 22
   on country living 130-1
   on homogenic attachment 130
Casanova, Pascale 17 n.1, 27, 28, 92, 119, 180
Casares, Adolfo Bioy 252
Cassin, Barbara 38, 168 n.23
Castillo, Debra 91
Cavell, Stanley 20 nn.31, 35
Cervantes, Miguel de 234
Césaire, Aimé 64, 118
Chakrabarty, Dipesh 85 n.19
Channing, Ellery 138 n.2
Chatterjee, Partha 92
Cheah, Pheng 17 n.1, 59, 121, 190, 192-3
   on migration 97
   on philosophical impact of world in literature 93
Chicago World (newspaper) 262
Chinese literature, significance of 176, 178-80
Chinese philosophy. *See* Confucian philosophy
Cioran, Emil 27

"Circular Ruins, The" (Borges) 252, 257
"Civil Disobedience" (Thoreau) 133, 138
Civilisation: Its Cause and Cure (Carpenter) 133
civilizing mission, of Africa 72
Cixous, Hélène 98
Clark, Nancy L. 85 n.12
Classic Asian Philosophy (Kupperman) 174, 175, 179
Clinton, Bill 9
Clive, Geoffrey 246 n.44
Cohen, Morris 269
Coleridge, Samuel Taylor 131, 139 n.20
Colli, Giorgio 165 n.2, 168 n.24
colonization 60, 62
color, significance of 213-14
combat literature 66
Combined and Uneven Development (WReC) 122
commodity fetishism 100
common property (*gemeingut*) 117
Communist Manifesto (Marx and Engels) 115, 117-22
   class cosmopolitanism and 117
   globalization and 124-5
   Goethean lesson about world literature in 120-1
   Industrial Revolution and 120
   phrasing and content and 122
   Puchner on 122
   translation as instance of equivalence and 123
   unity of 126
   world across class and culture and 117-18
compassion 135-6
conceptual space 123
Conference of Berlin 71, 82
Confucianism 56 n.9, 174-5
Confucius 174, 182 n.18
Conrad, Joseph 71
conscience and *Dasein* 242
continental tradition 1, 4, 257 n.1
   other 4-5
Contributions to a Critique of Language (*Beiträge zu einer Kritik der Sprache*) (Mauthner) 248-9
Cortázar, Julio 200, 204

cosmopolitanism 2, 92, 117, 118, 123
  love and 190
  visva sahitya and 193–4
Counterpath (Derrida and Malabou) 29
Cox, Gary 235
Crawford, Claudia 168 n.26
Creed of Kinship, The (Salt) 135
Creuzer, Friedrich 146–7, 166 n.5
Critique of Dialectical Reason (Sartre) 243–4
cruelty, significance of 111
Cuboniks, Laboria 95, 99
cultural persistence and cultural memory 223
curiosity, notion of 106

Dabashi, Hamid 166 n.5
Damrosch, David 17 n.1, 26, 37, 38, 92, 115, 119, 173
Danto, Arthur 26, 35
Dao De Jing (Chinese philosophy) 179
Dapía, Silvia G. 258 n.10
Darrow, Clarence 275 n.33
Dasein 187, 240, 241, 244 n.22
  call of conscience and 242
Dasenbrock, Reed Way 18 n.10
Dastur, François 166 n.5
Davidson, Arnold 56 n.22
Day, Jonathan C. 265
Death of Ivan Ilyich, The (Tolstoy) 239–42, 245–6 n.39, 246 n.44, 246 n.54
de Beauvoir, Simone 28, 91, 94, 173, 233
  on metaphysical novels 237
  on philosophical literature 235–8
deconstruction 5, 7, 16, 197
  aesthetic contracts and 205–6
  and *Arabesques* (see *Arabesques*)
  Derrida on 199–200
  into literature 220–5
  and *My Name is Red* (see *My Name is Red*)
  Rousseau and Derrida and 200–2
  significance of 198–9
  storytelling as 214–20
Defense of One's Own Life (*Apologia Pro Vita Sua*) (Newman) 270
Defoe, Daniel 23
Deleuze, Gilles 118

de Man, Paul 3, 4, 6, 18 n.8, 26, 223
demokratia 42
Derrida, Jacques 3–6, 18 nn.8, 10, 54, 56 n.22, 115, 211, 223, 226 n.20, 228–9 n.74
  arabesque and 215
  on curiosity 106
  on deconstruction 198–201
  on his identity 199–200
  on masterful writing 216
  on reason 41
  on translatability 36
  on translation 23, 25, 28, 29, 37, 38, 41
  and language 97–8
  Rousseau and 200–2
  on world as text 10, 19 n.22
Desai, Anita 180
Descartes, René 28, 79, 105, 234, 237, 247
desiring difference 106–8
deterritorialization, notion of 208
Dewey, John 269
Dhammapada, The (Indian philosophy) 175
dharma 195 n.10. *See also* sahitya; visva sahitya
Dialectic of Sex, The (Firestone) 99
dialectics and translation 38–9
dianoia (discursivity) 33
Dictionary of Untranslatables (Cassin) 38
Diderot, Denis 28, 234
Die heilige Sage (Rhode) 147
Differend, The (Lyotard) 35
Di Leo, Jeffrey R. 19 nn.23–4, 102 n.6
disalienation. *See* Fanon, Frantz
discontinuity 121, 159
Döblin, Alfred 212
Donne, John 24
Don Quixote (Cervantes) 234
Dooley, Mark 29
Dostoevsky, Fyodor 233
"Double Session, The" (Derrida) 198, 215
Douglas, Robert 176, 181 n.15
doxa, demystifying 108
dream metaphor 249
Drowning Eye, The (*L'OEil se noie*) (Fanon) 64

Durant, Ariel 265, 267, 275 nn.33, 41, 276 nn.46, 56
Durant, William James 261, 264, 270–2, 274 n.21, 275 nn.33, 41, 275–6 n.46, 276 nn.49, 53, 56–7
  controversies with 268–9
  Dewey on 269
  Haldeman-Julius and 265–7
  lecture career at Labor Temple 265
  on science and philosophy 271
  on specialists 270–1
Dussel, Enrique 79

Ear of the Other, The (Derrida) 25
Eckermann, Johann Peter 116
Eco, Umberto 204
Edwards, John 137
Edwards, Paul 274 n.16
Eighteenth Brumaire (Marx) 121
Einboden, Jeffrey 166 n.5
Ellis, John M. 20 n.27
Ellison, Ralph 233
Emerson, Ralph Waldo 133, 136
Engels, Friedrich 92, 115
epistemology 14, 59, 74, 80, 82, 105, 205. *See also individual entries*
  domestication and 107
  dualism and 149, 150, 153, 155, 158–9
  lying and 169 n.56
  philosophy and 264, 268, 269
  Plato and 48, 52–4
  poetics and 63–6
  of provenance 70 n.40
Escher, M. C. 198
essaying, significance of 107
Essay on the Origins of Language (Rousseau) 200, 201
Essays (Montaigne) 105
estrangement, notion of 194
  of world comparative literature 192
eternal feminine, notion of 169 n.57, 170 n.62
eternal recurrence doctrine 166 n.5, 168 n.19
eternity, desire for 156, 157
eudaimonistic ethics, rejection of 168 n.25
Eurocentric blindness 110
"exchange value," significance of 49

existentialism 15, 28, 53, 57 n.32, 70 n.40, 233
  Heidegger on Tolstoy and 238–43
  philosophical novel and 235–8
Existentialism from Dostoevsky to Sartre (Kaufmann) 235

Faith and Knowledge (Derrida) 29, 226 n.20
Fanon, Frantz 59, 68–9 n.22, 72, 82
  Bernasconi on 69–70 n.33, 70 n.40
  on combat literature 66
  global reception of 67 n.9
  on place of madness and 60–2
  on poetics as address 62–6
  on psychoanalysis 61
  on reading and writing 63
  on Sartre 65
  social therapies and 67 n.11, 68 n.18
Fanonian freedom 66
Farah, Nuruddin 121
feminism 91
  migration and 95–7
  problem of 91–4
  reproduction and catastrophe and 94–5
  technology and 99–100
  translation and 97–9
Ferguson, Frances 28
Fernández, Macedonio 249
Fervor the Buenos Aires (Borges) 250
Ficciones (Borges) 250
Firestone, Shulamith 99
Flesh of Words, The (Ranciere) 34, 35
Flies, The (*Les mooches*) (Sartre) 235
foreignness 38–9
Forget English! (Mufti) 119
Foucault, Michel 6, 57 n.29, 248, 249, 257 n.1
Fraser, Nancy 93
Friedman, Thomas 119, 123
From Socrates to Cinema (Di Leo) 270
fullness, sense of 156–7
Fundamental Concepts of Metaphysics, The (Heidegger) 29

Gadamer, Hans-Georg 40
Gadamerian hermeneutics 40
Gandhi, Mohandas 138
Gasché, Rodolphe 42

Gasset, José Ortega y 233
gastro-metaphor 78
Gay Science, The (Nietzsche) 80
Genet, Jean 215
George, Henry 130
"*German Ideology, The*" (Marx and Engels) 116, 117
Gift of Death, The (Patočka) 28
Giles, Peter 43 n.1
Gilmore, Jonathan 181 n.2
Girard, René 34
Gitanjali (Tagore) 178, 179
Glissant, Édouard 43, 82, 83
global and local, significance of 191
globalization 115–16, 119–21
  Communist Manifesto and 124–5
  as measured economically 125
Gödel, Escher, Bach (Hofstadter) 200
Goethe, Johann Wolfgang von 116, 117, 123, 147, 166 n.6, 169 n.57, 170 nn.62, 68, 192
Goetschel, Willi 43 n.14
Goldschmidt, Victor 57 n.38
González, José Eduardo 259 n.34
Goodman, Nelson 257 n.1
Goody, Jack 56 n.22
Graff, Gerald 7
Gravity's Rainbow (Pynchon) 200
Greek philosophy 32–3, 50
Green, Martin 138
Greenham, David 139 n.20
Grondin, Jean 40
Grosfoguel, Ramon 79
Gutiérrez, Edgardo 247

Hajnády, Zoltán 240
Haldeman, Marcet 262
Haldeman-Julius, Emanuel 261
  Durant and 265–7
  early life of 262
  family of 261–2
  Little Blue Books and 263–4, 266
  on Simon and Schuster 266–7
Haldeman-Julius Weekly (newspaper) 266
Hamid, Mohsin 120
Hampton, Cynthia 57 n.38
Haraway, Donna 94

Harding, Sue-Ann 67 n.9
Harding, Walter 129, 137
Harris, Kirsten 139 n.12
Hartman, Geoffrey H. 3–4, 18 nn.8, 12
Harvey, Samantha C. 139 n.20
Hatchet: The Life of Stephen the Great (Sadoveanu) 227 n.40
Havelock, Eric A. 56 n.22
Hegel: A Very Short Introduction (Singer) 270
Hegel, Georg Wilhelm Friedrich 30, 38–9, 74, 84 n.2, 117, 215, 234
Heidegger, Martin 10, 56 n.22, 86 n.48, 167 n.17, 170 n.70, 187
  being and 186
  on death 238–43
  existentialism and 233, 234, 236, 237, 244 n.22, 245 n.23, 246 n.47
  on idea 51
  on influence concept 245 n.30
  on Metaphysical universe 53
  on Tolstoy 238–43
  translation and 27, 29, 31–2
  on truth 50
  on Western philosophy 48–9
Hendrick, George 136, 138 n.7, 141 n.64
Hendrick, Willene 136, 138 n.7
"Henry David Thoreau" (Salt) 132
Heraclitus 257
hermeneutical Mafia 3, 18 n.8
hermeneutics and translation 40
hermeneutic skepticism 31
Herzog (Bellow) 200
Hester, Helen 94–5
heterosexual futurism 95
Hever, Hannan 209, 210
historical phantasmagoria 214
History of Western Philosophy, A (Russell) 256, 274 n.20
Hochschild, Adam 71, 84 n.5
Hofstadter, Douglas 198, 200, 207
Hölderlin 29, 32
holding environment 217, 228 n.55
Hopkins, Edward 176
Hopscotch (Cortázar) 200, 204
horizon, etymology and significance of 86–7 n.51
horizontal being-event 187

humanitarianism 132, 133
    Salt on 134–6
Humanitarian League 134–5
Husserl, Edmund 55 n.1
Hymn of Creation, The (Indian
    philosophy) 179
Hyndman, Henry 130

idea 53
    of the good 51
    of Platonism 52
ideai, notion of 53, 55
Iliad (Homer) 49, 50, 55
"Immortal, The" (Borges) 251
imperialism 77, 83, 84 n.9, 92, 100–1, 116
inauthenticity, significance of 239–41
Indian literature
    modern literature in 178–80
    significance of 175–6
Indian philosophy 175, 178
infinite time 146
International Socialist Review 262
Introducing Hegel (Spenser) 270
Irwin, William 239
islandology 23, 43
    significance of 24
isomorphic parallelism 216–17

Jacques the Fatalist and his Master (*Jacques
    le fataliste et son maître*) (Diderot) 234
James, William 274 n.22
Jameson, Fredric 92
Jaspers, Karl 27, 233, 243
Jeanson, Francis 63, 65
"John Wilkins' Analytical Language"
    (Borges) 248
Jones, Samuel A. 136
Journal (Thoreau) 129
joy, significance of 12, 35, 189–91, 193,
    194, 268
Joyce, James 23, 203, 212, 248
Joynes, James Leigh 130
Judaism 147
Jupp, William Jess 130
Justice (journal) 131

Kafka, Franz 208, 212, 214, 220, 233
Kamuf, Peggy 98

Kant, Immanuel 29, 43 n.14, 57 n.40, 58
    n.41, 74, 117, 169 n.38, 250
Kante, Božidar 239
Kaufmann, Walter 235, 239
Khalfa, Jean 59, 63, 67 n.11, 68 n.18
    on Fanonian freedom 66
Kierkegaard, Søren 78, 86 n.39, 233, 240,
    245 n.30
Kincaid, Jamaica 120
Kipling, Rudyard 255
Kirkpatrick, Sean 86–7 n.51
Klemm, Stephen 170 n.68
Kleuker, Johann Friedrich 146
Kopelin, Louis 262
Korrektur (Bernhard) 200
Krauze, Andrzej 270
Kupperman, Joel 174

"L'esprit du terrorisme" (Baudrillard) 9
Labat, Jean-Baptiste 71, 84 n.3
Lacan, Jacques 107, 253
Lacoue-Labarthe, Philippe 33
La Guerre du Golfe n'a pas en lieu
    (Baudrillard) 9
Lamming, George 83, 84 n.11
    on Prospero and Caliban 83
Lang, Berel 17 n.3
language 69 n.30, 84 n.11, 201. *See also* text
    analytical 248
    and corruption of social relations 68 n.12
    Mauthner on 248
    multiplicity and 75–8
    and readership 64–6
    reconstruction of self in 63
    rhythm and 81
    significance of 62–3
    surrealism and 64
    translation and 97–8
    world as subjective and 153–4
Lao She 180
Las Casas, Bartolomé de 112 n.4
Latour, Bruno 194
Lawall, Sarah 174
Lebensweise, notion of 202, 211, 213,
    217, 219
Lee, R. Alton 261, 263
Leibniz, Gottfried Wilhelm 34, 237
Leitch, Vincent 9, 19 n.24

Le Rider, Jacques 255, 258 n.10
Léry, Jean de 108
Lesevot, Typhaine 192
Lewis, David 173, 257 n.1
liberalism 114 n.45
"Library of Babel, The" (Borges) 256
Library of World's Best Literature, Ancient and Modern, A 174, 178, 181 n.16, 182 n.28
   on Confucian philosophy 174
   on Indian philosophy 175
   national literature idea in 176
Life of Henry David Thoreau (Salt) 138
lifeworld 189, 192
light and darkness, metaphysical dualism of 146–7
literary language and non-literary language, comparison of 37
literary theory, philosophy against 3–7
"Literature and Metaphysics" ("Littérature et métaphysique") (de Beauvoir) 235
logic 108, 122, 134, 179, 202, 216, 276 n.57
   of aesthetic contracts 206
   analytic thought and 234
   Aristotelian 252
   of being 47
   of genre 125
   institutional 119
   lateral 38
   mimetic 34
   of moments 157
   philosophy as 268
   structural 126
   of translation 38, 39, 123
   of world 116
Logics of Worlds (Badiou) 41
Longman Anthology of World Literature, The 179, 180
Los Angeles Citizen (newspaper) 262
Lotman, Juri 10
Luhmann, Niklas 27
Luo, Junjie 182 n.31
lying, as epistemic and ethical fault 169 n.56
Lyotard, Jean-François 35–6

McAllister, James 17 n.3
McGeehan, Justice 273–4 n.16

Macmillan Publishing 275 n.41
Maeterlinck, Maurice 182 n.18
Magee, Bryan 270
Make Kin Not Babies! slogan 94
Malabou, Catherine 29
Mallarmé, Stéphane 33, 34, 198, 215–16
Mandarins, The (*Les Mandarins*) (de Beauvoir) 235
Marshall, Donald 18 n.10
Marshall, Jim 173
Martinez, Guillermo 247
Marx, Karl 49, 92, 100, 115, 268
Masnavi (Rumi) 204
Masterpieces of the World's Literature, Ancient and Modern 174, 175
   national literature idea in 176
Mauthner, Fritz 248–9, 252, 254, 255, 258 n.10
Mbembe, Achille 72–3, 77, 82, 84 n.3
Meditations on First Philosophy (*Meditationes de prima philosophia*) 234
Medovoi, Leerom 93
Memoirs of the Blind (Derrida) 223
Mencius, The (Chinese philosophy) 179
Mendicino, Kristina 167 n.14
messianism 34
metaphysics, Western Philosophy as 48–9
midge metaphor 75
midnight/midday metaphor 157–8
Mifflin, Houghton 129
Mignolo, Walter D. 87 n.59
migration, in feminist context
   ideological position of 96
   NGOs and 97
   politics of 96
Miller, J. Hillis 6, 18 n.8
Miller, Webb 138
Milwaukee Leader (newspaper) 262
mimesis 34
mineness 244 n.22
Ministry of Utmost Happiness, The (Roy) 101–2
modernity 72, 82, 92, 101, 178, 211, 226 n.30
   broader 203, 226 n.15
   coloniality and 87 n.59

Communist Manifesto and 118, 119, 122, 124
   critique of 73–4
   European 83, 85 n.19
   globalization and 125
Monist, The (journal) 18 n.9
Monolingualism of the Other (Derrida) 29
Montaigne, Michel de 105
Montinari, Mazzino 165 n.2, 168 n.24
Moore, G. E. 276 n.57
moral dualism 147–8, 153, 161
Morality Matters (Di Leo) 276 n.64
moral judgments 149
More, Thomas 23, 43 n.1
Moretti, Franco 92, 124
Morris, Charles 175
Mudimbe, V. Y. 77, 80
Mufti, Aamir 17 n.1, 119
multiplicity, significance of 75–8, 86 n.33
My Name Is Red (Pamuk) 200, 209
   atelier motif in 202–4, 213, 220, 222
   blindness in 223–5, 229 n.74
   color significance in 213–14, 222–3
   contractual negotiations in 202–6
   decisive dialogue in 220–1
   miniature illustration in 202–5, 210, 214, 220–2, 224, 228 n.67
   visual sense in 222–4
mytheme 33

Name of the Rose, The (Eco) 204
Nancy, Jean-Luc 126
Narayan, R. K. 180
narrative phantasmagorias 211–12
national literature, idea of 104 n.49
natural attitude 47, 49–52
Nausea (*La nausée*) (Sartre) 235, 244 n.12
neoliberalism 9, 101, 116
Neumann, Birgit 119, 120
New Appeal (newspaper) 262
Newman, John Henry 270
"New Refutation of Time, A" (Borges) 251
New World, discourse of. *See* Cannibal
New York Call (newspaper) 262
Ngugi Wa Thiong'o 73, 82, 83
Nietzsche, Friedrich 10, 73, 85 n.13, 171 n.72, 233, 240, 256. *See also Thus Spake Zarathustra* (Nietzsche)
   on critique of modernity 73–4
   gastro-metaphor of 78
   on human being as both created and creative 85 n.26
   on illusion guiding knowledge in imperial sense 77
   on midge metaphor 75
   on nature's paradoxical task 78
   on poetic use of rhythm 80–1
   on poetry 81–2
   on rejecting Schopenhauer's dualism 148
   on shapes and rhythms 11, 72, 74–80, 87 n.51
   on time and space 74, 76, 80, 87 n.51
   on willful ignorance 78–9
   on will to power 79–81, 83
   worlding and 76
   and Zoroastrianism, relationship between 166 n.5
Noble Savage, myth of 109
No Exit (*Huit clos*) 235
nonbeing 31, 32, 60
Norton Anthology of World Literature, The 179, 180
Nuño, Juan 253

Oelschlaeger, Fritz 136, 141 n.64
"Of Cannibals" (Montaigne) 108
"Of Coaches" (Montaigne) 112 n.5
"Of Cripples" (Montaigne) 107
"Of Cruelty" (Montaigne) 110
"Of Experience" (Montaigne) 106, 112 n.9
Of Grammatology (Derrida) 200
"Of Moderation" (Montaigne) 110
Ong, Aihwa 07
Ong, Walter J. 56 n.22
"On Religion" (Schopenhauer) 147
On the Genealogy of Morals (Nietzsche) 78, 85 n.13
"On the Jewish Question" (Marx) 116
On the Nature of Things (*De rerum natura*) (Lucretius) 234
ontology 20 n.35, 52, 53, 119, 120
   Cannibal and 107, 108, 111, 112 n.4, 114 n.43
   of capitalist commodity production 49
   death and 244 n.22
   dualism and 150, 153, 155, 156, 158–9

existentialism and 237, 240–2, 245 n.31
mathematical 32
Platonist 48
poetic 32
On Truth and Lies in a Non-Moral Sense (Nietzsche) 75
Open Boat (Glissant) 82
Order of Things, The (Foucault) 248
Ordinary Language Philosophy (OLP) 34
Orientalism 13, 161, 165–6 n.4, 171 n.72. See also *Thus Spake Zarathustra* (Nietzsche)
Nietzsche's response to 145–9
origin, notion of 200–1
Oryx and Crake (Atwood) 101
Otherness 12, 97, 106, 111, 121
Otto, M. C. 264
Our Heritage of World Literature 176, 178
on Indian literature 178
Our Journal (*Notre Journal*) (Fanon) 63
Our Oriental Heritage (Durant) 272
Outline of History, The (Wells) 271
Oxford University Press 270

Packer, Barbara L. 139 n.20
Pamuk, Orhan 199, 200, 209, 220, 227 n.49, 228 nn.72, 74, 229 n.74. See also *My Name Is Red* (Pamuk)
Panchatantra (Indian literature) 178
Parallel Hands (*Les Mains parallèles*) 64
Parerga and Paralipomena (Schopenhauer) 147, 250
Pascal, Blaise 18 n.13
Passions of the Soul, The (Descartes) 105
passive resistance 138
Patočka, Jan 28
peasantry, significance of 226 n.30
"penitent of spirit" 170 n.67
Phaedrus (Plato) 34
phantasmagorias 211–12, 214
Phenomenology of Spirit (*Phänomenologie des Geistes*) (Hegel) 30, 38–40, 234
Philosophy and the Social Problem (Durant) 264, 267
"Philosophy as/and/ of Literature" (Danto) 26
"Pierre Menard, Author of the *Quixote*" (Borges) 251, 252

Pilpay 175
Pizer, John 170 n.68
Plato 32, 34, 47, 55, 58 n.41, 234; See also *Republic* (Plato)
Heidegger on 49
on idea 51, 53
Platonism and 47–8, 52, 53
"Plato's Pharmacy" (Derrida) 198, 215
Playing and Reality (Winnicott) 228 nn.54–5
Plea for Vegetarianism, A (Salt) 134, 138
pleasure/pain duality, significance of 169 n.41
Plot 33
poetic ontology 32
Poetics (Aristotle) 173
Poetics of Relation (Glissant) 43
Poetry of the Revolution (Puchner) 122
poiesis 60, 78
Pratt, Mary Louise 123
Preciado, Paul 99
on hormones 100
pregnancy, metaphor of 171 n.74
presence and absence, equating 150, 153, 156–8
Principia Mathematica (Russell) 268
Proust, Marcel 203, 218, 220, 228 n.65, 244 n.11
psychoanalysis 61, 99, 107, 114 n.45, 171 n.71, 228 nn.54–5
publicness 240
Puchner, Martin 122–3
Pynchon, Thomas 200

Rabinow, Paul 6
radical aloneness 153
Raghavan, V. 185
Ranciere, Jacques 34, 35
rasa, notion of 190, 191, 193, 194, 195 n.13
readership, significance of 64
Reagan, Ronald 9
reason 41–3
geopolitical voyage of 41
translation and 41–2
world universality 42
Recherche (Proust) 203, 220, 228 n.65
Reichenbach, Hans 19 n.16
repetition, paradox of 78, 86 n.39

representation (*Vorstellung*) 152
representational thinking and 49, 50, 54
Republic (Plato) 32, 49, 51
  Myth of the Cave 49–51, 54
"Requiem pour les Twin Towers"
  (Baudrillard) 9
ressentiment 79
reworlding 59, 66, 78
Rhode, J. G. 147
rhythm
  poetic use of 80–1
  and shapes 11, 72, 74–80, 87 n.51
  significance of 74
  will to power and 81
Rice-Sprout Song, The (Zhang) 180
Rilke, Rainer Maria 233
Rippl, Gabriele 119, 120
Rizal, José 124
Robbins, Bruce 93, 193
Robertson, Michael 130, 139 n.12
Roger, Sarah 259 n.45
romanticism 6, 7, 95, 131, 166 n.5, 203, 204, 228 n.72
Rorty, Richard 4, 5–6, 19 nn.22, 24, 118
  on philosophy 7–8
  and literature 173
  on textualism 6–7
Rose, Jenny 166 n.5
Rousseau, Jean-Jacques 109, 200
  Derrida and 200–2
Rousseau and Revolution (Durant and Durant) 267
Routledge 270
Rowbotham, Sheila 131, 139 n.12
Roy, Arhundhati 101–2
Rubin, Andrew 67 n.7
Rudrum, David 20 n.35
Rumi 204
Ruskin, John 132
Russell, Bertrand 256, 263, 268, 273–4 n.16, 274 nn.18, 20, 276 n.57
Ryan, William F. 274 n.18

Sadoveanu, Mihail 212, 227 n.40
sahitya
  being-event of 187, 193
  Dasein of 187
  dharma of 189
  etymology of 185–6
  event of 187
  sahit and 193
  significance of 186
  swadharma and 189–90
  Tagore on 188–92
  totality of 193
  world being of 187
  worlding and 192
Said, Edward 25, 36, 59, 67 n.7
Sakoontala (Indian literature) 178
Salt, Henry S. 130, 131, 138, 139 n.22, 141 n.64
  on humanitarianism 134–6
  on Thoreau 131–3, 137
  Thoreau biography and British Thoreau Centenary 136–7
  on vegetarianism 134
Salt, Kate 130, 139 n.22
sameness and difference, navigating between 108–11, 112 n.4
Sandburg, Carl 262
Sapiro, Gisele 92
Sartre, Jean-Paul 10, 28, 57 n.32, 173, 233, 234, 237, 241, 246 n.56
  Fanon on Negritude movement of 65
Sartre and Fiction (Cox) 235
Saussure, Ferdinand de 47
Schelling, Friedrich 148
Schlegel, Friedrich 26, 166 n.6
Schopenhauer, Arthur 147, 148, 168 n.24, 248–50
  influence on Borges 249–50, 255
  on self 249
Schuster, Lincoln 266
Schwab, Raymond 146
Schwartz, Samuel D. 275 n.33
Scruton, Roger 29
Searle, John 173
"Secret Miracle" (Borges) 251
self and ego, relationship between 167 n.14
self-presence/self-absence 150
Seventy Years among the Savages (Salt) 133
Shammas, Anton 199, 200
Shaw, George Bernard 130
She Came to Stay (*L'invitée*)
  (de Beauvoir) 235
Shell, Marc 23

Shklar, Judith 114 n.45
Simon, Richard 266
Simon and Schuster (publishing company) 267
"Simplification of Life" (Carpenter) 130, 131
Singer, Peter 134, 270
smandra 212, 219, 227 n.43
Snell, Bruno 56 n.22
Social Democrat (newspaper) 262
Social Democratic Federation 131
Socialist Catechism, The (Joynes) 130
social reproduction, in feminism context 91–3, 99–100
    catastrophe and 94–5
Socrates 57 n.33
Sorrows of Han, The (Chinese play) 178
sovereignty 11, 43, 79, 84 n.9, 92, 101, 111, 125, 210
    philosophical 23, 24, 42
Spenser, Lloyd 270
Spinoza, Baruch 248, 249, 253–4, 265
Spivak, Gayatri 42, 43, 102, 172 n.84
    on worlding and commodity fetishism 100–1
"Spring of Nations" 122
Staël, Germaine de 244 n.1
"Stakes of a World Literature, The" (Spivak) 42
Stanley, Henry Morton 71
Steger, Manfred B. 124
Stevenson, Robert Louis 251, 258 n.26
Stocking, Charles 50
Story, significance of 32–3
Story of Civilization, The (Durant) 267, 272, 275 n.46
Story of Philosophy, The (Durant) 266, 267–9
Story of Philosophy, The (Magee) 270
storytelling, significance of 219–20
style, in philosophy 17 n.2
subjective-objective, ambiguity of 151
surrealism 64
Sussman, Henry 226 n.15
swadharma and *sahitya* 189–90
Swift, Jonathan 71
Symbolism and Mythology of Ancient Peoples and in Particular the Greeks, The (Creuzer) 146

Tagore, Rabindranath 178, 188–94
"Task of the Translator, The" (Benjamin) 34
Taylor, Mark C. 19 n.16
technology, in feminist context 99–100
Temple Bar (magazine) 132, 136
temporal (in)determination, of world 156
text. *See also* language
    being of 188
    classical depiction of 19 n.23
    contemporary depiction of 19 n.23
    philosophical 35–6
    worldliness of 25, 26
textualism/textuality 8
    neoliberalism and 9
    Rorty's view on 6–8
Thatcher, Margaret 9
"Theses on the Philosophy of History" (Benjamin) 34
Thevet, André 108
"they-self" 240, 241
    Dasein and 242
Third World 100–1
"This Strange Institution Called Literature" (interview with Derrida) 10
Thoreau, Henry David 129, 131
    as American poet-naturalist 129–30
    influence on Gandhi 138
    passive resistance and 138
    Salt on 131–3, 137
        Thoreau biography and British Thoreau Centenary 136–7
    among socialists 131–3
    on vegetarianism 133
Thus Spake Zarathustra (Nietzsche) 145
    doubled perspectives of world in 151–8
    presence and absence motifs and 153, 156–8
    on literature 158
        negation of 160
        poets as deceptive 159–60
    Nietzsche's response to Orientalist discourse in 145–9
    self in 149–51
    "Of Old and New Tablets" 149, 151
    world iterature in 161–5
Timaeus (Plato) 256
Tiwari, Bhavya 186

"Tlön, Uqbar, Orbis Tertius"
(Borges) 253–4
Todorov, Tzvetan 105
Tolstoy, Leo 233, 234, 238
  on authenticity principle 241–3
  on inauthenticity principle 239–41
totality, notion of 155, 193, 194
Trakl, Georg 32
transitional objects 217, 228 n.54
translatability, significance of 25, 36–7
  ideal 37
translation 24, 119, 194
  as building toward commons 98–9
  as instance of equivalence 123
  language and 97–8
  philosophy and/as/or 38–40
  and philosophy's purview
    of universe 31–3
    of world 27–30
  philosophy's world as yet to come
    and 41–3
  philosophy's world language and 33–6
  on reproduction 98
  significance of 173, 254–5
  traveling philosophy and 36–8
  world philosophy and 24–6
"Traveling Theory" (Said) 25
truth 187. *See also individual entries*
  Badiou on 31
  compromising of 37
  essence of 50
  as idea 51
  and illusion 154
  representational thinking and 49, 50
  translatability and 36–7
  as vision 49
Truth and Method (Gadamer) 40
truth travels 33
Tsing, Anna 95

Übermensch (over-human), concept of 151, 160, 168 n.23
Ulysses (Joyce) 203
uncoveredness 187
"Undr" (Borges) 252
universal history 30, 34
universal philosophical language 34
universal truths 31

untranslatability, significance of 99, 168 n.23, 170 n.69
unworlding 82
Upanishads, The (Indian philosophy) 175, 179
Utopia (More) 23, 43 n.1
utopian language 23, 43 n.1

value-dualisms 149
van Eck, Caroline 17 n.3
vegetarianism 133, 134, 137
Venuti, Lawrence 119
Verkehr, concept of 123–4
vertical being-event 187
visva sahitya (World Literature) 185. *See also* sahitya
  aesthetic of 187
  cosmopolitanism and 193–4
  as ethical project 193
  Heidegger and 188
  as inherently anachronistic 192
  joy in 190–1
  as mode of estrangement 192
  poetic and 188
  totality of 194
  world-disclosures and 189, 191
"Visva Sahitya" (Tagore) 188
Voltaire 234, 237

Walden (Thoreau) 129, 131–3, 137, 138
"Walking" (Thoreau) 129
Walkowitz, Rebecca 119, 120
Walsh, Catherine 87 n.59
Warwick Research Collective (WReC) 122
Watt, Ian 56 n.22
Weep Not Child (Ngugi) 83
Weinbren, Dan 135
Weiss, Paul 269
Wells, H. G. 261, 271, 277 n.70
Welt 29–30
Western Democrat (newspaper) 262
What Can a Free Man Worship?
  (Russell) 263
What Is a World? (Cheah) 121
What Is World Literature? (Damrosch) 26
White, Hayden 6
Whitman, Walt 130, 131
Who's Afraid of Philosophy? (Derrida) 28

Why I Am Not a Christian (Russell) 263
Wilamowitz-Möllendorf, Ulrich von 145
"Wild Apples" (Thoreau) 129
will (*Ding An Sich*) 152
willful ignorance 72, 78
Williams, Raymond 98
Williamson, Edwin 249–50
Willis, Lonnie L. 137, 138
will to power, notion of 79–81, 83
Wilshire, Bruce W. 18 n.15
Winnicott, D. W. 228 nn.54–5
Wittgenstein, Ludwig 28, 34
Woolf, Virginia 91, 92, 101
Worger, William H. 85 n.12
world, as will and representation 255
world, doubled perspectives of 151–8
World, the Text, and the Critic, The
   (Said) 25
world-affirmation 152–3
World as Will and Representation, The
   (Schopenhauer) 250
world-disclosures 189, 191, 194
worlded literature, significance of 2
worlding
   acts of 40
   ambition and 30
   commodity fetishism and 100
   as embodied 96
   of European philosophy 41
   feminist 94–5
   for Heideggerian 29
   of migration 95
   Nietzsche and 76
   of philosophy 28, 34
   reproduction as 94
   sahitya and 192
world language, of philosophy 33–6
worldliness 115, 118, 152
   literature of 161
   of Marxism 12
   of Nietzsche 156, 161

quest for 93
of text 25, 26
of world 158
world literature. *See also individual entries*
   importance of 26
   and translatability 37–8
world-making 40, 59, 61, 82, 86 n.36,
   95, 120–1
   as forms of entering 189
   textual knowledge and 86 n.36
world philosophy, significance of 24–6
World Republic of Letters, The
   (Casanova) 27
world spirit 30
"World Systems and the Creole"
   (Spivak) 43
"worldwide-ization" 30
Wörterbuch der Philosophie
   (Mauthner) 248
Wretched of the Earth, The (*Les Damnés de
   la terre*) (Fanon) 60, 66, 70 n.41
Wright, Richard 233
writing, significance of 34–5, 63
Wyss Johann Rudolf 182 n.18

Yale school 6
Yelle, Robert A. 166 n.5
"Yes-Yet-Hegel's Oracle" (Mendicino)
   39
Yiannopoulou, Effie 95, 96
Young, Robert J. C. 63, 64, 30 n.69

Zadig (Voltaire) 234
Zend Avesta 145, 146
Zepp, Susanne 259 n.34
Zhang Ailing 180
Zhuangzi, The (Chinese philosophy) 179
Žižek, Slavoj 114 n.43
Zola, Émile 211, 212, 226 n.33
Zoroastrianism 145–7, 166 n.5
   as strict dualism 166 n.6

www.ingramcontent.com/pod-product-compliance
Lightning Source LLC
Chambersburg PA
CBHW072124290426
44111CB00012B/1773